Large Sample Theory and Statistics

Large Sample Theory and Statistics

Pankaj Dutta

RANDOM PUBLICATIONS
NEW DELHI (INDIA)

Large Sample Theory and Statistics

ISBN 978-93-5111-226-6

Published in 2014 in India by

RANDOM PUBLICATIONS

4376-A/4B, Gali Murari Lal, Ansari Road
New Delhi-110 002
Phone : +91-11-43580356, +91-11-23289044
e-mail: randomexports@gmail.com, sales@randompublications.com,
info@randompublications.com

Reprinted 2025

Type Setting by : Keystoneprintads, Delhi-110051
Digitally Printed at : Replika Press Pvt. Ltd.

Preface

"Large sample theory and statistics" is the title of this book. As we all know that statistics is one of the most important topics in today's world. Many books have been written in this topic. This modest effort is another pearl in the sequence. This book has been designed in mind the mentality of the general reader's language which is easy to understandable.

Large sample theory is a generic framework for assessment of properties of estimators and statistical tests. Within this framework it is typically assumed that the sample size n grows indefinitely, and the properties of statistical procedures are evaluated in the limit as $n \to \infty$.

In practical applications, asymptotic theory is applied by treating the asymptotic results as approximately valid for finite sample sizes as well. Such approach is often criticized for not having any mathematical grounds behind it, yet it is used ubiquitously anyway.

The importance of the asymptotic theory is that it often makes possible to carry out the analysis and state many results which cannot be obtained within the standard "finite-sample theory"

The objective of the book is to bring together a balanced selection of core concepts as well as new perspectives that collectively articulate a knowledge-based view of large sample theory and statistics.

This book is designed to be a comprehensive text on large sample theory and statistics for students in all over the world. This book covers a wide range of statistics issues, and attempt to introduce the subject in a comprehensive way.

It avoids the narrow focus and considerable complexity of many other books in this area where in depth treatment is required, students are recommended to read relevant texts by leading contributors to idea about large sample theory and statistics. We hope that the discussion made in this book will help the readers to understand and learnt about the different aspects of "Large Sample Theory and Statistics" in a most comprehensive way

I thank all members of my team who have helped in the preparation of the book. My special thanks go to "Random Publications" who have published the book.

– Pankaj Dutta

Contents

1

Introduction

STATISTICS

The word 'Statistics' is derived from the Latin word 'Statis' which means a "political state." Clearly, statistics is closely linked with the administrative affairs of a state such as facts and figures regarding defence force, population, housing, food, financial resources etc. What is true about a government is also true about industrial administration units, and even one's personal life.

The word statistics has several meanings. In the first place, it is a plural noun which describes a collection of numerical data such as employment statistics, accident statistics, population statistics, birth and death, income and expenditure, of exports and imports etc. It is in this sense that the word 'statistics' is used by a layman or a newspaper.

Secondly the word statistics as a singular noun, is used to describe a branch of applied mathematics, whose purpose is to provide methods of dealing with a collections of data and extracting information from them in compact form by tabulating, summarizing and analyzing the numerical data or a set of observations.

The various methods used are termed as statistical methods and the person using them is known as a statistician. A statistician is concerned with the analysis and interpretation of the data and drawing valid worthwhile conclusions from the same.

It is in the second sense that we are writing this guide on statistics.

Lastly the word statistics is used in a specialized sense. It describes various numerical items which are produced by using statistics (in the second sense) to statistics (in the first sense). Averages, standard deviation etc. are all statistics in this specialized third sense.

The word 'statistics' in the first sense is defined by Professor Secrit as follows:

"By statistics we mean aggregate of facts affected to a marked extent by multiplicity of causes, numerically expressed, enumerated or estimated according to reasonable standard of accuracy, collected in a systematic manner for a predetermined purpose and placed in relation to each other."

This definition gives all the characteristics of statistics which are:

- Aggregate of facts
- Affected by multiplicity of causes
- Numerically expressed
- Estimated according to reasonable standards of accuracy
- Collected in a systematic manner
- Collected for a predetermined purpose
- Placed in relation to each other.

The word 'statistics' in the second sense is defined by Croxton and Cowden as follows:–

"The collection, presentation, analysis and interpretation of the numerical data." This definition clearly points out four stages in a statistical investigation, namely:

- Collection of data
- Presentation of data
- Analysis of data
- Interpretation of data

In addition to this, one more stage i.e. organization of data is suggested.

USES

- To present the data in a concise and definite form: Statistics helps in classifying and tabulating raw data for processing and further tabulation for end users.
- To make it easy to understand complex and large data: This is done by presenting the data in the form of tables, graphs, diagrams etc., or by condensing the data with the help of means, dispersion etc.
- For comparison: Tables, measures of means and dispersion can help in comparing different sets of data..
- *In forming policies:* It helps in forming policies like a production schedule, based on the relevant sales figures. It is used in forecasting future demands.
- Enlarging individual experiences: Complex problems can be well understood by statistics, as the conclusions drawn by an individual are more definite and precise than mere statements on facts.
- In measuring the magnitude of a phenomenon:- Statistics has made it possible to count the population of a country, the industrial growth, the agricultural growth, the educational level (of course in numbers).

Limitations

- Statistics does not deal with individual measurements. Since statistics deals with aggregates of facts, it can not be used to study the changes that have taken place in individual cases. For example, the wages earned by a single industry worker at any time, taken by itself is not a statistical datum. But the wages of workers of that industry can be used statistically. Similarly the marks obtained by John of your class or the height of Beena (also of your class) are not the subject matter of statistical study. But the average marks or the average height of your class has statistical relevance.

- Statistics cannot be used to study qualitative phenomenon like morality, intelligence, beauty etc. as these can not be quantified. However, it may be possible to analyse such problems statistically by expressing them numerically. For example we may study the intelligence of boys on the basis of the marks obtained by them in an examination.
- *Statistical results are true only on an average:* The conclusions obtained statistically are not universal truths. They are true only under certain conditions. This is because statistics as a science is less exact as compared to the natural science.
- Statistical data, being approximations, are mathema-tically incorrect. Therefore, they can be used only if mathematical accuracy is not needed.
- Statistics, being dependent on figures, can be manipulated and therefore can be used only when the authenticity of the figures has been proved beyond doubt.

DISTRUST OF STATISTICS

It is often said by people that, "statistics can prove anything." There are three types of lies - lies, demand lies and statistics - wicked in the order of their naming. A Paris banker said, "Statistics is like a miniskirt, it covers up essentials but gives you the ideas." Thus by "distrust of statistics" we mean lack of confidence in statistical statements and methods. The following reasons account for such views about statistics.

- Figures are convincing and, therefore people easily believe them.
- They can be manipulated in such a manner as to establish foregone conclusions.
- The wrong representation of even correct figures can mislead a reader. For example, John earned $ 4000 in 1990 - 1991 and Jem earned $ 5000. Reading this one would form the opinion that Jem is decidedly a better worker than John. However if we carefully examine the statement, we might reach a different conclusion as Jem's earning period is unknown to us. Thus while working with statistics one should not only avoid outright falsehoods but be alert to detect possible distortion of the truth.

TYPES OF STATISTICS

For a layman or people in general, statistics means numbers - numerical facts, figures or information. The branch of statistics wherein we record and analyse observations for all the individuals of a group or population and draw inferences about the same is called "Descriptive statistics" or "Deductive statistics". On the other hand, if we choose a sample and by statistical treatment of this, draw inferences about the population, then this branch of statistics is known as Statical Inference or Inductive Statistics.

In our discussion, we are mainly concerned with two ways of representing descriptive statistics: Numerical and Pictorial.

- Numerical statistics are numbers. But some numbers are more meaningful such as mean, standard deviation etc.
- When the numerical data is presented in the form of pictures (diagrams) and graphs, it is called the Pictorial statistics. This statistics makes confusing and complex data or information, easy, simple and straightforward, so that even the layman can understand it without much difficulty.

COMMON MISTAKES COMMITTED IN INTERPRETATION OF STATISTICS

- *Bias:* Bias means prejudice or preference of the investigator, which creeps in consciously and unconsciously in proving a particular point.
- *Generalization:* Some times on the basis of little data available one could jump to a conclusion, which leads to erroneous results.
- *Wrong conclusion:* The characteristics of a group if attached to an individual member of that group, may lead us to draw absurd conclusions.
- *Incomplete classification:* If we fail to give a complete classification, the influence of various factors may not be properly understood.
- There may be a wrong use of percentages.
- Technical mistakes may also occur.
- An inconsistency in definition can even exist.
- Wrong causal inferences may sometimes be drawn.
- There may also be a misuse of correlation.

Glossary of Terms

Statistics: Statistics is the use of data to help the decision maker to reach better decisions. *Data:* It is any group of measurements that interests us. These measurements provide information for the decision maker.

- The data that reflects non-numerical features or qualities of the experimental units, is known as qualitative data.
- The data that possesses numerical properties is known as quantitative data.

Population: Any well defined set of objects about which a statistical enquiry is being made is called a population or universe. The total number of objects (individuals) in a population is known as the size of the population. This may be finite or infinite.

Individual: Each object belonging to a population is called as an individual of the population.

Sample: A finite set of objects drawn from the population with a particular aim, is called a sample. The total number of individuals in a sample is called the sample size.

Characteristic: The information required from an individual, from a population or from a sample, during the statistical enquiry (survey) is known as the characteristic of the individual. It is either numerical or non-numerical. For e.g. the size of shoes is a numerical characteristic which refers to a quantity, whereas the mother tongue of a person is a non-numerical characteristic which refers to a quality. Thus we have quantitative and qualitative types of characteristics.

Variate: A quantitative characteristic of an individual which can be expressed numerically is called a variate or a variable. It may take different values at different times, places or situations.

Attribute: A qualitative characteristic of an individual which can be expressed numerically is called an attribute. For e.g. the mother-tongue of a person, the colour of eyes or the colour of hair of a person etc.

Discretevariate: A variable that is not capable of assuming all the values in a given range is a discrete variate.

Continuous Variate: A variate that is capable of assuming all the numerical values in a given range, is called a continuous variate. Consider two examples carefully, viz. the number of students of a class and their heights. Both variates differ slightly, in the sense that, the number of students present in a class is a number say between 0 and 50; always a whole number. It can never be 1.5, 4.33 etc. This type of variate can take only isolated values and is called a discrete variate. On the other hand heights ranging from 140 cm to 190 cm can take values like 140.7, 135.8, 185.1 etc. Such a variate is a continuous variate.

Example:

Individual	*Characteristic*	*Type of Characteristic*
1. A person	Height in cm	→ Continuous variate
	Colour of eyes	→ Attribute
	Age	→ Continuous variate
	Weight in lbs	→ Continuous variate
	Sex	→ Attribute
	Mother tongue	→ Attribute
	Marks in statistics	→ Discrete variate
2. Mr. Brown's	Number of members	→ Discrete variate
family	Monthly income in dollars	→ Discrete variate
3. A washer	Diameter and thickness in cm	→ Continuous variate
	Defective or non-defective	→ Attribute

2

Classification and Tabulation

In any statistical investigation, the collection of the numerical data is the first and the most important matter to be attended. Often a person investigating, will have to collect the data from the actual field of inquiry.

For this he may issue suitable questionnaires to get necessary information or he may take actual interviews; personal interviews are more effective than questionnaires, which may not evoke an adequate response.

Another method of collecting data may be available in publications of Government bodies or other public or private organizations.

Sometimes the data may be available in publications of Government bodies or other public or private organizations. Such data, however, is often so numerous that one's mind can hardly comprehend its significance in the form that it is shown. Therefore it becomes, very necessary to tabulate and summarize the data to an easily manageable form. In doing so we may overlook its details. But this is not a serious loss because Statistics is not interested in an individual but in the properties of aggregates. For a layman, presentation of the raw data in the form of tables or diagrams is always more effective.

Sometimes the data may be available in publications of Government bodies or other public or private organizations. Such data, however, is often so numerous that one's mind can hardly comprehend its significance in the form that it is shown. Therefore it becomes, very necessary to tabulate and summarize the data to an easily manageable form. In doing so we may overlook its details. But this is not a serious loss because Statistics is not interested in an individual but in the properties of aggregates. For a layman, presentation of the raw data in the form of tables or diagrams is always more effective.

TABULATION

It is the process of condensation of the data for convenience, in statistical processing, presentation and interpretation of the information.

A good table is one which has the following requirements:

- It should present the data clearly, highlighting important details.

- It should save space but attractively designed.
- The table number and title of the table should be given.
- Row and column headings must explain the figures therein.
- Averages or percentages should be close to the data.
- Units of the measurement should be clearly stated along the titles or headings.
- Abbreviations and symbols should be avoided as far as possible.
- Sources of the data should be given at the bottom of the data.
- In case irregularities creep in table or any feature is not sufficiently explained, references and foot notes must be given.
- The rounding of figures should be unbiased.

CLASSIFICATION

"Classified and arranged facts speak of themselves, and narrated they are as dead as mutton" This quote is given by J.R. Hicks.

The process of dividing the data into different groups which are homogeneous within but heterogeneous between themselves, is called a classification.

It helps in understanding the salient features of the data and also the comparison with similar data. For a final analysis it is the best friend of a statistician.

METHODS OF CLASSIFICATION

The data is classified in the following ways:

- According to attributes or qualities this is divided into two parts:
  - Simple classification
  - Multiple classification.
- According to variable or quantity or classification according to class intervals:

Qualitative Classification: When facts are grouped according to the qualities (attributes) like religion, literacy, business etc., the classification is called as qualitative classification.

- *Simple Classification:* It is also known as classification according to Dichotomy. When data (facts) are divided into groups according to their qualities, the classification is called as 'Simple Classification'. Qualities are denoted by capital letters (A, B, C, D......) while the absence of these qualities are denoted by lower case letters (a, b, c, d.... etc.) For example,

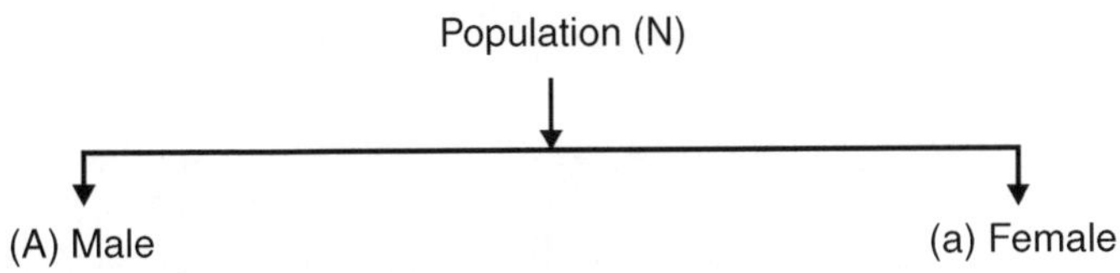

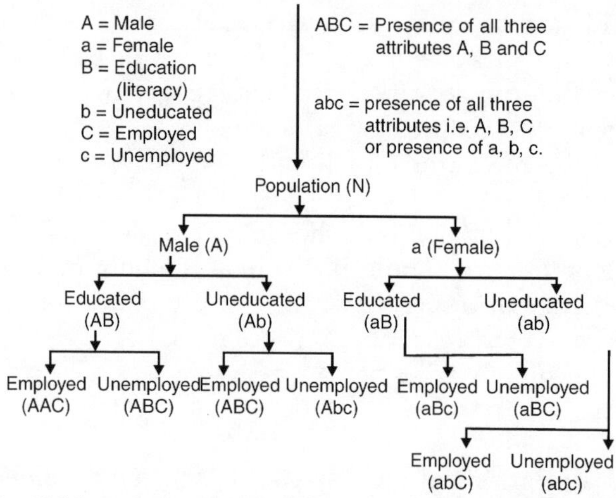

– *Manifold or multiple classification:* In this method data is classified using one or more qualities. First, the data is divided into two groups (classes) using one of the qualities. Then using the remaining qualities, the data is divided into different subgroups. For example, the population of a country is classified using three attributes: sex, literacy and business as,

Classification According to Class Intervals or Variables

The data which is expressed in numbers (quantitative data), is classified according to class-intervals. While forming class-intervals one should bear in mind that each and every item must be covered. After finding the least value of an item and the highest value of an item, classify these items into different class-intervals. For example if in any data the age of 100 persons ranging from 2 years to 47 years, is given, then the classification of this data can be done in this way:

Table:

Age in years	*No. of persons*
0-10	5
10-20	9
20-30	32
30-40	34
40-50	20

In deciding on the grouping of the data into classes, for the purpose of reducing it to a manageable form, we observe that the number of classes should not be too large.

If it were so then the object of summarization would be defeated. The number of classes should also not be too small because then we will miss a great deal of detail available and get a distorted picture. As a rule one should have between 10 and 25 classes, the actual number depending on the total frequency. Further, classes should be exhaustive; they should not be overlapping, so that no observed value falls in more than one class. Apart from exceptions, all classes should have the same length.

According to the Class-intervals in Classification the Following Terms are Used

Class-limits

A class is formed within the two values. These values are known as the class-limits of that class. The lower value is called the lower limit and is denoted by ℓ_1 while the higher value is called the upper limit of the class and is denoted by ℓ_2. In the example given above, the first class-interval has ℓ_1 = 0 and ℓ_2 = 10.

Magnitude of The Class-intervals

The difference between the upper and lower limits of a class is called the magnitude or length or width of a class and is denoted by 'i' or 'c'. Thus i $\equiv(\ell_2 - \ell_1)$.

Mid-value or Class-mark

The arithmetical average of the two class limits (i.e. the lower limit and the upper limit) is called the mid-value or the class mark of that class-interval.

For example, the mid-value of the class-interval (0 – 10) is

$$\frac{\ell_1+\ell_2}{2}=\frac{0+12}{2}=5,$$

$$(10 - 20) \text{ it is } \frac{10+20}{2}=15 \text{ and so on.}$$

Class frequency

The units of the data belong to any one of the groups or classes.

The total number of these units is known as the frequency of that class and is denoted by *fi* or simply *f*.

In the above example, the frequencies of the classes in the given order are 5, 9, 32, 34 and 40 respectively.

Classification is of two types according to the class-intervals–

- Exclusive Method
- Inclusive Method

Exclusive Method

In this method the upper limit of a class becomes the lower limit of the next class. It is called ' Exclusive ' as we do not put any item that is equal to the upper limit of a class in the same class; we put it in the next class, i.e. the upper limits of classes are excluded from them. For example, a person of age 20 years will not be included in the class-interval (10 – 20) but taken in the next class (20 – 30), since in the class interval (10 – 20) only units ranging from 10 – 19 are included. The exclusive-types of class-intervals can also be expressed as:

0 and below 10 or 0 – 9.9
10 and below 20 or 10 – 19.9
20 and below 30 or 20 – 29.9 and so on.

Inclusive Method

In this method the upper limit of any class interval is kept in the same class-interval. In this method the upper limit of a previous class is less by 1 from the lower limit of the next class interval. In short this method allows a class-interval to include both its lower and upper limits within it. For example:

Inclusive method		**Inclusive method**	
Class	Frequency	Class	Frequency
0 – 4	5	0 – 4.9	5
5 – 9	7	5 – 9.9	7
10 – 14	9	10 – 14.9	9
15 – 19	12	15 – 19.9	12
20 – 24	11	20 – 24.9	11
25 – 29	14	25 – 29.9	14

Class Boundaries

Weights are recorded to the nearest Kg The class-intervals 60 – 62 includes all measurements from 59.50000... to 62.50000... Kg; the variable being a continuous one. These numbers, indicated briefly by the exact numbers 59.5 and 62.5, are called class-boundaries or true class limits.

The smaller number 59.5 is the lower class boundary and the larger one 62.5 is the upper class boundary. In any problem if the class-intervals are given as the inclusive type, then they should first be converted into the exclusive-type. For this we require a correction factor.

Correction factor $=\frac{1}{2}$ (the upper limit of a class - the lower limit of the next class) which is generally 0.5.

Now you subtract it from the lower limits and add it to the upper limits of the class-intervals given in the inclusive-method.

The class-intervals given above can be written after correction as:

Class	Frequency
0 – 4.5	5
4.5 – 9.5	7
9.5 – 14.5	9
14.5 – 19.5	12
19.5 – 24.5	11
24.5 – 29.5	14

To obtain class-intervals when their mid-values are given, use the following formulae:

Lower limit (ℓ_1) = $m - i/_2$ and upper limit (ℓ_2) = $m + i/_2$

Where m = mid-value and i = class-length.

For example, we are given some mid-values as 72, 77, 82, 87.... Now, consider the first mid-value 72 and also the differences between successive mid-values.

We have 77 – 72 = 5, 82 – 77 = 5, 87 – 82 = 5....

which gives the class-length i = 5.

For the first class-interval, $\ell_1 = m - i/_2 = 72 - 5/_2 = 69.5$

and $\ell_2 = 72 + 5/_2 = 74.5$.

Thus the first class-interval is 69.5 – 74.5

and other class-intervals then are 74.5 – 79.5, 79.5 – 84.5, 84.5 – 89.5

Open-end Class Intervals

In any question when the lower limit of the first class-inteval or the upper limit of the last class-interval, are not given then subtract the class length of the next immediate class-interval from the upper limit. This will give us the lower limit of the first class-interval. Similarly add the same class length to the lower limit of the last class-interval. But always notice that the lower limit of the first class (i.e. the lowest class) must not be negative or less than 0. For example:

With open endsclasses	Completed ends	With open classes	Completed
Below 10	0 – 10	Below 10	0 – 10
10 – 20	10 – 20	10 – 25	10 – 25
20 – 30	20 – 30	25 – 40	25 – 40
30 – 40	30 – 40	40 – 70	40 – 70
40 – 50	40 – 50	above 70	70 – 100
above 50	50 – 60		

RELATIVE FREQUENCY DISTRIBUTION

The relative frequency of a class is the frequency of the class divided by the total number of frequencies of the class and is generally expresses as a percentage.

Example: The weight of 100 persons were given as under:

Weights (in Kgs)	60 – 62	63 – 63	66 – 68	69 – 71	72 – 74
No. of persons (f_i)	5	18	42	27	8

Solution:

Relative frequency table

Weight (in Kg.)	No. of persons (f_i)	Relative frequency
60 – 62	5	$\frac{5}{100} \times 5\%$ or 0.05
63 – 65	18	$\frac{18}{100} \times 18\%$ or 0.18
66 – 68	42	$\frac{42}{100} \times 42\%$ or 0.42
69 – 71	27	$\frac{27}{100} \times 27\%$ or 0.27
72 – 74	8	$\frac{8}{100} \times 8\%$ or 0.08
Total	$\Sigma f_i = 100$	

Note: The word frequency of a class means, the number of times the class is repeated in the data or the total number of items or observations of the data belongs to that class.

CUMULATIVE FREQUENCY

Many a times the frequencies of different classes are not given. Only their cumulative frequencies are given. The total frequency of all values less than or equal to the upper class boundary of a given class-interval is called the cumulative frequency up to and including that class interval. In this situation both the limits of a class-interval are not written; either lower or upper limit is written.

These cumulative frequencies are called less than or more than cumulative frequencies. For example,

Class-interval	0 – 10	10 – 20	20 – 30	30 – 40	40 – 50
Frequency	4	9	5	12	15

Less than cummulative frequency		**More than cumulative frequency**	
(Upper limits)	(cum. freq.)	(Lower limits)	(cum. freq.)
Less than 10	4	More than 0	45 = 41 + 4
Less than 20	4 + 9 = 13	More than 10	41 = 32 + 9
Less than 30	13 + 5 = 18	More than 20	32 = 27 + 5
Less than 40	18 + 12 = 30	More than 30	27 = 12 + 12
Less than 50	30 + 15 = 45	More than 40	15

Preparation of Frequency Distribution

We shall now study how to classify the raw data in a tabular form.

Consider the data collected by one of the surveyors, interviewing about 50 people. This is as follows:

Size of the shoes: 2, 5, 6, 8, 2, 5, 6, 7, 6, 8, 7, 4, 3.. This is called the raw data. Here some values repeat themselves. For instance the size 5 is repeated 10 times in 50 people. We say that the value of 5 of the variate has the frequency of 10.

Frequency means the number of times a value of the variate or an attribute, as the case may be, is repeated in the data. A table which shows each value of the characteristic with its corresponding frequency, is known as a Frequency Distribution.

The procedure of preparing such a table is explained as below:

Discrete variate

Consider the raw data which gives the size of shoes of 30 persons

2, 5, 6, 4, 5, 7, 4, 4, 6, 2
3, 5, 5, 4, 5, 6, 5, 4, 3, 2
4, 4, 5, 4, 5, 5, 3, 2, 4, 4

The least value is 2 and the highest is 7. All sizes are integers between 2 and 7 (both inclusive). We can prepare a frequency distribution table as follows:

Sizes of shoes	*Tally Marks*	*Frequency*
2	||||	4
3	|||	3
4	𝍸 𝍸	10
5	𝍸 𝍸	9
6	|||	3
7	|	1
Total		30

In this example the size difference from 2 to 7 is very small. If the range of a variate is very large, it is inconvenient to prepare a frequency distribution for each value of the variate.

In such a case we divide the variate into convenient groups and prepare a table showing the groups and their corresponding frequencies.

Such a table is called a grouped frequency distribution.

Consider the marks (out of 100) of 50 students as below:

40, 39, 43, 62, 30, 47, 33, 31, 17, 28

36, 29, 40, 32, 39, 24, 57, 42, 15, 30

50, 52, 47, 65, 31, 07, 37, 47, 17, 20

25, 53, 65, 85, 89, 56, 55, 41, 43, 10

44, 40, 69, 22, 40, 65, 39, 36, 71, 12

The range of the variate (marks) is very large. Also we are eager to know the performance of the students. The passing limit is 35 and above.

Marks between 35 and 44 form the third class (or grade). Marks ranging between 45 - 59 are considered as second class and 60 – 100 form the first class. Thus we have a grouped frequency distribution as:

Marks	**Tally Marks**	**Frequency**
0 – 34	𝍸 𝍸 𝍸 𝍷	16
35 – 44	𝍸 𝍸 𝍸 𝍷𝍷𝍷	18
45 – 59	𝍸 𝍷𝍷𝍷𝍷	9
60 – 100	𝍸 𝍷𝍷	7
Total		50

BIVARIATE FREQUENCY DISTRIBUTION

In table 7, we have classified students according to their marks in one subject. Suppose we have marks of a number of students in two subjects, say statistics and physics and we want to consider the variation of marks in both the subjects simultaneously. Then we have to prepare a table (known as a bivariate table) for the following data:

No. of students	1	2	3	4	5	6	7	8	9	10	11	12
Marks in statistics	60	56	42	33	40	13	27	12	19	50	23	16
Marks in physics	50	45	53	54	49	23	50	24	31	41	47	20

No. of students	13	14	15
Marks in statistics	32	42	30
Marks in physics	38	21	45

Marks in Statistics	Marks in Physics					
	10 – 20	20 – 30	30 – 40	40 – 50	50 – 60	
10 – 20		| | = 2	| = 1			3
20 – 30		| = 1		| = 1	| = 1	3
30 – 40			| = 1	| = 1	| = 1	3
40 – 50		| = 1		| = 1	| = 1	3
Total		4	2	4	5	15

Procedure

We have to consider a pair of data of observations.

We mark one stroke (the tally mark) for one pair.

Now consider the case of the 1st student.

Marks in statistics = 60

Marks in physics = 50

See the row along 50 – 60 → 5th row

and the column along 50 – 60 – 5th column

Therefore the stroke is marked in the cell (box) where the 5th row and the 5th column intersect each other.

In this way we mark the strokes for 15 pairs of marks for 15 students and we get the table – 8.

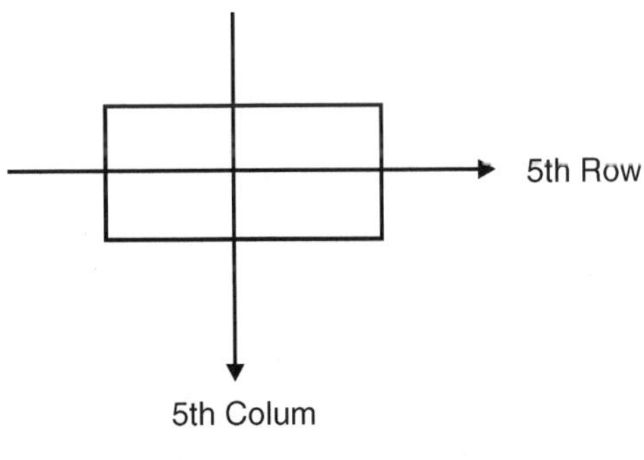

Example: Make a table showing the frequencies, cumulative frequencies (both less than and more than type) for the words having different numbers of letters in the following passage.

"In Asia the complications are likely to be greater still. There will be four major powers in the Asian balance: Russia, China, Japan and the United States.

To some extent, this increases the chance that the forces will emerge sufficient to contain China and it may lead to a real reapproachment between Russia and the West.

But who knows, with so many factors, what the pattern will be like, ten years from now ?"

Solution: We find that the smallest word ' a ' has one letter; and the longest word "re-approachment" has 14 letters.

We prepare a tally sheet by writing the number of letters in the first column from 1 to 14.

The table is as follows:

Number of letters	Tally-marks	Total
1	|	1
2	𝍸 𝍸 |	11
3	𝍸 𝍸 𝍸 |	16
4	𝍸 𝍸 𝍸 |	16
5	𝍸 ||||	9
6	𝍸 𝍸	10
7	𝍸 |	6
8	–	0
9	|	1
10	|	1
11	–	0
12	–	0
13	|	1
14	|	1
Total		73

Number of letters (xi)	Frequency	Cumulative frequency (< or = type)	Cumulative frequency (> or = type)
1	1	1	73
2	11	12	72
3	16	28	71
4	16	44	71
5	9	53	71
6	10	63	70
7	6	69	69
8	0	69	69
9	1	70	63
10	1	71	53
11	0	71	44
12	0	71	28
13	1	72	12
14	1	73	1
Total	73		

Example: The following gives the weights (to the nearest pounds) of 40 students of the 7th grade.

Construct a frequency distribution table giving frequencies and cumulative frequencies of two types. Tabulate the data into equal classes, the 1st class being 118 – 122. Also indicate the class boundaries and the class-marks.

144, 125, 149, 157, 132, 150, 164, 138,

146, 158, 140, 147, 168, 126, 138, 176,

136, 148, 142, 144, 163, 119, 154, 165,

146, 173, 161, 145, 135, 142, 142, 147,

135, 153, 140, 135, 150, 156, 128, 145

Solution: The successive classes are 118 – 122, 123 – 127....., 173 – 177. The lower and upper class boundaries for the 1st class will be 117.5 and 122.5 and the class-mark will be,

$$\frac{177.5+122.5}{2}=\frac{118+122}{2}=120$$

The class-boundaries and the class-marks will go on increasing by 5.

3

Central Tendency

We have studied how to collect raw data, its classification and tabulation in a useful form, which contributes in solving many problems of statistical concern. Yet, this is not sufficient, for in practical purposes, there is need for further condensation, particularly when we want to compare two or more different distributions. We may reduce the entire distribution to one number which represents the distribution.

A single value which can be considered as typical or representative of a set of observations and around which the observations can be considered as Centered is called an 'Average' (or average value) or a Centre of location. Since such typical values tends to lie centrally within a set of observations when arranged according to magnitudes, averages are called measures of central tendency.

In fact the distribution have a typical value (average) about which, the observations are more or less symmetrically distributed. This is of great importance, both theoretically and practically. Dr. A.L. Bowley correctly stated, "Statistics may rightly be called the science of averages."

The word average is commonly used in day-to-day conversations. For example, we may say that Abert is an average boy of my class; we may talk of an average American, average income, etc. When it is said, "Abert is an average student," it means is that he is neither very good nor very bad, but a mediocre student. However, in statistics the term average has a different meaning.

The fundamental measures of tendencies are:

- Arithmetic mean
- Median
- Mode
- Geometric mean
- Harmonic mean
- Weighted averages

However the most common measures of central tendencies or Locations are Arithmetic mean, median and mode. We therefore, consider the Arithmetic mean.

ARITHMETIC MEAN

This is the most commonly used average which you have also studied and used in lower grades. Here are two definitions given by two great masters of statistics. Horace Sacrist: Arithmetic mean is the amount secured by dividing the sum of values of the items in a series by their number.

W.I. King: The arithmetic average may be defined as the sum of aggregate of a series of items divided by their number.

Thus, the students should add all observations (values of all items) together and divide this sum by the number of observations (or items).

Ungrouped Data

Suppose, we have 'n' observations (or measures) $x_1, x_2, x_3......., x_n$ then the Arithmetic mean is obviously

$$\frac{x_1 + x_2 + x_3 + ... + x_n}{n}$$

We shall use the symbol x (pronounced as x bar) to denote the Arithmetic mean. Since we have to write the sum of observations very frequently, we use the usual symbol 'Σ' (pronounced as sigma) to denote the sum. The symbol x_i will be used to denote, in general the 'i' th observation. Then the sum, $x_1 + x_2 + x_3 + ... + x_n$ will be represented by or simply $\sum_{i=1}^{n} x_i$

or $\sum x_i$

Therefore the Arithmetic mean of the set $x_1 + x_2 + x_3 + ... + x_n$ is given by,

$$\overline{x} = \frac{\sum x_i}{n} = \frac{x_1 + x_2 + x_3 + ... + x_n}{n}$$

This method is known as the "Direct Method".

Example: A variable takes the values as given below. Calculate the arithmetic mean of 110, 117, 129, 195, 95, 100, 100, 175, 250 and 750.

Solution: Arithmetic mean $= \frac{\sum x_i}{n}$

$\sum x_i = 110 + 117 + 129 + 195 + 95 + 100 + 100 + 175 + 250 + 750 = 2021$ and $n =$

10

Indirect Method (Assumed Mean Method)

$$\overline{u} = \frac{\sum u_i}{n}$$

where,

$$u = x_i - A$$

A = Assumed Mean = $A + \overline{u}$
Calculations:
Let A = 175 then
Σu_i = –65, –58, –46, +20, –80, –75, –75, +0, +75, +575
= 670 – 399
= 271/10 = 27.1

$\overline{x} = A + \overline{u}$
= 175 + 27.1
= 202.1

Example: M.N. Elhance's earnings for the past week were:

Monday	\$ 450
Tuesday	\$ 375
Wednesday	\$ 500
Thursday	\$ 350
Friday	\$ 270

Find his average earning per day.

Solution: $\sum x_i$
= 450 + 375 + 500 + 350 + 270 = \$ 1945
$n = 5$

$$\text{Arithmetic mean} = \frac{\sum x_i}{n} = \frac{1945}{5} = \$389$$

Therefore, Elhance's average earning per day is \$389.

Short-cut Method:

Sometimes the values of x are very big and in that case, to simplify the calculation the short-cut method is used. For this, first you assume a mean (called as the assumed mean). Let it be A. Now find the deviations of all the values of x from A. We now get a new variable $u_i = x_i - A$

$$\text{Now find } \overline{u} = \frac{\sum u_i}{n}$$

$$\text{then } \overline{x} = A + \frac{\sum u_i}{n} \text{ or } \overline{x} = A + \overline{u}$$

Example: The expenditure of ten families in dollars are given below:

Family:	A	B	C	D	E	F	G	H	I	J
Expenditure: (in dollars).	300	700	100	750	500	80	120	250	100	370

Calculate the Arithmetic mean.

Solution: Let the assumed mean be $ 500. (as. = assume)

Families	Expenditure ($)	Deviation from as. mean
(x_i)		$(u_i = x_i - A)$
A	300	-200
B	700	200
C	100	-400
D	750	250
E	500	0
F	80	-420
G	120	-380
H	250	-250
I	100	-400
J	370	-130
n = 10		$\Sigma u_i = -2180 + 450$ $= -1730$

Calculations:

$$\bar{u} = \frac{\sum u_i}{n} = \frac{-1730}{10} = -173$$

$$\bar{x} = A + \bar{u}$$

$$\bar{x} = 500 + (-173) = 327$$

Discrete Series: There is a difference in the methods for finding the arithmetic means of the individual series and a discrete series. In the discrete series, every term (i.e. value of x) is multiplied by its corresponding frequency $(f_i x_i)$ and then their total (sum) is found $\left(\sum f_i x_i\right)$. The arithmetic mean is then obtained by dividing the total frequency $\left(\sum f\right)$ by the above sum so obtained $\left(\sum f_i x_i\right)$.

Therefore, if the observations $x_1 + x_2 + x_3 + ... + x_n$ are repeated $f_1 + f_2 + f_3 + ... + f_n$ times, then we have:

$$\text{Arithmetic mean } (\bar{x}) = \frac{\sum f_i x_i}{\sum f_i} \text{ i.e.}$$

$$\frac{f_1 + x_1 + f_2 + x_2 + f_3 x_3 + ... + f_n x_n}{f_1 + f_2 + f_3 + ... + f_n}$$

The formulae for Arithmetic mean by direct method and by the short-cut methods are as follows:

Direct method Short-cut method

$$\overline{x} = \frac{\sum f_i x_i}{\sum f_i}$$

$$\overline{x} = A + \overline{u}$$

where,

$$= \frac{\sum f_i u_i}{\sum f_i}$$

and $u = x_i - A$

Therefore,

Example: Find the mean of the following 50 observations.

19, 19, 20, 20, 20, 19, 20, 18, 21, 19,
20, 20, 19, 19, 20, 19, 21, 19, 19, 21,
18, 20, 18, 18, 17, 20, 20, 22, 20, 20,
20, 20, 20, 21, 20, 17, 23, 18, 17, 21,
20, 21, 20, 20, 20, 18, 21, 19, 20, 19

Solution: We may tabulate the given observations as follows.

Observations (x_i)	Frequency (f_i)	fx_i
17	3	$17 \times 3 = 51$
18	6	$18 \times 6 = 108$
19	11	$19 \times 11 = 209$
20	20	$20 \times 20 = 400$
21	8	$21 \times 8 = 168$
22	1	$22 \times 1 = 22$
23	1	$23 \times 1 = 23$
Total	$\sum f_i = 50$	$\sum f_i x_i = 981$

The arithmetic mean is $\overline{x}$

$$= \frac{\sum f_x}{\sum f} = \frac{981}{50} = 19.62$$

Example: Eight coins were tossed together and the number of times they fell on the side of heads was observed. The activity was performed 256 times and the frequency obtained for different values of x, (the number of times it fell on heads) is shown in the following table.

Calculate then mean by:

- Direct method
- Short-cut method

x:	0	1	2	3	4	5	6	7	8
f:	1	9	26	59	72	52	29	7	1

Solution:

No. of coins	**Frequency**	**Direct method**	**Short-cut method Dev. from A (4) i.e. $u_i = x_i - A$**	
x_i	f_i	$f_i x_i$	u_i	$\Sigma f_i u_i$
0	1	0	–4	–4
1	9	9	–3	–27
2	26	52	–2	–52
3	59	117	–1	–59
4	72	288	0	0
5	52	260	1	+52
6	29	174	2	+58
7	7	49	3	+21
8	1	8	4	+4
	$\Sigma f = 256$	$\Sigma fx = 1017$		+135 – 142 $\Sigma fu = -7$

Direct Method

Arithmetic mean

$$(\bar{x}) = \frac{\Sigma f_i x_i}{\Sigma f_i}$$

Therefore,

$$\text{Mean coins} = \frac{1017}{256}$$

$$\bar{x} = 3.97$$

Short-cut method

Arithmetic mean

$$(\bar{x}) = A + \frac{\Sigma f_i u_i}{\Sigma f_i}$$

Therefore,

$$\text{Mean coins} = 4 + \left(\frac{-7}{256}\right)$$

$$\bar{x} = 4 - 0.3$$

$$\bar{x} = 3.97$$

$$\boxed{\bar{x} = 3.97}$$

MEAN FOR GROUPED DATA

Continuous series:

The procedure of finding the arithmetic mean in this series, is the same as we have used in the discrete series. The only difference is that in this series, we are given class-intervals, whose mid-values (class-marks) are to be calculated first. Formula, Arithmetic mean,

$$(\bar{x}) = \frac{\sum f_i x_i}{\sum f_i}$$

where x = mid-value

Example: The weights (in gms) of 30 articles are given below:

14, 16, 16, 14, 22, 13, 15, 24, 23, 14, 20, 17, 21, 18, 18, 19, 20, 17, 16, 15, 11, 22, 21, 20, 17, 18, 19, 22, 23.

Form a grouped frequency table, by dividing the variate range into intervals of equal width, one class being 11-13 and then compute the arithmetic mean.

Solution:

Weights coins	Mid-values x_i	Frequency f_i	Direct method $f_i x_i$	Short-cut method A = 18 $u_i = x_i - A$	$f_i u_i$
11-13	12	3	36	−6	−18
13-15	14	4	56	−4	−16
15-17	16	5	80	−2	−20
17-19	18	6	108	0	0
19-21	20	5	100	+2	+10
21-23	22	4	88	+4	+16
23-25	24	3	72	+6	+18
Total		$\Sigma f_i = 30$	$\Sigma f_i x_i = 540$		$\Sigma f_i u_i = 0$

Direct Method

Arithmetic mean

$$(\bar{x}) = \frac{\Sigma f_i x_i}{\Sigma f_i}$$

$$\bar{x} = \frac{540}{30}$$

$$\bar{x} = 18$$

Short-cut method

Arithmetic mean

$$(\bar{x}) = A + \frac{\Sigma f_i u_i}{\Sigma f_i}$$

$$\bar{x} = 18 + \frac{0}{30}$$

$$\bar{x} = 18$$

Mean weight = 18 gms

Example: Find the arithmetic mean for the following:

Marks below: 10 20 30 40 50 60 70 80

No. of students: 15 35 60 84 96 127 198 250

Solution:

First, we have to convert the cumulative frequencies into frequencies of the respective classes.

Marks	Mid-values x_i	Frequencies c.f. f.	U = X − A A = 45	$f_i u_i$
0 – 10	5	15 15	−40	−600
10 –20	15	35 20	−30	−600
20 – 30	25	60 25	−20	−500
30 – 40	35	84 24	−10	−240

40 – 50	45 ⇒ A	96 12	0	0
50 – 60	55	127 31	+10	+310
60 – 70	65	198 71	+20	+1420
70 – 80	75	250 52	+30	+1560
Total		$\Sigma f = 250$		$\Sigma f_u = 1350$

Step-Deviation Method

Here all class intervals are of the same width say 'c'. This method is employed in place of the Short-cut method.

We measure all the class-marks (mid values) from some convenient value, say 'A', which generally should be taken as the class-mark of a class of maximum frequency or of a class which is the middle one.

All the class marks happen to be multiples of c, since all class intervals are equal. We consider class frequencies as if they are centered at the corresponding class-marks.

Theorem If $x_1, x_2, x_3 \ldots\ldots, x_n$ are n values of the class marks with frequencies $f_1, f_2, f_3 \ldots\ldots f_n$ respectively and if each xi is expressed in terms of the new variable ui by the relation x_i = A + cui then, with the usual notation, we have $\overline{x} = A + c\overline{u}$

where $\overline{u} = \dfrac{\sum fu_i}{\sum f_i}$ and $u_i = \dfrac{x_i - A}{c}$ This method is also known as the "Coding method."

Example: Calculate the arithmetic mean from the following data:

Age (years) below:	25	30	35	40	45	50	55	60
No. of employees:	8	23	51	81	103	113	117	120

Solution:

Age (years)	Mid-values x_i	Frequencies c.f	f_i	$u_i = \dfrac{x_i - A}{c}$	fu_i
20-25	22.5	8	8	–4	–32
25-30	27.5	23	15	–3	–45
30-35	32.5	51	28	–2	–59
35-40	37.5	81	30	–1	–30
40-45	42.5⇒A	103	22	0	0
45-50	47.5	113	10	+1	+10
50-55	52.5	117	4	+2	+8
55-60	57.5	120	3	+3	+9
Total			$\Sigma f = 120$		$\Sigma fu_i = -136$

Arithmetic mean $(\bar{x}) = A + c\bar{u}$

where $\bar{u} = \dfrac{\sum fu_i}{\sum f_i} = \dfrac{-136}{120}$ and c = 5 $\bar{x}$

$= 42.5 + \left(\dfrac{-136}{120}\right) \times 5\ \bar{x}$

= 42.5 – 5.67 $\bar{x}$

= 36.83 years

Example: From the following data, of the calculation of arithmetic mean, find the missing item.

wages in: 110 112 113 117 ? 125 129 130

No. of

workers 25 17 13 15 14 8 7 2

Mean wage $ 115.86

Solution:

Wages in $ x_i	Number of workers f_i	$f_i f_i x_i$
110	25	2750
112	17	1904
113	13	1496
117	15	1755
x	14	14x
125	8	1000
128	6	768
130	2	260
Total	Σf_i = 100	$\Sigma f_i x_i$ = 9906+14x

Now the arithmetic mean

$$(\bar{x}) = \frac{\sum f_i x_i}{\sum f_i}$$

Therefore, 115.86 $= \dfrac{9906 + 14x}{100}$

or 5115.86×100 = 9906 + 14x

11586 = 9906 + 14x

11586 – 9906 = 14x

1680 = 14x

$$\text{or} \quad x = \frac{1680}{14}$$

$$x = 120$$

Therefore the missing item is 120.

PROPERTIES OF ARITHMETIC MEAN

- The sum of the deviations, of all the values of x, from their arithmetic mean, is zero.

Justification: $\sum f_i(x_i - \bar{x}) \quad = \sum f_i x_i - \bar{x}\sum f_i = 0$

Since $\bar{x}$ is a constant, $\bar{x} = \dfrac{\sum f_i x_i}{\sum f_i} = \sum f_i x_i - = \bar{x}\sum f_i$

- The product of the arithmetic mean and the number of items gives the total of all items.

Justification: $\bar{x} = \dfrac{\sum f_i x_i}{\sum f_i} \Rightarrow \sum f_i x_i - = \bar{x}\sum f_i$

$$\text{or}\ \bar{x} = \frac{\sum x}{N} \Rightarrow \bar{x}.N = \sum x_i$$

- If $\bar{x}_1$ and $\bar{x}_2$ are the arithmetic mean of two samples of sizes n_1 and n_2 respectively then, the arithmetic mean $\bar{x}$ of the distribution combining the two can be calculated as

$$\bar{x} = \frac{n_1\bar{x}_1 + n_2\bar{x}_2}{n_1 + n_2}$$

This formula can be extended for still more groups or samples. $\bar{x}_1$

$$= \frac{\sum x_{1i}}{n_1} \Rightarrow \sum x_{1i} = n_1\bar{x}_1$$

Justification: $\bar{x}_1 = \dfrac{\sum x_{1i}}{n_1} \Rightarrow \sum x_{1i} = n_1\bar{x}_1$ = total of the observations of the first sample

Similarly $\sum x_{2i} = n_2\bar{x}_2$ = total of the observations of the first sample The combined mean of the two samples

$= \frac{\text{combined total}}{n_1 + n_2} \; \bar{x}$

$= \frac{n_1\bar{x}_1 + n_2\bar{x}_2}{n_1 + n_2}$

Example: The average marks of three batches of students having 70, 50 and 30 students respectively are 50, 55 and 45. Find the average marks of all the 150 students, taken together.

Solution:

Let x be the average marks of all 150 students taken together.

	Batch – I	Batch – II	Batch – III
	$\bar{x}_1$	$\bar{x}_2$	$\bar{x}_3$
A. marks:	= 50	= 55	= 45
No. of students	$n_1 = 70$	$n_2 = 50$	$n_3 = 30\,\bar{x}_1$

$= \frac{n_1\bar{x}_1 + n_2\bar{x}_2 + n_3\bar{x}_3}{n_1 + n_2 + n_3} = \frac{70 \times 50 + 50 \times 55 + 30 \times 45}{70 + 50 + 30}$

$= \frac{7600}{150} \; \bar{x}_1$

= 50.67 marks

Example: The mean of a certain number of observations is 40. If two or more items with values 50 and 64 are added to this data, the mean rises to 42. Find the number of items in the original data.

Solution:

Let 'n' be the number of observations whose mean $\bar{x} = 40.\ \bar{x}$

$= \frac{\sum x_i}{n} \quad \sum x_i = n\bar{x} = n(40) = 40n$ total of n values.

Two more items of values 50 and 64 are added therefore, total of $(n+2)$ values:

$= \sum x_i + 50 + 64$

$= 40n + 50 + 64$

$= 40n + 114$

Now new mean is 42.

$\text{New } \bar{x} = \frac{\text{New total of (n+2) value}}{n+2}$

$42 = \frac{40n + 14}{n+2}$

$42n + 84 = 40n + 114$
$2n = 30$
$n = 15$

Therefore, the number of items in the original data = 15.

Example: The sum of deviations of a certain numbers of observations measured from 4 is 72 and the sum of deviations of observations measured from 7 is –3. Find the number of observations and their mean.

Solution:

Let 'n' be the required number of observations $\sum (x_i - 4) = 72$, therefore, $\sum x_i - 4_n = 72$

Note $\sum 4 = 4n$ and $\sum (x_i - 7) = -3$, therefore,

$$\sum x_i - 7n = -3$$

Subtracting the two equations we get,

$$\sum x_i - 4n = 72$$
$$\sum x_i - 4n = -2$$
$$3n = 72$$

$n = 25$

Putting $n = 25$ in $\sum x_i - 4n = 72$, we get

$$\sum x_i - 4(25) = 72$$

$$\sum x_i = 72 + 100$$

$$\sum x_i = 172$$

Now Mean is given by $\bar{x} = \frac{\sum x_i}{n} = \frac{172}{25} = 6.88$

Example: The mean weight of 98 students is found to be 50 lbs. It is later discovered that the frequency of the class interval (30- 40) was wrongly taken as 8 instead of 10. Calculate the correct mean.

Solution:

Incorrect mean $(\bar{x})$ = 50 Kg and $\sum f_i = 98$

$$\text{Incorrect } \bar{x} = \frac{\text{Incorrect} \sum f_i x_i}{\sum f_i}$$

$$50 = \frac{\text{Incorrect} \sum f_i x_i}{98}$$

Therefore, Incorrect $\sum f_i x_i = 98 \times 50 = 4900$

Now correct

$\sum f_i x_i = \text{Incorrect} \sum f_i x_i - (8 \times 35) + (10 \times 35)$

Note that the class-mark of class interval (30 - 40) is 35 and for the calculation of the mean we consider class marks.

The correct $\sum f_i x_i$ = 4900 – 280 + 350 = 4970

Also the correct $\sum f_i$ = 98 + 2 = 100

Therefore, the correct mean $\overline{x}$

$$= \frac{\text{correct} \sum f_i x_i}{\text{correct} \sum f_i} = \frac{4970}{100} \overline{x}$$

= 49.701b

Example: The sum of the deviations of 'n' observation values of a variate from a constant 'a', is S. Show that the arithmetic mean is $a + \frac{S}{n}$.

Solution:

Dividing by n to get the mean

i.e. $\frac{\sum x_i}{n} - \frac{an}{n} = \frac{S}{n} \frac{\sum x_i}{n} = a + \frac{S}{n}$

But $\frac{\sum x_i}{n} = \overline{x}$

Therefore, $\overline{x} = a + \frac{S}{n}$

Merits

- It is rigidly defined. Its value is always definite.
- It is easy to calculate and easy to understand. Hence it is very popular.
- It is based on all the observations; so that it becomes a good representative.
- It can be easily used for comparison.
- It is capable of further algebraic treatment such as finding the sum

of the values of the observations, if the mean and the total number of the observations are given; finding the combined arithmetic mean when different groups are given etc.

- It is not affected much by sampling fluctuations.

Demerits

- It is affected by outliers or extreme values. For example, the average

(A.) mean of 10, 15, 25 and 500 is $\overline{x} = \dfrac{10+15+25+500}{4} = 137.5$

Now observe first three values whose A.mean is $\dfrac{10+15+25}{3} = 16.67$ (approx.)

Due to the outlier 500 the A. mean of the four numbers is raised to 137.5. In such a case A. mean is not a good representative of the given data.

- It is a value which may not be present in the given data.
- Many a times it gives absurd results like 4.4 children per family.
- It is not possible to take out the averages of ratios and percentages.
- We cannot calculate it when open-end class intervals are present in the data.

Newspaper: Punch, Quoted by Moroney

"The figure of 2.2 children per adult female was felt to be in some respect absurd and the Royal Commission suggested that the middle class is paid money to increase the average to a rounder and more convenient number."

MEDIAN

It is the value of the size of the central item of the arranged data (data arranged in the ascending or the descending order). Thus, it is the value of the middle item and divides the series in to equal parts.

In Connor's words - "The median is that value of the variable which divides the group into two equal parts, one part comprising all values greater and the other all values lesser than the median."

For example, the daily wages of 7 workers are 5, 7, 9, 11, 12, 14 and 15 dollars. This series contains 7 terms. The fourth term i.e. $11 is the median.

Median In Individual Series (ungrouped Data)

- Set the individual series either in the ascending (increasing) or in the descending (decreasing) order, of the size of its items or observations.
- If the total number of observations be 'n' then

A. If 'n' is odd,

The median = size of $\left(\frac{n+1}{2}\right)^{th}$ observation

B. If 'n' is even, the median

$$=\frac{1}{2}\left[\begin{array}{l}\text{size of}\left(\frac{n}{2}\right)^{th}\text{ observations}\\ +\text{size of}\left(\frac{n+2}{2}\right)^{th}\text{ observations}\end{array}\right]$$

Example: The following figures represent the number of books issued at the counter of a Statistics library on 11 different days. 96, 180, 98, 75, 270, 80, 102, 100, 94, 75 and 200. Calculate the median.

Solution:

Arrange the data in the ascending order as 75, 75, 80, 94, 96, 98, 100, 102,180, 200, 270.

Now the total number of items 'n'= 11 (odd)

Therefore, the median = size of $\left(\frac{n+1}{2}\right)^{th}$ item

$= \text{size of}\left(\frac{11+1}{2}\right)^{th}$ item

= size of 5th item

= 98 books per day

Example: The population (in thousands) of 36 metro-politan cities are as follows:

2468, 591, 437, 20, 213, 143, 1490, 407, 284, 176, 263, 19, 181, 777, 387, 302, 213, 204, 153, 733, 391, 176 178, 122, 532, 360, 65, 260, 193, 92, 672, 258, 239, 160, 147, 151. Calculate the median.

Solution:

Arranging the terms in the ascending order as:

20, 65, 92, 131, 142, 143, 147, 151, 153, 160, 169, 176, 178, 181, 193, 204, (213, 39), 258, 263, 260, 384, 302, 360, 387, 391, 407, 437, 522, 591, 672, 733, 777, 1490, 2488.

Since total number of items n = 36 (Even). the median

$$=\frac{1}{2}\left[\text{size of}\left(\frac{n}{2}\right)^{th}\text{ item}+\text{size of}\left(\frac{n+2}{2}\right)^{th}\text{ item}\right]$$

$$=\frac{1}{2}\left[\text{size of }18^{th}\text{ item}+\text{size of19th item}\right]$$

$$= \frac{1}{2}[213 + 239]$$

$$= \frac{1}{2}[252]$$

= 226 thousands

Median In Discrete Series

Steps:

- Arrange the data in ascending or descending order of magnitude.
- Find the cumulative frequencies.
- Apply the formula:

A. If 'n' = $\sum f_i$ (odd) then,

$$\text{Median} = \text{size of } \left(\frac{n+1}{2}\right)^{\text{th}} \text{ item}$$

B. If 'n' = $\sum f_i$ (even) then,

Median,

$$= \frac{1}{2}\left[\begin{array}{l}\text{size of}(n/2)^{\text{th}} \text{ item} \\ + \text{size of}\left(\frac{n+2}{2}\right)^{\text{th}} \text{ item}\end{array}\right]$$

Example: Locate the median in the following distribution.

Size: 8 10 12 14 16 18 20

Frequency: 7 7 12 28 10 9 6

Solution:

Size (x_i)	Frequency f_i	Cumulative frequency (c. f)
8	3	3
10	7	3 + 7 = 10
12	12	12 + 10 = 22
14	28	28 + 22 = 50
16	10	50 + 10 = 60
18	9	60 + 9 = 69
20	6	69 + 6 = 75
	$n = \Sigma f_i = 75$ (odd)	

$$\text{Therefore, the median} = \text{size of}\left(\frac{n+1}{2}\right)^{\text{th}} \text{ item}$$

$$= \text{size of} \left(\frac{75+1}{2}\right)^{\text{th}} \text{item}$$

= size of 38th item

In the order of the cumulative frequency, the 38th term is present in the 50th cumulative frequency, whose size is 14.

Therefore, the median = 14

Median In Continuous Series (grouped Data)

Steps:

- Determine the particular class in which the value of the median lies.

  Use as the rank of the median and not $\left(\frac{n+1}{2}\right)$

- After ascertaining the class in which median lies, the following formula is used for determining the exact value of the median.

Median,

$$= \ell_1 + \left[\frac{N/2 - c.f}{f}\right](\ell_2 - \ell_1)$$

where, ℓ_1 = lower limit of the median class, the class in which the middle item of the distribution lies.

ℓ_2 = upper limit of the median class

$c.f$ = cumulative frequency of the class preceding the median class

f = sample frequency of the median class

It should be noted that while interpolating the median value of frequency distribution it is assumed that the variable is continuous and that there is an orderly and even distribution of items within each class.

Example:: Calculate the median for the following and verify it graphically.

Age (years):	20-25	25-30	30-35	35-40	40-45
No. of person:	70	80	180	150	20

Solution:

Age (years) C.I.	No. of persons f_i	Cumulative frequency c.f.
20 - 25	70	70
25 - 30	80	70 + 80 = 150
30 - 35	180	150 + 180 = 330
35 - 40	150	330 + 150 = 480
40 - 45	20	480 + 20 = 500
	$n = \Sigma fi = 500$	

Now median = size of $(n/2)^{th}$ item

$$= \text{size of} \left(\frac{500}{2}\right)^{th}$$

= size of 250th item which lies in (30 - 35) class interval

$$\ell_1 + \left[\frac{N/2 - c.f}{f}\right](\ell_2 - \ell_1)$$

Here $\ell_1 = 30$, $\ell_2 = 35$, $= n/2\ 250$, $c.\,f. = 150$ and $f = 180$

Therefore, Median

$$= 30 + \left[\frac{250 - 150}{180}\right](35 - 30)$$

$$= 30 + \frac{10}{180} \times 5$$

= 32.78 years

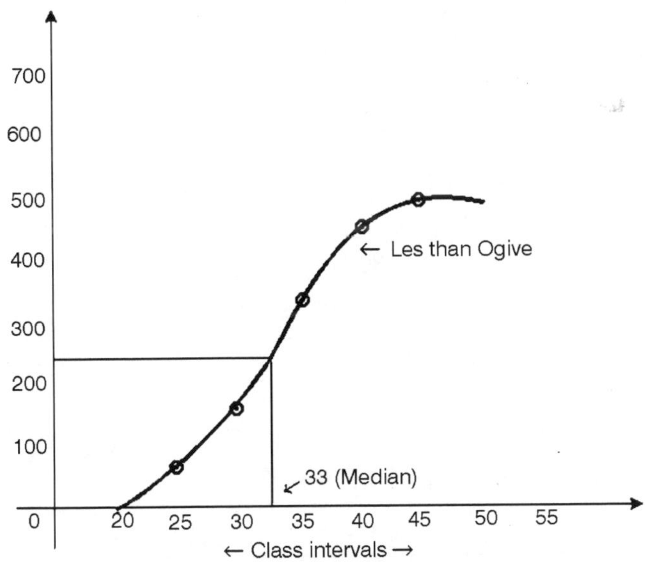

Sometimes the series is given in the descending order of magnitude. In this situation convert the series in the ascending order of magnitude and then using the regular formula, the median can be calculated or the series can be put in the descending order of the magnitude and an alternative formula be used to calculate the median.

Example:: Marks: 40-50 30-40 20-30 10-20 0-10

No. of students: 10 12 40 30 8

Solution:

Marks	No. of students	c.f
0 - 10	8	8
10 - 20	30	8 + 30 = 38
20 - 30	40	38 + 40 = 78
30 - 40	12	78 + 12 = 90
40 - 50	10	90 + 10 = 100
	$n = \Sigma f = 100$	

Median = size of $(n/2)^{th}$ item

$$= \text{size of } \left(\frac{500}{2}\right)^{th} \text{ item}$$

= size of 50th item which comes into class interval (20 - 30). By interpolation

$$= 20 + \left[\frac{50-38}{40}\right](30-20)$$

$$= 20 + \frac{12}{40} \times 10$$

$$= 20 + 3$$

$$\text{Median} = \ell_1 + \left[\frac{n/2 - c.f}{f}\right](\ell_2 - \ell_1)$$

Median = 23 marks

Marks	No. of students	Cumulative Frequency
40 - 50	10	10
30 - 40	12	22
20 - 30	40	62
10 - 20	30	92
0 - 10	8	100
	$n = \Sigma f = 100$	

Arranging the series in the descending order (as it is given) Median = size of $(n/2)^{th}$ item = size of 50th item which lies in (20 - 30) class-interval.

Alternative formula:

Median

$$= \ell_1 - \left[\frac{n/2 - c.f}{f}\right](\ell_2 - \ell_1)$$

$$=30-\left[\frac{50-22}{40}\right](30-20)$$

$$=30-\frac{28}{40}\times 10$$

= 23 marks

Note that, while calculating the median of a series, it must be put in the 'exclusive class-interval' form. If the original series is in inclusive type, first convert it into the exclusive type and then find its median.

Example:: The following distribution represents the number of minutes spent by a group of teenagers in watching movies. What is the median? Minutes/Weeks:0-99 100-199 200-299 300-399 400 - 499 500 - 599 600 & more

No. of teenagers: 27 32 65 78 58 32 8

Solution:

Minutes/ weeks	Real class intervals	Frequency	Cumulative frequency
0 - 99	0.5 - 99.5	27	27
100 - 199	99.5 199.5	32	27 + 32 = 59
200 - 299	199.5 - 299.5	65	59 + 65 = 124
300 - 399	299.5 - 399.5	78	124 + 78 = 202
400 - 499	399.5 - 499.5	58	202 + 58 = 260
500 - 599	499.5 - 599.5	32	260 + 32 = 292
600 &more	599.5 & more	82	92 + 8 = 300
		$n = \Sigma f_i = 300$	

Median = size of $(n/2)^{th}$ item

$$= \text{size of} \left(\frac{300}{2}\right)^{th} \text{item}$$

= size of 150th item which

lies in (299.5 – 399.5) class interval

By using interpolation

$$\text{Median} \quad =\ell_1-\left[\frac{n/2-c.f}{f}\right](\ell_2-\ell_1)$$

$$=299.5+\left[\frac{150-124}{78}\right](399.5-299.5)$$

$$=299.5+\left[\frac{26}{78}\right]\times 100$$

299.5 + 33.33 (approximately)

Median = 392.88 minutes/week

Merits of Median

- It is rigidly defined.
- It is easy to calculate and understand.
- It is not affected by extreme values like the arithmetic mean. For example, 5 persons have their incomes $2000, $2500, $2600, $3000, $5000. The median would be $2600 while the arithmetic mean would be $3020.
- It can be found by mere inspection.
- It is fully representative and can be computed easily.
- It can be used for qualitative studies.
- Even if the extreme values are unknown, median can be calculated if one knows the number of items.
- It can be obtained graphically.

Demerits of Median

- It may not be representative if the distribution is irregular and abnormal.
- It is not capable of further algebraic treatment.
- It is not based on all observations.
- It is affected by sample fluctuations.
- The arrangement of the data in the order of magnitude is absolutely necessary.

MODE

It is the size of that item which possesses the maximum frequency. According to Professor Kenney and Keeping, the value of the variable which occurs most frequently in a distribution is called the mode. It is the most common value. It is the point of maximum density.

Ungrouped Data

Individual series: The mode of this series can be obtained by mere inspection. The number which occurs most often is the mode.

Example: Locate mode in the data 7, 12, 8, 5, 9, 6, 10, 9, 4, 9, 9

Solution: On inspection, it is observed that the number 9 has maximum frequency. Therefore 9 is the mode. Note that if in any series, two or more numbers have the maximum frequency, then the mode will be difficult to calculate. Such series are called as Bi-modal, Tri-modal or Multi-modal series.

Grouped Data

Steps:

- Determine the modal class which as the maximum frequency.
- By interpolation the value of the mode can be calculated as -

$$\text{Mode} = \ell_1 - \left[\frac{f_1 - f_0}{2f_1 - f_0 - f_2}\right](\ell_2 - \ell_1)$$

where ℓ_1

= Lower limit of the modal class ℓ_2

= Upper limit of the modal class f_1

= Frequency of the modal class f_0

= Frequency of the class preceding to the modal class f_2

= Frequency of the class succeding the modal class

Example: Calculate the modal wages.

Daily wages in $:	20 -25	25-30	30-35	35-40	40-45	45-50
No. of workers:	1	3	8	12	7	5

Verify it graphically.

Solution:

Here the maximum frequency is 12, corresponding to the class interval (35 - 40) which is the modal class.

Therefore $\ell_1 = 35,\ \ell_2 = 40,\ \ell_0 = 8,\ \ell_1 = 12,\ \ell_2 = 7,$

By interpolation

$$\text{Mode} = \ell_1 - \left[\frac{f_1 - f_0}{2f_1 - f_0 - f_2}\right](\ell_2 - \ell_1)$$

$$= 40 + \left[\frac{12 - 8}{24 - 8 - 7}\right](40 - 35)$$

$$= 40 + \left[\frac{4}{9}\right] \times 5$$

= 40 + 2.22

= 37.22

Modal wages is $37. 22

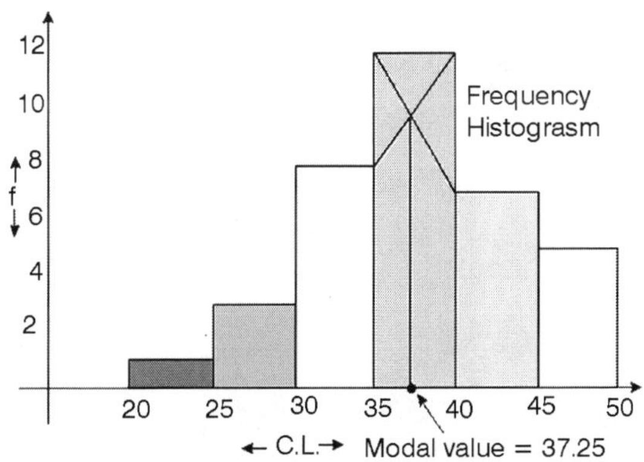

MERITS OF MODE

- It is simple to calculate.
- In individual or discrete distribution it can be located by mere inspection.
- It is easy to understand. Everyone is used to the idea of average size of a garment, an average American etc.
- It is not isolated like the median as it is the most common item.
- Like the Average mean, it is not a value which cannot be found in the series.
- It is not necessary to know all the items. What we need the point of maximum density frequency.
- It is not affected by sampling fluctuations.

DEMERITS

- It is ill defined.
- It is not based on all observations.
- It is not capable of further algebraic treatment.
- It is not a good representative of the data.
- Sometimes there are more than one values of mode.

EMPIRICAL RELATION BETWEEN MEAN, MEDIAN AND MODE

A distribution in which the values of mean, median and mode coincide (i.e. mean = median = mode) is known as a symmetrical distribution. Conversely, when values of mean, median and mode are not equal the distribution is known as asymmetrical or skewed distribution. In moderately skewed or asymmetrical distribution a very important relationship exists among these three measures of central tendency. In such distributions the distance between the mean and median is about one-third of the distance between the mean and mode, as will be clear from the diagrams 1 and 2. Karl Pearson expressed this relationship as:

Mode = mean –3 [mean – median]

Mode = 3 median –2 mean

and Median $= \text{mode} + \frac{2}{3}[\text{mean} - \text{mode}]$

Knowing any two values, the third can be computed.

Example:

Given median = 20.6, mode = 26 Find mean.

Solution:

Mode = 3 median – 2mean

$$\text{Mean} = \frac{1}{2}[3\,\text{median} - \text{mode}]$$

$$\text{Mean} = \frac{1}{2}[3(20.6) - (26)]$$

$$\text{Mean} = \frac{1}{2}[35.8]$$

$$\text{Mean} = 17.9$$

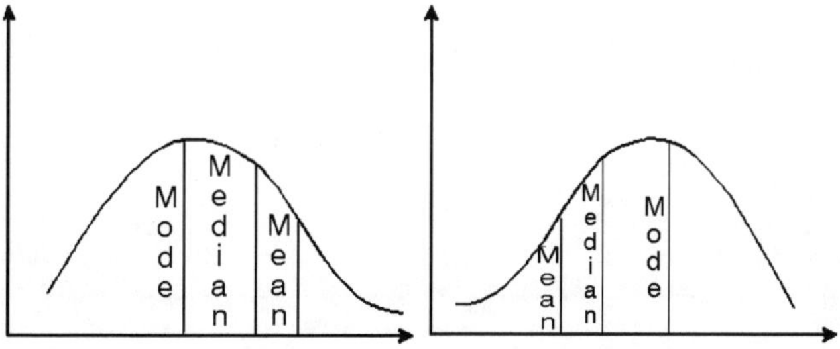

4

Dispersion

The measures of central tendencies (i.e. means) indicate the general magnitude of the data and locate only the centre of a distribution of measures. They do not establish the degree of variability or the spread out or scatter of the individual items and their deviation from (or the difference with) the means.

- According to Nciswanger, "Two distributions of statistical data may be symmetrical and have common means, medians and modes and identical frequencies in the modal class. Yet with these points in common they may differ widely in the scatter or in their values about the measures of central tendencies."
- Simpson and Kafka said, "An average alone does not tell the full story. It is hardly fully representative of a mass, unless we know the manner in which the individual item. Scatter around it.... a further description of a series is necessary, if we are to gauge how representative the average is."

From this discussion we now focus our attention on the scatter or variability which is known as dispersion. Let us take the following three sets.

Students	Group X	Group Y	Group Z
1	50	45	30
2	50	50	45
3	50	55	75
mean ⇒	50	50	50

Thus, the three groups have same mean i.e. 50. In fact the median of group X and Y are also equal. Now if one would say that the students from the three groups are of equal capabilities, it is totally a wrong conclusion then. Close examination reveals that in group X students have equal marks as the mean, students from group Y are very close to the mean but in the third group Z, the marks are widely scattered. It is thus clear that the measures of the central tendency is alone not sufficient to describe the data.

Definition of dispersion: The arithmetic mean of the deviations of the values of the individual items from the measure of a particular central tendency used. Thus the 'dispersion' is also known as the "average of the second degree." Prof. Griffin and Dr. Bowley said the same about the dispersion.

In measuring dispersion, it is imperative to know the amount of variation (absolute measure) and the degree of variation (relative measure). In the former case we consider the range, mean deviation, standard deviation etc.

In the latter case we consider the coefficient of range, the coefficient mean deviation, the coefficient of variation etc.

METHODS OF COMPUTING DISPERSION

- Method of limits:
  - The range
  - Inter-quatrile range
  - Percentile range
- Method of Averages:
  - Quartile deviation
  - Mean deviation
  - Standard Deviation and
  - Other measures.

Note that, we are going to study some of these and not all.

RANGE

In any statistical series, the difference between the largest and the smallest values is called as the range.

Thus Range (R) = $L - S \begin{cases} L = \text{Largest value of the series.} \\ S = \text{Smallest value of the series.} \end{cases}$

Coefficient of Range: The relative measure of the range. It is used in the comparative study of the dispersion co-efficient of Range = $\frac{\text{L}-\text{S}}{\text{L}+\text{S}}$

Example: (Individual series) Find the range and the co-efficient of the range of the following items:

110, 117, 129, 197, 190, 100, 100, 178, 255, 790.

Solution: R = L – S = 790 – 100 = 690

$$\text{Co-efficient of Range} = \frac{\text{L}-\text{S}}{\text{L}+\text{S}} = \frac{790-100}{790+100} = \frac{690}{890} = 0.78$$

Example: (Continuous series) Find the range and its co-efficient from the following data.

Size:	10-20	20-30	30-40	40-50	50-10
Frequency:	2	3	5	4	2

Solution: R = L – S = 100 – 10 = 90

$$\text{Co-efficient of range} = \frac{L-S}{L+S} = \frac{100-10}{100+10} = \frac{90}{110} = 0.82$$

MEAN DEVIATION

Average deviations (mean deviation) is the average amount of variations (scatter) of the items in a distribution from either the mean or the median or the mode, ignoring the signs of these deviations by Clark and Senkade.

Individual Series

Steps:

- Find the mean or median or mode of the given series.
- Using and one of three, find the deviations (differences) of the items of the series from them.

i.e. $x_i - x$, x_i – Me and x_i – Mo.
Me = Median and Mo = Mode.

- Find the absolute values of these deviations i.e. ignore there positive (+) and negative (-) signs.

i.e. $| xi - x |$, $| xi -$ Me $|$ and $xi -$ Mo $|$.

- Find the sum of these absolute deviations.

i.e. $S \mid xi - x \mid +$, $S \mid xi -$ Me $|$, and $S \mid xi -$ Mo $|$.

(5) Find the mean deviation using the following formula.

$$\text{M.D} = (\partial x) = \Sigma xi - x, \partial(\text{Me}) = \Sigma xi - \text{Me}$$

$$\text{or} \quad \partial(\text{Me}) = xi \text{ Mo}$$

Note that:

(i) generally M. D. obtained from the median is the best for the practical purpose.

$$\text{(ii) co-efficient of M. D.} = \frac{\partial \overline{x}}{\overline{x}} = \frac{\partial(\text{Me})}{\text{Me}} = \frac{\partial(\text{Mo})}{\text{Mo}}$$

Example: Calculate Mean deviation and its co-efficient for the following salaries:

$ 1030, $ 500, $ 680, $ 1100, $ 1080, $ 1740. $ 1050, $ 1000, $ 2000, $ 2250, $ 3500 and $ 1030.

S.No.	Salary ($) xi	Deviation from Me (1080) ± ignored
1	500	580
2	680	400
3	1030	50
4	1030	50
5	1050	50
6	1080	50

7	1100	30
8	1500	0
9	2000	420
11	2250	660
12	3500	920
		1170
		2420
$n = 13$		$\Sigma \mid xi - \text{Me} \mid = 6770$

Calculation:

i) Median (Me)

$$= \text{size of} \left(\frac{n+1}{2}\right)^{\text{th}} \text{ item}$$

$$= \text{size of } 7^{\text{th}} \text{ item}$$

ii) M. D. (δ Me) $= \dfrac{\Sigma \mid x_i - \text{Me}}{n}$

$$= \frac{6770}{13}$$

= $ 520.76

iii) co-efficient of δ Me.

$$= \frac{\delta\text{Me}}{\text{Me}} = \frac{520.76}{1080}$$

Example: (Discrete series) Calculate the mean deviation of the following series.

Size:	4	6	8	10	12	14	16
Frequency:	2	4	5	3	2	1	4

Solution:

Size(xi)	Frequency(f)	C.f.	I xi – Me I	I xi – Me I
4	2	2	I 8 – 4 I = 4	2 × 4 = 8
6	4	2 + 4 = 6	I 8 – 6 I = 2	4 × 2 = 8
8	5	6 + 5 = 11	I 8 – 8 I = 0	5 × 0 = 0
10	3	11 + 3 = 14	I 8 – 10 I = 2	3 × 2 = 6
12	2	14 + 2 = 16	I 8 – 12 I = 4	2 × 4 = 8
14	1	16 + 1 = 17	I 8 – 14 I = 4	1 × 6 = 6
16	4	17 + 4 = 21	I 8 – 16 I = 8	4 × 8 = 32
	$n = 21$			$\mid x_i - \text{Me} \mid = 68$

Calculations:

$$\text{i) Median (Me)} = \text{Size of} \left(\frac{n+1}{2}\right)^{\text{th}}$$

item = size of $\left(\frac{21+1}{2}\right)^{\text{th}}$ item

= Size of 11th item.

Therefore, Median (Me) = 8

ii) M. D. $= \frac{\Sigma |x_i - \text{Me}|}{\text{Me}} = \frac{68}{21} = 3.24$

Example: (Continuous series) Calculate the mean deviation and the coefficient of mean deviation from the following data using the mean.

Difference in ages between boys and girls of a class.

Diff. in years:	No.of students:
0 - 5	449
5 - 10	705
10 - 15	507
15 - 20	281
20 - 25	109
25 - 30	52
30 - 35	16
35 - 40	4

Solution:

Diff.in age	Mid-values (x_i)	frequency (f_i)	$f_i x_i$	$\lvert x_i - \bar{x}\rvert$	$f_i \lvert x_i - \bar{x}\rvert$
0 - 5	2.5	449	1122.5	8	3592
5 - 10	7.5	705	5287.5	3	2115
10 - 15	12.5	507	6337.5	2	1014
15 - 20	17.5	281	4917.5	7	1967
20 - 25	22.5	109	2452.5	12	884
25 - 30	27.5	52	1430.0	17	884
30 - 35	32.5	16	520.0	22	352
35 - 40	37.5	4	150.0	27	108
		n=2123	$\Sigma f_i x_i$= 22217.5		$\Sigma f_i \lvert x_i - \bar{x}\rvert$ = 11440

Calculation:

1) $X = \frac{\Sigma f_i x_i}{n} = \frac{22217.5}{2123} = 10.5$ (approx.)

2) M. D. $= \frac{\Sigma f_i |x_i - \bar{x}|}{n} = \frac{11440}{2123} = 5.4$

3) co - efficient of M. D. $= \frac{\text{M.D.}}{\bar{x}} = \frac{5.4}{10.5} = 0.514$

VARIANCE

The term variance was used to describe the square of the standard deviation R.A. Fisher in 1913. The concept of variance is of great importance in advanced work where it is possible to split the total into several parts, each attributable to one of the factors causing variations in their original series. Variance is defined as follows:

$$\text{Variance} = \frac{\Sigma(x_i - \bar{x})^2}{n}$$

Standard Deviation (s. d.)

It is the square root of the arithmetic mean of the square deviations of various values from their arithmetic mean. it is denoted by s.d. or σ.

Thus, s.d. $(\sigma x) = \sqrt{\frac{\Sigma(x_i - \bar{x})^2}{n}}$ for the ungrouped data

$= \sqrt{\frac{\Sigma f_i(x_i - \bar{x})^2}{n}}$ for the grouped data

where $n = \Sigma f_i$

Merits

- It is rigidly defined and based on all observations.
- It is amenable to further algebraic treatment.
- It is not affected by sampling fluctuations.
- It is less erratic.

Demerits

- It is difficult to understand and calculate.
- It gives greater weight to extreme values.

Note that variance $V(x) = \frac{\Sigma(x_i - \bar{x})^2}{n}$

and $s.\ d.\ (\sigma x) = \sqrt{\frac{\Sigma(x_i - \bar{x})^2}{n}}$ and $\sqrt{\frac{\Sigma f_i(x_i - \bar{x})^2}{n}}$

Then $V(x) = \sigma_x^2$

CO-EFFICIENT OF VARIATION (C. V.)

To compare the variations (dispersion) of two different series, relative measures of standard deviation must be calculated. This is known as co-efficient of variation or the co-efficient of s. d. Its formula is

$$\text{C. V.} = \frac{\sigma x}{\overline{x}} \times 100$$

Thus it is defined as the ratio s. d. to its mean.

Remark: It is given as a percentage and is used to compare the consistency or variability of two more series. The higher the C. V., the higher the variability and lower the C. V., the higher is the consistency of the data.

Example: Calculate the standard deviation and its co-efficient from the following data.

A	10
B	12
C	16
D	8
E	25
F	30
G	14
H	11
I	13
J	11

Solution:

No No.	x_i	$(x_i - x)$	$(x_i - x)^2$
A	10	-5	25
B	12	-3	9
C	16	+1	1
D	8	-7	49
E	25	+10	100
F	30	+15	225
G	14	-1	1
H	11	-5	16
I	13	-2	4
J	11	-4	16
$n = 10$	$\Sigma x_i = 150$		$\Sigma \mid x_i - x \mid 2 = 446$

Calculations:

$$\text{i) } \overline{x} = \frac{\Sigma x_i}{n} = \frac{150}{10} = 15$$

$$\text{ii) s.d.}(\sigma x) = \sqrt{\frac{\Sigma(x_i - \overline{x})^2}{n}} = \sqrt{\frac{446}{10}} = 6.7$$

$$\text{iii) co-efficient of s.d.} = \frac{\sigma x}{\overline{x}} = \frac{6.7}{15} = 0.45$$

Example: Prove that s.d. $(sx) = \sqrt{\frac{\Sigma xi^2}{n} - (\overline{x})^2}$

Solution: Now consider

$$\frac{\Sigma(x_i - \overline{x})^2}{n} = \frac{\Sigma(xi^2 - 2xi\overline{x} + \overline{x}^2)}{n}$$

$$= \frac{\Sigma xi^2}{n} - 2\overline{x}\frac{\Sigma xi}{n} + \overline{x}^2 \frac{\Sigma 1}{n}$$

$$= \frac{\Sigma x_i^2}{n} - 2\overline{x}(\overline{x}) + \overline{x}^2 . \frac{n}{n}$$

$$\ldots (\because \frac{\Sigma x_i}{n} = \overline{x} \text{ and } \Sigma 1 = n)$$

$$= \frac{\Sigma x_i^2}{n} - 2(\overline{x})^2 + (\overline{x})^2$$

Therefore, $\sigma x = \sqrt{\frac{\Sigma xi^2}{n} - (\overline{x})^2}$

This is known as a short-cut formula for standard deviation. The above problem can also be solved by this formula as:

Solution: We have $\Sigma x_i^2 = 2695$,

$n = 10$ and $\overline{x} = 15$ then

$$\text{s.d. } (s\ x) = \sqrt{\frac{2696}{10} - (15)^2}$$

$$= \sqrt{269.6 - 225} = \sqrt{44.6} = 6.67$$

Example: Calculate s.d. of the marks of 100 students.

Marks	No. of students(f_i)	Mid-values(x_i)	$f_i\ x_i$	$f_i\ x_i^2$
0-2	10	1	10	10
2-4	20	3	60	180
4-6	35	5	175	875
6-8	30	7	210	1470
8-10	5	9	45	405
	$n = 100$		$\Sigma f_i x_i =$ 500	$\Sigma f_i x_i^2$ =2940

Solution

$$1)\ \overline{x} = \frac{\Sigma f_i x_i}{n} = \frac{5990}{1000} = 5.99$$

$$\text{s.d.}(\sigma x) = \sqrt{\frac{\Sigma f_i x_i^2}{n} - (x)^2} = \sqrt{\frac{38770}{1000} - (5.99)^2}$$

2) $\sqrt{38.77 - 35.88} = \sqrt{2.89} = 1.7$ ($ in 100)

Example: Calculate s.d. of the marks of 100 students.

Marks	No. of students(f_i)	Mid-values(x_i)	$f_i\ x_i$	$f_i\ x_i^2$
0-2	10	1	10	10
2-4	20	3	60	180
4-6	35	5	175	875
6-8	30	7	210	1470
8-10	5	9	45	405
	$n = 100$		$\Sigma f_i x_i = 500$	$\Sigma f_i x_i^2 =$
		2940		

Solution:

$$(1)\ \frac{\Sigma f_i x_i}{n} = \frac{500}{1000} = 5$$

$$(2)\ \text{s.d.}(\sigma x) = \sqrt{\frac{\Sigma f_i x_i^2}{n} - (xy)^2}$$

$$= \sqrt{\frac{2940}{100} - (5)^2} = \sqrt{29.40 - 25} = \sqrt{4.40}$$

Combined Standard deviation: If two sets containing n_1 and n_2 items having means x_1 and x_2 and standard deviations σ_1 and σ_2 respectively are taken together then,

(1) Mean of the combined data is $\bar{x} = \dfrac{n_1\bar{x}_1 + n_2\bar{x}_2}{n_1 + n_2}$

(2) s.d. of the combined set is

$$\sigma = \frac{n_1\left(\sigma_1^2 + d_1^2\right) + n_2\left(\sigma_2^2 + d_2^2\right)}{n_1 + n_2}$$

Where $d_1 = \bar{x}_1 - \bar{x}$ and $d_2 = \bar{x}_2 - \bar{x}$

Example: Adistribution consists of three parts, characterized as follows:

Part	No. of items	Arithmetic mean	Standard deviation
1	200	25	3
2	250	10	4
3	300	15	5

Show that the combined mean of the three parts together is 16 and s.d. is 7.2 approximately. Also calculate its combined coefficient of variation.

Solution:

Part	Number	Mean s.d.
1	$n_1 = 200$	$\overline{x}_1 = 25 \sigma_1 = 3$
2	$n_2 = 500$	$\overline{x}_2 = 10 \sigma_2 = 4$
3	$n_3 = 300$	$\overline{x}_3 = 25 \sigma_3 = 5$

(1) (Combined mean)123

$$= \frac{n_1\overline{x}_1 + n_2\overline{x}_2 + n_3\overline{x}_3}{n_1 + n_2}$$

$$= \frac{(23 \times 200) + (10 \times 250) + (15 \times 300)}{200 + 250 + 300}$$

$$= \frac{12000}{750} = 16$$

(2) $d_1 = \overline{x}_1 - \overline{x} = 25 - 16 = 9,$

$d_2 = \overline{x}_2 - \overline{x} = 16 - 10 = 6$

and $d_3 = \overline{x}_3 - \overline{x} = 16 - 16 = 1$

and $d_1^2 = 81,\ d_2^2 = 36$ and $d_3^2 = 1$

(3) Combineds.d (σ) =

$$\sqrt{\frac{n_1\left(\sigma_1^2 + d_2^2\right) + n_2\left(\sigma_2^2 + d_2^2\right) + n_3\left(\sigma_3^2 + d_3^2\right)}{n_1 + n_2 + n_3}}$$

$$= \sqrt{\frac{200(9 + 81) + 250(16 + 36) + 300(25 + 1)}{200 + 250 + 300}}$$

$$= \sqrt{\frac{38880}{750}} = \sqrt{51.73} = 7.2$$

Combined coefficient of variation (C.V.)

$$= \frac{\sigma x}{\overline{x}} \times 100$$

$$= \frac{7.2}{16} \times 100$$

$= 45\%$

Example: The mean and s.d. of the marks of a group of 100 students in atest in Mercantile Law were given to be 40 and 3 respectively. It was afterwards found that the marks of one student were wrongly recorded as 37 in stead of 73. Calculate the correct mean and s.d.

Solution: (1) Incorrect mean = 40, n = 100

Using $\overline{x} = \frac{\Sigma x_i}{n}$ we get

Incorrect $\Sigma x_i = n\overline{x} = 100 \times 40 = 4000$

Therefore, correct mean $(\overline{x}) = \frac{\text{Correct } \Sigma x_i}{n}$

$$= \frac{4036}{100} = 40.36 \text{ marks}$$

(2) s. d. $(\sigma x) = \sqrt{\frac{\Sigma x_i^2}{n} - (\overline{x})^2}$

Squaring we get $(\sigma x)^2 = \frac{\Sigma x_i^2}{n} - (\overline{x})^2$

Therefore, $\Sigma x_i^2 = n[(\sigma x)^2 + (\overline{x})^2]$

Incorrect $\Sigma x_i^2 = 100[(3)^2 + (40)^2]$

$= 100[9 + 1600]$

$= 160900$

Correct Σx_i^2 = Incorrect Σx_i^2

$- (37)^2 + (73)^2$

$= 160900 + 3960$

$= 164860$

Correct $\sigma x = \sqrt{\frac{164860}{100} - (40.36)^2}$

$= \sqrt{19.6} = 4.43$

Example: The score of two teams A and B in 10 matches are as:

A:	B:
40	21
32	14

0	29
40	13
30	5
7	12
13	10
25	13
14	30
5	0

Find the variance for both the series. Which team is more consistent ?

A			B		
x_i	$x_i - \bar{x}$	$(x_i - \bar{x})^2$	y_i	$(y_i - \bar{y})$	$(y_i - \bar{y})^2$
40	19	361	21	4	16
32	11	121	14	-3	9
0	-21	441	14	12	144
40	19	361	30	13	169
30	9	81	5	-12	144
7	-8	196	12	-5	25
13	-8	64	10	-7	49
25	4	16	13	-4	16
14	-7	49	30	13	169
9	-12	144	6	-11	121
$\Sigma x_i = 210$		$\Sigma(x_i - \bar{x})^2 = 1834$	$\Sigma x_i = 110$		$\Sigma(x_i - \bar{y})^2 = 862$

Example: Calculate the coefficient of variation of a series on the basis of the following results:

$n = 50$, $\Sigma(x_i - 75) = -10$, $\Sigma(x_i - 7.5)2 = 400$

Solution: (1) $\Sigma(x_i - 75) = \Sigma x_i - 375 = -10...$

(since $\Sigma 7.5 = 7.5n = 7.5 \times 50 = 375$)

$\Sigma x_i = -10 + 375 = 365$

Therefore, $\bar{x} = \dfrac{\Sigma x_i}{n} = \dfrac{365}{50} = 7.3$

(2) $\Sigma(x_i - 7.5)^2 = \Sigma(x_i - 7.3 - 0.2)^2$

$= \Sigma(x_i - 7.3 - 0.2)^2$

$- 0.4\ \Sigma(x_i - 7.3) + 0.04_n$

$= \Sigma(x_i - \bar{x})^2 - 0.4\Sigma(x_i - \bar{x})$

$+ 0.04 \times 50$

But $\Sigma(x_i - \bar{x}) = 0$

$\Sigma(x_i - 7.5)^2 = \Sigma(x_i - \bar{x})^2 - 0.4\,\Sigma$

$(0) + 2 = 400$

$\Sigma(x_i - \bar{x})^2 = 398$

$$\text{Now } \sigma\, x = \sqrt{\frac{\Sigma(x_i - \bar{x})^2}{n}} = \sqrt{\frac{398}{50}}$$

$$= 2.8213$$

$$\text{(3) C. V.} \quad = \frac{2.8213}{7.3} \times 100 = 38.65\%$$

Solution:

$$(1)\, \bar{x} = \frac{\Sigma xi}{n} = \frac{210}{10} \text{ and } \bar{y} = \frac{\Sigma yi}{n} = \frac{170}{10} = 17$$

$$\sigma x = \sqrt{\frac{\Sigma(x_i - \bar{x})^2}{n}} \sqrt{\frac{1834}{10}} = \sqrt{183.4} = 13.54$$

$$\text{Also } \sigma y = \sqrt{\frac{\Sigma(y_i - \bar{y})^2}{n}} = \sqrt{\frac{864}{10}} = \sqrt{86.2} = 9.28$$

$$\text{Therefore, } (\text{C.V})_A = \frac{13.54}{21} \times 100 = 64.47\%$$

$$\text{and } (\text{C.V})_B = \frac{9.28}{17} \times 100 = 54.69\%$$

Since $(\text{C.V.})_A < (\text{C.V.})_B$
The base ball team A is more consistent.

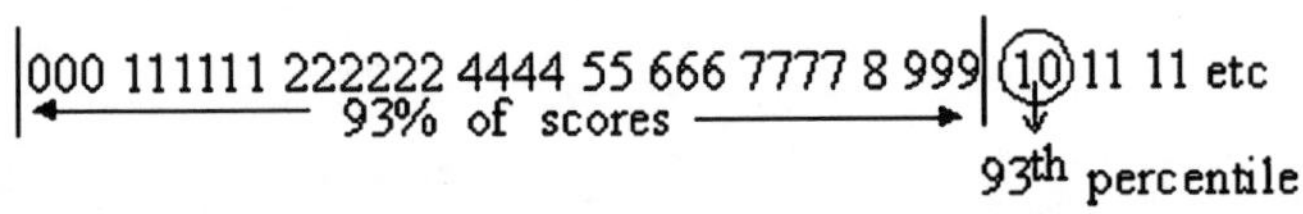

PERCENTILE

The nth percentile is that value (or size) such that n% of values of the whole data lies below it. For example, a score of 7% from the topmost score would be 93 the percentile as it is above 93% of the other scores.

Percentile Range

It is used as one of the measure of dispersion. it is a set of data and is defined as = *P*90 – *P*10 where *P*90 and *P*10 are the 90th and 10th percentile respectively.

The semi - percentile range,

i.e. $\left(\frac{P_{90} - P_{10}}{2}\right)$ can also be used but it is not common in use.

QUARTILES AND INTERQUARTILE RANGE

If we concentrate on two extreme values (as in the case of range), we don't get any idea about the scatter of the data within the range (i.e. the two extreme values). If we discard these two values the limited range thus available might be more informative. For this reason the concept of interquartile range is developed. It is the range which includes middle 50% of the distribution. Here 1/4 (one quarter of the lower end and 1/4 (one quarter) of the upper end of the observations are excluded.

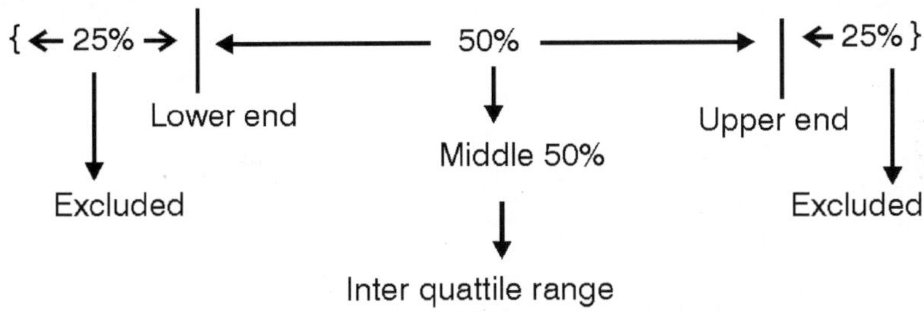

Now the lower quartile (Q_1) is the 25th percentile and the upper quartile (Q_3) is the 75th percentile. It is interesting to note that the 50th percentile is the middle quartile (Q_2) which is in fact what you have studied under the title ' Median". Thus symbolically

Inter quartile range = $Q_3 - Q_1$

If we divide ($Q_3 - Q_1$) by 2 we get what is known as Semi-Iinter quartile range.

i.e. $\frac{Q_3 - Q_1}{2}$. It is known as Quartile deviation (*Q. D* or SI *QR*).

Therefore *Q. D.* (*SIQR*) $= \frac{Q_3 - Q_1}{2}$. It is known as Quartile deviation (*Q. D* or *SIQR*).

Consider the marks obtained by 19 students in an examination as - (of course arranged in the ascending order of magnitude)

20, 27, 29, (33) Q_3, 37, 40, 42, 48, 50,

(53) Q_2, 55, 62, 81, 83, (88) Q_3, 90, 91, 95, 100

Now n = 19 thus $Q_1 = \frac{n+1}{4} = \frac{19+1}{4}$ = 5th obs. = 37 marks.

$Q_2 = \frac{n+1}{2}$ = 10th obs. (Median) = 53 marks.

$$Q_3 = \frac{3(n+1)}{4} = 15^{th} \text{ obs.} = 88 \text{ marks.}$$

Note that as $n = 10$ (odd) instead of $\frac{n}{4}, \frac{n}{2}$ or $\frac{3n}{4}$ we have take

$\frac{n+1}{4}, \frac{n+1}{2}$ and $\frac{3(n+1)}{4}$ respectively.

Therefore, $I.\ R. = Q_3 - Q_1 = 88 - 37 = 51$ marks

and $Q.\ D.$ or $S.\ I.\ Q.\ R. = \frac{Q_3 - Q_1}{2} = \frac{51}{2} = 25.50$

Also note that Q_1 and Q_3 are equidistance from the median. In any perfect symmetrical distribution).

Median $- Q_1 = Q_3 -$ Median.

i.e. 2 Median $= Q_3 + Q_1 \Rightarrow$ Median $= \frac{Q_3 - Q_1}{2}$ which covers exactly 50% of the observations.

For continuous series (grouped data), the formula for calculating Q_1 and Q_3 are same as the median (Q_2)

$$\text{i.e. } Q_1 = \ell_1 + \left[\frac{n/4 - c.f}{f}\right](\ell_2 - \ell_1)$$

$$= \ell_1 + \left[\frac{3n/4 - c.f}{f}\right](\ell_2 - \ell_1)$$

where (11, 12) are lower quartile and upper quartile class - intervals respectively.

SKEWNESS, MOMENTS AND KURTOSIS

The voluminous raw data cannot be easily understood, Hence, we calculate the measures of central tendencies and obtain a representative figure. From the measures of variability, we can know that whether most of the items of the data are close to our away from these central tendencies.

But these statical means and measures of variation are not enough to draw sufficient inferences about the data. Another aspect of the data is to know its symmetry. This symmetry is well studied by the knowledge of the "skewness."

Still one more aspect of the curve that we need to know is its flatness or otherwise its top. This is understood by what is known as "Kurtosis."

Skewness

It may happen that two distributions have the same mean and standard deviations. For example, see the following diagram.

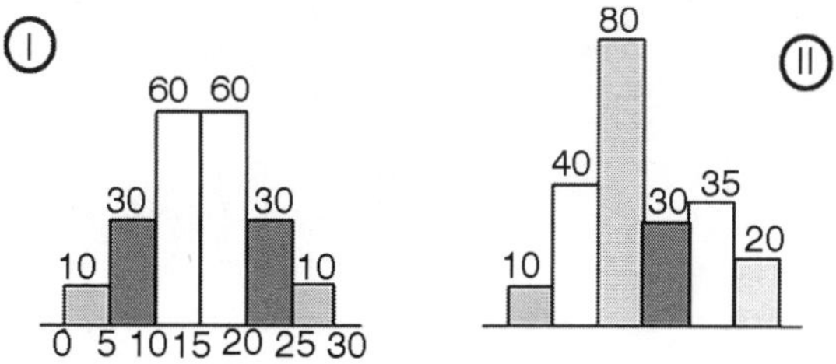

Although the two distributions have the same means and standard deviations they are not identical. Where do they differ?

They differ in symmetry. The left-hand side distribution is symmetrical one where as the distribution on the right-hand is asymmetrical or skewed. For a symmetrical distribution, the values, of equal distances on either side of the mode, have equal frequencies.

Thus, the mode, median and mean - all coincide. Its curve rises slowly, reaches a maximum (peak) and falls equally slowly.

But for a skewed distribution, the mean, mode and median do not coincide. Skewness is positive or negative as per the positions of the mean and median on the right or the left of the mode.

A positively skewed distribution curve rises rapidly, reaches the maximum and falls slowly.

In other words, the tail as well as median on the right-hand side.

A negatively skewed distribution curve rises slowly reaches its maximum and falls rapidly. In other words, the tail as well as the median are on the left-hand side.

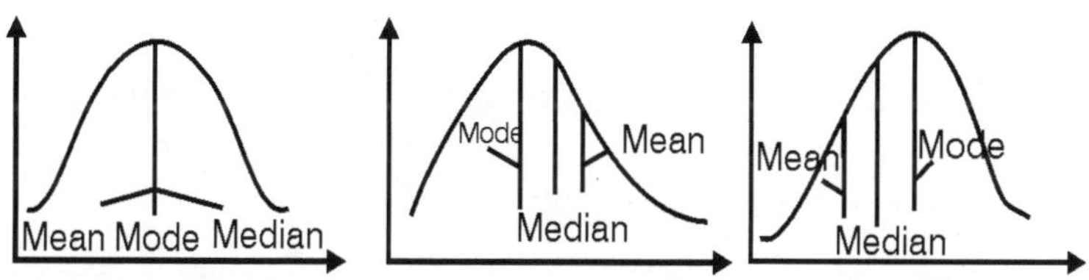

Size	Frequency	Size	Frequency	Size	Frequency
1	12	1	4	1	3
2	13	2	6	2	7
3	14	3	12	3	8
4	15	4	10	4	10
5	14	5	8	5	12
6	13	6	7	6	6
7	12	7	3	7	4

Tests Of Skewness

1. The values of mean, median and mode do not coincide. The more the difference between them, the more is the skewness.

2. Quartiles are not equidistant from the median. i.e. (Q_3 – Me) [1] (Me – Q_1).
3 The sum of positive deviations from the median is not equal to the sum of the negative deviations.
4. Frequencies are not equally distributed at points of equal deviation from the mode.
5. When the data is plotted on a graph they do not give the normal bell-shaped form.

Measure Of Skewness

1. First measure of skewness It is given by Karl Pearson
Measure of skewness Co-efficient of skewness

Skp = Mean - Mode $J = \frac{\overline{x} - Mo}{\overline{x}}$

i.e. Skp $= \overline{x} - Mo$

Pearson has suggested the use of this formula if it is not possible to determine the mode (Mo) of any distribution,

(Mean - Mode) = 3 (mean - median)

Skp = 3 ($\overline{x}$ $- Mo$) Thus $J = \frac{3(\overline{x} - Me)}{\sigma \overline{x}}$

Note: i) Although the co-efficient of skewness is always within ± 1, but Karl Pearson's co-efficient lies within ± 3.

ii) If J = 0, then there is no skewness

iii) If J is positive, the skewness is also positive.

iv) If J is negative, the skewness is also negative.

Unless and until no indication is given, you must use only Karl Pearson's formula.

Example: Find Karl Pearson's coefficient of skewness from the following data:

Marks above:	No.of students:
0	150
10	140
20	100
30	80
40	80
50	70
60	30
70	14
80	0

Solution:

Marks (x_i)	Mid-value (x_i)	No. students (f_i)	Deviation $u_i = \frac{x_i - A}{10}$	$f_i u_i$	$f_i u_i^2$
0 - 10	5	10	-4	-40	160
10 - 20	15	40	-3	-120	360
20 - 30	25	20	-2	- 40	80
30 - 40	35	0	-1	0	0
40 - 50	45 ⇒ A	10	0	0	0
50 - 60	55	40	+1	+ 40	40
60 - 70	65	16	+2	+ 32	64
70 - 80	75	14	+3	+ 42	126
		$n=\Sigma f_i=150$		$n=\Sigma f_i=150$	$\Sigma f_i u_i=830$

Note: You will always find the different values of J when calculated by Karl Pearson's and Bowley's formula. But the value of J by Bowley's formula always lies with ± 1.

Example: The following table gives the frequency distribution of 291 workers of a factory according to their average monthly income in 1945 – 55.

Income group ($):	No.of workers:
Below 50	1
50-70	16
70-90	39
90-110	58
110-130	60
130-150	46
150-170	22
170-190	15
190-210	15
210-230	9
230 & above	10

(ii) Q_1 = size of $\left(\frac{n+1}{4}\right)^{th}$ item = size of $\left(\frac{292}{4}\right)^{th}$ item = size of 73^{IC} item

which lies in (90 – 110) class – interval.

$$Q_1 = \ell_1 + \left[\frac{n/4 - c.f.}{f}\right](\ell_2 - \ell_1)$$

$$= 90 + \left[\frac{73 - 56}{58}\right](20) = 95.8 \text{ dollars}$$

(iii) Q_3 = Size of $\left(\frac{n+1}{4}\right)^{th}$ item

= Size of 219th item which lies in (130 – 150) class – interval.

$$Q_3 = \ell_1 + \left[\frac{\frac{3n}{4} - c.f.}{f}\right](\ell_2 - \ell_1)$$

$$= 130 + \left[\frac{219 - 174}{46}\right](20) = 149.2 \text{ marks}$$

(iv) By Bowley's formula, J_Q

$$= \frac{Q_3 + Q_1 - 2Me.}{Q_3 - Q_1}$$

$$= \frac{149.2 - 95.8 - 2 \times 12.5}{149.2 - 95.8}$$

$$= \frac{245 - 241}{53.4}$$

$$= 0.75$$

(3) Third measure of Skewness: It is credited to "King." It is a better measure but to the complexity that arises in calculations, is not so much in common use.

Individual series	Grouped data
$SK_3 = \sqrt[3]{\frac{\Sigma d^3}{n}}$	$SK_3 = \sqrt[3]{\frac{\Sigma fd^3}{n}}$
$J = \sqrt[3]{\frac{\Sigma d^3}{n}} \Big/ \sigma$	$J = \sqrt[3]{\frac{\Sigma fd^3}{n}} \Big/ \sigma$

KURTOSIS

It has its origin in the Greek word "Bulginess." In statistics it is the degree of flatness or 'peakedness' in the region of mode of a frequency curve. It is measured relative to the 'peakedness' of the normal curve.

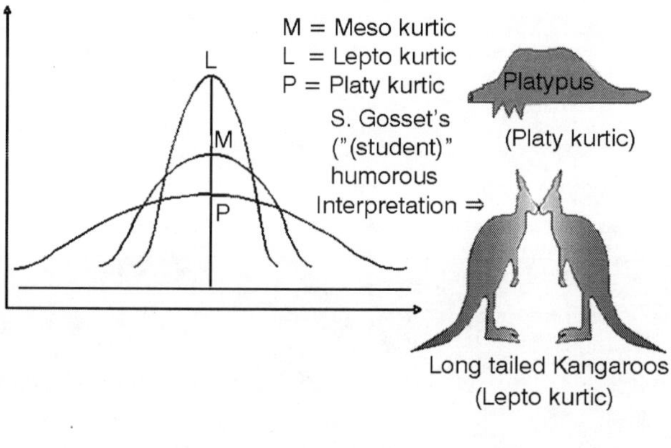

It tells us the extent to which a distribution is more peaked or flat-topped than the normal curve. If the curve is more peaked than a normal curve it is called 'Lepto Kurtic.' In this case items are more clustered about the mode. If the curve is more flat-toped than the more normal curve, it is Platy-Kurtic. The normal curve itself is known as "Meso Kurtic."

Moments

Moment is a familiar mechanical term for the measure of a force with reference to its tendency to produce rotation. In statistics moments are used to describe the various characteristics of a frequency distribution like centre tendency, variation, skewness and kurtosis.

Moments are calculated using the arithmetic mean. According to Waugh, the arithmetic mean of the various powers of these deviations in any distribution are called the moments of the distribution.

Let 'x' be the deviation of any item in a distribution from the arithmetic mean of that distribution. The arithmetic mean of the various powers of these deviations is the moments of the distribution.

If we take the mean of the 1st power of the deviations, we get the 1st moment about the mean, the mean of the squares of the deviations gives the second moment about the mean, the mean of the cubes gives the third moment about the mean and so on. The moments about mean are called the "central moment" and are denoted by μ1, μ2, μ3, μ4....

Symbolically $\mu 1 \frac{\Sigma(x-\overline{x})}{n}$ or $\frac{\Sigma x}{n}$ ...1st central moment = 0

Since sum of deviations of items from the arithmetic mean is always zero.

$$\mu 2 = \frac{\Sigma(x-\overline{x})^2}{n} \text{ or } \frac{\Sigma x^2}{n} \quad [\mu 2 = \sigma^2]$$

$$\mu 3 = \frac{\Sigma(x-\overline{x})^3}{n} \text{ or } \frac{\Sigma x^3}{n} \text{ and so on}$$

For frequency Distribution,

$$\mu 1 = \frac{\Sigma f(x-\overline{x})}{n} \text{ or } \frac{\Sigma fx}{n}$$

$$\mu 2 = \frac{\Sigma f(x-\overline{x})^2}{n} \text{ or } \frac{\Sigma fx^2}{n}$$

$$\mu 3 = \frac{\Sigma f(x-\overline{x})^3}{n} \text{ or } \frac{\Sigma fx^3}{n}$$

$$\mu 4 = \frac{\Sigma f(x-\bar{x})^4}{n} \text{ or } \frac{\Sigma fx^4}{n} \quad \text{where } n = \Sigma f \text{ and so on}$$

In many cases it is very difficult to calculate moments about actual moment, particularly when actual mean is in fractions. In such case we first compute moments about an arbitrary origin 'A' and then convert these moments into moments about actual mean. These are called ' raw moments ' which are denoted by *n*.

Thus we have

$$v_1 = \frac{\Sigma f(x-A)}{n}, \; v_2 = \frac{\Sigma f(x-A)^2}{n},$$

$$v_3 = \frac{\Sigma f(x-A)^3}{n}, \; v_4 = \frac{\Sigma f(x-A)^4}{n}$$

and so on. For frequency distribution

$$v_1 = \frac{\Sigma fi(x-A)}{n}, \; v_2 = \frac{\Sigma fi(x-A)^2}{n},$$

$$v_3 = \frac{\Sigma fi(x-A)^3}{n}, \; v_4 = \frac{\Sigma fi(x-A)^4}{n} \text{ and so on.}$$

Now to obtain the central moment as

$\mu = v - v = \sigma$

$\mu = v - 3v.\ v + 2v$

$\mu = v - 4v.\ v + 6v\ v - 3v$

Pearson's β and ν coefficients. Karl Pearson defined the following four coefficients, based upon four moments about the mean.

β coefficients

$$\begin{cases} \beta_1 = \dfrac{\mu_3^2}{\mu_2^3} = \dfrac{\mu_3^2}{\sigma^6} \\[2ex] \beta_2 = \dfrac{\mu_4}{\mu_2^2} = \dfrac{\mu_4}{\sigma^4} \end{cases}$$

ν coefficient

$$\begin{cases} v_1 + \sqrt{\beta_1} = \dfrac{\mu_3}{\sigma^3} \\[2ex] v_2 + \beta_2 - 3 = \dfrac{\mu_4}{\sigma^2} - 3 = \dfrac{\mu_{4-3\sigma^2}}{\sigma^4} \end{cases}$$

These are pure numbers and they provide information about the shape of the curve obtained from the frequency distribution.

For symmetrical distribution, the moments of odd order about the mean vanish and therefore $\mu_3 = 0$ rendering $\beta_1 = 0$ thus β_1 gives the measure of departure from symmetry and also defines a measure of skewness. Also $\beta_2 = \frac{\mu_4}{\mu_2}$ gives the measure of flatness of the mode and also defines the measure of Kurtosis or convexity of the curve.

Note: (1) If $\beta_2 = 3$ i.e. $v_2 = 0$ then the curve is normal which is neither flat nor peaked i.e. Meso kurtic.

(2) If $\beta_2 > 3$ i.e. $v_2 > 0$ then the curve is more peaked than a normal curve and is called Lepto kurtic.

(3) If $\beta_2 < 3$ i.e. $v_2 <> 0$ then curve is flatter than a normal curve and is called Platy kurtic.

5

Correlation and Regression

So far we have considered only univariate distributions. By the averages, dispersion and skewness of distribution, we get a complete idea about the structure of the distribution. Many a time, we come across problems which involve two or more variables.

If we carefully study the figures of rain fall and production of paddy, figures of accidents and motor cars in a city, of demand and supply of a commodity, of sales and profit, we may find that there is some relationship between the two variables.

On the other hand, if we compare the figures of rainfall in America and the production of cars in Japan, we may find that there is no relationship between the two variables. If there is any relation between two variables i.e. when one variable changes the other also changes in the same or in the opposite direction, we say that the two variables are correlated.

W. J. King: If it is proved that in a large number of instances two variables, tend always to fluctuate in the same or in the opposite direction then it is established that a relationship exists between the variables. This is called a "Correlation."

CORRELATION

It means the study of existence, magnitude and direction of the relation between two or more variables. in technology and in statistics. Correlation is very important.

The famous astronomist Bravais, Prof. Sir Fanci's Galton, Karl Pearson (who used this concept in Biology and in Genetics). Prof. Neiswanger and so many others have contributed to this great subject.

TYPES OF CORRELATION

- Positive and negative correlation
- Linear and non-linear correlation

A) If two variables change in the same direction (i.e. if one increases the other also increases, or if one decreases, the other also decreases), then this is called a positive correlation. For example: Advertising and sales.

B) If two variables change in the opposite direction (i.e. if one increases, the other decreases and vice versa), then the correlation is called a negative correlation. For example: T.V. registrations and cinema attendance.

- The nature of the graph gives us the idea of the linear type of correlation between two variables. If the graph is in a straight line, the correlation is called a "linear correlation" and if the graph is not in a straight line, the correlation is non-linear or curvi-linear.

For example, if variable x changes by a constant quantity, say 20 then y also changes by a constant quantity, say 4. The ratio between the two always remains the same (1/5 in this case). In case of a curvi-linear correlation this ratio does not remain constant.

DEGREES OF CORRELATION

Through the coefficient of correlation, we can measure the degree or extent of the correlation between two variables. On the basis of the coefficient of correlation we can also determine whether the correlation is positive or negative and also its degree or extent.

Perfect correlation:

If two variables changes in the same direction and in the same proportion, the correlation between the two is perfect positive. According to Karl Pearson the coefficient of correlation in this case is + 1. On the other hand if the variables change in the opposite direction and in the same proportion, the correlation is perfect negative. its coefficient of correlation is –1. In practice we rarely come across these types of correlations.

Absence of correlation:

If two series of two variables exhibit no relations between them or change in variable does not lead to a change in the other variable, then we can firmly say that there is no correlation or absurd correlation between the two variables. In such a case the coefficient of correlation is 0.

Limited degrees of correlation:

If two variables are not perfectly correlated or is there a perfect absence of correlation, then we term the correlation as Limited correlation. It may be positive, negative or zero but lies with the limits ± 1.

High degree, moderate degree or low degree are the three categories of this kind of correlation. The following table reveals the effect (or degree) of coefficient or correlation.

Degrees	Positive	Negative
Absence of correlation →	Zero	0
Perfect correlation →	+ 1	-1
High degree →	+ 0.75 to + 1	–0.75 to –1

Moderate degree →	+ 0.25 to + 0.75	–0.25 to –0.75
Low degree →	0 to 0.25	0 to –0.25

METHODS OF DETERMINING CORRELATION

We shall consider the following most commonly used methods.(1) Scatter Plot (2) Kar Pearson's coefficient of correlation (3) Spearman's Rank-correlation coefficient.

Scatter Plot (Scatter diagram or dot diagram):

In this method the values of the two variables are plotted on a graph paper. One is taken along the horizontal ((x-axis) and the other along the vertical (y-axis). By plotting the data, we get points (dots) on the graph which are generally scattered and hence the name 'Scatter Plot'.

The manner in which these points are scattered, suggest the degree and the direction of correlation. The degree of correlation is denoted by 'r' and its direction is given by the signs positive and negative.

- If all points lie on a rising straight line the correlation is perfectly positive and $r = +1$

① 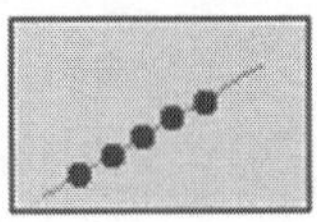 r = +1

- If all points lie on a falling straight line the correlation is perfectly negative and $r = -1$

② 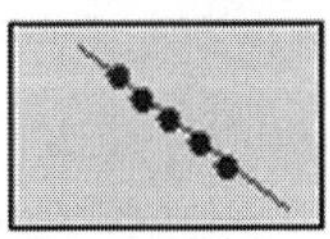 r = –1

- If the points lie in narrow strip, rising upwards, the correlation is high degree of positive

③ 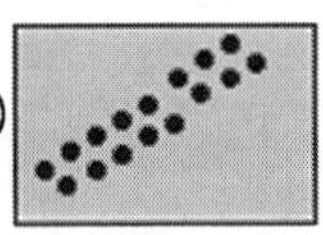 r = + ↑High

- If the points lie in a narrow strip, falling downwards, the correlation is high degree of negative

④ 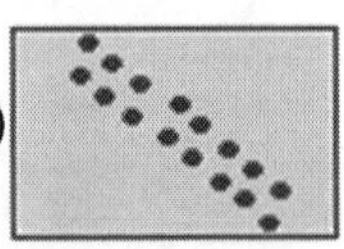 r = –↓High v)

- If the points are spread widely over a broad strip, rising upwards, the correlation is low degree positive

⑤ 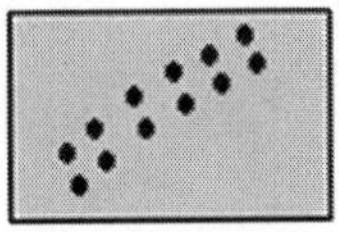 r = +↑ Low

- If the points are spread widely over a broad strip, falling downward, the correlation is low degree negative

⑥ 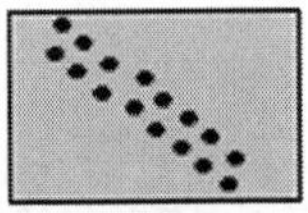 r = −↓ Low

- If the points are spread (scattered) without any specific pattern, the correlation is absent. i.e. $r = 0$.

⑦ 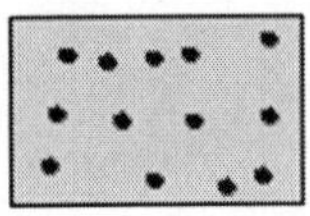 r = 0

Though this method is simple and is a rough idea about the existence and the degree of correlation, it is not reliable. As it is not a mathematical method, it cannot measure the degree of correlation.

Karl Pearson's coefficient of correlation:

It gives the numerical expression for the measure of correlation. it is noted by 'r'. The value of 'r' gives the magnitude of correlation and sign denotes its direction. It is defined as,

$$r = \frac{\Sigma xy}{n\sigma x \sigma y}$$

$x = (x_i - \bar{x}), y = (y_i - \bar{y}), \sigma_x$ = s.d. of x and where σ_y = s.d. of y.
N = Number of pairs of observation.
Note: r is also known as product-moment coefficient of correlation.

$$\text{OR } r = \frac{\Sigma xy}{\sqrt{\Sigma x^2} \times \sqrt{\Sigma y^2}} \quad \text{since } \sigma_x = \sqrt{\frac{\Sigma x^2}{n}} \text{ and } \sigma_y = \sqrt{\frac{\Sigma y^2}{n}}$$

$$\text{OR } r = \frac{\Sigma x.y - \left(\frac{\Sigma y.\Sigma y}{n}\right)}{\sqrt{\Sigma x^2 - \frac{\Sigma x^2}{n}} . \sqrt{\Sigma y^2 - \frac{\Sigma y^2}{n}}}$$

Now covariance of x and y is defined as,

$$\text{cov}(x, y) = \frac{\Sigma(x_i - \bar{x})(y_i - \bar{y})}{n} \quad r = \frac{\text{cov}(x, y)}{\sigma_x \sigma_y}$$

Example: Calculate the coefficient of correlation between the heights of father and his son for the following data.

Height of father (cm):	165	166	167	168	167	169	170	172
Height of son (cm):	167	168	165	172	168	172	169	171

Solution: $n = 8$ (pairs of observations)

Height of father x_i	Height of son y_i	$x = x_i - x$	$y = y_i - y$	xy	x^2	y^2
165	167	–3	-2	6	9	4
166	168	–2	-1	2	4	1
167	165	-1	-4	4	1	16
167	168	-1	-1	1	1	1
168	172	0	3	0	0	9
169	172	1	3	3	1	9
170	169	2	0	0	4	0
172	171	4	2	8	16	4
Σx_i=1344	Σy_i=1352	0	0	Σxy=24	Σx^2=36	Σy^2=44

Calculation: $\bar{x} = \frac{\Sigma x_i}{n} = \frac{1344}{8}$

$= 168\text{cm and } \sigma_x = \sqrt{\frac{\Sigma x^2}{n}} = \sqrt{\frac{36}{8}}\quad \bar{y} = \frac{\Sigma y_i}{n} = \frac{1352}{8}$

$= 169\text{cm and } \sigma_y = \sqrt{\frac{\Sigma y^2}{n}} = \sqrt{\frac{44}{8}}$

Note: r is also known as product-moment coefficient of correlation.

$$\text{OR } r = \frac{\Sigma xy}{\sqrt{\Sigma x^2} \times \sqrt{\Sigma y^2}} \quad \text{since } \sigma_x = \sqrt{\frac{\Sigma x^2}{n}} \text{ and}$$

$$\text{OR } r = \frac{\Sigma x.y - \left(\frac{\Sigma y.\Sigma y}{n}\right)}{\sqrt{\Sigma x^2 - \frac{\Sigma x^2}{n}}.\sqrt{\Sigma y^2 - \frac{\Sigma y^2}{n}}}$$

Now covariance of x and y is defined as,

$$\text{cov }(x, y) = \frac{\Sigma(x_i - \bar{x})(y_i - \bar{y})}{n} \quad r = \frac{\text{cov}(x, y)}{\sigma_x \sigma_y}$$

Example: Calculate the coefficient of correlation between the heights of father and his son for the following data.

Height of father (cm):	165	166	167	168	167	169	170	172
Height of son (cm):	167	168	165	172	168	172	169	171

Solution: n = 8 (pairs of observations)

Height of father x_i	**Height of son y_i**	**$x = x_i - x$**	**$y = y_i - y$**	**xy**	**x^2**	**y^2**
165	167	–3	-2	6	9	4
166	168	–2	-1	2	4	1
167	165	-1	-4	4	1	16
167	168	-1	-1	1	1	1
168	172	0	3	0	0	9
169	172	1	3	3	1	9
170	169	2	0	0	4	0
172	171	4	2	8	16	4
Σx_i=1344	Σy_i=1352	0	0	Σxy=24	Σx^2=36	Σy^2=44

Calculation: $\bar{x} = \frac{\Sigma x_i}{n} = \frac{1344}{8}$

$= 168\text{cm and } \sigma_x = \sqrt{\frac{\Sigma x^2}{n}} = \sqrt{\frac{36}{8}} \; \bar{y} = \frac{\Sigma y_i}{n} = \frac{1352}{8}$

$= 169\text{cm and } \sigma_y = \sqrt{\frac{\Sigma y^2}{n}} = \sqrt{\frac{44}{8}}$

Now,

$$r = \frac{\Sigma xy}{n\sigma_x \sigma_y} = \frac{24}{8\sqrt{\frac{36}{8}} \times \sqrt{\frac{44}{8}}} = \frac{24}{\sqrt{36 \times 44}} = +0.6029$$

Since r is positive and 0.6. This shows that the correlation is positive and moderate (i.e. direct and reasonably good).

Example: From the following data compute the coefficient of correlation between x and y.

		x	y
No. of items	→	15	15
Arithmetic mean	→	25	18
$\Sigma(x_i - \bar{x})^2.\Sigma(y_i - \bar{y})^2$	→	136	138

$\Sigma(x_i - \overline{x}).\Sigma(y_i.\overline{y}) \quad \rightarrow \quad 122$

Solution: Given, $n = 15, \overline{x} = 25, \overline{y} = 18$

$\Sigma(x_i - \overline{x})^2$ i.e. $\Sigma x^2 = 136, \Sigma(y_i - \overline{y})^2$
i.e. $\Sigma y^2 = 138$

and $\Sigma(x_i - \overline{x}).\Sigma(y_i - \overline{y}) = \Sigma xy = 122$

Using $r = \frac{\Sigma xy}{\sqrt{\Sigma x^2} \times \sqrt{\Sigma y^2}}$ we get

$$r = \frac{122}{\sqrt{136} \times \sqrt{138}} = \frac{122}{136.9} = 0.891$$

Example: If covariance between x and y is 12.3 and the variance of x and y are 16.4 and 13.8 respectively. Find the coefficient of correlation between them.

Solution: Given – Covariance = cov (x, y) = 12.3
Variance of x (σ_x^2) = 16.4
Variance of y (σ_y^2) = 13.8
Now,

$$r = \frac{\text{cov}.(x, y)}{\sigma_x \sigma_y} = \frac{12.3}{\sqrt{16.4} \times \sqrt{13.8}} = \frac{12.3}{4.05 \times 3.71} = 0.82$$

Example: Find the number of pair of observations from the following data. $r = 0.25$, $\Sigma(x_i - x)(y_i - y) = 60$, $\sigma_y = 4$, $\Sigma(x_i - x)2 = 90$.
Solution: Given – $r = 0.25$

$$\Sigma(x_i - \overline{x})(y_i - \overline{y}) = \Sigma xy = 60$$

$$\sigma_x = \sqrt{\frac{\Sigma x^2}{n}} = \sqrt{\frac{\Sigma(x_i - \overline{x})^2}{n}} = \sqrt{\frac{90}{n}}$$

$$\sigma_y = 4 = \sqrt{\frac{\Sigma y^2}{n}}$$

$$\text{Now, } r = \frac{\Sigma xy}{n\sigma_x.\sigma_y} = \frac{60}{n\sqrt{\frac{20}{n}} \times 4} = \frac{15}{\sqrt{90n}}$$

$$0.25 = \frac{15}{\sqrt{90n}}$$

$$0.25 \times \sqrt{90n} = 15$$

On squaring,

$0.0625 \times 90n = 225$

$90n = \dfrac{225}{0.0625}$

$90n = 3600$

$n = 40$

Therefore, the number of pairs of observations = 40

If the values of x and y are very big, the calculation becomes very tedious and if we change the variable x to $u = \dfrac{x_1 - x_0}{c}$ and y to $v = \dfrac{y_1 - y_0}{c}$ where x_0 and y_0 are the assumed means for variable x and y respectively, then $r_{xy} = ruv$

The formula for r can be simplified as,

$$r_{xy} = r_{uv} = \frac{\Sigma uv - \left(\dfrac{(\Sigma u)(\Sigma v)}{n}\right)}{\sqrt{\Sigma u^2 - \dfrac{(\Sigma u)^2}{n}} \times \sqrt{\Sigma v^2 - \dfrac{(\Sigma v)^2}{n}}}$$

Example: Marks obtained by two brothers FRED and TED in 10 tests are as follows:

FRED:	44	80	76	48	52	72	68	56	60	64
TED:	48	75	54	60	63	69	72	51	57	66

Find the coefficient of correlation between the two.

Solution: Here $x_0 = 60$, $c = 4$, $y_0 = 60$ and $d = 3$

FRED	TED	$u = \dfrac{x_i - x_0}{c}$	$v = \dfrac{x_i - x_0}{c}$	uv	u^2	v^2
44	48	-4	-4	16	16	16
80	75	5	5	25	25	25
76	54	4	-2	-8	16	4
48	60	-3	0	0	9	0
52	63	-2	1	-2	4	1
72	69	3	3	9	9	9
68	72	2	4	8	4	16
56	51	-1	-3	3	1	9
60	57	0	-1	0	0	1
64	66	1	2	2	4	4
Total		$\Sigma u = 5$	$\Sigma v = 5$	$\Sigma uv = 53$	$\Sigma u^2 = 85$	$\Sigma v^2 = 85$

Calculation:

$$r_{xy} = r_{uv} = \frac{\Sigma uv - \dfrac{(\Sigma u)(\Sigma v)}{n}}{\sqrt{\Sigma u^2 - \dfrac{(\Sigma u)^2}{n}} \times \sqrt{\Sigma v^2 - \dfrac{(\Sigma v)^2}{n}}}$$

$$= \frac{53 - \frac{(5)(5)}{10}}{\sqrt{85 - \frac{(5)^2}{10}} \times \sqrt{85 - \frac{(5)^2}{10}}}$$

$$= \frac{53 - 2.5}{\sqrt{82.5} \times \sqrt{82.5}}$$

$$= \frac{50.5}{82.5} = 0.61$$

COEFFICIENT OF CORRELATION FOR BIVARIATE GROUPED DATA

When the number of observations is very large, we need to arrange the data into different classes, which are either discrete or continuous. Items having values falling in a particular class are placed together and those having values falling in another class are placed together.

Due to this the whole data is divided into horizontal rows and vertical columns, with one variable placed horizontally and the other placed vertically.

The table so obtained is a two-way frequency distribution table and is called the correlation table or Bi-variate frequency distribution table. The formula for calculating and for bi-variate distribution is given by

$$r = \frac{\Sigma fuv - \frac{(\Sigma fu)(\Sigma fv)}{n}}{\sqrt{\Sigma fu^2 - \frac{(\Sigma fu)^2}{n}} \times \sqrt{\Sigma fv^2 - \frac{(\Sigma fv)^2}{n}}}$$

PROBABLE ERROR

It is used to help in the determination of the Karl Pearson's coefficient of correlation ' r '. Due to this ' r ' is corrected to a great extent but note that ' r ' depends on the random sampling and its conditions. it is given by

$$\text{P. E.} = 0.6745 \frac{1 - r^2}{\sqrt{n}^2}$$

- If the value of r is less than P. E., then there is no evidence of correlation i.e. r is not significant.
- If r is more than 6 times the P. E. ' r ' is practically certain.i.e. significant.
- By adding or subtracting P. E. to ' r ', we get the upper and Lower limits within which ' r ' of the population can be expected to lie.

Symbolically $e = r \pm P.\ E.$

P = Correlation (coefficient) of the population.

Example: If $r = 0.6$ and $n = 64$ find out the probable error of the coefficient of correlation.

Solution: $\text{P. E.} = 0.6745\left[\dfrac{1-r^2}{\sqrt{n}}\right]$

$$= 0.6745\left[\frac{1-(-0.6)^2}{\sqrt{64}}\right]$$

$$= \frac{0.6745-0.64}{8} = 0.57$$

SPEARMAN'S RANK CORRELATION COEFFICIENT

This method is based on the ranks of the items rather than on their actual values. The advantage of this method over the others in that it can be used even when the actual values of items are unknown. For example if you want to know the correlation between honesty and wisdom of the boys of your class, you can use this method by giving ranks to the boys. It can also be used to find the degree of agreements between the judgements of two examiners or two judges.

The formula is:

$$R = 1 - \frac{6\Sigma D^2}{N\left(N^2-1\right)}$$

where R = Rank correlation coefficient

D = Difference between the ranks of two items

N = The number of observations.

Note: $-1 \le R \le 1$.

i) When $R = +1 \Rightarrow$ Perfect positive correlation or complete agreement in the same direction

ii) When $R = -1 \Rightarrow$ Perfect negative correlation or complete agreement in the opposite direction.

iii) When $R = 0 \Rightarrow$ No Correlation.

Computation:

- Give ranks to the values of items. Generally the item with the highest value is ranked 1 and then the others are given ranks 2, 3, 4.... according to their values in the decreasing order.
- Find the difference $D = R_1 - R_2$

where R_1 = Rank of x and R_2 = Rank of y

Note that $S\ D = 0$ (always)

- Calculate D^2 and then find $S\ D^2$
- Apply the formula.

Note:

In some cases, there is a tie between two or more items. in such a case each items have ranks 4th and 5th respectively then they are given $\frac{4+5}{2}$ = 4.5th rank. If three items are of equal rank say 4th then they are given $\frac{4+5+6}{3}$ = 5th rank each. If m be the number of items of equal ranks, the factor $\frac{1}{12}(m^3 - m)$ is added to $S\ D^2$. If there are more than one of such cases then this factor added as many times as the number of such cases, then

$$R = 1 - \frac{6\left\{\Sigma D^2 + \frac{1}{12}(m_1^3 - m_1) + \frac{1}{12}m_2^3 - m_2) + \ldots\right\}}{N(N^2 - 1)}$$

Example: Calculate ' R ' from the following data.

Student No.:	1	2	3	4	5	6	7	8	9	10
Rank in Maths:	1	3	7	5	4	6	2	10	9	8
Rank in Stats:	3	1	4	5	6	9	7	8	10	2

Solution:

StudentNo.	**Rank in Maths (R_1)**	**Rank in Stats (R_2)**	**$R_1 - R_2$ D**	**$(R_1 - R_2)^2$ D^2**
1	1	3	–2	4
2	3	1	2	4
3	7	4	3	9
4	5	5	0	0
5	4	6	–2	4
6	6	9	–3	9
7	2	7	–5	25
8	10	8	2	4
9	9	10	–1	1
10	8	2	6	36
$N = 10$			$S\ D = 0$	$S\ D^2 = 96$

Calculation of R:

$$R = 1 - \frac{6\Sigma D^2}{N(N^2 - 1)} \qquad = 1 - \frac{6(96)}{10(100 - 1)}$$

$$=1-\frac{6\times 96}{10\times 99}=0.4181$$

Example:: Calculate ' R ' of 6 students from the following data.

Marks in Stats: 40 42 45 35 36 39

Marks in English: 46 43 44 39 40 43

Solution:

Marks in Stats	R_1	Marks in English	R_2	$R_1 - R_2$	$(R_1 - R_2)^2 = D^2$
40	3	46	1	2	4
42	2	43	3.5	–1.5	2.25
45	1	44	2	–1	1
35	6	39	6	0	0
36	5	40	5	0	0
39	4	43	3.5	0.5	0.25
$N = 6$				$S D = 0$	$S D^2 = 7.50$

Here $m = 2$ since in series of marks in English of items of values 43 repeated twice.

$$R=1-\frac{6\left\{SD^2+\frac{1}{12}(2^3-2)\right\}}{N(N^2-1)}=1-\frac{6\left\{7.5+\frac{1}{12}(8-2)\right\}}{6(36-6)}$$

$$R=1-\frac{6(7.5+0.5)}{210}=0.771$$

Example: The value of Spearman's rank correlation coefficient for a certain number of pairs of observations was found to be 2/3. The sum of the squares of difference between the corresponding rnks was 55. Find the number of pairs.

Solution: We have

$$R=1-\frac{6SD^2}{N(N^2-1)} \text{ but } R = 2/3 \text{ and } SD^2 = 55\frac{2}{3}$$

$$=1-\frac{6\times 55}{N(N^2-1)}\quad -\frac{1}{3}=-\frac{6\times 55}{N(N^2-1)}$$

$N(N^2 - 1) = 6 \times 55$

Now $N(N^2 - 1) = 990$

$N(N^2 - 1) = 10 \times 99 = 10(100 - 1)$

$N(N^2 - 1) = 10(10^2 - 1) \Rightarrow N = 10$

Therefore, there were 10 students.

LINEAR REGRESSION

Correlation gives us the idea of the measure of magnitude and direction between correlated variables. Now it is natural to think of a method that helps us in estimating the value of one variable when the other is known. Also correlation does not imply causation.

The fact that the variables x and y are correlated does not necessarily mean that x causes y or vice versa. For example, you would find that the number of schools in a town is correlated to the number of accidents in the town. The reason for these accidents is not the school attendance; but these two increases what is known as population.

A statistical procedure called regression is concerned with causation in a relationship among variables. It assesses the contribution of one or more variable called causing variable or independent variable or one which is being caused (dependent variable). When there is only one independent variable then the relationship is expressed by a straight line. This procedure is called simple linear regression.

Regression can be defined as a method that estimates the value of one variable when that of other variable is known, provided the variables are correlated. The dictionary meaning of regression is "to go backward." It was used for the first time by Sir Francis Galton in his research paper "Regression towards mediocrity in hereditary stature."

Lines of Regression: In scatter plot, we have seen that if the variables are highly correlated then the points (dots) lie in a narrow strip. if the strip is nearly straight, we can draw a straight line, such that all points are close to it from both sides. such a line can be taken as an ideal representation of variation. This line is called the line of best fit if it minimizes the distances of all data points from it. This line is called the line of regression. Now prediction is easy because now all we need to do is to extend the line and read the value.

Thus to obtain a line of regression, we need to have a line of best fit. But statisticians don't measure the distances by dropping perpendiculars from points on to the line. They measure deviations (or errors or residuals as they are called) (i) vertically and (ii) horizontally.

(1) Line of regression of y on x

Its form is $y = a + b\,x$

It is used to estimate y when x is given

(2) Line of regression of x on y

Its form is $x = a + b\,y$

It is used to estimate x when y is given.

They are obtained by graphically - by Scatter plot (ii) Mathematically-by the method of least squares.

ii. Let $y = a + b\,y$ where a and b are given by the normal equations

$\Sigma\, y = n\,a + b\,\Sigma\, x$

Sxy $= a\,\Sigma\, x + b\,\Sigma\, x^2$

where 'n' be the number of pairs of values of x and y.

Equation (2) can be written as $\dfrac{\Sigma y}{n} = a + b\dfrac{\Sigma x}{n}$ but $\dfrac{\Sigma y}{n}$

$= \bar{y}$ and $\frac{\Sigma x}{n} = \bar{x}$ .... means of y & x respectively.

Therefore, we have $\bar{y} = a + b\bar{x}$

Thus the line passes through the point $(\bar{x}, \bar{y})$

Shifting the origin to $(\bar{x}, \bar{y})$ we get $y - \bar{y}$

$= a + b(x - \bar{x})$

and (2) reduces to $\Sigma(y - \bar{y}) = n\,a + b\Sigma(x - \bar{x})$.

But $\Sigma(y - \bar{y}) = 0$ and $\Sigma(x - \bar{x}) = 0$

Therefore, $a = b$

Also becomes $\Sigma(x - \bar{x})\,(y - \bar{y}) = b\,\Sigma(x - \bar{x})^2$

$a = 0$

or $\Sigma xy = b\,\Sigma x^2$ where $x = x - \bar{x}$ and

$y = y - \bar{y}$ are deviations.

$$b = \frac{\Sigma xy}{x^2} = \frac{\Sigma xy}{n\sigma x^2} \text{ .... since}$$

$$\sigma x = \sqrt{\frac{\Sigma x^2}{n}} \Rightarrow n\sigma x^2 = \Sigma x^2$$

$$\text{But } r = \frac{\Sigma xy}{n\sigma x \sigma y}$$

Therefore, $b = r.\frac{\Sigma xy}{\sigma x}$ Also denoted by b_{yx}

Putting values of 'a' and 'b' in (5) we get

$$y - \bar{y} = r.\frac{\sigma y}{\sigma x}(x - \bar{x})$$

i.e. $y - \bar{y} = b_{yx}(x - \bar{x})$

Equation is the equation of the line of regression of y on x.

$b_{yx} = r.\frac{\sigma y}{\sigma x}$ is called the coefficient of regression of y on x which is obviously the slope of this line. Interchanging x and y in equation (6), the equation of the line of regression of x and y is given by

$$x - \bar{x} = r.\frac{\sigma x}{\sigma y}(y - \bar{y})$$

i.e. $x - \bar{x} = b_{xy}(y - \bar{y})$

Naturally b_{xy} is the slope of this line which is equal to $\frac{1}{r} \cdot \frac{\sigma y}{\sigma x}$

Note:

i) The point of intersection of these regression line is the point $(\bar{x}, \bar{y})$.

ii) $b_{xy} \times b_{yx} = r\frac{\sigma y}{\sigma x} \times r\frac{\sigma x}{\sigma y} = r^2$

$$r = \pm\sqrt{b_{xy} \times b_{yx}}$$

iii) $$b_{yx} = \frac{\Sigma uv - \frac{(\Sigma u)(\Sigma v)}{n}}{\Sigma u^2 - \frac{(\Sigma u)^2}{n}}$$

$$= \frac{\Sigma xy}{\Sigma x^2} \text{ for ungrouped data}$$

$$b_{yx} = \frac{\Sigma uv - \frac{(\Sigma fu)(\Sigma fv)}{n}}{\Sigma fu^2 - \frac{(\Sigma fu)^2}{n}}$$

$$= \frac{\Sigma xy}{\Sigma x^2} \text{ for grouped data}$$

and $$b_{xy} = \frac{\Sigma uv - \frac{(\Sigma u)(\Sigma v)}{n}}{\Sigma fu^2 - \frac{(\Sigma u)^2}{n}}$$

$$= \frac{\Sigma xy}{\Sigma y^2} \text{ for ungrouped data}$$

$$b_{xy} = \frac{\Sigma uv - \frac{(\Sigma fu)(\Sigma fv)}{n}}{\Sigma fu^2 - \frac{(\Sigma fv)^2}{n}}$$

$$= \frac{\Sigma xy}{\Sigma y^2} \text{ for grouped data}$$

Example: A panel of two judges A and B graded dramatic performance by independently awarding marks as follows:

Performance No.	:	1	2	3	4	5	6	7	8
Marks by A	:	36	32	34	31	32	32	35	38
Marks by B	:	35	33	31	30	34	32	36	?

Solution:

Sr.No.	x_i	x - x x	x^2	y_i	y - y y	y^2	xy 6
1	36	+3	9	35	+2	4	0
2	32	-1	1	33	0	0	-2
3	34	1	1	31	-2	4	6
4	31	-2	4	30	-3	9	-1
5	32	-1	1	34	1	1	1
6	32	-1	1	32	-1	1	6
7	35	2	4	36	3	9	
n = 7	$\Sigma x_i = 135$		$\Sigma x^2 = 21$	$\Sigma y_i = 231$		$\Sigma y^2 = 28$	$\Sigma xy = 16$

$\overline{x}$

$$= \frac{\Sigma x}{n} = \frac{232}{7} = 33 \text{ and } \overline{y} = \frac{\Sigma y}{n} = \frac{231}{7} = 33$$

Now $$r = \frac{\Sigma xy}{\sqrt{x^2} \times \sqrt{y^2}} = \frac{16}{\sqrt{21} \times \sqrt{18}}$$

$$= \frac{16}{\sqrt{588}} = \frac{16}{24.22} = 0.65$$

Also $$\sigma x = \sqrt{\frac{\Sigma x^2}{n}} = \sqrt{\frac{21}{7}} = \sqrt{3} = 1.73$$

$$\sigma y = \sqrt{\frac{\Sigma y^2}{n}} = \sqrt{\frac{28}{7}} = 2$$

The equation of the line of regression of y on x

$$y - \overline{y} = r.\frac{\sigma y}{\sigma x}(x - \overline{x})$$

Inserting $x = 38$, we get

$y - 33 = 0.74\ (38 - 33\ )$

$y - 33 = 0.74 \times 5$

$y - 33 \quad = 3.7$

$y \quad = 3.7 + 33$

$y \quad = 36.7 = 37$

Therefore, the Judge B would have given 37 marks to 8th performance.

Example: The two regression equations of the variables x an y are $x = 19.13 - 0.87\ y$ and $y = 11.64 - 0.50\ x$

Find (1) Mean of x's

(2) Mean of y's

(3) Correlation coefficient between x and y

Solution:

- Calculation of Mean

Since lines of regression pass through means

i.e. $(\overline{x} - \overline{y})$

$\overline{x} + 0.87\overline{y} \qquad = 19.13..........(1)$

$50\overline{x} + \overline{y} \ = 11.64$

i.e. $\overline{x} + 2\overline{y} \ = 23.28..........(2)$

Subtracting (1) from (2) we get

$1.13\overline{y} = 4.15$ or $\qquad \overline{y} \qquad = 3.67$

Inserting $\overline{y} = 3.67$ in (2) we get $\overline{x} = 15.94$

Mean of x's = 15.94 and Mean of y's = 3.67

- Calculation of ' r '

$x = 19.93 - 0.87\ y$

Therefore, $b_{xy} = r.\dfrac{\sigma x}{\sigma y} = -\ 0.87............(3)$

and $y = 11.64 - 0.50\ x$

Therefore, $b_{yx} = r.\dfrac{\sigma y}{\sigma x} = -0.50............(4)$

From (3) and (4)

$$r^2 = \pm\sqrt{b_{xy} \times b_{yx}} \qquad = \pm\sqrt{-0.87 \times -0.50}$$

$r \quad = \pm\ 0.66$

But regression coefficient are negative

$r \quad = -0.66$

Example: In a partially destroyed laboratory record of an analysis of correlation data, the following results are legible:

Variance of $x \qquad = 9$

Regression equations: $8\ x - 10y + 66 = 6$

$40x - 18y \qquad = 214$

What are (1) Means of x's and y's (2) the coefficient of correlation between x and y (3) the standard deviation of y?

Solution:

- Means:

$8x - 10y = -66$ ...(1)

$40x - 18y = 214$ ...(2)

Solving (1) and (2) as

$40x - 50y = -330$ ...(1)

$40x - 18y = 214$ ...(2)

$-32y = -544$

$y = 17$

Mean of y's $(\bar{y})$ 17

Substituting $y = 17$ in (1) we get $8x - 10 \times 17 = -66$

or $8x = 104$ $x = 13$

Mean of x's $(\bar{x}) = 13$

- Coefficient of correlation between x and y

$40x = 18y + 214$

$$x = \frac{18}{40}y + \frac{214}{40}$$

$$b_{xy} = \frac{18}{40} = 0.45$$

Also $-10\,y = -8x - 66$

$$y = \frac{8}{10}x + \frac{66}{10}$$

$$b_{yx} = \frac{8}{10} = 0.8$$

Therefore, $r = \sqrt{b_{xy} \times b_{yx}} = \sqrt{.45 \times .8} = 0.6$

- Standard deviation of y

Variance of x i.e. $\sigma x^2 = 9$ $\sigma x = 3$

Now $b_{yx} = r.\dfrac{\sigma y}{\sigma x}$ or $0.8 = 6 \times \dfrac{\sigma y}{3} = 2\sigma y$

$\sigma y = 0.4$

Example: From 10 observations of price x and supply y of a commodity the results obtained $\Sigma x = 130$, $\Sigma y = 220$, $\Sigma x^2 = 2288$, $\Sigma xy = 3467$

Compute the regression of y on x and interpret the result. Estimate the supply when the price of 16 units.

Solution: The equation of the line of regression of y on x

$y = a + b\,x$

Also from normal equations

$\Sigma y = n\,a + b\,\Sigma\,x$ and $\Sigma\,xy = a\,\Sigma\,x + b\,\Sigma\,x^2$

we get

220 $= 10a + 130b \Rightarrow (1)$

3467 $= 130a + 2288 \Rightarrow (2)$

Solving (1) and (2) as

2860 $= 130a + 1690b$

3467 $= 130a + 2288b$

On subtraction

607 $= 598b\ b = 1.002$

Putting $b = 1.002$ in $220 = 10a + 130b$, we get $a = 8.974$.

Hence the 3 equation of the line of regression of y on x is

$y = 8.974 + 1.002x$

When $x = 16$, we get

$y = 8.974 + 1.002\,(16)$

$y = 25.006$

Example: If q is the acute angle between the two regression lines in the case of two variables x and y show that

$$\tan\theta = \frac{1-r^2}{r} \times \frac{\sigma x \sigma y}{\sigma x^2 + \sigma y^2}$$

with usual meanings. Explain the significance when $r = 0$ and $r = \pm 1$.

Solution: The slopes of the two regression lines are

$$m_1 = b_{yx} = r.\frac{\sigma y}{\sigma x} \text{ and } b_{xy} = r.\frac{\sigma x}{\sigma y} \text{ or } \frac{1}{r}.\frac{\sigma y}{\sigma x} = m_2$$

$$\tan\theta = \left|\frac{m_1 - m_2}{-+m_1.m_2}\right|$$

$$\tan\theta = \left|\frac{r\frac{\sigma y}{\sigma x} - \frac{1}{r}\frac{\sigma y}{\sigma x}}{1+\frac{\sigma y}{\sigma x}.\frac{1}{r}\frac{\sigma y}{\sigma x}}\right|$$

$$\tan\theta = \left|\frac{\frac{\sigma y}{\sigma x}\left(r-\frac{1}{r}\right)}{1+\left(\frac{\sigma y}{\sigma x}\right)^2}\right| = \left|\frac{\frac{r^2-1}{r}.\frac{\sigma y}{\sigma x}}{\frac{\sigma x^2+\sigma y^2}{\sigma x^2}}\right|$$

$$\tan\theta = \frac{(1-r^2)}{r} \times \frac{\sigma x \sigma y}{\sigma x^2 + \sigma y^2}$$

If $r = \theta$ then $\tan\theta = \infty$ or $\theta = \pi/2$ i.e. there is no relationship between two variables i.e. independent or uncorrelated. If $r = \pm 1$ then $\theta = 0$. The two regression lines are coincident or parallel and the correlation is perfect.

6

Probabilities

The theory of probability was developed towards the end of the 18th century and its history suggests that it developed with the study of games and chance, such as rolling a dice, drawing a card, flipping a coin etc.

Apart from these, uncertainty prevailed in every sphere of life. For instance, one often predicts: "It will probably rain tonight."

"It is quite likely that there will be a good yield of cereals this year" and so on. This indicates that, in layman's terminology the word 'probability' thus connotes that there is an uncertainty about the happening of events.

To put 'probability' on a better footing we define it. But before doing so, we have to explain a few terms."

TRIAL

A procedure or an experiment to collect any statistical data such as rolling a dice or flipping a coin is called a trial.

Random Trial or Random Experiment

When the outcome of any experiment can not be predicted precisely then the experiment is called a random trial or random experiment.

In other words, if a random experiment is repeated under identical conditions, the outcome will vary at random as it is impossible to predict about the performance of the experiment.

For example, if we toss a honest coin or roll an unbiased dice, we may not get the same results as our expectations.

SAMPLE SPACE

The totality of all the outcomes or results of a random experiment is denoted by Greek alphabet Ω or English alphabets and is called the sample space. Each outcome or element of this sample space is known as a sample print.

Event

Any subset of a sample space is called an event. A sample space S serves as the universal set for all questions related to an experiment 'S' and an event A w.r.t it is a set of all possible outcomes favorable to the even t A

For example,
A random experiment:- flipping a coin twice
Sample space:- Ω or $S = \{(HH), (HT), (TH), (TT)\}$
The question: "both the flipps show same face"
Therefore, the event A: $\{(HH), (TT)\}$

Equally Likely Events

All possible results of a random experiment are called equally likely outcomes and we have no reason to expect any one rather than the other. For example, as the result of drawing a card from a well shuffled pack, any card may appear in draw, so that the 52 cards become 52 different events which are equally likely.

Mutually Exclusive Events

Events are called mutually exclusive or disjoint or incompatible if the occurrence of one of them precludes the occurrence of all the others. For example in tossing a coin, there are two mutually exclusive events viz turning up a head and turning up of a tail. Since both these events cannot happen simultaneously. But note that events are compatible if it is possible for them to happen simultaneously. For instance in rolling of two dice, the cases of the face marked 5 appearing on one dice and face 5 appearing on the other, are compatible.

Exhaustive Events

Events are exhaustive when they include all the possibilities associated with the same trial. In throwing a coin, the turning up of head and of a tail are exhaustive events assuming of course that the coin cannot rest on its edge.

Independent Events

Two events are said to be independent if the occurrence of any event does not affect the occurrence of the other event. For example in tossing of a coin, the events corresponding to the two successive tosses of it are independent.

The flip of one penny does not affect in any way the flip of a nickel.

Dependent Events

If the occurrence or non-occurrence of any event affects the happening of the other, then the events are said to be dependent events.

For example, in drawing a card from a pack of cards, let the event A be the occurrence of a king in the 1st draw and B be the occurrence of a king in the 1st draw and B be the occurrence of a king in the second draw.

If the card drawn at the first trial is not replaced then events A and B are independent events.

Note: (1) If an event contains a single simple point i.e. it is a singleton set, then this event is called an elementary or a simple event.

(2) An event corresponding to the empty set is an "impossible event."

(3) An event corresponding to the entire sample space is called a 'certain event'.

Complementary Events

Let S be the sample space for an experiment and A be an event in S. Then A is a subset of S. Hence $\overline{A}$, the complement of A in S is also an event in S which contains the outcomes which are not favorable to the occurrence of A i.e. if A occurs, then the outcome of the experiment belongs to A, but if A does not occur, then the outcomes of the experiment belongs to $\overline{A}$

It is obvious that A and $\overline{A}$ are mutually exclusive. $A \cap \overline{A} = \phi$ and $A \cup \overline{A} = S$.

If S contains n equally likely, mutually exclusive and exhaustive points and A contains m out of these n points then $\overline{A}$ contains $(n - m)$ sample points.

DEFINITIONS OF PROBABILITY

We shall now consider two definitions of probability:

(1) Mathematical or a priori or classical.

(2) Statistical or empirical.

1. Mathematical (or A Priori or Classic) Definition

If there are 'n' exhaustive, mutually exclusive and equally likely cases and m of them are favorable to an event A, the probability of A happening is defined as the ratio m/n

Expressed as a formula:-

$$P(A) = \frac{m}{n} = \frac{\text{number of favorable outcomes}}{\text{total number of possible outcomes}}$$

$$P(A) = \frac{n(A)}{n(S)}$$

This definition is due to 'Laplace.' Thus probability is a concept which measures numerically the degree of certainty or uncertainty of the occurrence of an event.

For example, the probability of randomly drawing taking from a well-shuffled deck of cards is 4/52. Since 4 is the number of favorable outcomes (i.e. 4 kings of diamond, spade, club and heart) and 52 is the number of total outcomes (the number of cards in a deck).

If A is any event of sample space having probability P, then clearly, P is a positive number (expressed as a fraction or usually as a decimal) not greater than unity. $0 \leq P \leq 1$ i.e. 0 (no chance or for impossible event) to a high of 1 (certainty). Since the number of cases not favorable to A are $(n - m)$, the probability q that event A will not happen is, $\frac{n-m}{n}$ q = or q = 1 – m/n or $q = 1 - p$. Now note that the probability q is nothing but the probability of the complementary event A i.e.

Thus $p(\overline{A}) = 1 - p$ or $p(\overline{A}) = 1 - p(\overline{A})$

so that $p(A) + p(\overline{A}) = 1$ i.e. $p + q = 1$

Relative Frequency Definition

The classical definition of probability has a disadvantage i.e. the words 'equally likely' are vague. In fact, since these words seem to be synonymous with "equally probable". This definition is circular as it is defining (in terms) of itself. Therefore, the estimated or empirical probability of an event is taken as the relative frequency of the occurrence of the event when the number of observations is very large.

2. Van Mise's Statistical (or Empirical) Definition

If trials are to be repeated a great number of times under essentially the same condition then the limit of the ratio of the number of times that an event happens to the total number of trials, as the number of trials increases indefinitely is called the probability of the happening of the event.

It is assumed that the limit exists and finite uniquely. Symbolically $p(A) = p = \lim_{n\to\infty} \frac{m}{n}$ provided it is finite and unique.

The two definitions are apparently different but both of them can be reconciled the same sense.

Example: Find the probability of getting heads in tossing a coin.
Solution: Experiment: Tossing a coin
Sample space: $S = \{H, T\} \Rightarrow n(S) = 2$
Event A: getting heads
$A = \{\text{H}\} \Rightarrow n(A) = 1$

Therefore, $p(A) = \frac{n(A)}{n(S)}$ or 0.5

Example: Find the probability of getting 3 or 5 in throwing a die.
Solution: Experiment: Throwing a dice
Sample space: $S = \{1, 2, 3, 4, 5, 6\} \Rightarrow n(S) = 2$
Event A: getting 3 or 6

$A = \{3, 6\} \Rightarrow n(A) = 2$

Therefore, $p(\text{A}) = \dfrac{n(A)}{n(S)} = \dfrac{2}{6} = \dfrac{1}{3} 0.33$

Example: Two dice are rolled. Find the probability that the score on the second die is greater than the score on the first die.

Solution: Experiment: Two dice are rolled

Sample space: $S = \{(1, 1), (1, 2), (1, 3), (1, 4), (1, 5), (1, 6)$ $(2, 1), (2, 2), (2, 3), (2, 4), (2, 6)\}$...

$(6, 1), (6, 2)$ $(, 3), (6, 4), (6, 5), (6, 6)\}$

$n(S) = 6 \times 6 = 36$

Event A: The score on the second die > the score on the 1st die.

i.e. $A = \{(1, 2), (1, 3), (1, 4), (1, 5), (1, 6)$ $(2, 3), (2, 4), (2, 5), (2, 6)$ $(3, 4), (3, 5), (3, 6)$ $(4, 5), (4, 6)$ $(5, 6)\}$

$n(A) = 15$

Therefore, $p(A) = \dfrac{n(A)}{n(S)} = \dfrac{15}{36} = \dfrac{5}{12}$ or 0.42

Example: A coin is tossed three times. Find the probability of getting at least one head.

Solution: Experiment: *A* coin is tossed three times.

Sample space: $S = \{(H\,H\,H), (H\,H\,T), (HTH), (HTT), (THT), (TTH), (THH), (TTT)\}$

$\Rightarrow n(S) = 8$

Event A: getting at least one head

so that A: getting no head at all

$\overline{A} = \{(TTT) \Rightarrow n(\overline{A}) = 1$

$P(\overline{A}) = \dfrac{n(\overline{A})}{n(S)} = \dfrac{1}{8}$

Therefore, $P(A) = 1 - P(A) = 1 - \dfrac{1}{8} = \dfrac{7}{8}$

$= \dfrac{2}{7}$ = 0.29(approximately)

Example: A ball is drawn at random from a box containing 6 red balls, 4 white balls and 5 blue balls. Determine the probability that the ball drawn is (i) red (ii) white (iii) blue (iv) not red (v) red or white.

Solution: Let R, W and B denote the events of drawing a red ball, a white ball and a blue ball respectively.

$$P(R) = \frac{\text{Number of favorabel outcomes}}{\text{Total number of outcomes}} = \frac{n(R)}{n(S)}$$

$$= \frac{6}{6+4+5} = \frac{6}{15} = \frac{2}{5} = 0.4$$

(ii) $P(W) = \frac{4}{6+4+5} = \frac{4}{15} = 0.26\overline{6}$

(iii) $P(B) = \frac{5}{6+4+5} = \frac{5}{15} = \frac{1}{3} = 0.3\overline{3}$

(iv) $P(\overline{R}) = 1 - P(R) = -\frac{2}{3} = \frac{3}{5} = 0.6$

(v) $P(R + W) = P(R) + P(W) = \frac{2}{5} + \frac{4}{15} = \frac{2}{3} = 0.6\overline{6}$

Note: The two events R and W are 'disjoint' events.

Example: What is the chance that a leap year selected at random will contain 53 Sundays?

Solution: A leap year has 52 weeks and 2 more days.

The two days can be:

Monday - Tuesday

Tuesday - Wednesday

Wednesday - Thursday

Thursday - Friday

Friday - Saturday

Saturday - Sunday and

Sunday - Monday.

There are 7 outcomes and 2 are favorable to the 53rd Sunday.

Now for 53 Sundays in a leap year, $P(A) = \frac{n(A)}{n(S)}$

$= \frac{2}{7}$ = 0.29 (approximately)

Example: If four ladies and six gentlemen sit for a photograph in a row at random, what is the probability that no two ladies will sit together?

4 ladies + 6 gentlemen = 10 persons in all.

They can sit in a row in ${}^{10}P_{10} = 10!$ ways

Thus $n(S) = 10!$

Solution: Now if no two ladies are to be together, the ladies have 7 positions, 2 at ends and 5 between the gentlemen

Arrangement L, G1, L, G2, L, G3, L, G4, L, G5, L, G6, L

The 4 ladies can occupy these 7 seats in ${}^{7}P_{4}$ ways and 6 gentlemen can occupy 6 seats in ${}^{6}P_{6}$ ways. Therefore, the total number of these arrangements $= {}^{7}P_{4} \times {}^{6}P_{4}$ ways.

Therefore, the required,

$$\text{probability} = \frac{\text{No of favorabel outcomes}}{\text{Total no. of outcomes}}$$

$$= \frac{{}^7P_4 \times {}^6P_4}{10!}$$

$$= \frac{1}{6} \text{ or } 0.17 \text{ (approximately)}$$

Example: In a class there are 13 students. 5 of them are boys and the rest are girls. Find the probability that two students selected at random will be both girls.

Solution: Two students out of 13 can be selected in ${}^{13}C_2$ ways and two girls out of 8 can be selected in ${}^8C_2$ ways.

Therefore, required probability

$$= \frac{{}^8C_2}{{}^{13}C_2} = \frac{14}{39} = 0.36 \text{ (approximately)}$$

Example: A box contains 5 white balls, 4 black balls and 3 red balls. Three balls are drawn randomly. What is the probability that they will be (i) white (ii) black (iii) red ?

Solution: Let *W*, *B* and *R* denote the events of drawing three white, three black and three red balls respectively.

THE LAWS OF PROBABILITY

So far we have discussed probabilities of single events. In many situations we come across two or more events occurring together. If event *A* and event *B* are two events and either *A* or *B* or both occurs, is denoted by $A \cap B$ or $(A + B)$ and the event that both *A* and *B* occurs is denoted by $A \cap B$ or *AB*. We term these situations as compound event or the joint occurrence of events. We may need probability that *A* or *B* will happen.

It is denoted by $P(A \cap B)$ or $P(A + B)$. Also we may need the probability that *A* and *B* (both) will happen simultaneously. It is denoted by $P(A \cap B)$ or $P(AB)$.

Consider a situation, you are asked to choose any 3 or any diamond or both from a well shuffled pack of 52 cards. Now you are interested in the probability of this situation.

It is denoted by $P(A \cup B)$ or $P(A + B)$. Also we may need the probability that *A* and *B* (both) will happen simultaneously. It is denoted by $P(A \cap B)$ or $P(AB)$.

Consider a situation, you are asked to choose any 3 or any diamond or both from a well shuffled pack of 52 cards. Now you are interested in the probability of this situation.

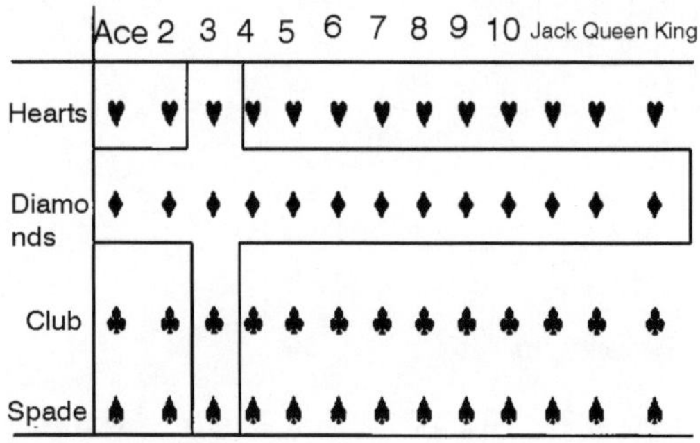

Now count the dots in the area which fulfills the condition any 3 or any diamond or both. They are 16.

$$= \frac{\text{No.of favorable outcomes}}{\text{Total no.of outcomes}}$$

$$= \frac{16}{52} \text{ or } 0.31$$

Thus the required probability

In the language of set theory, the set any 3 or any diamond or both is the union of the sets 'any 3 which contains 4 cards ' and 'any diamond' which contains 15 cards.

The number of cards in their union is equal to the sum of these numbers minus the number of cards in the space where they overlap. Any points in this space, called the intersection of the two sets, is counted here twice (double counting), once in each set. Dividing by 52 we get the required probability.

= P(any 3) + P(any diamond) – P(3 of diamond)

$$= \frac{4}{52} + \frac{13}{52} - \frac{1}{52}$$

$$= \frac{16}{32} \text{ or } 0.31$$

Thus P(any 3 or any diamond or both)

In general, if the letters A and B stands for any two events, then,

$$\left\{ \begin{array}{c} P(A \cup B) = P(A) + P(B) - P(A \cap B) \\ OR \\ P(A + B) + P(A) + P(B) - P(AB) \end{array} \right\}$$

Addition Law

Clearly, the outcomes of both A and B are non-mutually exclusive.

Example: Two dice are rolled. Find the probability that the score is an even number or multiple of 3.

Solution: Two dice are rolled.

Sample space = {(1, 1), (1, 2)............, (6, 6)}

$n(S) = 6 \times 6 = 36$

Event E: The score is an even number or multiple of 3.

Note here score means the sum of the numbers on both the dice when they land. For example (1, 1) has score 1 + 1 = 2.

It is clear that the least score is 2 and the highest score (6, 6) $\Rightarrow 6 + 6 = 12$

i.e. score 2, 3, 4, 5, 6, 7, 8, 9, 10, 11, 12

Let Event A: Score is an even numbers

A = {(1, 1), (1, 3), (1, 5), (2,2), (2, 4), (2, 6), (3, 1), (3, 3) (3, 5), (4, 2), (4, 4), (4, 6), (5, 1), (5, 3), (5, 5), (6, 2), (6, 4), (6, 6)}

Therefore $n(A) = 18$

Let Event B: The score is the multiple of 3

Let Event B: The score is the multiple of 3

i.e. 3, 6, 9, 12

B = {(1, 2), (1, 5), (2, 4), (2, 1) (3, 6) (3, 3) (4,2), (4, 5), (5, 1), (5,4), (6, 3), (6, 6)}

$n(B) = 12$

Let Event $A \cap B$:The score is an even number and multiple of 3 or (i.e. common to both A and B) AB

AB = {(2, 4), (4, 2), (33,3), (4,2), (5, 1), (6,6)}

$n(AB) = 6$

Now $P(A + B) = P(A) + P(AB)$ where $E = A + B$

$$= \frac{n(A)}{n(S)} + \frac{n(B)}{n(S)} - \frac{n(AB)}{n(S)}$$

$$= \frac{18}{36} + \frac{12}{36} - \frac{6}{36}$$

$$= \frac{14}{36} \quad = \frac{2}{3} \text{ or } 0.67 \text{ (approximately)}$$

Corollary

You are flipping a coin and wanting to find the probability of at least one head or at least one tail. Now it is clear that the probability of one coin flip landing heads is 1/2 and that of one coin flip landing tails is also 1/2. Now these two events are mutually exclusive as you cannot expect a coin land both heads and tails in one trial. Therefore you can determine the required probability by the mere addition of the two probabilities: $\frac{1}{2} + \frac{1}{2} = 1$ (or certainty).

Thus if A and B are two mutually exclusive events then the probability that either A or B will happen is the sum of the probabilities of A and B i.e. $P(A + B) = P(A) + P(B)$

Odds In Favour And Against

If P is the probability that an event will occur and $q(= 1 - p)$ is the probability of the non-occurrence of the event; then we say that the odds in favour of the event occurring are $p: q$

(p to q) and the odds against its occurring are $q: p$.

For example, if the event consists of drawing a card if club from the deck of 52 cards, then the odds in favour are $\frac{13}{52}:\frac{39}{52}$ i.e. $\frac{1}{4}:\frac{3}{4}$ i.e. 1: 3;

Similarly the odds against a card of diamond would be 3: 1. The odds in favour of 4 or 6 in a single toss of a fair die are $\frac{1}{3}:\frac{2}{3}$; i.e. 1: 2 and the odds against are 2: 1.

Multiplication Law of Probability

If there are two independent events; the respective probability of which are known, then the probability that both will happen is the product of the probabilities of their happening respectively $P(AB) = P(A) \times P(B)$

To compute the probability of two or even more independent event all occurring (joint occurrence) extent the above law to required number.

For example, first flip a penny, then the nickle and finally flip the dime.

On landing, probability of heads $\frac{1}{2}$ is for a penny

probability of heads is $\frac{1}{2}$ for a nickle

probability of heads is $\frac{1}{2}$ for a dime

Thus the probability of landing three heads will be $\frac{1}{2}\times\frac{1}{2}\times\frac{1}{2}=\frac{1}{8}$ or 0.125.

(Note that all three events are independent)

Example: Three machines I, II and III manufacture respectively 0.4, 0.5 and 0.1 of the total production. The percentage of defective items produced by I, II and III is 2, 4 and 1 percent respectively for an item randomly chosen, what is the probability it is defective ?

Solution:

The defective items produced by machine

$$\text{I} = \frac{0.4 \times 2}{100} = \frac{8}{100}$$

The defective items produced by machine

$$II = \frac{0.5 \times 4}{100} = \frac{2}{100}$$

The defective items produced by machine

$$II = \frac{0.1 \times 1}{100} = \frac{0.1}{100}$$

The total defective items produced by all three machines

$$= \frac{0.8}{100} + \frac{2}{100} + \frac{0.1}{100}$$

$$= 0.029$$

Thus the requiered probability

$$= \frac{0.029}{1}$$

$$= 0.029$$

[A case of addition Law of mutually exclusive events]

Example: In shuffling a pack of cards, 4 are accidentally dropped one after another. Find the chance that the missing cards should be one from each suit.

Solution: Probability of 4 missing cards from different suits are as follows:

Let H, D, C and S denote heart, diamond, club and spade cards respectively

then $P(H) = \frac{13C_1}{52C_1}$

$$P(D) = \frac{13C_1}{52C_1},\ P(C) = \frac{13C_1}{52C_1} \text{ and } P(S) = \frac{13C_1}{52C_1}$$

Since all the four events are independent, using multiplication Law, we get Required probability = $P(H) \times P(D) \times P(C) \times P(S)$

$$= \frac{13C_1}{52C_1} \times \frac{13C_1}{52C_1} \times \frac{13C_1}{52C_1} \times \frac{13C_1}{52C_1}$$

$$= \frac{1}{4} \times \frac{1}{4} \times \frac{1}{4} \times \frac{1}{4}$$

$$= \frac{1}{256}$$

Example: A problem in statistics is given to three students A, B and C whose chances in solving it are $\frac{1}{2}, \frac{3}{4}$, and $\frac{1}{4}$ respectively. What is the probability that the problem will be solved?

Solution: The probability that A can solve the problem = 1/2
The probability that B cannot solve the problem = 1 – 1/2 = 1/2

Similarly the probabilities that B and C cannot solve problem are $\left(1-\frac{3}{4}\right)$ and $\left(1-\frac{1}{4}\right)$ respectively.

The probability that *A, B, C* cannot solve the problem

$=\left(1-\frac{1}{2}\right)\left(1-\frac{3}{4}\right)\left(1-\frac{1}{4}\right)$ .... ($\because$ indepemdent events)

$= \frac{1}{2}\times\frac{1}{4}\times\frac{3}{4}=\frac{3}{22}$

Hence the probability that the problem can be solved

$= 1-\frac{3}{22}$

$= \frac{29}{32} = 0.90625$

Example: Tom and his wife Jenny appear in an interview for two vacancies in the same post. The chance of Tom's selection is 1/7 and that of Jenny's selection is 1/5. What is the probability that (i) both of them will be selected (ii) only one of them will be selected (iii) none of them will be selected.

Solution: *P* (Tom's selection) = 1/7 *P*(wife Jenny's selection) = 1/5

(i) $P(\text{both selected}) = \frac{1}{7}=\frac{1}{5}=\frac{1}{35}$ or 0.03

(ii) *P*(only one is selected) = *P*(only Tom is selected)
P(Jenny's selection)

$= \left(\frac{1}{7}\times\frac{4}{5}\right)+\left(\frac{1}{5}\times\frac{6}{7}\right)$

$= \frac{10}{35}=\frac{2}{7}$

Note that when we say only Tom is selected. Simultaneously we mean Jenny is rejected. Thus the two events become independent and hence multiplication rule is applied. Also Tom's selection and Jenny's selection in this case is a mutually exclusive. Hence finally addition rule is applied.

(iii) $P(\text{none of them will be selected}) = \frac{6}{7}\times\frac{4}{5}=\frac{24}{35}$ or 0.69

CONDITIONAL PROBABILITY

In many situations you get more information than simply the total outcomes and favorable outcomes you already have and, hence you are in position to make yourself more informed to make judgements regarding the probabilities of such situations. For example, suppose a card is drawn at random from a deck of 52 cards. Let *B* denotes the event 'the card is a diamond' and *A* denotes the event 'the card is red'. We may then consider the following probabilities.

(i) $P(B) = \frac{13C_1}{52C_1} = \frac{13}{52}$

(ii) $P(A) = \frac{26C_1}{52C_1} = \frac{26}{52}$

(iii) $P(AB)$ = The probability that the card is both adiamond and a red card $= \frac{13C_1}{52C_1} = \frac{13}{52}$

(iv) The probability that the card is a diamond knowing that it is red. Since there are 26 red cards of which 13 are diamonds, the probability that the card is diamond is $\frac{13}{26}$. In other words the probability of event *B* knowing that *A* has occurred is $\frac{13}{26}$.

The probability of *B* under the condition that *A* has occurred is known as condition probability and it is denoted by $P(B/A)$. Thus $P(B/A) = \frac{13}{26}$. It should be observed that the probability of the event B is increased due to the additional information that the event A has occurred.

Conditional probability found using the formula $P(B/A) = \frac{P(AB)}{P(A)}$

Justification:- $P(A/B) = \frac{P(AB)}{P(A)} = \frac{13}{26} = \frac{13/52}{26/52} = \frac{P(AB)}{P(B)}$

Similarly $P(A/B) = \frac{P(AB)}{P(A)}$

In both the cases if *A* and *B* are independent events then $P(A/B) = P(A)$ and $P(B/A) = P(B)$

Therefore $P(A) = \frac{P(AB)}{P(B)} \Rightarrow P(AB) = P(A).\,P(B)$

or $P(B) = \frac{P(AB)}{P(A)} \Rightarrow P(AB) = P(A).\,P(B)$

Propositions

- If A and B are independent events then A and B' are also independent where B' is the complementary event B.
- If A and B are independent events then A' and B' are also independent events.
- Two independent events cannot be mutually exclusive.
- De Morgan's Laws: $P(A \cup B)' = P(A' \cap B')$

$P(A \cap B)' = P(A' \cup B')$

Example: A bag contains 6 red and 4 blue balls. One ball is drawn at random from the first bag and put into the second bag. A ball is then drawn from the second bag. What is the probability that is red ?

Solution:

Let A = Getting a red ball from the 1st bag.

B = Getting a blue from the first bag.

C = Getting a red ball from the second bag after the ball drawn from the first bag is put into it.

Since there are 10 balls in the first bag out of which 6 are red and 4 are blue.

$P(A) = \frac{6}{10}$ and $P(B) = \frac{4}{10}$

Suppose that A has occurred. Then a red ball is transferred into second bag. The probability of getting a red ball from the second bag when a red ball is got from the first is $P(C/A) = 5/11$

The probability of getting a red ball from the first bag and a red ball from the second is $P(A \cap C) = P(A).\,P(C/A) = \frac{6}{10} \times \frac{5}{11} = \frac{30}{110}$ Now, suppose the event B has occurred then a blue ball is transferred into the second bag. There are now 11 balls in the second bag out of which 4 are red.

$$P(C/B) = \frac{4}{11}$$

$$P(B \cap C) = P(B).\,P(C/B) = \frac{4}{10}.\frac{4}{11} = \frac{16}{110}$$

Since $A \cap C$ and $B \cap C$ are mutually exclusive events

$$P(A \cap C) \cup P(B \cap C) = P(A \cap C) + P(B \cap C)$$

$$= \frac{30}{110} + \frac{16}{110} = \frac{23}{25} \text{ i.e. } 0.92$$

Example: In a certain school, 25% of the boys and 10% of the girls are studying French. The girls constitute 60% of the students boy. If a student is selected at random and is studying French, determine the probability that the student is a girl.

Solution: Let there be 100 students. 60% of which are girls.

i.e. number of girls is 60 and number of boys is 40.

Then 25% of 40 $= \frac{25}{100} \times 40 = 10$

and 10% of 60 $= \frac{10}{100} \times 60 = 6$

students are studying 'French'

Let A = a student studying French $\Rightarrow n(A) = 16$

and $P(A) = \frac{n(A)}{n(S)} = \frac{16}{100}$

Let B = a girl student. $A \cap B$ = a girl student studying French

Now, $n(A \cap B) = 6$, $P(A \cap B) = \frac{n(A \cap B)}{n(S)} = \frac{6}{100}$

Now $P(B/A)$ = Probability that a selected student is a girl studying French

Now $P(B/A) = \frac{P(A \cap B)}{P(A)} = \frac{6/100}{16/100} = \frac{3}{8} = 0.375$

Example: In a school competition, the probability of hitting the target by Dick is 1/2, by Betty is 1/3 and by Joe is 3/5. If all of them fire independently at the same target, calculate the probability that

- The target will be hit
- Only one of them will hit the target and
- Dick hits, given that only one hits the target.

Solution:

P(Dick hits the target) = 1/2, P(Betty hits the target) = 1/3 and P (Joe hits the target) = 3/5

Now the probabilities of their nothitting the target are

Let P(not-Dick hits the target) $= 1 - \frac{1}{2} = \frac{1}{2} = P(D')$

P(not-Betty hits the target) $= 1 - \frac{1}{3} = \frac{2}{3} = P(B')$

$P(\text{not-Joe hits the target}) = 1 - \frac{3}{5} = \frac{2}{5} = P(J')$

(i) Since original probabilities are independent events,

$\overline{D}, \overline{B}$ and $\overline{J}$ are also independent events.

Hence $P(\overline{D}.\overline{B}.\overline{J}) = P(\overline{D}).P(\overline{B}).P(\overline{J})$

$= \frac{1}{2} \times \frac{2}{3} \times \frac{2}{5} = \frac{2}{15}$

The target will be hit if at least one of them hits the target. Therefore, the probability of hitting the target by at least one of them is $1 - P(\overline{D}.\overline{B}.\overline{J})$

$= 1 - \frac{2}{15} = \frac{13}{15}$

(ii) Dick hits but Betty and Joe do not i.e. $D \cap \overline{B} \cap \overline{J}$

Betty hits but not Dick and Joe i.e. $\overline{B} \cap D \cap \overline{J}$

Joe hits but not Dick and Betty i.e. $\overline{J} \cap \overline{D} \cap \overline{B}$

Therefore, P(event of hitting the target by only one of Dick, Betty and Joe).

$P(A) = P(\overline{D})\ P(\overline{B})\ P(\overline{J}) + P(\overline{D})\ P(\overline{B}).P(\overline{J})$

$+ P(\overline{D})\ P(\overline{B})\ P(\overline{J})$

Since these events are mutually exclusive and also independent.

$P(A) = \frac{1}{2} \times \frac{2}{3} \times \frac{2}{5} + \frac{1}{2} \times \frac{1}{3} \times \frac{2}{5} + \frac{1}{2} \times \frac{2}{3} \times \frac{3}{5} = \frac{2}{5}$

(iii) We have to find the probability of Dick with the added information that the event discussed in part (ii) i.e. A.

We have $P(\text{Dick} \cap A) = D \cap \overline{B} \cap \overline{J}$

$$P(D \cap \overline{B} \cap \overline{J}) = P(D)P(\overline{B})P(\overline{J}) = \frac{2}{15}$$

$$P(D/A) = \frac{(D \cap A)}{P(A)} = \frac{2/15}{2/5} = \frac{1}{3}$$

Example: A purse contains 6 silver coins and 3 copper coins. Another purse contains 4 silver coins and 5 copper coins. A purse is selected at random and a coin is drawn from it. What is the probability that it is a silver coin?

Solution:

Let A = the first purse selected

B = the second purse is selected
C = a silver coin is drawn from the purse
Since there are two purses

$P(A) = \frac{1}{2}$ and $P(B) = \frac{1}{2}$

Suppose the event A has occurred. Since there are 6 silver coins out of 9

$P(C/A) = \frac{6}{9}$

The probability of getting the first purse and a silver coin from it is

$$P(A \cap C) = P(A).\ P(C/A) = \left(\frac{1}{2}\right)\left(\frac{6}{9}\right) = \frac{6}{18}$$

Similarly, suppose B has occurred then $P(C/B) = \frac{4}{9}$

$$P(B \cap C) = P(B)\ P(C/B) = \left(\frac{1}{2}\right)\left(\frac{4}{9}\right) = \frac{4}{18}$$

Now $A \cap C$ and $B \cap C$ are mutually exclusive.

$$P(A \cap C \cup B \cap C) = P(A \cap C) + P(B \cap C) = \frac{6}{18} + \frac{4}{18} = \frac{5}{9}$$

Example: A student takes his examination in for subjects A, B, C and D. He estimates that his chances of passing A is $\frac{4}{5}$, in B as $\frac{3}{4}$, in C as $\frac{5}{6}$ and in D as $\frac{2}{3}$. To qualify he must pass in A and atleast two other subjects. What is the probability that he passes?

Solution:

Given that, $P(A) = \frac{4}{5}$ $P(\bar{A}) = 1 - P(A) = 1 - \frac{4}{5} = \frac{1}{5}$

$P(B) = \frac{3}{4}$ $P(\bar{B}) = 1 - P(B) = 1 - \frac{3}{4} = \frac{1}{4}$

$P(C) = \frac{5}{6}$ $P(\bar{C}) = 1 - P(C) = 1 - \frac{5}{6} = \frac{1}{6}$

and $P(D) = \frac{2}{3}$ $P(\bar{D}) = 1 - P(D) = 1 - \frac{2}{3} = \frac{1}{3}$

- Probability of passing *B*, *C* and failing in *D*

$$= P(B).P(C).P(\overline{D})$$

$$= \frac{3}{4} \times \frac{5}{6} \times \frac{1}{3}$$

- Probability of passing *C*, *D* and failing in *B*

$$= P(C).P(D).P(\overline{B})$$

$$= \frac{5}{6} \times \frac{2}{3} \times \frac{1}{4} = \frac{5}{36}$$

- Probability of passing *D*, *B* and failing in *C*

$$= P(D).P(B).P(\overline{C})$$

$$= \frac{2}{3} \times \frac{3}{4} \times \frac{1}{6} = \frac{1}{12}$$

Probability of passing *B*, *C* and *D*

$$= P(B).\ P(C).\ P(D)$$

$$= \frac{3}{4} \times \frac{5}{6} \times \frac{2}{3} = \frac{5}{12}$$

Thus probability of passing at least two subjects

$$= \frac{5}{24} + \frac{5}{36} + \frac{1}{12} + \frac{5}{12} = \frac{61}{72}$$

Therefore, probability of passing *A* and at least two subjects $= \frac{4}{5} \times \frac{61}{72} = \frac{61}{90}$

Example: Probability that a man will be alive 25 years is 0.3 and that his wife will be alive 25 years is 0.4. Find the probability that 25 years hence (1) Both will be alive (2) Only man will be alive (3) Only wife will be alive (4) At least one of them will be alive.

Solution:

Let *A*: the man will be alive 25 years hence $P(A) = 0.3$

Let *B*: His wife will be alive 25 years hence $P(B) = 0.4$

- $P(\text{both will be alive}) = P(A) \times P(B)$
  $= 0.3 \times 0.4 = 12$
- $P(\text{only man will be alive}) = P(A) \times P(B)$
  $= P(A) \times [1 - P(B)]$
  $= 0.3 \times [1 - 0.4]$
  $= 0.3 \times 0.6$
  $= 0.18$
- $P(\text{only wife will be alive}) = P(B) \times P(A)$

$= P(B) \times [1 - P(A)]$
$= 0.4 \times [1 - 0.3]$
$= 0.4 \times 0.7$
$= 0.28$

- P(at least one of them will be alive)
$= 1 - P(A).\ P(B)$
$= 1 - (0.7)\ (0.6)$
$= 1 - 0.42$
$= 0.58$

Example: A box contains 6 white and 4 black balls. Two balls are drawn at random one after the other. Replace the first ball after noting its colour. Find the probability that (1) both are white (2) both are black (3) the first is white, the second is black (4) the first black the second white (5) one white and one black.

Solution: Since the first ball is replaced, the outcome of the second draw is no way affected i.e. the events are independent.

Case (I) P(both white) $= P(W).\ P(W)$

$$= \frac{6}{10} \cdot \frac{6}{10} = 0.36$$

Case (II) P(both black) $= P(B).\ P(B)$

$$= \frac{4}{10} \cdot \frac{4}{10} = 0.16$$

Case (III) P(first white, second black) $= P(W).\ P(B)$

$$= \frac{6}{10} \cdot \frac{4}{10} = 0.24$$

Case (IV) P (first black, second white) $P(B).\ P(W)$

$$= \frac{4}{10} \cdot \frac{6}{10} = 0.24$$

Case (V) P(one white and one black)

$= 0.24 + 0.24 = 0.48$

Example: From a deck of 52 cards, cards are drawn randomly without replacement. What is the probability of drawing a King of hearts at the third attempt ? If it was drawn at the 15th attempt, what was the probability ?

Solution: Since the cards are not replaced,

P(getting the card at third attempt) = P(not getting at first) × P(not getting at second) × P(getting it a third attempt)

$$= \frac{51}{52} \times \frac{50}{51} \cdot \frac{1}{50} = \frac{1}{52}$$

Similarly, the probability of getting King of hearts, at the 15th attempt will be also $\frac{1}{52}$

Example: One card is drawn randomly from a pack of 52 cards and put aside. What is the probability of drawing an ace or a king in a single draw, from the remaining 51 cards?

Solution: The probability of the required draw depends upon the results of the first draw. There are three cases (1) First card is an ace (2) a king (3) neither an ace nor a king.

(1) $P(A) = \frac{4C_1}{52C_1}$, if the first card is an ace.

Now in the remaining lot of 51 cards, there are 3 aces and 4 kings.

$$\text{P(B/A)} = \frac{7C_1}{51C_1}$$

Therefore, P (an ace or a king in the second draw)
= *P*(ace in first draw). *P*(ace or king in the second draw)

$$= P(A).\ P(B/A) = \frac{4}{52}\cdot\frac{7}{51}$$

(2) $P(A) = \frac{4C_1}{52C_1}$, if the first card is a king.

Now in the remaining lot of 51 cards, there are now 4 aces and 3 kings.

$$P(B/A) = \frac{7C_1}{51C_1}$$

Therefore, P_2 (an ace or a king in the second draw)
= *P*(a king in the first draw). *P*(ace or king in the second draw)

$$= P(A).\ P(B/A) = \frac{4}{52}\cdot\frac{7}{51}$$

(3) If the first draw shows neither an ace nor a king,

$P(A) = \frac{44C_1}{52C_1}$ [Note 52 – (4 kings + 4 aces)] = 44.

There are now 4 aces and 4 kings left in 52 cards

$$P(B/A) = \frac{8C_1}{51C_1}$$

Therefore P_3 (ace or king in the second draw)
= *P*(Neither an ace nor a king) × P(ace or king in the second draw).

$$= P(A).\ P(B/A) = \frac{44}{52}\cdot\frac{8}{51}$$

$$= P_1 + P_2 + P_3 \text{ (why?)}$$

$$= \frac{28}{52.51} + \frac{28}{52.51} + \frac{352}{52.51}$$

$$= \frac{408}{52.51} = \frac{2}{13}$$

Required probability

Example: The odds in favour of *A* winning a race against *B* are 5: 2. If three races are attended, what are the odds in favour of *A* winning at least one race?

Solution: $P(A \text{ winning}) = \frac{2}{5+2} = \frac{2}{7}$

$P(A \text{ losing}) = \frac{2}{5+2} = \frac{2}{7}$

P(*A* winning the race at least once)

= 1 – *P* (*A* losing all)

= 1 – *P* (*A* losing first) × *P*(*A* losing second) × *P*(*A* losing third)

$$= 1 - \frac{8}{343} = \frac{335}{343} \qquad = \frac{335}{335+8}$$

$$=1 - \left(\frac{2}{7}\right)\left(\frac{2}{7}\right)\left(\frac{2}{7}\right)$$

i.e. odds in favour of A winning at least one race are 335.8.

Example: A book contains 1000 pages. A page is chosen randomly. what is the chance the sum of the digits on a page is equal to 9?

Solution: A page is selected randomly out of thousand pages

$n(s) = 1000C1 = 1000$

Let *A: A* page selected which has a sum of digits on it be 9.

Number of favorable ways of getting a page, showing the no of the digits on it 9 is.... {9, 18, 27, 36, 45........900}

$n(A) = 100$

Note that the sequence in the bracket is an A.P.

With $a = 9$, $l = 900$ and $d = 9$

Then $l = a + (n - 1)\, d$ gives

$900 = 9 + (n - 1).\, 9 \frac{891}{9}$

$= n - 1$

$99 = n - 1$

$100 = n$

$$P(A) = \frac{n(A)}{n(S)} = \frac{100}{1000} = 0.1$$

THEORETICAL DISTRIBUTIONS

Random variable and probability distributions

Random variables:

When we assign a number to each point of a sample space, we have a function which is defined on the sample space. This function is called a random variable (or stochastic variable).

It is usually denoted by bold letters like X or Y.

Consider two independent tosses of a fair coin

$S = \{(HH), (HT), (TH), (TT)\}$

Let X denote the number of heads.

Then $X(HH) = 2$, $X(HT) = 1$, $X(TH) = 1$ and $X(TT) = 0$

i.e. $X = 0, 1, 2$. Here X is known as a random variable. Thus a random variable is one, which denotes the numerical value of an outcome, of a random experiment.

- If the random variable X takes only finite values or countably infinite values, then X is known as a 'discrete variable'
- If the random variable takes the uncountably infinite values between a specified range or limit, it is called as 'continuous random variable'.

For example: X denotes the age of a person.

Discrete probability distribution

Return to the above given example of tossing of a fair coin twice.

$S = \{(HH), (HT), (TH), (TT)\}$

Then $X(HH) = 2$, $X(HT) = 1$, $X(TH) = 1$ and $X(TT) = 0$

Also $P(HH) = \frac{1}{4}$, $P(HT) = \frac{1}{4}$, $P(TH) = \frac{1}{4}$ and $P(HH) = \frac{1}{4}$

The probability distribution:– Number of Heads

X $P(x)$

$0 \rightarrow \frac{1}{4}$ or 0.25

$1 \rightarrow \frac{1}{4} + \frac{1}{4} = \frac{1}{2}$ or 0.50

$2 \rightarrow \frac{1}{4}$ or 0.25

The probability graph can be obtained by using a bar chart as shown in figure 1 or a Histogram as shown in figure 2.

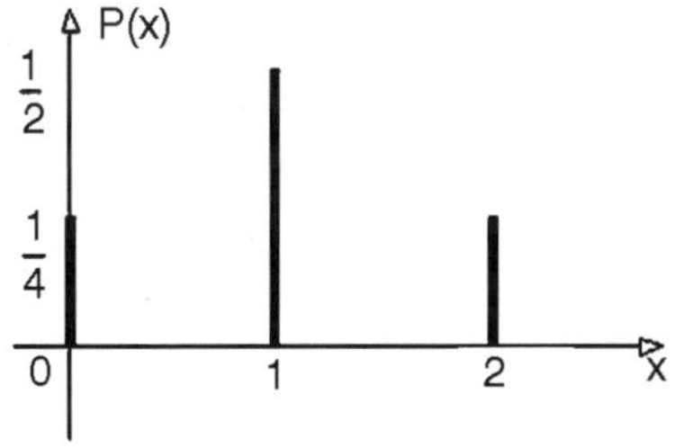

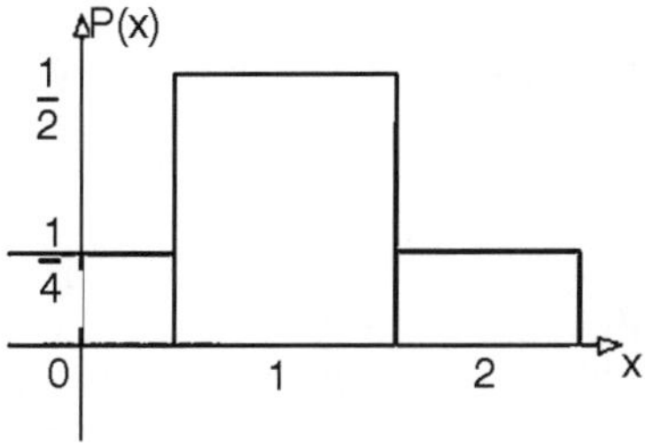

Total of probabilities of discrete random variables:

As you have noted from the probability distribution table or from the bar chart (in which the sum of ordinates i.e. heights of bar is 1) and from the Histogram (in which sum of the rectangular area is 1), the sum (total) of probabilities of all values of X always equal to 1.

Thus, if the random variable $X = X_1, X_2, X_3 \ldots\ldots X_i \ldots\ldots X_n$ and X_i each is associated with a number P_i i.e. X_1 with P_1, X_2 with $P_2 \ldots\ldots$, $X_n = P_n$. Then P_i is called probabilities of X_i and is denoted by $P(X_i)$ or simply $P(X)$ which satisfies

(1) $P(X_i) > 0$

(2) $\sum_{i=1}^{n} P(X_i) = 1$ then $P(X_i)$ or $P(X)$ is called the probability mass function of the discrete random variable X.

i.e. $X \quad X_1 \quad X_2 \quad X_3 \ldots\ldots\ldots Xn$

$P(X) \quad P_1 \quad P_2 \quad P_3 \ldots\ldots\ldots Pn$

Mathematical Expression of a discrete random variable

If $X = x_i$ is a discrete random variable.

Taking $X = x_1, x_2 \ldots\ldots, x_n$ with respective probabilities

$P_i = P_1, P_2 \ldots\ldots\ldots, P_n$ then

The mathematical expression of X is denoted by $E(X)$ and denoted by,

$$E(X) = P_1X_1 + P_2 X_2 + \ldots\ldots + P_n X_n = \sum_{i=1}^{n} P_i X_i$$

Mean and Standard deviation:

If the random variable X, assumes the values $x_1, x_2..., x_n$ with associated probabilities as $P_1, P_2 .... P_n$ respectively then,

$$\text{Mean } (X \text{ or } m) = \frac{\sum_{i=1}^{n} P_i X_1}{\sum_{i=1}^{n} P_1}$$

$$\text{Therefore } \overline{X} \text{ or } \mu = \sum_{i=1}^{n} P_i X_i = E(X)$$

i.e. Mean = $E(X)$ = Expected value.

$$\text{Also variance } (X) = \sigma x^2 = \sum_{i=1}^{n} (X_i - \overline{X})^2 P_i$$

On simplification, we get, the standard deviation,

$$\text{i.e. } \sigma x^2 = \sqrt{\sum_{i=1}^{n} P_1 X_i - (\overline{X})^2}$$

Example:: *A* business can make a profit of \$2000/- with the probability 0.4 or it can have a loss of \$1000/- with the probability 0.6. What is the expected profit?

Solution: The discrete random variable '*x*' is

x_1 = \$ 2000 (profit)

x_2 = – \$1000 (loss)

With probabilities $P_1 = 0.4$ and $P_2 = 0.6$ respectively

Then expected profit is given by,

$E(x) = P_1 x_1 + P_2 x2$

= (0.4) (2000) + (0.6) (-1000)

= \$ 200

Example: What is the expected value of the number of points that will be obtained in a single throw of an ordinary dice?

Solution: The discrete random variable '*x*', in this problem assume values

$x_1 = 1, x_2 = 2, x_3 = 3, x_4 = 4, x_5 = 5$ and $x_6 = 6$

With probabilities $P_1 = P_2 = P_3 = P_4 = P_5 = P_6 = 1/6$ (each)

Expected value of the number of points is given by,

$E(x) = P_1 x_1 + P_2 x_2 + P_3 x_3 + P_4 x_4 + P_5 x_5 + P_6 x_6$

$$= \frac{1}{6} \times 1 + \frac{1}{6} \times 2 + \frac{1}{6} \times 3 + \frac{1}{6} \times 4 + \frac{1}{6} \times 5 + \frac{1}{6} \times 6 = \frac{21}{6} = 3.5$$

Example: Two dice are thrown. Find the mathematical expression of the sum of the points obtained.

Solution: Let X = sum of points obtained.

$$\therefore \quad S=\{(1,1),(1,2),(1,3),\ ....,(6,5),(6,6)\}$$

$$\downarrow \quad \downarrow \quad \downarrow \qquad\quad \downarrow \quad \downarrow$$

$$\text{Therefore } X=\{2,\quad 3,\quad 4,\ ....,\quad 11,\quad 12\}$$

Their corresponding probabilities are

$$P(X_i)=\left\{\frac{1}{36},\frac{2}{36},\frac{3}{36},\frac{4}{36},\frac{4}{36},\frac{5}{36},\frac{6}{36},\frac{5}{36},\frac{4}{36},\frac{3}{36},\frac{2}{36},\frac{1}{36}\right\}$$

Now the expected sum of points is,

$$E(x)=\left(\frac{1}{36}\right)(2)+\left(\frac{2}{36}\right)(3)+\left(\frac{3}{36}\right)(4)+\left(\frac{4}{36}\right)(5)+\left(\frac{5}{36}\right)(6)$$

$$+\left(\frac{6}{36}\right)(7)\left(\frac{5}{36}\right)(8)+\left(\frac{4}{36}\right)(9)+\left(\frac{3}{36}\right)(10)+\left(\frac{22}{36}\right)(11)+\left(\frac{1}{36}\right)(1)$$

$E(x) = 7$

Example:: Given the following probability distribution.

x: 0, 1, 2, 3, 4, 5, 6, 7

P_i: 0, 2λ, 2λ, λ, 3λ, λ^2, $2\lambda^2$, $7\lambda^2+1$

Find (1) λ (2) Evaluate $P(x \geq 5)$ (3) Evaluate $P(x < 4)$

Solution: (1) We know that $\sum_{i=1}^{n} P_i = 1$

Therefore, $0 + 2\lambda + 2\lambda + \lambda + 3\lambda + \lambda^2 + 2\lambda^2 + 7\lambda^2 + 1 = 1$

$10\lambda^2 + 9\lambda - 1 = 0$

$10\lambda^2 + 10\lambda - \lambda - 1 = 0$

$$\frac{10\lambda(\lambda+1)-1(\lambda+1)=0}{(10\lambda-1)(\lambda+1)=0}$$

$\lambda = 1/10$ or $\lambda = -1$ (discarded)

$\lambda = 1/10$

(2) $P(x \geq 5) = P(5) + P(6) + P(7)$

$= \lambda^2 + 2\lambda^2 + 7\lambda^2 + 1$

$= 10\lambda^2 + 1$

$$=10\left(\frac{1}{10}\right)^2+\frac{1}{10}=\frac{2}{10}=0.2$$

(3) $P(x < 4) = P(3) + P(2) + P(1) + P(0)$

$= \lambda + 2\lambda + 2\lambda + 0$
$= 51$

$$= 5\left(\frac{1}{10}\right) = 0.5$$

BINOMIAL DISTRIBUTION

Bernoulli's trials:

A series of independent trials which can be resulted in one of the two mutually exclusive possibilities 'successes' or 'failures' such that the probability of the success (or failures) in each trials is constant, then such repeated independent trials are called as "Bernoulli's trials".

A discrete variable which can results in only one of the two outcomes (success or failure) is called Binomial. For example, a coin flip, the result of an examination success or failures, the result of a game - win or loss etc. The Binomial distribution is also known as Bernoulli's distribution, which expresses probabilities of events of dichotomous nature in repeated trials. When do we get a Binomial distribution ? The following are the conditions in which probabilities are given by binomial distribution.

- A trial is repeated '*n*' times where n is finite and all 'n' trials are identical.
- Each trial (or you can call it an event) results in only two mutually exclusive, exhaustive but not necessarily equally likely possibilities, success or failure.
- The probability of a "success" outcome is equal to some percentage which is identified as proportion, π(or p)
- This proportion π(or p), remains constant throughout all events (or trials). It is defined as the ratio of the number of successes to the number of trials.
- The events (or trials) are independent.
- If probability of success is p or π, then the probability of failures is $1 - p$ or $1 - p$ this is denoted by q. Thus $p + q = 1$.

Suppose a coin is flipped twice. Let p (or p) be the probability of getting heads and q the probability of tails, such that $p + q = 1$ (note that $p = q = 1/2$ if the coin is fair) Then there are three possible outcomes which are given below.

Sr.No.	First Flip	Second Flip	Probability
(1)	Tail	Tail	$q \times q = q^2$
(2)	Head or Tail	Tail	$\left.\begin{matrix} p \times q \\ \text{or} \\ q \times p \end{matrix}\right] = 2pq$
(3)	Head	Head	$p \times p = p^2$

The sum of all these probabilities is

$$q^2 + 2\,pq + p^2 = (q + p)^2.$$

The terms of $(q + p)^2$ in its expansion give the probabilities of getting 0, 1, 2 heads.

The result obtained above can be generalized to find the probability of getting 'r' heads in flipping n coins simultaneously.

The probabilities of getting 0, 1, 2, 3....., r..... n heads in a flip of 'n' coins are the terms of the expansion $(q + p)^n$. Since the expansion is given by the Binomial Theorem, the distribution is called Binomial Distribution.

Thus the Binomial formula is,

$$p(x = r) = {}^nC_r q^{n-r}.p^r$$

i.e. $$p(x = r) = \frac{n!}{r!(n-r)!} q^{n-r}.p^r$$

or $$p(x = r) = \frac{n!}{r!(n-r)!} (1-\pi)^{n-r}.\pi^r$$

where $n\,! = n\,(n-1)\,(n-2)$............ 3. 2. 1

Properties of the Binomial distribution:

We get below some important properties of the Binomial distribution without derivations.

- If x denotes the Binomial variate, expression of x i.e. the mean of the distribution is given by,
  $E(x) = \mu = np$ or $E(x) = \mu = n\mu$
- The standard deviation of the Binomial distribution is determined by, $\sigma = \sqrt{npq}$ or $\sigma = \sqrt{n\pi(1-\pi)}$
- If in experiment, each of n trials, is repeated N times then expression of r successes i.e. the expected frequency of r successes in N experiment is given by, Frequency = $N^nC_r\, q^{n-r}.\, \pi^r$
  Frequency = $N.\, {}^nC_r\, \pi^r(1-\pi)^{n-r}$

Example: What is the expression of heads if an unbiased coin is tossed 12 times.

Solution: Since the expression of x in a binomial distribution is given by, $E(x) = np$ where $n = 12$ and $p = 0.5$.

We could expect 12 ′ 0.5 = 6 heads.

Example: For a Binomial distribution, mean is 2 and standard deviation is 1. Find all the constants of the distribution.

Solution: We are given, Mean $(\mu) = n\,p = 2$

and $S.D. = \sqrt{npq}$

Therefore, $\frac{npq}{np} = \frac{1}{2}$ $\quad q = 0.5$

Also, $p = 1 - q = 1.0.5 = 0.5$
Again $np = 2 \Rightarrow n \times 0.5 = 2 \qquad n = 4$
Hence the constants of the distribution are $n = 4$, $p = 0.5$ and $q = 0.5$

Example: If the probability of a defective bulb is 0.4. Find the mean and the standard deviation for the distribution of the defective bulbs in a lot of 1000 bulbs. What is the expected number of defective bulbs in the lot?

Solution:
We have $p = 0.4$, $n = 1000$ and $q = 1 - p = 1 - 0.4 = 0.6$
Mean (μ) = $np = 1000 \times 0.2 = 200$

$$S.D.\ (\sigma) = \sqrt{npq} = \sqrt{1000 \times 0.4 \times 0.6} = \sqrt{240} = 15.49$$

Expected number = $np = 0.4 \times 1000 = 400$

Example: Six dice are thrown 729 times. How many times do you expect at least three dice to show 5 or 6?

Solution: Let P = probability (showing 5 or 6) = 2/6 = 1/3
$q = 1 - p = 1 - 1/3 = 2/3$
$n = 6$ and $r = 3$
Also $p(x = r)$ = probability (at least 3 dice will show 5 or 6 in one trial)
Using the 'complement' theorem
$p(x = r) = 1 - [p(x = 0) + p(x = 1) + p(x = 2)]$

$$= 1 - \left[{}^{n}C_0 \left(\frac{2}{3}\right)^6 \left(\frac{1}{3}\right)^0 + {}^{6}C_1 \left(\frac{2}{3}\right)^5 \left(\frac{1}{3}\right)^1 + {}^{6}C_2 \left(\frac{2}{3}\right)^4 \left(\frac{1}{3}\right)^2 \right]$$

$$= 1 - \left[1.\left(\frac{2}{3}\right)^6 \left(\frac{1}{3}\right)^0 + 6\left(\frac{2}{3}\right)^5 \left(\frac{1}{3}\right)^1 + 15\left(\frac{2}{3}\right)^4 \left(\frac{1}{3}\right)^2 \right]$$

$$= 1 - \left(\frac{2}{3}\right)^4 \left[\frac{4}{9} + \frac{12}{9} + \frac{15}{9}\right]$$

$$= 1 - \frac{16}{9} \times \frac{31}{9} \qquad = 1 - \frac{496}{729} \qquad = \frac{233}{729}$$

Therefore in 729 trials, the expression $= 729 \times \dfrac{233}{729} = 233$

Example: Take 100 sets of tosses of 10 flips of a fair coin. In how many cases do you expect to get 7 heads at least?

Solution: We have $N = 100$ sets. $n = 10$ trials in each set $p = 0.5$ and $q = 1 - p = 0.5$

Probability (getting at least 7 heads) in one set
$= p(x = 7) + p(x = 8) + p(x = 9) + p(x = 10)$
$= {}^{10}C_7\ (0.5)^7\ (0.5)^3 + {}^{10}C_8\ (0.5)8\ (0.5)2$

$+ {}^{10}C_9 (0.5)^9 (0.5)^1 + {}^{10}C_{10} (0.5)^{10} (0.5)^1$

$= (0.5)10[{}^{10}C_7 + {}^{10}C_8 + {}^{10}C_9 + {}^{10}C_{10}]$

$= (0.5)^{10} [120 + 45 + 10 + 1]$

$= (0.5)^{10} [176]$

Therefore in 100 sets = $Np(r) = 100 \times (0.171) \cong 17$ times you can expect to get at least 7 heads.

Example: If the probability of success is $\frac{1}{20}$. How many trials are required in order that the probability of getting at least one success, is just greater than $\frac{1}{2}$?

Solution: Here $p = \frac{1}{20}$ $q = 1 - \frac{1}{20} = \frac{19}{20}$

Let '*n*' be the required number of trials to get the probability of at least one success which is,

$1 - {}^nC_0 P^0 Q^{n-0}$ [since probability (at least one success) = $1 - p(x = 0)$ i.e. 1 – probability (No success)]

$= 1 - 1 \times 1 \times qn$

$= 1 - \text{qn} = 1 - \left(\frac{19}{20}\right)^n$

Now we need $1 - \left(\frac{19}{20}\right)^n > \frac{1}{2}$ i.e. $-\left(\frac{19}{20}\right)^n > -\frac{1}{2}$

i.e. $\left(\frac{19}{20}\right)^n > \frac{1}{2}$ i.e. $\ln\left(\frac{10}{20}\right)^n < \ln\left(\frac{1}{2}\right)$

i.e. n[log 10 – 1r. 20] < ln (0.5)

i.e. n[1–0.022] < –0.3010

i.e. $n \geq \frac{0.3010}{0.022}$

i.e. $n \geq 13.95$ i.e. n = 14

Therefore 14 trials are necessary

Example: *A* and *B* play a game in which *A*'s chance of winning is 2/9. In a series of 8 games, what is the chance that *A* will win at least 9 games?

Solution: Here *A*'s chance of winning = $p = 2/9$

Therefore $q = 1 - p = 1 - 2/9 = 7/9$, $n = 8$

The probability (*A* will win at least 6 games in a series of 8 games)

$= p(x = 6) + p(x = 7) + p(x = 8)$

$$= {}^8C_6\left(\frac{2}{9}\right)^6\left(\frac{7}{9}\right)^2 + {}^8C_7\left(\frac{2}{9}\right)^7\left(\frac{7}{9}\right)^1 + {}^8C_6\left(\frac{7}{9}\right)\left(\frac{2}{9}\right)^8\left(\frac{7}{9}\right)^0$$

$$= \left(\frac{2}{9}\right)^6\left[{}^8C_6\left(\frac{7}{9}\right)^2 + {}^8C_7\left(\frac{2}{9}\right)\left(\frac{7}{9}\right) + {}^8C_8\left(\frac{2}{9}\right)^2 \times 1\right]$$

$$= \left(\frac{2}{9}\right)^6\left[28\times\frac{49}{81} + 8\times\frac{14}{81} + 1\times\frac{4}{81}\right]$$

$$= \left(\frac{2}{9}\right)^6\left[\frac{1372}{81} + \frac{112}{81} + \frac{4}{81}\right]$$

$$= \left(\frac{2}{9}\right)^6\left[\frac{1488}{81}\right]$$

$$= \frac{1024}{2187} = 0.4682.$$

Example: Assuming half of a population is vegetarian the chance of an individual being a vegetarian is 0.5.

Assuming that 100 investigators take a sample of 10 individuals to see whether they are vegetarians, how many investigators do you expect will report that three or less were vegetarian?

Solution: For one investigator,

$p = 0.5 \Rightarrow q = 0.5$ and $n = 10$

Then, probability of 3 or less vegetarian is $p(x \le 3)$

Now $\pi(x \le 3) = p(x = 0) + p(x = 1) + p(x = 2) + p(x = 3)$

$= {}^{10}C_0\,(0.5)^0\,(0.5)^{10} + {}^{10}C_1\,(0.5)^1\,(0.5)^9$

$+ {}^{10}C_2\,(0.5)^2\,(0.5)^8 + {}^{10}C_3\,(0.5)^3\,(0.5)^7$

$= (0.5)^{10}[{}^{10}C_0 + {}^{10}C_1 + {}^{10}C_1 + {}^{10}C_2 + {}^{10}C_3]$

$= (0.5)^{10}[1 + 10 + 45 + 120]$

$= (0.5)^{10}\,[176] \qquad = 0.1719$

For 100 investigators we expect $100 \times p(x \le 3)$

$= 100 \times 0.1719$

$= 17.19$ i.e. 17 individuals were vegetarians

Example: The incidence of occupational disease in an industry is such that the workmen have 20% chance of suffering from it.

What is the probability of 4 or more workmen out of 6 contacting the disease?

Solution: Here $n = 6$, $p = 0.2$ therefore $q = 1 - 0.2 = 0.8$

Probability of out of 6, 4 or more workmen will contact the disease,

$= p(x \geq 4)$

$= p(x = 4) + p(x = 5) + p(x = 6)$

$= {}^6C_4(0.2)^4 (0.8)^2 + {}^6C_5 (0.2)^5 (0.8)^1 + {}^6C_6 (0.2)^6 (0.8)^0$

$= 15 \times 0.0016 \times 0.4 + 6 \times 0.00032 \times 0.8 + 1 \times 0.000064$

Example: Assume that the probability of a bomb dropped from an aeroplane, striking a target is 1/5. If 6 bombs are dropped, find the probability that

- Txactly two will strike.
- At least two strikes the target.

Solution:

$$n = 6, = \frac{1}{5} \text{ and } q = 1 - \frac{1}{5} = \frac{4}{5}$$

$$(1)\ p(x = 2) = {}^6C_2 \left(\frac{1}{5}\right)^2 \left(\frac{4}{5}\right)^4 = 0.2458$$

(2) p(at least two bombs strike the target)

$= 1 - [p(0) + p(1) + p(2)]$

$$= 1 - \left[{}^6C_0 \left(\frac{1}{5}\right)^0 \left(\frac{4}{5}\right)^6 + {}^6C_1 \left(\frac{1}{5}\right)^1 \left(\frac{4}{5}\right)^5 \right]$$

$$= 1 - \left(\frac{4}{6}\right)^5 \left[1 \times 1 \times \frac{4}{5} + 6 \times \frac{1}{5} \right]$$

$$= 1 - \left(\frac{4}{6}\right)^5 \left[\frac{4}{5} + \frac{6}{5} \right]$$

$$= 1 - \left(\frac{4}{6}\right)^5 \times 2 = 0.3446$$

E1xample: The probability of a man hitting a target is 1/3. How many must he fire so that the probability of hitting the target, at least once, is more than 90%?

Solution: Here $p = 1/3$ and $q = 2/3$ and $n = ?$

Now, p(hitting the target at least once) > 90%

$p(x \geq 1) = 1 - p(x = 0)$ must be greater than 90%

$$\text{i.e. } 1 - {}^nC_0 \left(\frac{1}{6}\right)^0 \left(\frac{2}{3}\right)^{n-0} > 90\%$$

i.e. $1-1\times1\times\left(\frac{2}{3}\right)^n > 0.9$ i.e. $1-\left(\frac{2}{3}\right)^n > 0.9$

i.e. $\left(\frac{2}{3}\right)^n > -0.1$ i.e. $\left(\frac{2}{3}\right)^n < 0.1$

or $n > \frac{\log(0.1)}{\log(2/3)} = 5.6789 \approx 6$

i.e. $1-\left(\frac{2}{3}\right)^n > 0.9$ i.e. $n > 6$

Therefore, he must fire at least 6 times so that the probability of hitting the target at least once is more than 90%

Example: If an average 8 ships out of 10 trials arrive safely at a port. Find the mean and standard deviation of the number of ships arriving safely out of the total of 1600 ships.

Solution: $p = 0.8$ therefore $q = 1 - p = 1 - 0.8 = 0.2$ and $n = 1600$

Mean (μ) = $np = 1600 \times 0.8 = 1280$

S.D. (σ) = $\sqrt{npq} = \sqrt{1280\times0.2} = \sqrt{256} = 16$

Hence the mean and standard deviation of ships, returning safely respectively 1280 and 16.

Example: In a hurdle race, a player has to cross 10 hurdles. The probability that he will clear each hurdle is 5/6. What is the probability that he will knock down fewer than 2 hurdles?

Solution: $n = 10$, q = probability that he will clear each hurdle = 5/6

p = probability that he will knock down = 1 – 5/6 = 1/6

Therefore, p(knocking down fewer than 2 hurdles) = p (0) + p(1)

$$= {}^{10}C_0\left(\frac{1}{6}\right)^0\left(\frac{5}{6}\right)^{10} + {}^{10}C_1\left(\frac{1}{6}\right)^1\left(\frac{5}{6}\right)^9$$

$$= 1\times1\times\left(\frac{5}{6}\right)^{10} + 10\left(\frac{1}{6}\right)\left(\frac{5}{6}\right)^9$$

$$= \left(\frac{5}{6}\right)^9\left[\frac{5}{6}+\frac{10}{6}\right] = \frac{5}{2}\left(\frac{5}{6}\right)^9$$

Example: The probability that a man aged 60 will live to be 70 is 0.65. What is the probability that out of 10 men, now 60, at least 7 will live to be 70?

Solution: P = The probability that a man aged 60 will live to be 70 = 65

$q = 1 - P = 1 - 0.65 = 0.35$

Number of men (n) = 10
Probability that at least 7 men will live to 70
= P(7 or 8 or 9 or 10)
= P(7 or 8 or 9 or 10)
$= 10C_7\, q^3P^7 + 10C_8\, q^2\, P^8 + 10C_9\, qP_9 + 10C_9\, q^0\, P^{10}$
$= 10C_7\, (0.35)^3\, (.65)^7 + 10C_8\, (0.35)^2\, (.65)^8 + 10C_9$
$(0.35)\, (.65)^9 + 10C_{10}\, (0.35)\, (.65)^{10}$
$= (.65)^7\, [120(.35)3 + 45(.35)2\, (.65) + 10(.35)\, (.65)$
$+ 1 \times 1(0.65)]$
$= (.65)^7 \times 125[120 \times (0.07)^3 + 45 \times (0.07)^2\, (0.13)$
$+ 10 \times (0.07)\, (0.13)^2 + (0.13)^3]$
$= 0.04901 \times 125[0.04116 + 0.028665 + 0.011830$
$+ 0.002197]$
$= 6.12625 \times 0.083852 \qquad = 0.5137$

Example: A and B take turns in throwing dice. The first to throw 10 is awarded the prize, show that if A has the first throw, their chance of winning are in the ratio 12: 11.

Solution: The combinations of throwing 10 from two dice can be (6 + 4), (4 + 6), (5 + 5).

The number of combination is 3
Total combinations from two dice = 6 × 6 = 36

The probability of throwing 10 = $P = \frac{3}{36} = \frac{1}{12}$

$$q = 1 - P = 1 - \frac{1}{12} = \frac{11}{12}$$

If A is to win, he should throw 10 in either the first, the third, the fifth... throws. Their respective probabilities

are $P_1\, Q^2\, P,\, Q^4P_1$.....

$$= \frac{1}{12}, \left(\frac{11}{12}\right)^2 . \frac{1}{12}, \left(\frac{11}{12}\right)^4 . \frac{1}{12}, \ldots..$$

A's total probability of winning

$$\frac{1}{12} + \left(\frac{11}{12}\right)^2 . \frac{1}{12} + \left(\frac{11}{12}\right)^4 . \frac{1}{12} + \ldots..$$

[This is infinite Geometric series, its sum $= \frac{a}{1-r}$

where $a = \frac{1}{12}$ and $r = \frac{1}{12}$]

$$= \frac{\frac{1}{12}}{1-\left(\frac{11}{12}\right)^2} = \frac{12}{13}$$

B can in either 2nd, 4th, 6th..... throws.

so B's total chance of winning

$= qP + q^3P + q^5P + ...$

$$= \left(\frac{11}{12}\right)\left(\frac{1}{12}\right) + \left(\frac{11}{12}\right)^3\left(\frac{1}{12}\right) + \left(\frac{11}{12}\right)^5\left(\frac{1}{12}\right) + ...$$

$$= \frac{\left(\frac{11}{12}\right)\left(\frac{1}{12}\right)}{1+\left(\frac{11}{12}\right)^2} \qquad = \frac{11}{23}$$

Hence A's chance to B's chance $= \frac{12}{13} : \frac{11}{13}$ = 12: 11

NORMAL DISTRIBUTION

The normal distribution developed by Gauss is a continuous distribution of maximum utility. If we know a curve such that the area under the curve from,

$$x = a \text{ to } x = b$$

is equal to the probability that x will take a value between a and b and that the total area under the curve is unity, then the curve is called the probability curve.

If the curve is described by a relation $y = \phi(x)$ then $y = \phi(x)$ is called a probability density or simply probability function.

Among all the probability curves, the normal curve is the most important one. The corresponding function is called the normal probability function and the probability distribution is called the normal distribution.

The normal distribution can be considered as the limiting form of the Binomial Distribution, however n, the number of trials, is very large and neither P nor q is very small.

The normal distribution is given by

$$y = \frac{1}{\sigma\sqrt{2\pi}} . e^{-(x-\mu)^2/2\sigma^2}$$

where y = ordinate, x = abscissa of a point on the curve, u = the mean of x, σ = $S. D.$of x.

x = a constant = 3.1416 and e = a constant = 2.7183.

Example: Find P, mean and the standard deviation of the normal distribution given by

$$y = Pe^{-\left[\frac{x^2}{8} - x + 2\right]}$$

$$\text{Now } \frac{x^2}{8} - x + 2 = \frac{1}{2}\left[\frac{x^2}{4} - 2x + 4\right]$$

$$= \frac{1}{2}\left[\frac{x^2 - 8x + 16}{4}\right] = \frac{1}{2}\left[\frac{(x-4)^2}{4}\right]$$

$$y = Pe^{-1/2\left[\frac{(x-4)2}{4}\right]}$$

$$\text{Comraring with } y = \frac{1}{\sigma\sqrt{2\pi}} e^{-(x-\mu)^2/2\sigma^2}$$

$$P = \frac{1}{\sigma\sqrt{2\pi}}, \mu = 4 \text{ and } \sigma = 2$$

Solution:

The Normal Curve: The shape of a normal curve is like a bell. It is symmetrical about the maximum ordinate If P and Q are two points on the x-axis, the shaded are $PQRS$, bounded by the portion of the curve RS, the ordinates at P and Q and the x-axis is equal to the probability that the variate x lies between $x = a$ and $x = b$ at P and Q respectively. We have already seen that the total area under a normal curve is unity.

Any probability distribution, defined this way is known as the normal distribution. The distribution can be completely known if we know the values of μ and σ. Therefore μ and σ are known as the parameters of the distribution. The normal distribution with mean μ and standard deviation σ is denoted by $N(\mu, \sigma)$.

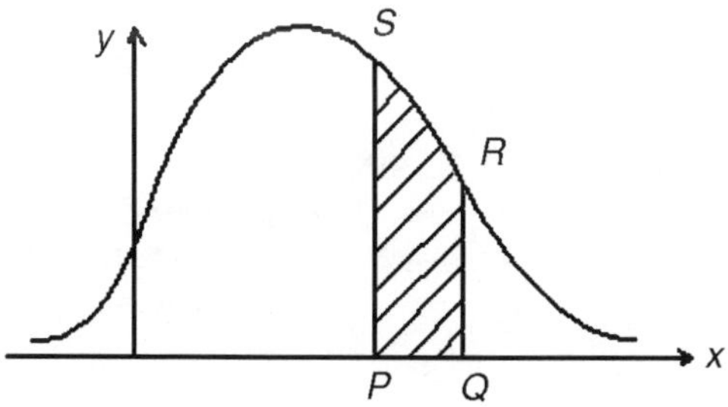

Properties of the normal distribution (Normal curve)

- The normal curve is bell-shaped and symmetrical about the maximum ordinate at $x = \mu$, the mean. This ordinate divides the curve into two equal parts. The part on one side is the mirror image of the other side. it has the maximum height at $x = \mu$. Thus the mode of the distribution is also μ. The ordinate $x = \mu$ divides the whole area under the curve into two equal parts. Hence the median is also $x = \mu$. Thus for the normal distribution, the mean, mode and median coincide. i.e. mean = median = mode = μ.
- We know that the area under the normal curve is equivalent to the probability of randomly drawing a value in the given range. The area is the greatest in the middle, where the "hump" (where mean, mode and median coincide) and then thin out towards out on the either sides of the curve, i.e. tails, but never becomes zero. In other words, the curve never intersects x-axis at any finite point. i.e. x-axis is its Asymptote.
- Since the curve is symmetrical about mean. The first quartile Q_1 and the third quartile Q_3 lie at the same distance on the two sides of the mean μ. The distance of any quartile from μ is 0.6745 σ units. Thus,

$$Q_1 = \mu - 0.6745\,\sigma \text{ or } \mu - \frac{2}{3}\sigma \text{ and}$$

$$Q_3 = \mu + 0.67566 \text{ or } \mu + \frac{2}{3}\sigma$$

Hence, middle 50% observations lie between

$$\mu - \frac{2}{3}\sigma \text{ and } \mu + \frac{2}{3}\sigma$$

- Since the normal curve is symmetrical its skewness is zero and kurtosis is 3. The curve is meso kurtic.
- The mean deviation is $\frac{4}{5}\sigma$ approximately.
- As discussed earlier, the probability for the variable to lie in any interval (a, b) in the range of variable is given by the are under the normal curve, the two ordinates $x = a$ and $x = b$, and the x-axis.

The area under the normal curve is distributed as follows:

- The area between $x = \mu - \sigma$ and $x = \mu + \sigma$ is 18.27%
- The area between $x = \mu - 2\sigma$ and $x = \mu + 2\sigma$ is 95.45%
- The area between $x = \mu - 3\sigma$ and $x = \mu + 3\sigma$ is 99.73%

These areas are shown in the following figure.

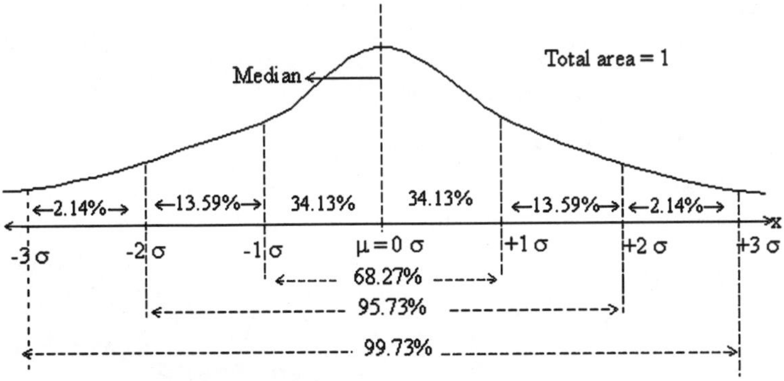

i.e. $P(\mu - \sigma < x < \mu + \sigma) = 68.27\%$
$P(\mu - 2\sigma < x < \mu + 2\sigma) = 95.73\%$
$P(\mu - 3\sigma < x < \mu + 3\sigma) = 99.73\%$

- $\mu \pm 1s$ are points of inflexons

Example: For a normal distribution the mean 50 and the standard deviation is 15. Find i) Q_1 and Q_3 ii) Mean deviation and also the interquartile range.

Solution: For a normal distribution

$$\text{(i) } Q_1 = \mu - \frac{2}{3}\sigma = 50 - \frac{2}{3} \times 15 = 40$$

$$\text{Also } Q_3 = \mu + \frac{2}{3}\sigma - 50 + \frac{2}{3} \times 15 = 60$$

(ii) The mean deviation is = $4/5\sigma = 4/5 \times 15 = 12$
(iii) Inter quartile range = $Q_3 - Q_1 = 60 - 40 = 20$

The Standard Normal Variate (Z-Score):

The problem of finding the probability reduces to finding the area between the two ordinates. For different values of μ and σ we get different normal curves, which multiplies it into too many problems if we are to find the area between the given values for different curves with different μ and σ.

All such problems can be reduced to a single one by reducing all normal distributions to a single normal distribution called 'Standardized Normal Distribution' or to what is known as the z-score.

To convert a value to a z-score is to express it in terms of how many standard deviations it is above or below the mean. This actually amounts to the shifting of the origin to μ and reducing its scale by σ.

Thus,

$$z = \frac{x - \mu}{\sigma}$$

where x = the value to be converted, μ = the population mean and σ = the population standard deviation. obviously the $\mu = 0$ and $\sigma = 1$ for the Normal standard distribution. it is denoted by N (0,1). The areas under the curve between $x = 0$ and various ordinate $x = a$ are in a table of standard normal probabilities. This area is equal to the probability that x will assume a value between $x = 0$ and $x = a$.

How to use Table: The table gives the areas from the ordinate $x = 0$ to $x = 3.09$ which covers more than 0.499 units of area on one side i.e. more than 0.99 units of area on both sides, the total area being 1, and it is 0.5 on both sides.

If the variate is not standardized first then convert it into a standardized normal variate i.e. z-score, using $z = \frac{x-\mu}{\sigma}$ and find the limits of z-score corresponding to the given limits of the variate.

If we want to find the probability of x between $x = \alpha$, and $x = \beta$, we find z from $z = \frac{x-\mu}{\sigma}$

Suppose those values are a and b. Then referring to the table we find the area between $z = \alpha$ and $z = \beta$. This is the required probability.

- If both limits α and b are positive or negative, we find the areas corresponding to $z = \alpha$ and $z = \beta$ and then the required area is the Difference between them.
- If one limit say α is negative and other say β is positive then the areas from $z = -\alpha$ to $z = 0$ is the same as from $z = 0$ to $z = \alpha$. We find it from the table and also from $z = 0$ to $z = \beta$ from the table. Then the required area is the SUM of these two areas.
- If we want to find the expected frequency of variate x within certain limits when the experiment is carried for N times. Then first we find probability P which is equal to the area between the limits. Thus it is NP.

Example: For the z-score, find the probability that z lies between (i) 0 and 1.98 (ii) –0.68 and 0 (iii) 1.35 to 2.18 (iv) –2.18 to – 1.35 (v) To the left of – 0.6 (vi) To the right of $z = -1.28$ (vii) –2.18 to 1.35

Solution: Here we are given z-scores, we have only to refer to the table and find the areas corresponding to these numbers and add or subtract accordingly as the numbers are negativeor positive.

(i) From the table $z = 1.98$ gives $z = 1.98$ is 0.4762

Thus $P(0 \leq z \leq 1.98) = 0.4762$ i.e. 47% of area.

Note: For $z = 1.18$ looking into the table of z-score, first find 4.9 in the first column and move to your right along the same horizontal row till you get column with head 0.08. The intersection of the two is 0.4762

See this → First column 0.01 0.02 ....0.08 0.09

z) 1.9 0.4713 0.4719 .....0.4762 0.4767

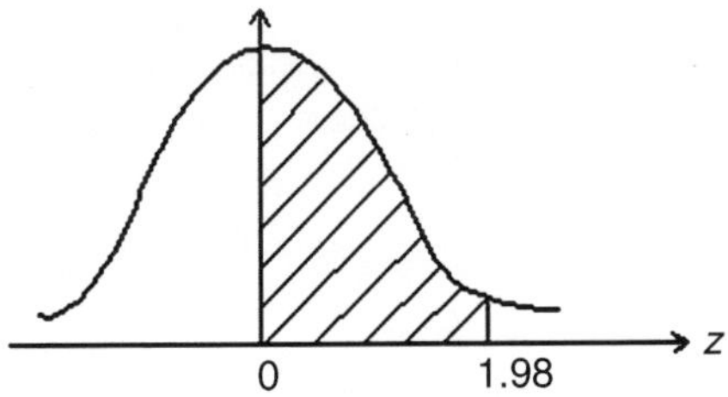

ii. Area from $z = -0.68$ to 0 is the same as from 0 to 0.68 by symmetry. hence for $z = 0.68$ it is 0.2518.

$P(-0.68 \leq z \leq 0 = 0.2518$ i.e. 25% of area.

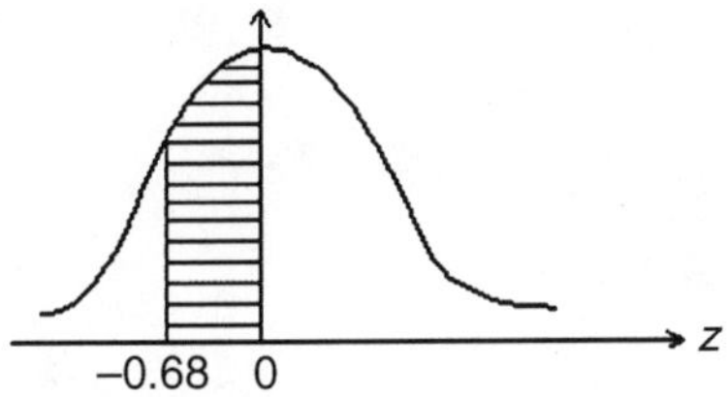

iii. Area from 0 to 1.35 is 0.4115 and from 0 to 2.18 is 0.4854. The required area is the difference between the two areas.

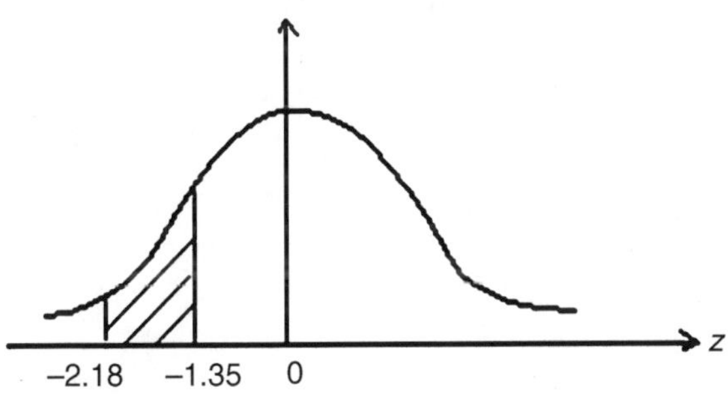

$P(1.35 \leq z \leq 2.18$

$= 0.4854 - 0.4115$

$= 0.739$

i.e. 7% of area.

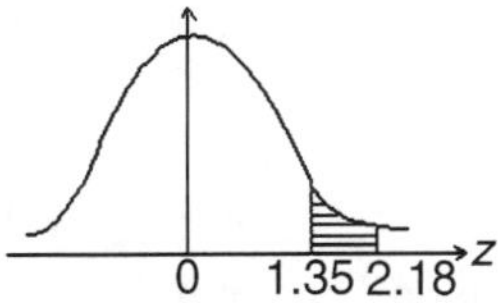

iv) Area from –2.18 to – 1.35 is the same from 1.35 to 2.18.

$P(-2.18 \leq z \leq -1.35\ ) = 0.4854 - 0.4115$

$= 0.0739$ i.e. ≈ 7% of area.

v) Required area = 0.5 – Area between z = 0 to z = 0.6 (to the left of –0.6)

$= 0.5 - P(o \leq z \leq 0.6)$

$= 0.5 - (0.2257)$
$= 0.2743 \approx 27\%$ of area.s

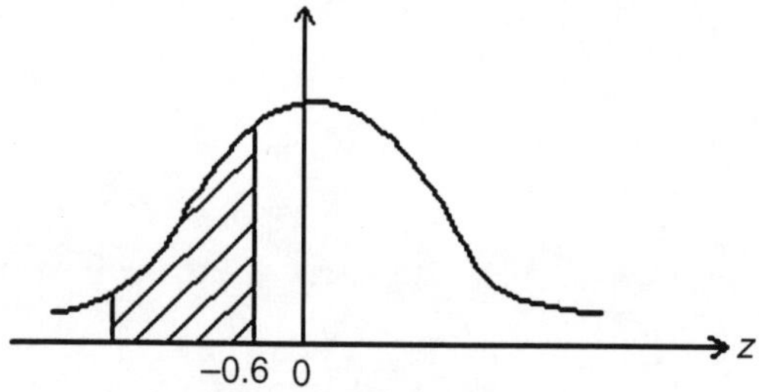

vi) Required area = (Area between $z = 0$ and $z = -1.28$) + 0.5
= (Area between $z = 0$ and $z = -1.28$) + 0.5
$= 0.3997 + 0.5$
$= 0.8997 \approx 90\%$ of area.
vii) Area from – 2.18 to 0 is the same as

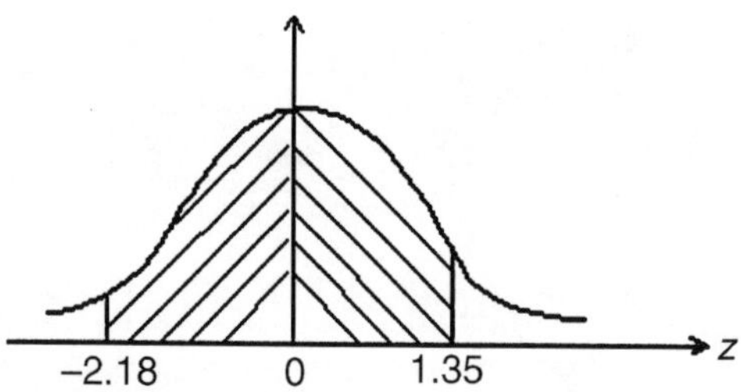

from 0 to 2.18 which is
$P(-2.18 \leq z \leq 0)$
$= P(0 \leq z \leq -2.18) = 0.4864$
and area from 0 to 1.35 is
$P(0 \leq z \leq -1.35) = 0.4115$
Thus the required area is the sum of two
i.e. $P(-2.18 \leq z \leq -1.35) = 0.4854 + 0.4115$
$= 0.8969 \approx 90\%$ of area

Example: For z, find the probability (i) z^3 1.68, (ii) $z \leq 1.68$, (iii) $z \leq -1.68$, and (iv) $| z | \geq 1.68$.

Solution: (i) $P(z \geq 1.68) = 0.5 - P(0 \leq 0 \leq 1.68)$
$= 0.5 - 4535 = 0.0465 \approx 5\%$ of area.

(ii) The probability that $z \leq 1.68$ is equal to the area to the left of $z = 1.68$. Hence the required area $= 0.5 + 4.4535 = 0.9535$.

(iii) The probability that $z \leq -1.68$ is equal to the area to left of $z = -1.68$ = the area to the right of $(z = 1.68) = 0.5 - 0.4535 = 0.0465$

(iv) We know that $| z | \geq 1.68 \Rightarrow z \geq$
1.68 or $-z \geq 1.68$
i.e. $z \geq 1.68$ or $z \leq 1.68$
i.e. z is to the right of 1.68 or z is to the left of -1.68 <

$P(z \geq 1.68) = 0.0465$ and $P(z \leq -1.68)$
$= 0.0465$
Therefore $P(|z| \geq 1.68) = 2 \times 0.0465 = 0.093$

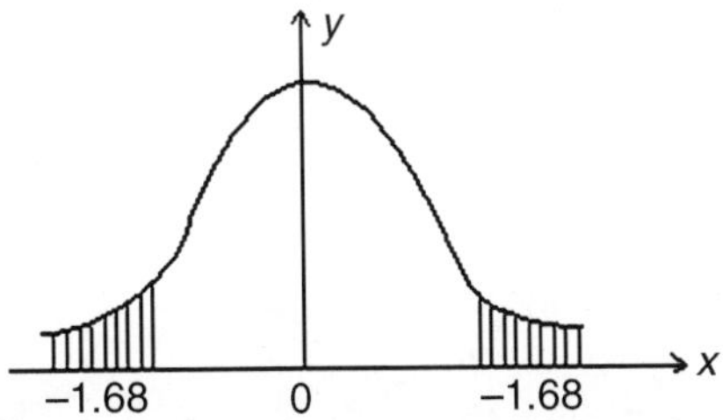

Example: In a sample of 1000 cases, the mean of a certain test is 14 and standard deviation is 2.5. Assuming the distribution to be normal.

1) How many students score between 14 and 15?
2) How many score above 18?
3) How many score below 18?
4) How many score 16?

Solution: $n = 1000$, $\mu = 14$ and $\sigma = 2.5$

1) $z_1 = \dfrac{x-\mu}{\sigma} = \dfrac{12-14}{2.5} = -0.8$ and

$z_2 = \dfrac{x-\mu}{\sigma} = \dfrac{15-14}{2.5} = -0.4$

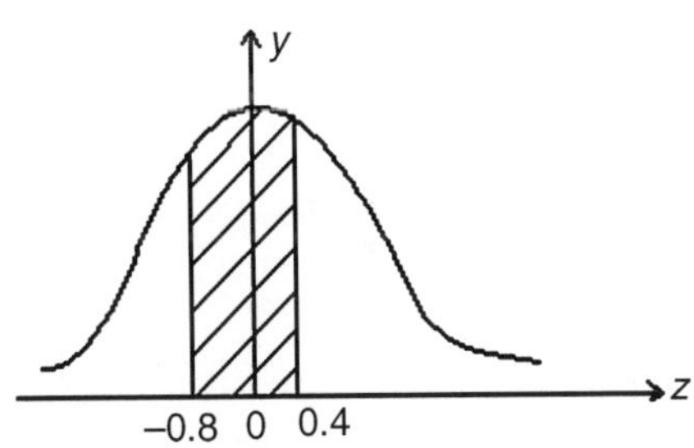

The area lying between – 0.8 to 0.4
= Area ($z = 0$ to $z = 0.8$) + Area ($z = 0$ to $z = 0.4$)
$= P(0 \leq x \leq 0.8) + P(0 \leq x \leq 0.4)$
$= 0.2881 + 0.1554$
$= 0.4435$
The required number of students score between 14 and 15
= NP = 1000 ′ 0.4435 = 443.5 = 444.

2) $z = \dfrac{x-\mu}{\sigma} = \dfrac{18-14}{2.5} = 1.6$

Area right to 1.6
= 0.5 – Area ($z = 0$ to $z = 1.6$)

$= 0.5 - P(0 \leq z \leq 1.6)$
$= 0.5 - 0.4452$
$= 0.0548$
Therefore, the number of students score above 16 = nP
$= 1000 \times 0.0548$
$= 54.8 = 55$

3) $z = \dfrac{x-\mu}{\sigma} = \dfrac{18-14}{2.5} = 1.6$
Area left to $z = -2.4$
$= 0.5 -$ Area ($z = 0$ to $z = 2.4$)
$= 0.5 - 0.4918 = 0.0082$
Therefore, the number of students score below 8 = NP
$= 1000 \times 0.0082$
$= 8.2 \quad = 8$
4) Exactly 16 means between $x = 15.5$ and $x = 16.5$

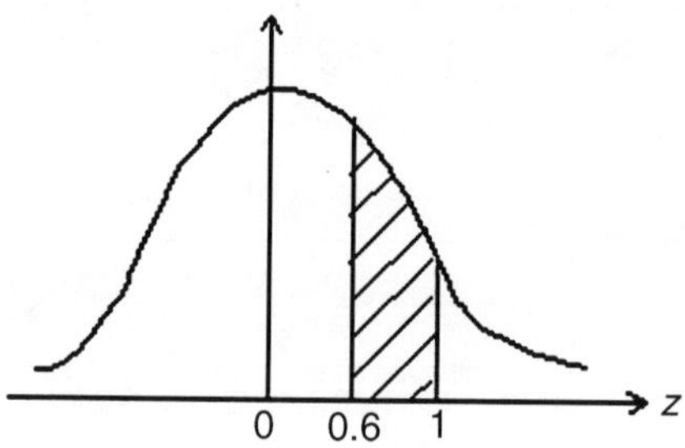

$$z_1 = \frac{15.5-14}{2.5} = 0.6 \text{ and } z_2 = \frac{16.5-14}{2.5} = 1$$
The area lying between $z = 0.6$ and $z = 1$
= Are ($z = 0$ to $z = 1$) – Area ($z = 0$ to $z = 0.6$)
$= 0.3413 - 0.225$
$= 0.1156$
The number of students score exactly 16 = NP
$= 1000 \times 0.1156$
$= 115.6$
$= 116$

Example: Ten thousand candidates appeared in a certain examination, having maximum marks as 100. It was found that the marks are normally distributed with mean as 39.5 and S. D. as 12.5. Determine approximately the number of candidates who secured a first class for which a minimum of 60 marks is necessary. You may see the given table below:

$z = x/6$	1.5	1.6	1.7	.8
A	0.93319	0.94520	0.95543	0.96407

Solution: $m = 39.5$, $s = 12.5$ and $x = 60$
then $z =$
Now Area for $z = 1.6$ is 0.94520
Area for $z = 1.7$ is 0.95543
Therefore difference for 0.1 is 0.01023
Therefore difference for 0.4 is 0.004092

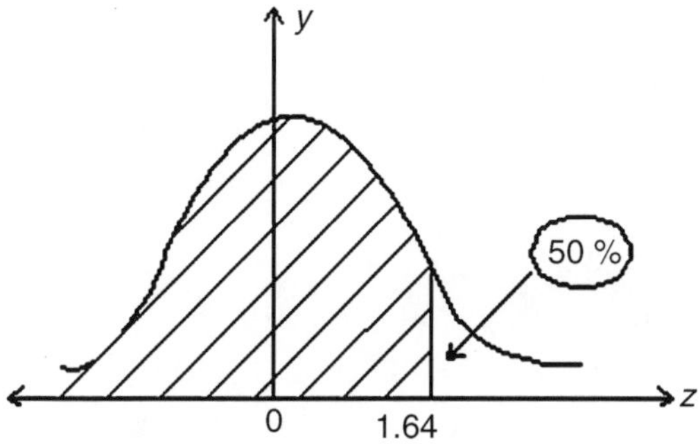

Area for 1.64 = 0.94520 + 0.004092
= 0.949292
Area right to $z = 1.64 = 1 - 0.949292 = 0.050708$
Therefore the number of candidates who
secured 60 marks or more (i.e. 1st class) = NP
= 1000 × 0.50708
= 507.08
= 507

Example: In a distribution exactly normal 7% of the items are under 35 and 89% are under 63. What are the mean and standard deviations of the distribution?

Solution: If x is normally distributed, N(μ, σ), then it is given that $P(x < 35) = 0.07$ and $P(x < 63) = 0.89$ or $P(x > 63) = 0.11$

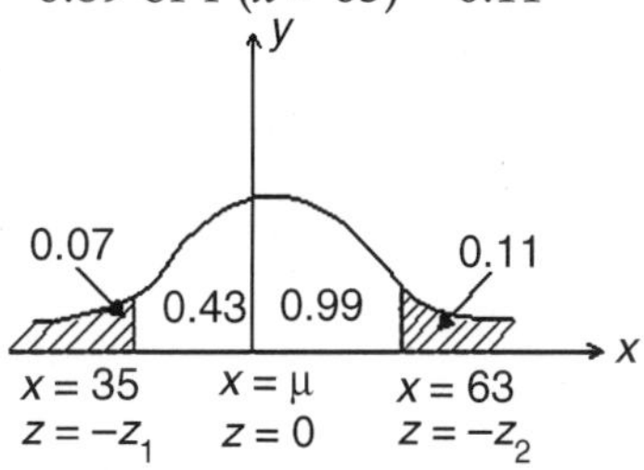

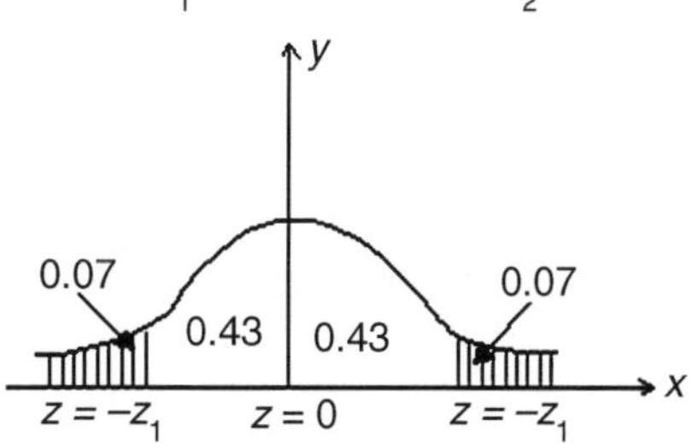

The points $x = 63$ and $x = 35$ are shown in (figure 1). Since $x = 35$ is located to the left of mean $x = m$ the corresponding value of z is negative. When $x =$ 63, z is given by

$z_2 = \dfrac{63-\mu}{\sigma}$ and when $x = 35$, $z_1 = \dfrac{35-\mu}{\sigma}$

From (figure 1) and (figure 2), we have

$P(0 < z < z_2) = 0.39$ and $P(0 < z < z_1) = 0.43$

From the table we have $z_2 = 1.23$ and $z_1 = 1.48$

$1.23 = \dfrac{63-\mu}{\sigma}$ and $-1.48 = \dfrac{35-\mu}{\sigma}$

$1.23\,\sigma + \mu = 63 \Rightarrow (1)$ and $-1.486 + \mu = 35 \Rightarrow (2)$

on solving (1) and (2) we get $\mu = 50.3$ and $\sigma = 10.33$

7

Sampling Theory

POPULATION

Any well defined set (group) of objects about which a statistical enquiry is being made is called a population or universe.

The total number of objects (individuals or members) in a population is known as the size of the population which may be finite or infinite.

The population can refer to things as well as people.

For example,

- All members of the cultural society of your city.
- All students of mathematics of Ithaca college.
- All Americans who saw 'TITANIC' last year.
- Heights of all students of your school.
- Weights of all the citizens of city of New York above 20 years of age.
- Mileages of automobiles tyres of Dunlop. etc.

A population is finite if it contains finite numbers of individuals. For example, the ages of 20 boys of your class. A population is infinite if it contains infinite number of individuals. For example, the pressures at various points in the atmosphere.

SAMPLE

A finite set of objects drawn from the population with an aim is called a sample. Even in every day life we make many of our decisions based on samples taken, though we are not aware of it. We just take a little from a gunny bag of rice, we judge its quality and then we purchase the whole bag.

If we want to taste milk, we just take a glassful of milk from the can and taste it. Note that taking a sample is easy in many cases where the population is uniform or homogeneous. When the population is heterogeneous (not uniform), the selection of a sample is not very easy.

The fundamental assumption underlying most of the theory of sampling is random sampling. This consists of the selection of individuals from the population in such a way that each individual of the population has an equal chance of being selected i.e. a sample so selected must be a true representative of the population. The process of such selection is called random sampling.

The aim of the theory of sampling is to get as much information as possible, ideally all the information about the population from which the sample has been drawn.

From the parent population, in particular, we would like to estimate the parameters of the population or specify the limits or ranges within which the population parameters are expected to lie with a specified degree of confidence. The logic of the sampling theory is the logic of induction, that is, we go from particular (i.e sample) to general (i.e. population).

Naturally all results will have to be expressed in terms of probability. In the theory of sampling, we often come across two words, 'parameters' and 'statistics'.

PARAMETERS AND STATISTICS

The word 'Parameters' is associated with the population and it is understood as the measure of the characteristics of the population, such as mean and standard deviation etc.

The word 'Statistics' is used for a random sample and it is understood as the measure of the characteristics of the random sample, such as mean and standard deviation etc.

Note: Different symbols are used to denote parameters and statistics.

Characteristic	Mean	Standard deviation
Sample Statistics	$\overline{x}$	δ ro s.d.
Parameters of the population	m(read: Mu)	s (read: sigma) Or S.D.

Inferential or inductive statistics helps us in making an educated guess about the population parameters based on the statistics of its random sample.

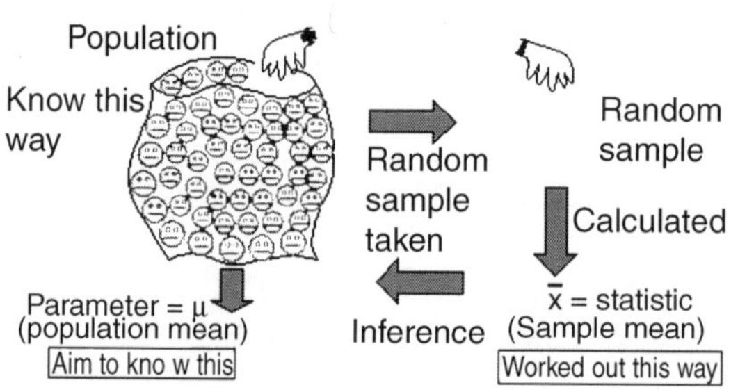

For instance, say

Aim to know: The average (mean) income of families living in the area "Park avenue" in the year 1997-1998. i.e. The population parameter μ (in dollars). *Work out this way*: Draw a random sample of 200 families and compute their mean income. i.e. the statistic of sample x say $ 120000.

Conclusion (or inference): The population mean (parameter) is close to sample mean (statistic)i.e. mean income of the families living in the area 'Park Avenue' is \$ 120000.

SAMPLING DISTRIBUTION

Consider a finite population of 4000 students of a certain college. Of this 200 students are selected randomly and their mean weight is calculated. It was computed as $x = 135$ lbs. If we draw 20 different samples of 200 students, instead of just one as we did previously. We can't expect the same mean weight of these 20 samples chosen randomly. It is due to sampling variability i.e. each sample drawn randomly from the same population differs from each other in their computed 'statistic'.

The means computed is listed as

130 137 140 131 132133 128 125 129 138

133 134 142 145 136134 128 143 137 136

These 20 values form what is known as a part of the sampling distribution of a statistic "mean" weight. Therefore, the sampling distribution is the statistic calculated for a large number of random samples drawn from the same population. Alternatively, consider all possible samples of size 'n' which can be drawn randomly from the same population, and for each one, compute the aimed statistic. In this manner we obtain the distribution of the statistic, which is the sampling distribution.

Now we compute mean of this sampling distribution which is 134.55 lb (note that is obtained using the formula,

$$\bar{x} = \frac{\Sigma x_i}{n} = \frac{2691}{20} = 134.55$$

Now we are told that the population mean (μ) i.e. mean weight of 4000 students is 134.21 lb (In case of infinite population, this is not known). Therefore, 135 lb is not a bad estimate of the population mean. But 134.55 lb is a still better estimation.

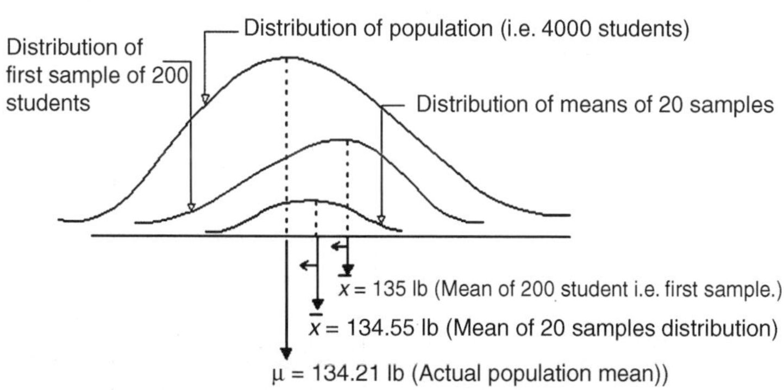

We thus conclude that the more the sample means (statistics) included in the sampling distribution, the more correct the chances of the mean of the sampling distribution becoming an estimate of the population mean (parameter). The following graphical representation supports this argument.

Now recall the list of means computed for 20 random samples. We observe that the 20 sample means differed form the true population mean m = 134.21 lbs.

The means 137, 140, 138, 133, 142, 142, 136, 143, 147, 136 are clearly above the true mean while 130, 131, 133, 132, 128, 125, 129, 133, 134, 134, 128 are below the true mean. These deviations or differences from true value is due to the variability of samples. This is known as 'Random error' in statistical estimation. Note that the mean of 20 random sample means is slightly greater than the true population mean. If we take 20 more samples of 200 students, the mean of this new sampling distribution might be lower than the true population mean.

Other than random error, error arises due to the tendency of consistent under estimating or over estimating a true value. This is known as systematic error or bias. Suppose, in the example discussed above, an investigator is investigating only those students who are healthy and fit. He would most likely overestimate the population mean. Generally healthy bodies have reasonable weights. Clearly the investigator's choice is one of bias.

This is an example from one of the bias that occurs in estimation.

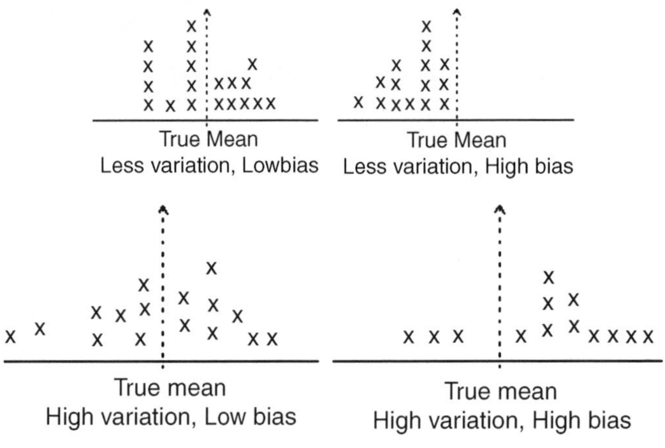

8.5 SAMPLING ERROR

There is generally some difference between a statistic i.e. the value obtained from a sample and its corresponding parameter of the population. In above example, discussed the mean of the weights of 200 students taken (first sample) is slightly different from the mean of the weights of 4000 students i.e. the population.

This difference is called sampling error (whose types and situations are discussed). This error can be minimized by increasing the size of the sample and by taking sample of extremely random in nature. If the size of sample is large the sampling error is small. The accuracy of the sample increases as the square root of the size 'n' of the sample i.e. according to $\sqrt{n}$. Hence we take samples of sufficiently large in size.

CENTRAL LIMIT THEOREM

What we have discussed above with an example, is stated as a theorem called Central limit theorem. It states that 'when the size of the sample increases and becomes sufficiently large the distribution of the sample means tends to Normal Distribution'.

Now here we must take one thing in our notice that the theorem is equally valid for both normal and strongly non-normal. We restate the central limit theorem as: "Even if the population distribution is strongly non-normal, its sampling distribution of means tends to normal distribution for large sample size". The natural question that comes to one's mind is as to what will be the size which can be taken as the large size? The following diagrams show how sampling distribution of means approaches normal distribution even if the parent distribution is not normal.

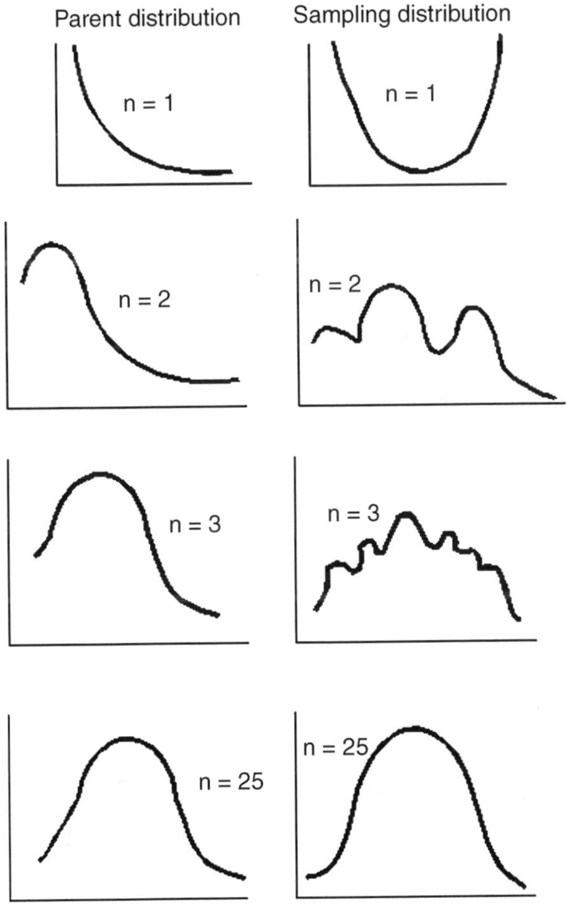

The answer to the above question is that the "large sample size" means $n > 30$ i.e. over 30. We have seen that the sample mean $\overline{x}$ is distributed normally with mean m, the mean of the population which is an unbiased estimator. It can be shown that the standard deviation of the sample means, called Standard error (S.E.) is equal to $\sigma/\sqrt{n}$

Thus $\mu_{\overline{x}} = \mu$ and

$$\sigma_{\overline{x}} = \frac{\sigma}{\sqrt{n}}$$

If we put, $z = \dfrac{\overline{x} - \mu}{\sigma/\sqrt{n}}$ then z - score is called a standard n ormal variate, with the mean as zero and the standard deviation as 1. If m is the population mean and $\overline{x}$ is the sample mean then $\overline{x} - \mu$ is the deviation of the sample mean from the population mean.

When this deviation is divided by $\sigma/\sqrt{n}$, the ratio $\dfrac{\overline{x} - \mu}{\sigma/\sqrt{n}}$ is called the relative deviation of the sample mean from the population mean.

CRITICAL REGION

Now $\dfrac{\overline{x} - \mu}{\sigma/\sqrt{n}}$ i.e. the relative deviation of sample is a standard normal variate from which it is extremely useful to draw statistical inference.

We know that the standard normal variate is our z - score. 95% area under the curve lies between –1.96 and +1.96, 99% lies between –2.58 and +2.58 and 99.73% lies between –3 and +3. In other words, only 5% area under the normal curve lies beyond ± 1.96, 1%, beyond ± 2.58 and 0.27% lies beyond ±3. These areas also indicate the probabilities that the z - score exceeds these values i.e. the probability that z - score will exceed 1.96 numerically is 0.05.

$P(z < -1.96 \text{ or } z > 1.96) = 0.05$

$P(|z| > 1.96) = 0.05$

This means that the probability that z - score will lie in the shaded region is 0.05 which is very small.

Similarly $P(|z| > 2.58) = 0.01$ and $P\ P(|z| > 3) = 0.0027$.

Return to our z - score formula $z_1 = \dfrac{\overline{x} - \mu_0}{\sigma/\sqrt{n}}$ where mean of sample is for which z-score is z_1.

Now 95 out of 100 values of z_1 will lie between –1.96 and +1.96. For $z_1 > 1.96$ or $z_1 < 1.96$, a rare event has taken place because $p(|z_1| > 1.96) = 0.05$

which is very small. The z - score (z_1 of x_1 from μ_0 is so significant that it can not due to sample fluctuations alone.

If $p(|\ z_1\ | > 2.58) = 0.01$, then very unusual event has taken place because this probability is extremely small (remote). Again we can firmly say that the deviation of x_1 from μ_0 (i.e. z - score) is significant and it is not due to the sample fluctuations alone.

From this discussion we come to a strong conclusion that the levels marked by the probabilities 0.05 or 0.01 which determine the significance of an event are called Levels Of Significance and are always expressed in percentages as 5% level of significance or 1% level of significance. The corresponding regions are called Critical Regions.

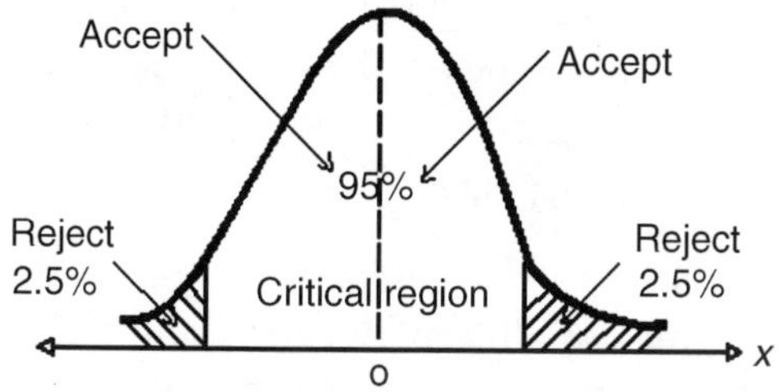

The limits within which we expect z-score lies with specified probabilities are called 'Confidence limits'. Thus $p\ (|\ z\ | > 1.96\ ) = 0.05$ and the bounding values are $\pm$ 1.96 are the confidence limits or fiducial limits. It means we are confident that 95 cases out of 100, the sample mean x will be such that z lies between –1.96 and +1.96.

Main objects of sampling theory are (i) Estimation (ii) Testing a hypothesis.

TESTING OF HYPOTHESIS

For testing a hypothesis:

Many a time, we strongly believe some results to be true. but after taking a sample, we notice that one sample data does not wholly support the result. The difference is due to (i) the original belief being wrong and (ii) the sample being slightly one sided.

Tests are therefore, needed to distinguish between the two possibilities. These tests tells about the likely possibilities and reveal whether or not the difference can be due to chance elements. If the difference is not due to chance elements it is significant and therefore, these tests are called tests of significance. The whole procedure is known is Testing of Hypothesis.

A hypothesis is a statement supposed to be true till it is proved false. It may be based on previous experience or may be derived theoretically. First a statistician or the investigator forms a research hypothesis that an exception is to be tested. Then he derives a statement which is opposite the research hypothesis (noting as H_0). The approach here is to set up an assumption that there is no contraction between the believed result and the sample result and that the difference therefore can be ascribed solely to chance. Such a hypothesis is called a null hypothesis (H_0). It is the null hypothesis that is actually tested, not the research hypothesis. The object of the test is to see whether the null hypothesis should be rejected or accepted.

If the null hypothesis is rejected, that is taken as evidence in favour of the research hypothesis which is called as the alternative hypothesis (denoted by H_a). In usual practice we do not say that the research hypothesis has been "proved" only that it has been supported.

For example, if it is assumed that the mean of the weights of the population of a college is 110 lb, then the null hypothesis will be the mean of the population that is 110 lbs. i.e. H_0: m = 110 lbs (Null hypothesis). In terms of alternative hypothesis (i) $H\alpha$: $\mu\alpha \neq 110$ lbs (ii) $H\alpha$: $\mu\alpha > 110$ lbs (iii) $H\alpha$: $\mu\alpha < 110$ lbs.

Setting Up levels of Significance

Once the null hypothesis is set up, the next job is to set the limits within which we expect (the null hypothesis) m lies. The idea behind it is to ensure that the difference between the sample value and the hypothesis should arise due to sampling fluctuations alone. If this difference does not exceeds this limit then the sample supports the null hypothesis and the sample is accepted. If it exceeds this limit the sample does not support the hypothesis and it is rejected. Now fixing the limits totally depends upon the accuracy desired. Generally the limits are fixed such that the probability that the difference will exceeds the limits is 0.05 or 0.01. These levels are known as the 'levels of significance' and are expressed as 5% or 1% levels of significance. Rejection of null hypothesis does not mean that the hypothesis is disproved.

It simply means that the sample values does not support the hypothesis. Also, acceptance does not mean that the hypothesis is proved. It means simply it is being supported.

Confidence Limits

The limits (or range) within which the hypothesis should lie with specified probabilities are called the confidence limits or fiducial limits. It is customary to take these limits as 5% or 1% levels of significance. If sample values lies between the confidence limits, the hypothesis is accepted; if it does not, the hypothesis is rejected at the specified level of significance.

ERRORS IN TESTING OF HYPOTHESIS

In testing any hypothesis, we get only two results: either we accept or we reject it. We do not know whether it is true or false. Hence four possibilities may arise.

- The hypothesis is true but test rejects it (Type I error)

- The hypothesis is false but test accepts it (Type II error)
- The hypothesis is true and test accepts it (correct decision)
- The hypothesis is false and test rejects it (correct decision)

In a statistical hypothesis testing experiment, a Type I error is committed when the null hypothesis is rejected though it is true. In terms of probability, Type I error is denoted by α (alpha) where

α = probability of type I error

= probability (rejecting H_o/ H_α is true).

A Type II error is committed by not rejecting (i.e. accepting) the null hypothesis, when it is false. The probability of Type II error is denoted by β (beta) where

β = probability of Type - II error

= probability (accepting H_o/ H_α is false)

Now consider that the difference between two population means is actually zero i.e. H_o: $\mu_1 - \mu_2 = 0$. But our test says that the difference is significant. Here we make a Type I error.

On the other hand, suppose there is true difference between the population means i.e. H_o: $\mu_1 - \mu_2 \neq 0$, but our test says the difference is not significant. Here we commit a Type II error.

Hypothesis (H_o)	Decision Accept (H_o)	Reject (H_o)
True	Correct decision	Type I error
False	Type II error	Correct decision

Now suppose Murray, a manufacturer produces some type of articles of good quality. A purchaser by chance selects a sample randomly. It so happens that the sample contains many defective articles and it leads the purchaser to reject the whole product. Now, Murray suffers a loss even though he has produced a good article of quality. Therefore, this Type I error is called "producers risk".

On the other hand, if we accept the entire lot on the basis of a sample and the lot is not really good, the consumers are put in loss. Therefore, this Type II error is called the "consumers risk".

In practical situations, still other aspects are considered while accepting or rejecting a lot. The risks involved for both producer and consumer are compared. Then Type I and Type II errors are fixed; and a decision is reached.

POWER OF A HYPOTHESIS TEST

The measure of how well the test of hypothesis is working, is called the 'power of the test'. In hypothesis testing both α (the probability of Type-I error) and β (the probability of Type II error) should be small.

Type I error occurs when we reject H_o which is true and a (the significance level of the test) is the probability of making type I error. Once the significance level is fixed, nothing can be done about a. Type II error occurs when we accept H_o which is false. The probability of type II error is β. The smaller the value of β, the better is the test. Alternately (1 – β) i.e. the probability of rejecting H_o when it is false should be as large as possible.

Rejecting H_0 when it is false is exactly what a good test must do. A high value of (1 – β), mostly close to 1, means that the test is working in high gear. A low value of (1 – β), mostly close 0, means that the test is working poorly.

Thus (1 – β) is the measure of the power of the test. If we plot the values of (1 – β) for each value of μ f_2 for which Ha is true, the resulting curve is known as a power curve.

You can see from the figure given below that the power is simply (1 – β). In testing of a hypothesis high power is desirable. As we know that the Type I error or a is usually set in advance by a researcher but the Type II error or b for a given test is harder to know as it requires estimation of the distribution of H_a, which is unknown in most of the cases. So like β, the power can be difficult to estimate accurately, but increasing the sample size n, we can increase the power of the test.

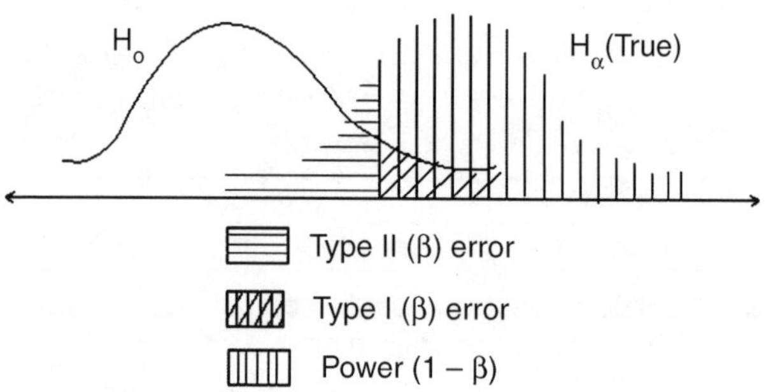

SAMPLING OF VARIABLES

The sample mean $\overline{x}$ is normally distributed with mean μ and standard deviation $\sigma/\sqrt{n}$ where μ is the mean of the population and σ is the standard deviation of the population. This results will help us in testing a hypothesis about the population mean.

1. Testing the hypothesis that the population mean $\mu = \mu_0$ which is a specified value.

Now σ = S.D. of the population is known.

In notations:-

The null hypothesis: $\mu = \mu_0$ i.e. $\mu - \mu_0 = 0$.

First calculate $| z | = \left| \dfrac{\overline{x} - \mu}{\sigma / \sqrt{n}} \right|$

i. If $| z | < 1.96$, the difference is not significant at 5% level and H_o is accepted, otherwise rejected.

ii. If $| z | < 2.58$, the difference is not significant at 1% level and H_o is accepted, otherwise rejected.

Note: We have assumed that σ is known. If however σ is not known, we take σ to be equal to the S.D. of the sample.

Example: A random sample of 400 male students have average weight of 55 kg. Can we say that the sample comes from a population with mean 58 kg. with a variance of 9 kg. ?

Solution: The null hypothesis H_0 is that the sample comes from the given population.

In notations: H_0: $\mu = 58$ kg. and $H\alpha$: $\mu \neq 58$ kg.

Now $|z| = \left|\frac{\bar{x}-\mu}{\sigma/\sqrt{n}}\right|$. Insert $\bar{x}$ = sample mean = 55kg.

μ = population mean = 58 kg. n = 400 and σ = population S.D. = 3

$$\text{Therefore } |z| = \left|\frac{55-58}{3/\sqrt{400}}\right| = 20 > 2.58$$

This value is highly significant. We will reject H_0 on the basis of this sample. The sample therefore, is not likely to be from the given population.

Example: A random sample of 400 tins of vegetable oil and labeled "5 kg. net weight" has a mean net weight of 4.98 kg. with standard deviation of 0.22 kg. Do we reject the hypothesis of net weight of 5 kg. per tin on the basis of this sample at 1% level of significance?

Solution: The null hypothesis H_0 is that the net weight of each tin is 5 kg.

In notations $H_{0:}$ $\mu = 5$ kg.

Inserting, $\bar{x} = 4.98$ kg., $\mu = 5$ kg. $\sigma = 0.22$ kg. and n = 400

$$\text{In } |z| = \left|\frac{\bar{x}-\mu}{\sigma/\sqrt{n}}\right| \text{ we get}$$

$$|z| = \left|\frac{4.98-5}{0.22/\sqrt{400}}\right| = 1.8 < 2.58$$

Hence H_0 is accepted at 1% level of significance.

Example: A stenographer claims that she can take dictation at the rate of 120 words per minute. Can we reject her claim on the basis of 100 trials in which she demonstrated a mean of 116 words with standard deviation of 15 words?

Solution: The hypothesis to be tested is that her claims to be accepted.

In notations $H_{0:}$ $\mu = 120$ and $H\alpha$: $\mu \neq 120$

Substituting, $\bar{x} = 116$, $\sigma = 15$, n = 100 in

$$|z| = \left|\frac{\bar{x}-\mu}{\sigma/\sqrt{n}}\right| \text{ we get}$$

$$| z | = \left| \frac{116-120}{15/\sqrt{100}} \right|$$

The difference is not significant at both 5% and 1% level of significance i.e. the value of z - score 2.67 is highly significant. Hence H_0 is rejected i.e. her claim is to be rejected.

If somebody is interested in the number of trials on the basis of which, with the same figure, her claim would not have been rejected, he can proceed as

$$| z | = \left| \frac{116-120}{15/\sqrt{n}} \right| = \left| \frac{-4}{15/\sqrt{n}} \right| \leq 1.96$$

$$\text{i.e.} = \frac{4\sqrt{n}}{15} \leq 1.96 \text{ i.e. } \sqrt{n} \leq 0.49 \times 15$$

$$\text{i.e. } \sqrt{n} \leq 7.35 \text{ i.e. } \sqrt{n} \leq (7.35)^2 \text{ i.e. } \sqrt{n} \leq 54.02$$

i.e. n = 54 trials.

Example: An automatic machine was designed to pack exactly 2 kg. of tea. A sample of 100 packs was examined to test the machine. The average weight was found to be 1.94 kg. with standard deviation of 0.10 kg. is the machine working properly?

Solution: The null hypothesis to be tested is that the machine is working properly.

In notations $H_{0:}$ μ = 2kg. and $H_{a:}$ μ ≠ 2kg.

Substituting, $\bar{x}$ = 1.94, s = 0.10, n = 100 in

$$| z | = \left| \frac{\bar{x}-\mu}{\sigma/\sqrt{n}} \right| = \left| \frac{1.94-2}{0.10/\sqrt{100}} \right| = 6.1 > 2.58$$

The z-score is highly significant, hence, we reject H_0 on the basis of this sample i.e. the machine is not working properly.

SAMPLING OF ATTRIBUTES

Characteristics like religion, language, locality etc. cannot be measured in numbers as they are attributes. We can only say whether a particular attribute is present or absent in an individual.

The sampling of attributes means drawing a sample from the population, of which every member possesses a particular attribute or does not have it.

In many cases, we are interested in knowing how many in the population possess the attribute.

For instance, Brooke wants to know how many from his area are smokers i.e. he is interested in the number or proportion of smokers in his area. Now we shall see how to test a hypothesis about the number or proportion of the individuals of the population possessing an attribute. Testing the hypothesis that population proportion $p = P_o$

In notations: $H_{0:}$ population proportion $= P_o$

Now P' = sample proportion is normally distributed with mean P_o and standard deviation

$$\text{Hence } z = \left| \frac{P' - P_0}{\sqrt{\frac{P_0 q_0}{n}}} \right|$$

i. If $| z | > 1.96$ a rare event has taken place.

If $P(| z | > 1.96) = 0.05$ we reject the hypothesis $= P_o$ at 5% level of significance.

ii. If $| z | > 1.96$ a usual event has happened and accept the hypothesis that $P = P_o$ at 5% level of significance.

iii. If $| z | > 2.58$ a rare (unusual) event has taken place. Now $P(| z | > 2.58) = 0.01$. We then reject the hypothesis $P = P_o$ at 1% level of significance.

iv. If $| z | > 2.58$, an unusual event occurred and we accept the hypothesis at 1% level of significance.

Example: A sample of 600 persons selected at random from a large city shows that there are 53% smokers. Is there any reason to doubt the hypothesis that smokers and non-smokers are equal in number in the city?

Solution: The null hypothesis is that the smokers and non smokers are equal in numbers.

$H_{0:}\ P = P_o$ and Ha: $P \neq P_o$

where $P_o = 0.5 \Rightarrow q_o = 1 - P_o = 0.5$

Also the sample proportion is

$$P' = 53\% = 0.53 \text{ and } n = 600.$$

$$| z | = \left| \frac{P' - Po}{\sqrt{\frac{P_o q_o}{n}}} \right| = \left| \frac{0.53 - 0.5}{\sqrt{\frac{0.5 \times 0.5}{600}}} \right| = 1.5 > 1.96$$

Hence the hypothesis H_o is accepted at 5% level of significance. i.e. we can undoubtedly say that both smokers and non-smokers are equal in numbers in that city.

Example: When flipped 1000 times, a coin landed 515 times heads up. Does it support the hypothesis that the coin is unbiased?

Solution: The null hypothesis is that the coin is unbiased.

In notations $H_{0:}\ P = P_o$ where $P_o = 0.5$ and

$$q_o = 1 - P_o = 0.5$$

$$\text{Now the sample proportion is } P' = \frac{515}{1000} = 0.515$$

$$| z | = \left| \frac{P' - Po}{\sqrt{\frac{P_o q_o}{n}}} \right| = \left| \frac{0.515 - 0.5}{\sqrt{\frac{0.5 \times 0.5}{100}}} \right| = 3.9 < 2.58 \text{ or even } 3$$

We then reject the null hypothesis. The coin is not unbiased.

Example: While throwing 5 die 40 times, a person got success 25 times - getting a 4 was called success. Can we consider the difference between expected value and observed value as being significantly different?

Solution: If we carefully examine the data then the hypothesis can be stated that the dice is unbiased.

In notation $H_{o:}\ P = P_o$ where $P_0 = 5C_1 \left(\frac{1}{6}\right)\left(\frac{5}{6}\right)^4 = \left(\frac{5}{6}\right)^5 = 0.4019$

i.e. $H_{o:}\ P = 0.4019$ and $H_{a:}\ P \neq 0.4019$

The sample proportion $P' = \frac{25}{40} = 0.625$

$$| z | = \left| \frac{P' - P_o}{\sqrt{\frac{P_o q_o}{n}}} \right| = \left| \frac{0.625 - 0.4019}{\sqrt{\frac{0.4019 \times 0.4019}{40}}} \right| = 3.49 < 2.58$$

Hence the hypothesis H_o is to be rejected at 1% level of significance or we can say that the value obtained is highly significant. The given data do not support H_o. Thus the dice is not unbiased.

Example: A patented medicine claimed that it is effective in curing 90% of the patients suffering from malaria.

From a sample of 200 patients using this medicine, it was found that only 170 were cured. Determine whether the claim is right or wrong. (Take 1% level of significance).

Solution: The null hypothesis is that the claim is quite right.
i.e. $H_{o:}\ P = P_o$ where $P_o = 90\% = 0.9$ and H_α: $P \neq 0.9$.
Also $q_o = 0.1$ and $n = 200$.

The sample proportion $P' = \frac{170}{200} = 0.85$

$$| z | = \left| \frac{P' - p_o}{\sqrt{\frac{P_o q_o}{n}}} \right| = \left| \frac{0.85 - 0.9}{\sqrt{\frac{0.9 \times 0.1}{200}}} \right| = 2.36 < 2.58$$

The null hypothesis H_o is quite right at 1% level of significance and that the claim is justified.

ESTIMATION

We have studied so far how to test the hypothesis about Mean or Population proportion from a given sample. Now we are going to determine the Mean or proportion of the population.

This is known as estimation. The following types of estimations are possible: (1) Point estimate and (2) Interval estimate.

Point Estimation:

i) The best estimate of population mean (μ) is the sample mean (x) and ii) The best estimate of population proportion (P) is the sample proportion (P').

For example i) If the average weight of 50 students of a school of 500 students is found to be 50 kg. We estimate that the average weight of all 500 students is also 50 kg.

ii) We are given a sample of 100 workers from a population of 1000 workers. If 53% smoke then we estimate that the proportion of smokers in the given population is also 53%.

Interval Estimation:

1) Population mean:

Consider | z | < 1.96 i.e. $\left|\dfrac{\bar{x}-\mu}{\sigma/\sqrt{n}}\right| < 1.96$

i.e. $|\bar{x}-\mu| < 1.96\sigma/\sqrt{n}$ or $\bar{x}-\mu > 1.96\sigma/\sqrt{n}$

i.e. $\dfrac{\bar{x}-1.96\sigma/\sqrt{n} < \mu < \bar{x}+1.96\sigma/\sqrt{n}}{OR}$

$\bar{x}-1.96 S.E. \mu < \bar{x}+1.96 S.E.$

at 5% level of significance.

This gives us the interval in which we estimate x to lie with 95% confidence. They are called confidence or fiducial limits.

1) $\bar{x}$ ± 1.96 S.E. at 95% confidence level.

2) $\bar{x}$ ± 2.58 S.E. at 99% confidence level.

3) $\bar{x}$ ± 3 S.E. at 99.73% confidence level (which is almost certainly).

Note: S. E. = Standard Error $= \sigma/\sqrt{n}$

However, if population S.D. (σ) is not known then replace s by s.d. of the sample.

Example: A random sample of 100 girls of 8 graders of a school gave the following results:

Mean weight = 60 kgs. S.D. = 5 kgs. Find the limits within which the mean weight of the school (for girls only) almost certainly lies.

Solution: 99.73% confidence limits of mean are $x \pm 3$ S.E.

Now S.E. $= \sigma/\sqrt{n} = 5/\sqrt{100} = 0.5$ and $\bar{x} = 60$kgs.

Therefore the limits are $60 - 3 \times 0.5 = 58.5$ kgs and $60 + 3 \times 0.05 = 61.5$ kgs

Example: The mean height obtained from a random sample of size 100 is 64 inches. The standard deviation of the distribution of height of the population is known to be 3 inches. Test the statement that the mean height of the population is 67 inches at 5% level of significance. Also set up 99% limits of the mean heights of the population.

Solution: The null hypothesis is that the mean height of the population is 67 inches.

In notation: $H_{0:}$ $\mu = 67$ inches and H_a: $\mu \pm 67$ inches

Given that $\mu = 67$, $x = 64$ and $n = 100$ with $\sigma = 3$

Therefore, H_o is rejected at 5% level of significance. Hence mean height of the population could not be 67 inches. 99% probable limits of the mean of population is given by ± 2.58 S.E.

Now S.E. $= \sigma/\sqrt{n} = 3/\sqrt{100} = 0.3$

Therefore, we have 64 ± 2.58 (0.3) inches.

= 64 – 2.58 (0.3) = 63.2 inches to 64 + 2.58 (0.3) = 64.8 inches.

Example: A random sample of 400 workers from the Lorson and Lorson was drawn for estimating the average salary. The sample mean was $ 800 and S.D. was $100. Find 95% confidence interval.

Solution: 95% confidence limits are $\bar{x} \pm 1.96$ S.E.

$$\text{Now S.E.} = \sigma/\sqrt{n} = \frac{100}{400} = \$5 \text{ and } \bar{x} = \$800$$

Therefore we have $\bar{x} \pm 1.96$ S. E. = 800 ± 1.96 (5)

i.e. 800 – 1.96(5) = $ 809 + 0

800 + 1.96(5) = $ 890

Population Proportion

For population proportion the limits are

1) P' ± 1.96 S.E. at 95% confidence level.

2) P' ± 2.58 S.E. at 99% confidence level.

3) P' ± 3 S.E. at 99.73% confidence level.

When, instead of proportion, if we required the number in the size N of the population, from the sample of size 'n' the intervals are just multiplied by N.

i.e. N (P' ± 1.96 S.E.) for 9.5% confidence level etc.

Example: A dice is thrown 9000 times and a throw of 5 or 6 considered success, was obtained 3240 times. Show that the dice is not unbiased and find the limits between which the probability of a throw of 5 or 6 lies.

Solution: The null hypothesis is that the dice is not unbiased.
In notation: $H_{0:}\ P_o = 0.5$ i.e. $H\alpha$: $P_o \neq 0.5$
$P_o = 0.5$ then $q_o = 0.5$, $n = 9000$

Also, sample proportion $= \dfrac{3240}{9000} = 0.36 = P'$

$$\text{Now, } |z| = \left|\frac{P' - P_o}{\sqrt{\dfrac{P_o q_o}{n}}}\right| = \left|\frac{0.36 - 0.5}{\sqrt{\dfrac{0.5 \times 0.5}{9000}}}\right| = 5.93 > 2.58$$

Thus H_0 is rejected i.e. the dice is not unbiased. The 99.73% confidence limits are $P' \pm 3$ S.E. where $P' = 0.36$ and

$$\text{S.E.} \sqrt{\frac{P_o q_o}{n}} = \sqrt{\frac{0.5 \times 0.5}{9000}} = \frac{0.5}{\sqrt{9000}} = 0.00527$$

Therefore, $P' \pm 3$ S.E. $= 0.36 \pm 0.00527$.
i.e. $0.36 - 0.00527 = 0.35473$ to
$0.36 + 0.00527 = 0.36527$

Example: In a sample of 900 stock-holders of companies, 400 stated that their major aim in holding stocks is capital appreciation. What is the 90% confidence range within which lies the population proportion of stock-holders who hold stocks for capital appreciation?

Solution: The 90% confidence range is given by $P' \pm 1.64$ S.E. where S.E.

$$= \sqrt{\frac{p'q'}{n}}$$

$$\text{Now } P' = \frac{400}{900} = \frac{4}{9} \text{ and } q' = 1 - p = \frac{5}{9}$$

$$\text{Hence the range is given by } \frac{4}{9} \pm 1.64\sqrt{4/9.5/9/900}$$

$$= \frac{4}{9} \pm 1.64\sqrt{\frac{20}{270}} = 0.4444 \pm 0.0272$$

Hence the range is $0.4444 + 0.0272 = 0.4716$ and
$0.4444 - 0.0272 = 1.4172$
ie. (0.4172 to 0.4716).

* Note that when we do not know p_o and q_o then we can use p' and q' in their places respectively.

Example: Out of consignment of 10000 tennis balls, 400 were selected randomly and examined. it was found that 20 of these were defective. How many defective balls you can reasonably expect to have in the whole consignment at 95% confidence level?

Solution: $P' = \frac{20}{400} = 0.05$ and $q' = 1 - p = 0.95$

The limits are (at 95% confidence level) = $p' \pm 1.96$ S.E.

where S. E. = $\sqrt{\frac{p'q'}{n}} = \sqrt{\frac{0.05 \times 0.95}{400}} = 0.01089$

Therefore, $0.05 \pm 1.96 \times 0.01089$ i.e. 0.05 ± 0.0213

Therefore p' lies between 0.0713 to 0.0287.

The expected number lies between

NP' = 10000 × 0.0713 = 7130 and

NP' = 10000 × 0.0287 = 2870.

TESTING THE DIFFERENCE BETWEEN MEANS

If $\bar{x}_1$ and $\bar{x}_2$ denote the means of the samples drawn from the first and second population respectively, having means μ_1 and μ_2 and standard deviations σ_1 and σ_2 and if the sizes of the samples are n_1 and n_2, then it can be proved that the distribution of the difference between the means $(\bar{x}_1 - \bar{x}_2)$ is normal with mean $(\mu_1 - \mu_2)$ and S.D. is given by

$$S = \sqrt{\frac{\sigma_1^2}{n_1} + \frac{\sigma_2^2}{n_2}}$$

Therefore, $$z = \frac{(\bar{x}_1 - \bar{x}_2) - (\mu_2 - \mu_2)}{\sqrt{\frac{\sigma_1^2}{n_1} + \frac{\sigma_2^2}{n_2}}}$$

Further, under the hypothesis $H_{o:}\ \mu_1 = \mu_2$ or $H_{o:}\ \mu_1 - \mu_2 = 0$ We see that

$$z = \frac{\bar{x}_1 - \bar{x}_2}{\sqrt{\frac{\sigma_1^2}{n_1} + \frac{\sigma_2^2}{n_2}}}$$

When the two samples belong to the same population, we have $\sigma_1 = \sigma_2 = \sigma$ then,

$$z = \frac{\bar{x}_1 - \bar{x}_2}{\sqrt{\frac{1}{n_1} + \frac{1}{n_2}}}$$

Similarly, the confidence limits for $(\mu_1 - \mu_2)$ at various levels of confidence are:

1) $(\bar{x}_1 - \bar{x}_2) \pm 1.96$ S at 95% level of confidence
2) $(\bar{x}_1 - \bar{x}_2) \pm 2.58$ S at 99% level of confidence
3) $(\bar{x}_1 - \bar{x}_2) \pm 3.$ S at 99.73% level of confidence.

Note: Here $S = S.E. = \sigma\sqrt{\frac{1}{n_1} + \frac{1}{n_2}}$

For the samples drawn from the same population.

2. Note: If S.D. of two populations i.e. σ_1, σ_2 are unknown, we use s.d. of samples in their places.

Example: A group of 200 students have the mean height of 154 cms. Another group of 300 students have the mean height of 152 cms. Can these be from the same population with S.D. of 5 cms?

Solution: $H_{o:}\ \mu_1 = \mu_2$, the samples are from the same population.

$H_{a:}\ \mu_1 \neq \mu_2$, here $\bar{x}_1 = 154$ cms, $\bar{x}_2 = 152$ cms, s = 5 cms, $n_1 = 200$ and $n_2 = 300$.

$$\text{Now, } |z| = \left|\frac{\bar{x}_1 - \bar{x}_2}{\sigma\sqrt{\frac{1}{n_1} + \frac{1}{n_2}}}\right| = \left|\frac{154 - 152}{5\sqrt{\frac{1}{200} + \frac{1}{300}}}\right| = 4.4 > 3$$

i.e. the z-score is highly significant. Therefore, we reject H_o i.e. it is not likely that the two samples are from the same population.

Example: Random samples from two population gave the following results:

	Population A	*Population B*
Mean	490	500
S.D.	50	40
Size	300	300

Is the difference between the means significant?

Solution: $H_{o:}\ \mu_1 = \mu_2$, the difference between the two means is not significant. i.e. $H_{a:}\ \mu_1 \neq \mu_2$.

We have $\bar{x}_1 = 490$, $\bar{x}_2 = 500$, $\sigma_1 = 50$, $\sigma_2 = 40$, $n_1 = 300$ and $n_2 = 300$.

$$|z| = \left|\frac{\bar{x}_1 - \bar{x}_2}{\sqrt{\frac{\sigma_1^2}{n_1} + \frac{\sigma_2^2}{n_2}}}\right| = \left|\frac{490 - 500}{5\sqrt{\frac{(50)^2}{300} + \frac{(40)^2}{300}}}\right|$$

$$= \left| \frac{-10}{\sqrt{\frac{2500}{300} + \frac{1600}{300}}} \right|$$

$$= \left| \frac{-10}{\sqrt{\frac{4100}{300}}} \right| = \left| \frac{-10}{\sqrt{\frac{41}{3}}} \right| = \left| \frac{-10}{13.66} \right| = 0.7315 < 1.96$$

Therefore, the null hypothesis H_o is accepted i.e. the difference between the two means is not significant.

Example: Two samples of 100 electric bulbs each has a means 1500 and 1550, standard deviations are 50 and 60. Can it be concluded that two brands differ significantly in equality at 1% level of significance?

Solution: $H_{o:}\ \mu_1 - \mu_2$ i.e. there is no significant difference in the mean life of two brands of bulbs. We have = 1500, = 1500, $\sigma_1 = 50$, $\sigma_2 = 60$, $n_1 = 100$ and $n_2 = 100$.

$$|\ z\ | = \left| \frac{\bar{x}_1 - \bar{x}_2}{\sqrt{\frac{\sigma_1{}^2}{n_1} + \frac{\sigma_2{}^2}{n_2}}} \right| = \left| \frac{1500 - 1500}{5\sqrt{\frac{(50)^2}{100} + \frac{(60)^2}{100}}} \right|$$

$$= \left| \frac{-50}{7.81} \right| = 6.4 > 2.58$$

Therefore, the null hypothesis H_o is rejected. Hence there is a significant difference in the mean life of the two brands of bulbs.

Example: Two populations have their means equal but the standard deviation of one is twice of the other. If samples of size 2000 are drawn from each population, show that the difference between the means will almost not exceed 0.15 s′ where s′ is the smaller S.D.

Solution: We have

$$s_1 = \sigma',\ \sigma_2 = 2\sigma',\ n_1 = 2000,\ n_2 = 2000$$

Therefore

$$S = \sqrt{\frac{\sigma_1{}^2}{n_1} + \frac{\sigma_2{}^2}{n_2}} = \sqrt{\frac{\sigma'^2}{200} + \frac{4\sigma'^2}{200}} = \sigma'\sqrt{\frac{5}{200}} = 0.056'$$

$$\text{Now} \left| \frac{\bar{x}_1 - \bar{x}_2}{\sqrt{\frac{\sigma_1{}^2}{n_1} + \frac{\sigma_2{}^2}{n_2}}} \right| = \left| \frac{\bar{x}_1 - \bar{x}_2}{0.056'} \right| < 3$$

$|\bar{x}_1 - \bar{x}_2| < 3 \times 0.056\sigma'$

i.e. $|\bar{x}_1 - \bar{x}_2| < 0.156\sigma'$

Example: The data of a certain trace element in blood is as under:

	Sample - I	*Sample - II*
Mean	28 ppm	32 ppm
S. D.	14 ppm	10 ppm
Size	75 male	60 female

What is the likelihood that the population means of the concentration of the elements are the same for male and female (at 95% confidence level)?

Solution: The null hypothesis is $H_{o:}\ \mu_1 - \mu_2$ and the alternative hypothesis $H\alpha$: $\mu_1 \neq \mu_2$.

We have $\bar{x}_1 = 28, \bar{x}_2 = 32, \sigma_1 = 14, \sigma_2 = 10, n_1 = 75$ and $n_2 = 60$.

$$|z| = \left| \frac{\bar{x}_1 - \bar{x}_2}{\sqrt{\frac{\sigma_1{}^2}{n_1} + \frac{\sigma_2{}^2}{n_2}}} \right| = \left| \frac{28 - 32}{5\sqrt{\frac{(14)^2}{75} + \frac{(10)^2}{60}}} \right|$$

$$= \left| \frac{-4}{\sqrt{2.61 + 1.67}} \right| = 1.07 > 1.96$$

Thus H_o is accepted i.e. the population means of the concentrations of the elements are the same for both male and female.

Example: In a certain school there are 6th graders and 7th graders. The average weight of students in a sample of 250 in 6th graders was found to be 120 lbs with s.d. of 12 lbs. While the corresponding figures in a sample of 400 students from 7th graders were 124 lbs and 141 lbs. Is the difference significant? Also find 99% confidence limits for the difference in the average weights of students in the two graders.

Solution: We have $H_{o:}\ \mu_1 - \mu_2$ and $H_{a:}\ \mu_1 \neq \mu_2$. $\bar{x}_1$

$= 120$, $\sigma_1 = 1_2$, $n_1 = 250 \rightarrow$ For 6th graders $\bar{x}_2$

$=124$, $\sigma_2 = 14$, $n_2 = 400 \rightarrow$ For 7th graders

$$|z| = \left| \frac{\bar{x}_1 - \bar{x}_2}{\sqrt{\frac{\sigma_1{}^2}{n_1} + \frac{\sigma_2{}^2}{n_2}}} \right| = \left| \frac{120 - 124}{5\sqrt{\frac{144}{250} + \frac{196}{400}}} \right|$$

$$= \left| \frac{-4}{\sqrt{0.576 + 0.490}} \right| = \left| \frac{-4}{\sqrt{1.0324}} \right|$$

$| z | = 3.87 > 3$

Hence, the difference between two samples is significant as we have rejected H_o.

Now 99% confidence limits are given by $(x_1 - x_2) \pm 2.585$

$= (4) \pm 2.58 \times 1.0324$

$= 4 \pm 2.66$ which are (1.34, 6.66).

TEST FOR DIFFERENCE BETWEEN PROPORTIONS

If two samples are drawn from different populations, we may be interested in finding out whether the difference between the proportion of successes is significant or not. Let x_1 and x_2 be the number of items possessing the attribute A, in the random sampling of sizes n_1 and n_2 from two populations respectively.

Then the sample proportions of successes are $P_1 = \frac{x_1}{n_1}$ and $P_2 = \frac{x_2}{n_2}$ if P_1 and P_2 are proportion of successes in the two populations and $Q_1 = 1 - P_1$, $Q_2 = 1 - P_2$ then

$$z = \frac{(P_1 - P_2) - (P_1 - P_2)}{\sqrt{\frac{P_1Q_1}{n_1} + \frac{P_2Q_2}{n_2}}}$$

Under the hypothesis that the proportions in two populations are equal. i.e. $P_1 = P_2 = P \Rightarrow Q_1 = Q_2 = Q$ (say) then

$$z = \frac{(P_1 - P_2) - 0}{\sqrt{\frac{PQ}{n_1} + \frac{PQ}{n_2}}} = \frac{P_1 - P_2}{\sqrt{PQ\left(\frac{1}{n_1} + \frac{1}{n_2}\right)}}$$

In general, however, we do not know the population's proportion of success.

In such a case we can replace P by its best estimate P = the pooled estimate of the actual proportion in the population, where

$$\text{Pooled estimate } (P) = \frac{n_1P_1 + n_2P_2}{n_1 + n_2} \quad \text{or } P = \frac{x_1 + x_2}{n_1 + n_2}$$

Example: A machine produced 20 defective articles in a batch of 500. After overhauling it produced 3 defective in a batch of 100. Has the machine improved?

Solution: $H_{o:}$ $P_1 = P_2$ i.e. The machine has not improved after overhauling
$H_{a:}$ $P_1 \neq P_2$

Now $P_1 = \frac{16}{500} = 0.032$ and $P_2 = \frac{3}{100} = 0.030$

Pooled estimate of actual proportion in the population is given by P

$$= \frac{x_1 + x_2}{n_1 + n_2} = \frac{16+3}{500+100} = 0.032$$

$Q = 1 - P = 0.968$

$$|z| = \frac{P_1 - P_2}{\sqrt{PQ\left(\frac{1}{n_1} + \frac{1}{n_2}\right)}} = \left|\frac{0.032 - 0.030}{\sqrt{0.032 \times 0.968}\left(\frac{1}{500} + \frac{1}{100}\right)}\right|$$

$$|z| = \left|\frac{0.002}{0.019}\right| = 0.105 < 1.96 \text{ (at 5\% level)}$$

H_o is true i.e. the machine has not improved significantly.

Example: In two large populations there are 30% and 25% fair haired people respectively.

Is the difference likely to be hidden in sample of 1200 and 900 respectively from the two populations?

Solution: $P_1 = 30\% = 0.30$ and $P_2 = 25\% = 0.25$ & $q_1 = 0.70$ and $q_2 = 0.75$ $n_1 =$ 1200 and $n_2 = 900$.

$$|z| = \left|\frac{P_1 - P_2}{\sqrt{\frac{P_1 q_1}{n_1} + \frac{P_2 q_2}{n_2}}}\right| = \left|\frac{0.30 - 0.25}{\frac{(.3)(.7)}{1200} + \frac{(.25)(.75)}{900}}\right|$$

$$= \left|\frac{0.05}{0.0195}\right| = 2.56$$

Therefore, $|z| > 1.96$ (i.e. at 5% level of significance). Hence it is unlikely that the real difference will be hidden.

Note: At times you may be interested in the comparison of proportions of persons possessing an attribute in a sample with proportion given by the population. In that case use:

$$|z| = \left|\frac{P_1 - P_2}{\sqrt{P_2 q_2 \times \frac{n_2}{n_1 + n_2}}}\right|$$

where P_2 = Population proportion. $q_2 = 1 - P_2$

n_1 = Number of observations in the sample

$n_1 + n_2$ = Size of population

n_2 = (Size of population $- n_1$)

Example: There are 1000 students in a college out of 20000 students in the whole university. In a study 200 were found smokers in the college and 1000 in the university. Is there a significant difference between the proportion of smokers in the college and in the university?

Solution: $H_{o:}$ $P_1 = P_2$ i.e. there is no significant difference in the college and university in case of proportion of smokers. $H\alpha$: $P_1 \neq P_2$.

$$\text{Proportion of smokers in college } P_1 = \frac{200}{1000} = 0.20$$

$$\text{Proportion of smokers in the university } P_2 = \frac{1000}{20000} = 0.05$$

$q_2 = 1 - P2 = 0.95$
Also $n_1 = 1000$ and $n_1 + n_2 = 20000$. $n_2 = 19000$.

$$| z | = \left| \frac{0.20 - 0.05}{0.05 \times 0.95 \left(\dfrac{19000}{1000 + 20000} \right)} \right|$$

$$| z | = \left| \frac{0.15}{0.0067} \right| = 22.39 > 3$$

Since the value is highly significant, it could not have arisen due to sample fluctuations.

Rejecting H_o we say that there is a significant difference between proportion of smokers in the college and the university.

TWO TAILED AND ONE TAILED TESTS

While testing a hypothesis, we often talk of two-tailed tests and one-tailed tests. In the previous tests the critical region lay along both the tails of the distributions. That is, we did not want sample statistic (say mean) to be away from the population parameter (say mean) in either direction.

The test for such a hypothesis is non-directional or two-sided or two-tailed. A two-tailed test of hypothesis will reject the null hypothesis H_o, if the sample statistic is significantly higher than or lower than the hypothesized population parameter. Thus in two-tailed test the rejection (critical) region is located in both the tails.

For example, suppose you suspect that a particular 6th grader's performance on a test in Mathematics is not a true representative of the students who have appeared. The national mean score in this test was found to be 75. The alternative (or research) hypothesis is:

$H_{a:}$ $\mu \neq 75$ while the null hypothesis is: $H_{o:}$ $\mu = 75$.

Now our pre-determined probability level is 95% i.e. 5% level of significance for this test. Both tests have the rejection (or critical) region of 5%

i.e. 0.05. Now this rejection region is divided between both the tails of the distribution i.e. 2.5% or 0.25 in the upper tail and 2.5% or 0.25 in the upper tail and 2.5% or 0.25 in the lower tail since your hypothesis gives only a difference and not a direction. You will reject the null hypothesis on the basis that the sample mean falls into the area beyond 1.96 S.E. Otherwise if it falls into area 0.475 corresponds to 1.96 S.E. you can accept the null hypothesis.

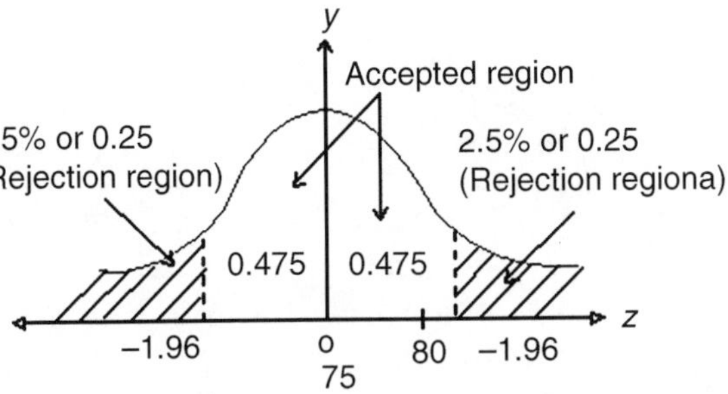

Suppose you want to reduce the risk of committing a Type I error, reduce the size of the rejection region. If the hypothesis is treated at 1% i.e. 0.01 level of significance. If we consult the table of areas under the normal curve, we find the acceptance region of 0.495 ((one half of.99) is equal to 2.58 S.E. from μ_H i.e. z-score = 0.

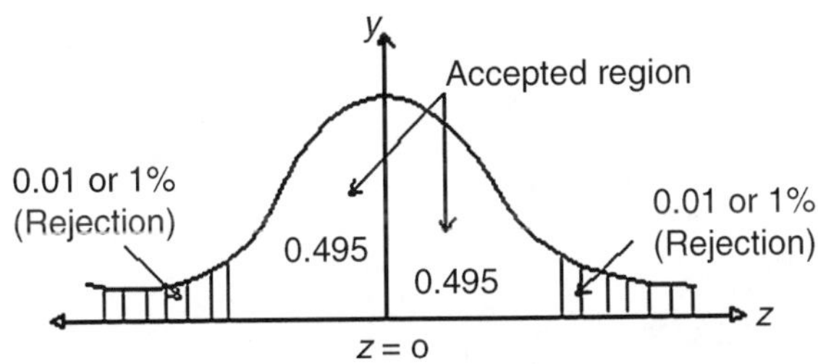

You will still reject the null hypothesis of no difference, if the class sample is either much higher or much lower than our population mean of 75.

As distinguished from the two-tailed test, we can apply a directional - one sided i.e. one-tailed test also because in some cases it is necessary to guard against only small values of $\overline{x}_1$ (i.e. sample mean). One-tailed test is so called because the rejection region will be located in only one-tail, which may either be on the upper or the lower side of the distribution depending upon the alternative (H_a) hypothesis formula. For example, we want to test a hypothesis that the average income per household is greater than $ 5000 against the alternative hypothesis that the income is $ 1000 or more. We will place all α risk on the upper-side of the theoretical sampling distribution and the test will be one-tailed. On the other hand, if we are testing that the average income per household is $ 5000 against H_a that the income is less than $ 5000 or less, the α risk is on the lower side of the distribution and the test will be one sided.

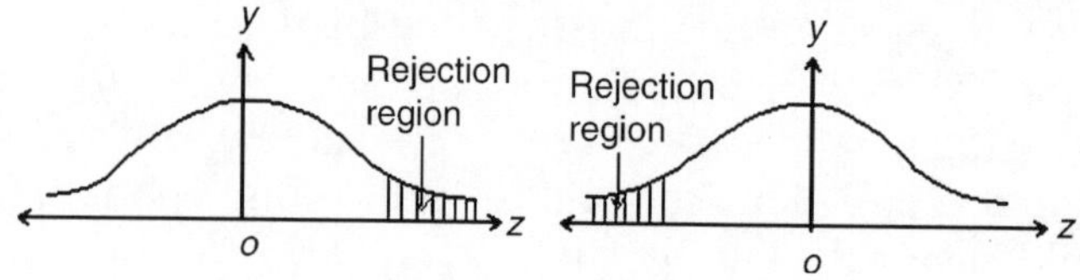

Summing up, if the population as specified mean say μo then the null hypothesis would be $H_{0:}\ \mu = \mu_o$ and alternative (researcher's) hypothesis could be:

1) $H_{a:}\ \mu \neq \mu_o$ (i.e. $\mu > \mu_o$ or $\mu < \mu_o$)
2) $H_{a:}\ \mu > \mu_o$
3) $H_{a:}\ \mu < \mu_o$

Example: Past records show that the mean marks of students taking statistics are 60 with standard deviation of 15 marks. A new method of teaching is adopted and a random sample of 64 students is chosen. After using the new method, the sample gives the mean marks of 65. Is the new method better?

Solution: Here we are interested in knowing whether the marks increased on using the new teaching method. Therefore, we use the one-tailed method:

The null hypothesis is: $H_{0:}\ \mu = 60$

The alternative hypothesis is: $H_{a:}\ \mu > 60$.

We have $\bar{x} = 65$, $\mu = 60$, $\sigma = 16$ and $n = 64$ then

$$z = \frac{\bar{x} - \mu}{\sigma / \sqrt{n}} = \frac{65 - 60}{16 / \sqrt{64}} = 2.5$$

Now suppose the researcher had predetermined the level of significance which is 0.01 or 1% for his decision. Then 2.5 > 2.33 (Here z-score is 2.33 for 0.01 level on the upper-tail of distribution). Therefore, the observed value is highly significant. That is H_0 is rejected and H_a is accepted. This means the new teaching method is better.

Example: A manufacturer of an antibiotic claimed that his antibiotic was 90% effective in curing a certain type of V. D. if used for a duration of 8 weeks. In a sample of 200 people who tried this, 160 people were cured. Determine whether his claim is legitimate.

Solution: Let P = Probability for curing the V. D. by the use of the manufacturer's antibiotic.

Setting two types of hypothesis as:

Null hypothesis: $H_{0:}\ P = 0.9 \Rightarrow$ claim is supported.

Researcher's hypothesis: $H_{a:}\ P < 0.9 \Rightarrow$ claim is rejected.

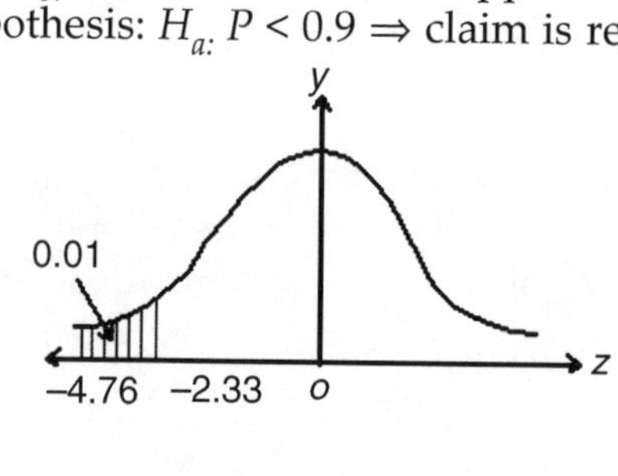

Now P' = Proportion of success in the given sample $= \frac{160}{200} = 0.8$

Now $P = 0.9 \Rightarrow q = 0.1$

Therefore, $\sqrt{\frac{Pq}{n}} = \sqrt{\frac{(0.9)(0.1)}{200}} = 0.021$

Thus the corresponding z-score will be

$$z = \frac{P' - P}{\sqrt{\frac{Pq}{n}}} = \frac{0.8 - 0.9}{0.021} = \frac{-0.1}{0.021} = 4.76$$

which is much less than –2.33. Thus by our decision rule H_0 is rejected and H_a is accepted stating that his claim is not legitimate and that the sample results are highly significant (at 0.01 level of significance).

Example: The breaking strengths of metal rods, produced by a certain company, have mean as 820 kg. and standard deviation as 50 kg. When a new manufacturing process is adopted, it is claimed that the breaking strength can be improved. A sample of 100 rods is tested and the results indicates that the breaking strength as 840 kg. Can we support this claim at a 1% level of significance?

Solution: Setting up the two hypotheses as:

Null hypothesis: $H_{0:}\ \mu = 820$ kg. $\Rightarrow$ there is no change.

Researcher's hypothesis: $H_{\alpha:}\ \mu < 820$ kg. $\Rightarrow$ Breaking strength is improved.

A one-tailed test should be used at 0.01 level of significance for decision making rule.

Now $\mu = 820, \overline{x} = 840$, n = 100 and $\sigma = 50$ then

$$z = \frac{\overline{x} - m}{s/\sqrt{n}} = \frac{840 - 820}{50/\sqrt{100}} = \frac{20}{50/10} = 0.04$$

Now z-score 4 > 2.33 i.e. the null hypothesis H_0 is rejected and the researchers hypothesis is accepted stating that we support the claim "Breaking strength is improved by the new manufacturing process".

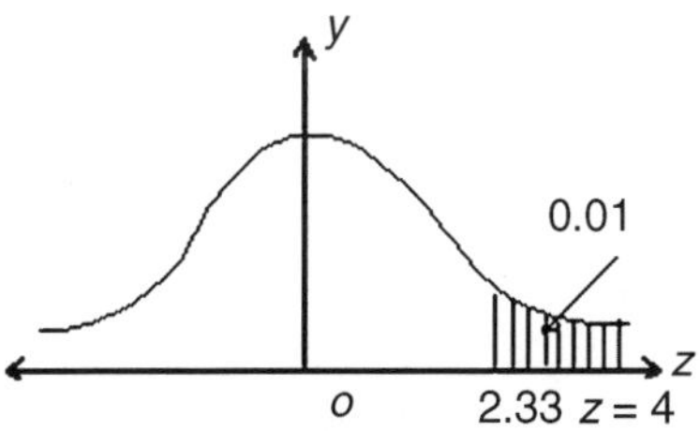

Note: In practice, one should adopt a 'one tailed test' only when he has enough reasoning to expect that the difference will be in a specified direction.

A two-tailed test is conservative than a one-tailed test. Since it uses more extreme test statistic for the rejection of the null hypothesis.

TEST OF SIGNIFICANCE FOR SMALL SAMPLES

So far we have discussed problems belonging to large samples. When a small sample (size < 30) is considered, the above tests are inapplicable because the assumptions we made for large sample tests, do not hold good for small samples. In case of small samples it is not possible to assume (i) that the random sampling distribution of a statistics normal and (ii) the sample values are sufficiently close to population values to calculate the S.E. of estimate.

Thus an entirely new approach is required to deal with problems of small samples. But one should note that the methods and theory of small samples are applicable to large samples but its converse is not true.

Degree of freedom (df)

By degree of freedom we mean the number of classes to which the value can be assigned arbitrarily or at will without voicing the restrictions or limitations placed.

For example, we are asked to choose any 4 numbers whose total is 50. Clearly we are at freedom to choose any 3 numbers say 10, 23, 7 but the fourth number, 10 is fixed since the total is 50 [50 – (10 + 23 + 7) = 10]. Thus we are given a restriction, hence the freedom of selection of number is 4 – 1 = 3.

The degree of freedom (df) is denoted by ν (nu) or df and it is given by $\nu = n - k$, where n = number of classes and k = number of independent constrains (or restrictions).

In general for a Binomial distribution, $\nu = n - 1$

For Poisson distribution, $\nu = n - 2$ (since we use total frequency and arithmetic mean).

For normal distribution, $\nu = n - 3$ (since we use total frequency, mean and standard deviation) etc.

STUDENT'S T-DISTRIBUTION

This concept has been introduced by W. S. Gosset (1876 – 1937). He adopted the pen name "student." Therefore, the distribution is known as 'student's t-distribution'.

It is used to establish confidence limits and test the hypothesis when the population variance is not known and sample size is small (< 30).

If a random sample $x_1, x_2, \ldots\ldots, x_n$ of n values be drawn from a normal population with mean μ and standard deviation s then the mean of sample

$$\bar{x} = \frac{\Sigma x_i}{n}$$

Estimate of the variance: Let s^2 be the estimate of the variance of the sample then s^2 given by,

$s^2 = \frac{\Sigma(x_i - \overline{x})^2}{n-1}$ $(n - 1)$ as denominator in place 'n'.

(I) The statistic 't' is defined as

$$t = \frac{|\overline{x} - \mu|}{\sqrt{\frac{s^2}{n}}} \text{ or } \frac{|\overline{x} - \mu|}{s}\sqrt{n}$$

Where x = sample mean, μ = actual or hypotheticalmean of population, n = sample size, s = standard deviation of sample.

$$\text{Where } s = \sqrt{\frac{\Sigma(x_i - \overline{x})^2}{n-1}}$$

Note: 't' is distributed as the student distribution with $(n - 1)$ degree of freedom (df).

(II) 1) The variable 't' distribution ranges from minus infinity to plus infinity.

2) Like standard normal distribution, it is also symmetrical and has mean zero

3) σ2 of t-distribution is greater than 1, but becomes 1 as 'df' increases and thus the sample size becomes large. Thus the variance of t-distribution approaches the variance of the normal distribution as the sample size increases for ν (df) = ∞, the t-distribution matches with the normal distribution. (observe the adjoining figure).

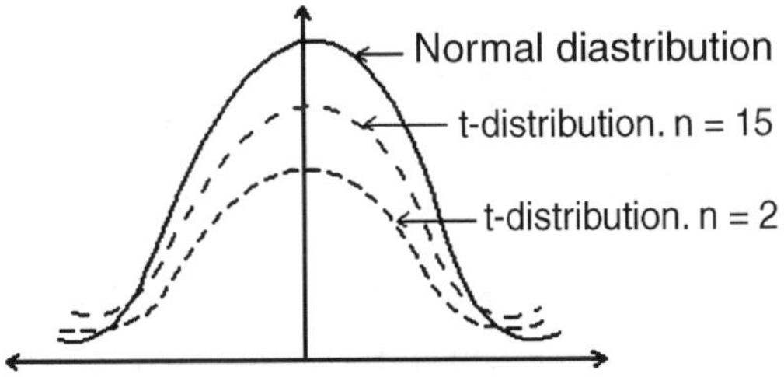

Also note that the t-distribution is lower at the mean and higher at the tails than the normal distribution. The t-distribution has proportionally greater area at its tails than the normal distribution.

(III) 1) If | t | exceeds $t_{0.05}$ then difference between x and μ is significant at 0.05 level of significance.

2) If | t | exceeds $t_{0.01}$, then difference is said to highly significant at 0.01 level of significance.

3) If $|t| < t_{0.05}$ we conclude that the difference between $\overline{x}$ and μ is not significant and the sample might have been drawn from a population with mean = μ i.e. the data is consistent with the hypothesis.

Fiducial Limits of Population Mean

For 95%, $\bar{x} \pm \frac{S}{\sqrt{n}} r_{0.05}$

For 99%, $\bar{x} \pm \frac{S}{\sqrt{n}} r_{0.01}$

Example: A random sample of 16 values from a normal population is found to leave a mean of 41.5 and standard deviation of 2.795. On this basis is there any reason to reject the hypothesis that the population mean μ = 43? Also find the confidence limits for μ.

Solution: Here

$$n = 16 - 1 = 15, \bar{x} = 41.5, \sigma = 2.795 \text{ and } \mu = 43.$$

Now $t = \frac{|\bar{x} - \mu|}{s}\sqrt{n} = \frac{1.5 \times \sqrt{15}}{2.795} = 2.078$

From the t-table for 15 degree of freedom, the probability of t being 0.05, the value of $t = 2.13$. Since 2.078 < 2.13. The difference between $\bar{x}$ and μ is not significant.

Now, null hypothesis: $H_{0:}$ μ = 43 and
Alternative hypothesis: $H_{\alpha:}$ μ ≠ 43.

using for 95%, $\bar{x} \pm \frac{S}{\sqrt{n}} t_{0.05}$

$= 41.5 \pm \frac{2.795}{\sqrt{16}} \times 2.13$

$= 41.5 \pm (0.6988)(2.13)$

= (40.011, 42.988)

Thus there is no reason to reject H_0. To find the limits,

Example: Ten individuals are chosen at random from the population and their heights are found to be inches 63, 63, 64, 65, 66, 69, 69, 70, 70, 71. Discuss the suggestion that the mean height in the universe is 65 inches given that for 9 degree of freedom the value of student's '*t*' at 0.05 level of significance is 2.262.

Solution: x_i = 63, 63, 64, 65, 66, 69, 69, 70, 70, 71 and
$n = 10$ $\bar{x}$

$= \frac{\Sigma x_i}{n} = \frac{670}{10} = 67$

and $S = \sqrt{\frac{\Sigma(x_i - \bar{x})^2}{n-1}} = \sqrt{\frac{88}{9}} = 3.13$ inches

The null hypothesis *Ho*: μ = 65 inches

The alternative hypothesis $H\alpha$: $\mu \neq 65$ inches
The df = $n - 1 = 10 - 1 = 9$

$$t = \frac{|\overline{x} - \mu|}{S}\sqrt{n} = \frac{67-65}{3.13}\sqrt{10} = 2.02$$

But $t_{0.05}$ at df = 9 = 2.02
$t = 2.02 < 2.262$
(xi – x)2
(63 – 67)2 = 16
(63 – 67)2 = 16
(64 – 67)2 = 9
(66 – 67)2 = 1
(69 – 67)2 = 4
(69 – 67)2 = 4
(70 – 67)2 = 9
(70 – 67)2 = 9
(71 – 67)2 = 16
(63 – 67)2 = 9

The difference is not significant at a t 0.05 level thus H_o is accepted and we conclude that the mean height is 65 inches.

Example: Nine items of a sample have the following values 45, 47, 50, 52, 8, 47, 49, 53, 51, 50. Does the mean of the 9 items differ significantly from the assumed population mean of 47.5? Given that for degree of freedom = 8. P = 0.945 for t = 1.8 and P = 0.953 for t = 1.9.

Solution: Given that for degree of freedom = 8. P = 0.945 for t = 1.8 and P = 0.953 for t = 1.9.

$\Sigma\, xi = 45 + 47 + 52 + 48 + 47 + 49 + 53 + 51 + 50 = 442$

$n = 9\,\overline{x}$

$$= \frac{\Sigma x_i}{n} = \frac{442}{n} = 49.11$$

$$\text{Also } S = \sqrt{\frac{\Sigma(x_i - \overline{x})^2}{n-1}} = \sqrt{\frac{54.89}{9-1}} = 2.62$$

Let the null hypothesis H_o: $\mu = 47.5$ and the alternative hypothesis H_α: $\mu \neq 47.5$

$$\text{Now } t = \frac{\overline{x} - \mu}{S}\sqrt{n} = \frac{49.11 - 47.5}{2.62} \times \sqrt{9} = 1.843$$

With the given data, we interpret the value of P for t = 1.83
for t = 1.9 $\quad$ P = 0.953

$$\frac{\text{for } t = 1.8}{\text{Difference } of\ t = 0.1} \qquad \frac{P = 1.8}{\text{Difference } of\ P = 0.008}$$

Therefore for difference of t = 0.043, the difference of $P = 0.0034$. Hence for $t = 1.843$, $P = 0.9484$. Therefore the probability of getting a value of $t > 1.43$ is (1 – 0.9484) = 0.051 which is in fact 2 × 0.051 = 0.102 and it is greater than 0.05. Thus H_0 is accepted, i.e. the mean of 9 items differ significantly from the assumed population mean.

Example: A certain stimulus administered to each of 12 patients resulted in the following increments in 'Blood pressure' 5, 2, 8, –1, 3, 0, 6, –2, 1, 5, 0, 4. Can it be concluded that the stimulus will in general be accompanied by an increase in blood pressure, given that for all df the value of t0.05 = 2.201?

$$\textit{Solution:}\ \bar{x} = \frac{\Sigma x_i}{n} = \frac{31}{12} = 2.583 \approx 2.6$$

$$\text{Also, } S = \sqrt{\frac{\Sigma(x_i - \bar{x})^2}{n-1}} = \sqrt{\frac{104.92}{12-1}} = 3.08$$

The null hypothesis $H_{0:}\ \mu = 0$ i.e. assuming that the stimulus will not be accompanied by an increase in blood pressure (or the mean increase in blood pressure for the population is zero).

$$\text{Now } t = \frac{\bar{x} - \mu}{S}\sqrt{n} = \frac{2.6 - 0}{3.08}\sqrt{12} = 2.924$$

The table value, $t_{0.05}$, $n = 11 = 2.201$

Therefore, 2.924 > 2.201

Thus the null hypothesis H_0 is rejected i.e. we find that our assumption is wrong and we say that as a result of the stimulus the blood pressure will increase.

DISTRIBUTION OF 'T' FOR COMPARISON OF TWO SAMPLES

Let $x1i$ (i = 1, 2, 3....., n_1) and $x2i$ (i = 1, 2, 3....., n_2) be two random independent samples drawn from two normal populations with mean μ_1 and μ_2 respectively but with same variance σ^2. Let $\bar{x}_1$ and $\bar{x}_2$ be sample means and let

$$S_1^2 = \frac{1}{n_1 - 1}\sum_1^{n_1}(x_i - \bar{x}_1)^2 \text{ and } S_2^2 = \frac{1}{n_2 - 1}\sum_1^{n_2}(x_i - \bar{x}_2)^2$$

Then the static t is given by

$$t = \frac{(\bar{x}_1 - \bar{x}_2) - (\mu_1 - \mu_2)}{\sqrt{S_P^2\left(\frac{1}{n_1} + \frac{1}{n_2}\right)}}$$

Where $S_P^2 = \dfrac{(n_1 - 1)S_1^2 + (n_2 - 1)S_2^2}{n_1 + n_2 - 2}$, is called the pooled estimate of the population variance.

Example: Two types of drugs were used on 5 and 7 patients for reducing their weights in Jerry's 'slim-beauty' health club. Drug A was allopathic and drug B was Herbal. The decrease in the weight after using drugs for six months was as follows:

Drug *A*: 10 12 13 11 14

Drug *B*: 8 9 12 14 15 10 9

Is there a significant difference in the efficiency of the two drug? If not which drug should you buy?

Solution:

Let the null hypothesis $H_{o:}\ \mu_1 = \mu_2$ or $H_{o:}\ \mu_1 - \mu_2 = 0.$

Alternative hypothesis $H_{\alpha:}\ \mu_1 \neq \mu_2$ or H_α: $\mu_1 - \mu_2 \neq 0$

x_{1i}	$(x_1 - \bar{x}_1)$	$(x_1 - \bar{x}_1)^2$	x_{2i}	$(x_2 - \bar{x}_2)$	$(x_2 - \bar{x}_2)^2$
10	-2	4	8	-3	9
12	0	0	9	-2	4
13	1	1	12	1	1
11	-1	1	14	3	9
14	2	4	15	4	16
			10	-1	1
			9	-2	4
$x_{1i} = 60$	$(x_1 - \bar{x}_1)^2 = 10$		$x_{2i} = 77$	$(x_2 - \bar{x}_2)^2 = 44$	

$$\text{Now } \bar{x}_1 = \frac{Sx_{1i}}{n} = \frac{60}{5} = 12 \text{ and } \bar{x}_2 = \frac{Sx_{2i}}{n} = \frac{77}{7} = 11$$

$$\text{Also } S_P^2 = \frac{(n_1 - 1)S_1^2 + (n_2 - 1)S_2^2}{n_1 + n_2 - 2}$$

$$\text{Where } S_1^2 = \frac{\Sigma(x_1 - \bar{x}_1)^2}{n_1 - 1} = \frac{10}{5 - 1} = 2.5 \text{ and}$$

$$S_2^2 = \frac{\Sigma(x_2 - \bar{x}_2)^2}{n_2 - 1} = \frac{44}{7 - 1} = 7.3$$

$$\text{Therefore, } S_P^2 = \frac{(5-1)2.5 + (7-1)7.3}{5 + 7 - 2}$$

$$= \frac{4 \times 2.5 + 6 \times 7.3}{10} = 5.38$$

Then using the formula

$$t = \frac{\bar{x}_1 - \bar{x}_2 - (\mu_1 - \mu_2)}{\sqrt{S_P^2\left(\frac{1}{n_1} + \frac{1}{n_2}\right)}} \quad \text{where } \mu_1 - \mu_2 = 0,$$

we get

$$t = \frac{12-11}{\sqrt{5.38\left(\frac{1}{5}+\frac{1}{7}\right)}} = \frac{1}{\sqrt{5.38 \times \frac{12}{35}}} = \frac{1}{\sqrt{5.38 + 0.342}} = 0.735$$

Now $\nu(\text{df}) = n_1 + n_2 - 2 = 10$
For $\nu = 10$, $t_{0.05} = 2.228$
Therefore, $0.735 < 2.228$

Thus the null hypothesis is accepted. Hence there is no significance in the efficiency of the two drugs. Since drug B is Herbal and there is no difference in efficiency between the two with no side effects, we should buy the Herbal drug.

Example: Two types of batteries are tested for their length of life and following results are obtained.

	No. of sample (n)	Mean (x)	Variance (σ_2)
Battery A	10	500 hours	100
Battery B	10	560 hours	121

Is there a significant difference in the two batteries?

Solution: The null hypothesis

$$H_{o:}\ \mu_1 = \mu_2 \text{ or } H_{o:}\ \mu_1 - \mu_2 \neq 0$$

Alternative hypothesis $H_{\alpha:}\ \mu_1 \neq \mu_2$ or $H_{\alpha:}\ \mu_1 - \mu_2 \neq 0$
i.e. there is no significant difference in the two batteries.

Now $n_1 = 10$, $s_1 = \sqrt{100} = 10$, $\bar{x}_1 = 500$, $n_2 = 10$, s_2

$= \sqrt{121} = 11$ and $\bar{x}_2 = 560$

$$\text{Thus } S_P^2 = \frac{(n_1-1)S_1^2 + (n_2-1)S_2^2}{n_1+n_2-2}$$

$$= \frac{(10-1)(10)^2 + (10-1)(11)^2}{10+10-2}$$

$$\text{Using the formula } t = \frac{\bar{x}_1 - \bar{x}_2 - (\mu_1 - \mu_2)}{\sqrt{S_P^2\left(\frac{1}{n_1} + \frac{1}{n_2}\right)}}$$

where

$$\mu_1 - \mu_2 = 0$$

we get $t = \dfrac{500-560}{\sqrt{122.8\left(\dfrac{1}{10}+\dfrac{1}{10}\right)}} = 12.2$

The degree of freedom ν(df) = 10 + 10 – 2 = 18
For $\nu = 18$, $t_{0.05} = 2.1$
Therefore, 12.2 > 2.1 (much higher)
Thus the difference is highly significant (rejection of H_o)

Example: To test the effect of a fertilizer on rice production, 24 equal plots of a certain land are selected. Half of them were treated with fertilizer leaving the rest untreated. Other conditions were the same.

The mean production of rice on untreated plots was 4.8 quintals with standard deviation of 0.4 quintal, while the mean yield on the treated plots was 5.1 quintals with a standard deviation of 0.36 quintal. Can we say that there is significant improvement in the production of rice due to use of fertilizer at 0.05 level of significance?

Solution: The null hypothesis $H_{o:}\ \mu_1 = \mu_2$ or $H_{o:}\ \mu_1 - \mu_2 = 0$
Alternative hypothesis $H_{\alpha:}\ \mu_1 \neq \mu_2$ or $H_{\alpha:}\ \mu_1 - \mu_2 \neq 0$
or $H_{\alpha:}\ \mu_1 > \mu_2$ and the fertilizer improved the yield.

Given $\bar{x}_1 = 4.8$, $n_1 = 12$, $s_1 = 0.4$. $\bar{x}_2 = 5.1$,

$n_2 = 12$, $s_2 = 0.36$ S_P^2

$$= \frac{(n_1-1)S_1^2+(n_2-1)S_2^2}{n_1+n_2-2}$$

$$= \frac{(12-1)(0.4)^2+(12-1)(0.36)^2}{12+12-2} \quad S_P^2$$

= 0.2704

Using the formula $t = \dfrac{\bar{x}_1-\bar{x}_2-(\mu_1-\mu_2)}{\sqrt{S_P^2\left(\dfrac{1}{n_1}+\dfrac{1}{n_2}\right)}}$

we get $t = \dfrac{5.1-4.8-0}{\sqrt{0.2704\left(\dfrac{1}{12}+\dfrac{1}{12}\right)}} = 1.44$

For n (df) = 12 + 12 – 2 = 22, $t_{0.05} = 2.07$
Therefore, 1.44 < 2.07

Thus we accept H_0 i.e. there is no significant difference in rice production due to the use of fertilizer.

DIFFERENCE BETWEEN MEANS OF TWO DEPENDENT SAMPLES

Two samples are said to be dependent on each other when the elements of one are related to those of the other in any significant or meaningful manner.

In fact the two samples consists of observations made of the same objects, individuals or more generally, on the same selected population elements.

The ' t ' test is often used to compare 'before' and 'after' scores in experiments for the determination of the significant change that has occurred. We may carry out some experiment, say, to find the training effect on some students, to find out the efficacy of coaching class, efficacy of two drugs. Often the use of dependent or paired samples will enable us to perform a more precise analysis.

The ' t ' test is defined by the formula:

$$t = \frac{\overline{x} - \Delta}{S}\sqrt{n} \text{ where } \Delta = 0 \text{ (for testing equal means)}$$

$$\text{and } S = \sqrt{\frac{\Sigma d^2}{n-1}} \text{ where } d = \text{Deviationfrom the } 'm'$$

where m = mean of the differences.

Example: Two laboratories carry out independent estimates of fat content in the ice-cream of a certain company. A sample is taken from each batch, halved and the separate halves were tested in the two laboratories. They obtain the following results:

% of fat content in ice-cream

Batch No.	1	2	3	4	5	6	7	8	9	10
Lab A	7	8	7	3	8	6	90	4	7	8
Lab B	9	8	8	4	7	7	9	6	6	6

Is the testing reliable?

Solution: The null hypothesis

$$H_{o:}\ \mu_1 - \mu_2 \text{ or } H_{o:}\ \mu_1 - \mu_2 = 0$$

i.e. If the testing is reliable the mean of the difference in the results should not be significantly differ from 0.

Difference of results (Lab A – Lab B)	Deviation from mean (m) (d)	d^2
+2	+1.7	2.89
0	–0.3	0.09
+1	+0.7	0.49
+1	+0.7	0.49
–1	–1.3	1.69
+1	+0.7	0.49
0	–0.3	0.09

+2	−1.7	2.89
−1	−1.3	1.69
−2	−2.3	5.29
$\Sigma m = +3$		$Sd2 = 16.10$

Mean of the difference $\overline{x} = \frac{\Sigma m}{n} = \frac{3}{10} = 0.3$

Standard deviation of the differences

$$S = \sqrt{\frac{\Sigma d^2}{n-1}} = \sqrt{\frac{16.1}{10-1}} = 1.33$$

Using the formula $t = \frac{\overline{x} - \Delta}{S}\sqrt{n}$ where $\Delta = 0$

we get,

$$t = \frac{0.3 - 0}{1.33}\sqrt{10} = 0.71$$

For $v = 10 - 9 = 9$, $t\ 0.05 = 2.57$. Therefore, $0.71 < 2.57$.

The null hypothesis is accepted i.e. the testing is reliable.

Example: Boys from a certain class were given a test in statistics. They were given a six month's further extra coaching and a second test of an equal level was held. Do the marks give evidence that the students have benefitted by the extra coaching?

Boys	1	2	3	4	5	6	7	8	9	10	11
Marks (1st test)	23	20	19	21	18	20	18	18	23	16	19
Marks (2nd test)	24	19	22	18	20	22	20	20	23	20	17

Solution: The null hypothesis $Ho: \mu_1 - \mu_2$ or $Ho: \mu_1 - \mu_2 = 0$ i.e. $\Delta = 0$ alternative hypothesis $H\alpha: \mu_1 \neq \mu_2$ or $H\alpha: \mu_1 - \mu_2 \neq 0$

Boys	**Difference of marks (Test 2 – Test 1) = m**	**Deviations from 'm' (d)**	d^2
1	+1	0	0
2	−1	−2	4
3	+3	2	4
4	−3	−4	16
5	+2	1	1
6	+2	1	1
7	+2	1	1
8	+3	2	4
9	0	−1	1
10	+4	3	9
$n = 11$	$\Sigma m = 11$		$\Sigma d^2 = 50$

$$\text{Mean of difference } \bar{x} = \frac{\Sigma m}{n} = \frac{11}{11} = 1$$

$$\text{Standard deviation of the difference } S = \sqrt{\frac{\Sigma d^2}{n-1}}$$

$$= \sqrt{\frac{50}{11-1}} = 2.24$$

$$\text{Now } t = \frac{\bar{x} - \Delta}{S}\sqrt{n} = \frac{1-0}{2.24}\sqrt{11} = 1.482$$

The number of degree of freedom is 11 – 1 = 10

$t_{0.05}$, $\nu = 10 = 2.228$.

Thus, 1.482 < 2.228 i.e. the calculated value of t - it considerably less than the table value. Hence we accept null hypothesis *Ho*, that the marks do not give any evidence that the boys have been benefitted by the extra coaching.

Example: A dietitian decided to try out a new type of diet programme on 10 boys. Before applying this programme, he recorded their weights. Three months later, he recorded their weights again. The weight would have grown by an average of 6 kgs. during this period even without this special diet programme

- Did this special diet programme help? Use 0.05 level of significance.

Boys	1	2	3	4	5	6	7	8	9	10
Before weight	36	32	31	36	23	28	25	26	35	28
After weight	45	37	39	45	31	34	29	36	42	35

Solution: The null hypothesis

$$H_{o:}\ \mu_1 \neq \mu_2 \text{ or } H_{o:}\ \mu_1 - \mu_2 \neq 0$$

or more clearly $H_{o:}\ \mu_1 - \mu_2$ i.e. $\Delta \leq 6$

alternative hypothesis $H_{\alpha:}\ \Delta > 6$

Boys	Difference of marks (Test 2 – Test 1) = m	Deviations from 'm' (d)	d^2
1	+9	+1.5	2.25
2	+5	–2.5	6.25
3	+8	+0.5	0.25
4	+9	+1.5	2.25
5	+8	+0.5	0.25
6	+8	+0.5	0.25
7	+4	–2.5	6.25
8	+10	+2.5	6.25
9	+7	–0.5	0.25
10	+7	–0.5	0.25
$n = 10$	$\Sigma m = 75$		$\Sigma d^2 = 24.50$

$$\text{Mean of difference } \bar{x} = \frac{\Sigma m}{n} = \frac{75}{10} = 7.5$$

Star. dard deviation of the difference

$$S = \sqrt{\frac{\Sigma d^2}{n-1}} = \sqrt{\frac{24.50}{10-1}} = 1.65$$

Therefore, $t = \frac{\overline{x} - \Delta}{S}\sqrt{n} = \frac{7.5-6}{1.65}\sqrt{10} = \frac{1.5\sqrt{10}}{1.65} = 2.87$

The degree of freedom ν (df) = 10 – 1 = 9. The test is one-tailed because we are asked only whether the new diet programme increases the weight and not whether it reduces it.

Now $t_{0.05}$, ν = 9 = 2.26 (i,e. $t_{0.025}$, ν = 9 = 2.25 for one tailed test) Because 2.87 > 2.26. The null hypothesis can be rejected. Thus the test has provided evidence that the new diet programme caused the weight increase in boys. Though the amount of actual increase was not large (1.6 kgs over normal weight) but is was statistically significant.

CHI-SQUARE

Tests like z-score, *t*, *F* are based on the assumption that the samples were drawn from normally distributed populations or more accurately that the sample means were normally distributed. As these tests require assumption about the type of population or parameters, these tests are known as 'parametric tests.'

There are many situations in which it is impossible to make any rigid assumption about the distribution of the population from which samples are drawn. This limitation led to search for non-parametric tests. Chi-square (Read as Ki - square) test of independence and goodness of fit is a prominent example of a non-parametric test. The chi-square (χ^2) test can be used to evaluate a relationship between two nominal or ordinal variables.

χ^2 (chi-square) is measure of actual divergence of the observed and expected frequencies. In sampling studies we never expect that there will be a perfect coincidence between actual and observed frequencies and the question that we have to tackle is about the degree to which the difference between actual and observed frequencies can be ignored as arising due to fluctuations of sampling.

If there is no difference between actual and observed frequencies then χ^2 = 0. If there is a difference, then χ^2 would be more than 0.

But the difference may also be due to sample fluctuation and thus the value of χ^2 should be ignored in drawing the inference.

Such values of χ^2 under different conditions are given in the form of tables and if the actual value is greater than the table value, it indicates that the difference is not solely due to sample fluctuation and that there is some other reason. On the other hand, if the calculated χ^2 is less than the table value, it indicates that the difference may have arisen due to chance fluctuations and can be ignored. Thus χ^2-test enable us to find out the divergence between theory and fact or between expected and actual frequencies is significant or not.

If the calculated value of χ^2 is very small, compared to table value then expected frequencies are very little and the fit is good.

If the calculated value of χ^2 is very large as compared to table value then divergence between the expected and the observed frequencies is very big and the fit is poor.

We know that the degree of freedom r (df) is the number of independent constraints in a set of data.

Suppose there is a 2 × 2 association table and actual frequencies of the various classes are as follows:

	A	a	
B	AB	aB	60
	–22	–38	
b	Ab	ab	40
	–8	–32	
	30	70	100

Now the formula for calculating expected frequency of any class (cell)

$$= \frac{\text{Row total for row containing the cell} \times \text{column total for column containing the cell}}{\text{The total number of observation}}$$

In notations: Expected frequency $= \dfrac{R \times C}{N}$

For example, if we have two attributes A and B that are independent then the expected frequency of the class (cell) AB would be $\dfrac{30 \times 60}{100} = 18$

Once the expected frequency of cell (AB) is decided the expected frequencies of remaining three classes are automatically fixed.

Thus for class (aB) it would be 60 – 18 = 42

for class (Ab) it would be 30 – 18 = 12

for class (ab) it would be 70 – 42 = 28

This means that so far as 2 × 2 association (contingency). Table is concerned, there is 1 degree of freedom.

In such tables the degrees of freedom are given by a formula $n = (c - 1)(r - 1)$

where c = Number of columns

r = Number of rows

Thus in 2 ′ 2 table df = (2 – 1) (2 – 1) = 1

3 ′ 3 table df = (3 – 1) (3 – 1) = 4

4 ′ 4 table df = (4 – 1) (4 – 1) = 9 etc.

If the data is not in the form of contingency tables but as a series of individual observations or discrete or continuous series then it is calculated by $n = n - 1$ where n is the number of frequencies or values of number of independent individuals.

$$\chi^2 = \Sigma\left[\frac{(\text{observed frequency - expected frequency})^2}{\text{expected frequency}}\right]$$

$$\chi^2 = \Sigma\left[\frac{(O-E)^2}{E}\right]$$

where O = observed frequency and E = expected frequency.

Example: The following table shows the age groups of people interviewed according to their age-group and the number in each group estimated to have T. B.

Age group	**Nos. ingterviewed**	**T.B. cases**
15 – 20	199	1
20 – 25	300	8
25 – 35	1128	38
35 – 45	1375	96
45 – 55	1089	105
55 – 65	625	56
65 – 73	155	12
Total	4871	316

Do these figures justify the hypothesis that T. B. is equally popular in all age groups?

Solution: If T.B. equally popular in all groups then in each age group.

$$\left[\frac{316}{4871}\times 100 = 65\% \text{ of the people suffer from it}\right]$$

On this basis the observed and expected frequencies would be as

Age group	**Observed Cases**	**Expected cases**
15 - 20	1	13
20 - 25	8	19.5
25 - 35	38	73
35 - 45	96	89
45 - 55	105	71
55 - 65	56	40.5
65 - 75	12	10

Using Formula, we get,

$$\chi^2 = \frac{(1-13)^2}{13} + \frac{(8-19.5)^2}{19.5} + \frac{(38-73)^2}{73} + \frac{(96-89)^2}{89}$$

$$+\frac{(105-71)^2}{71}+\frac{(56-40.5)^2}{40.5}+\frac{(12-10)^2}{10}$$

Therefore, $\chi^2 = 57.6$

Also n (df) = $(c - 1)(n - 1) = (7 - 1)(2 - 1) = 6$

From the $c2$ – table, $c2$ 0.05, $n = 6 = 12.59$

Since 57.6 > 12.59 at 0.05 level of significance for 6 degree of freedom, the difference is significant and the hypothesis is not justified.

Example: 12 die were thrown 4096 times and a throw of 6 was reckoned as a success. The observed frequencies were as given below:

Number of successes 0 1 2 3 4 5 6 7 and over Total

Frequencies 447 1145 1181 796 380 115 24 8 – 4096

Find the value of $c2$ on the hypothesis that the dice were unbiased and hence show that the data is consistent with the hypothesis so far as the $c2$ test is concerned.

Solution: On the hypothesis of unbiased dice the theoretical frequencies in 4096 throws are the terms in the Binomial expansion of 4096 (5/6 + 1/6)2 and are given below:

Number of successes 0 1 2 3 4 5 6 7 and over Total

Theoretical

Frequencies 459 1102 1212 808 364 116 27 8 - 4096

Using the formula:

$$\chi^2 = \frac{(O_1-E_1)^2}{E_1}+\frac{(O_2-E_2)^2}{E_2}+$$

$$\frac{(O_3-E_3)^2}{E_3}+.....+\frac{(O_8-E_8)^2}{E_8}$$

We get

$$\chi^2 = \frac{(447-459)^2}{459}+\frac{(1145-1102)^2}{1102}+....+\frac{(8-8)^2}{8}$$

$\chi^2 = 5.811$

The number of classes is 8 but the total of the observed and theoretical frequencies agree. Therefore n (df) = 8 – 1 = 7. From the table $c^2_{0.05}$, $n = 7 =$ 14.07 i.e. the calculated value of c^2 is not significant and thus the observed frequency distribution is consistent with the hypothesis.

Example: Two hundreds digits were chosen at random from a set of tables. The frequencies of the digits are as below:

Digit	Frequency
0	18
1	19

2	23
3	21
4	16
5	25
6	21
7	20
8	21
9	15

Use χ^2 test to assess the correctness of the hypothesis that the digits were distributed in an equal manner in the tables from which they are chosen.

Solution: Our hypothesis is that the digit were distributed equally in the tables as correct. The expected frequencies of the digits would be:

Digit	0	1	2	3	4	5	6	7	8	9
Expected Frequency	20	20	20	20	20	20	20	20	20	20

Formula:

$$\chi^2 = \frac{(O_1 - E_1)^2}{E_1} + \frac{(O_2 - E_2)^2}{E_2} + ... + \frac{(O_{10} - E_{10})^2}{E_{10}}$$

$$\chi^2 = \frac{(18 - 20)^2}{20} + \frac{(19 - 20)^2}{20} + ... + \frac{(15 - 20)^2}{20}$$

$$\chi^2 = \frac{1}{20}[4 + 1 + 9 + 1 + 16 + 4 + 0 + 1 + 25]$$

$\chi^2 = 4.3$

The numbers of degree of freedom r (df) = $(c - 1)(r - 1)$

$= (10 - 1)(2 - 1)$

$= 9$

From the table, $\chi^2_{0.03}, n = 9 = 16.919$

Therefore, $4.3 < 16.919$

Thus calculated value of χ^2 is less than table value of $\chi^2_{0.05}, n = 9$. Hence our hypothesis is correct.

Example: In a certain town 100 persons were randomly chosen and interviewed for their educational stature. The results are as

		Education			
		Middle	High School	College	Total
Male	→	10	15	25	50
Female	→	25	10	15	50
Total		35	25	40	100

Can you say that education depends on the sex of the individual?

Solution: The null hypothesis: That there is no association between education and sex. On this hypothesis the expected frequencies are as below:

	Middle	High School	College	Total
Male	17.5	12.5	20	50
Female	17.5	12.5	20	50
Total	35	25	40	100

$$\chi^2 = \frac{(10-17.5)^2}{17.5} + \frac{(15-12.5)^2}{12.5} + \frac{(25-20)^2}{20}$$

$$+\frac{(25-17.5)^2}{17.5} + \frac{(10-12.5)^2}{12.5} + \frac{(15-20)^2}{20}$$

The numbers of degree of freedom $\nu = (c-1)(r-1)$
$\chi^2 = 9.93$ (approx.) $= (3-1)(2-1)$
$= 2$
From the table $\chi^2 0.05, \nu = 2 = 5.99$ and χ^2 $0.01, \nu = 2 = 9.21$

Thus the calculated value of χ^2 is highly significant and the null hypothesis which stated that, education does not depend on sex is, discredited.

Example: The following table is published in a memoir written by 'Karl Pearson'

Eye colour in sons		not light	light	
Eye colour in fathers	no light	230	148	378
	light	151	471	622
Total		381	619	1000

Test whether the colour of son's eyes is associated with that of father's.

Solution: The null hypothesis: The eye colour of sons and eye colour of father's are independent. If this is true the expected frequencies are

Eye colour in sons		not light	light
Eye colour in fathers	no light	144	234
Total	light	237	385

$$\text{Therefore, } \chi^2 = \frac{(230-144)^2}{144} + \frac{(184-234)^2}{234}$$

$$+\frac{(151-237)^2}{237} + \frac{(471-385)^2}{385}$$

$\chi^2 = 133.37$

The nos. of degree of freedom $v = (c - 1)(r - 1)$
$= (2 - 1)(2 - 1)$
$= 1$

The table value of χ^2 at 0.05 level of significance for df = 1 is 3.841 which is extremely poor compared to the calculated 133.37. Thus we reject the null hypothesis saying that there is high association between the sons's eyes and that of the father.

Example: In an experiment on the immunization of goats from anthrax, the following results were obtained. Derive the you inference on the efficacy of the vaccine.

	Died of anthrax	**Survived**	**Total**
Inoculated	2	10	12
Non-inoculated	6	6	12
Total	8	16	24

Solution: The null hypothesis: Inoculation of vaccine and survival are independent attributes. The expected frequencies would be:

	Died of anthrax	Survived	Total
Inoculated	4	8	12
Non-inoculated	4	8	12
Total	8	16	24

Therefore, by formula,

$$\chi^2 = \frac{(2-4)^2}{4} + \frac{(10-8)^2}{8} + \frac{(6-4)^2}{4} + \frac{(6-8)^2}{8}$$

$\chi^2 = 3$

The nos. of degree of freedom $n = (c - 1)(r - 1)$
$= (2 - 1)(2 - 1)$
$= 1$

From the table $\chi^2 0.05$, $v = 1 = 3.841$. Thus the calculated value is less than table value. Hence the hypothesis is accepted,

Note: Brandt and Snedecor gave a simple formula for 2 × 2 contingency table, in order to calculate c^2. Representing th (2 × 2) fold contingency table as:

b_1	b_2	T_b
c_1	c_2	T_c
T_1	T_2	T

$$X_1 = \frac{(b_1c_2 - c_1b_2)^2}{T_1 \times T_2 \times T_b \times T_c}$$

We Multiply diagonal frequencies and find the difference between the two products $(b_1c_2 - c_1b_2)$

Square this i.e. $(b_1c_2 - c_1b_2)^2$

Multiply by the grand total i.e. $(b_1c_2 - c_1b_2)^2 \times T$

Divide the above result by the product of all the sub totals i.e. $T_1 \times T_2 \times T_b \times T_c$, In our problem,

2	10	12
6	6	12
8	16	24

Therefore, $\chi^2 = \dfrac{[(2\times 6)] - (6\times 10)^2]\times 24}{8\times 16\times 12\times 12} = 3$

SAMPLING THEORY OF CORRELATION

By using the sampling correlation coefficient, you often have to estimate the population correlation coefficient. To do so one must know the sampling distribution of the coefficient of correlation. If the population coefficient of correlation = 0, this distribution is symmetric and the statistic having student's 't' - distribution can be used. Otherwise the distribution is skewed. For such a case a transformation, given by Fisher, which produces a statistic which is nearly normally distributed is used.

1) In case of large sample (> 30) the standard error of coefficient of correlation 'r' is calculated by $\dfrac{\sqrt{1-r^2}}{\sqrt{n}}$

2) In case of small samples the S. E. of the coefficient of correlation is calculated in the way as in the large samples, with the difference of $1 - r^2, \sqrt{1-r^2}$ is used. Instead of $\sqrt{\text{n}} - 2$ is used because in the calculation of coefficient of correlation, 2 degree of freedom are lost and therefore ν (df) = $n - 2$. Thus the S. E. of the coefficient of correlation in small samples is given by $\dfrac{\sqrt{1-r^2}}{\sqrt{n-2}}$

The value of 't' is calculated by finding out the ratio between the coefficient of correlation and its S. E.

Thus $t = \dfrac{r\sqrt{n-2}}{\sqrt{1-r^2}}$

Example: Use 't' test to find whether a correlation coefficient of 0.5 is significant if $n = 51$.

Solution: $r = 0.5$ and $n = 51$ then $t = \dfrac{\sqrt{n-2}}{\sqrt{1-r^2}}$ will be

$$t = \frac{0.5\sqrt{51-2}}{\sqrt{1-(0.5)^2}} = 4.07$$

From the table $t_{0.05}$, $r = 49 = 2.01$

Thus the calculated value is much higher than table value of ' t ', then the correlation is significant.

Example: A random sample of 15 from a normal population given the coefficient of correlation of –0.5. is this significant of the existence of correlation of the population?

Solution: $r = -0.5$ and $n = 15$

Inserting it $= \frac{r\sqrt{n-2}}{\sqrt{1-r^2}}$ we get $t = \frac{-0.5\sqrt{15-2}}{\sqrt{1-(-0.5)^2}} = 2.07$

The df $= n - 2 = 15 - 2 = 13$

From the table t0.05, $r = 13 = 2.16$.

Thus $t = -2.07 < 2.16$. hence correlation of is not significant to warrant an existence of correlation in the population.

Example: What is the least size of a sample that is appropriated to conclude that a correlation coefficient of 0.32 is significantly greater than 0 and 0.05 level?

Solution: Let the sample size for t0.05 is ' n ', which is least.

Using One-sided test of ' t ' –distribution at 0.05 level, $\frac{0.32\sqrt{n-2}}{\sqrt{1-(0.32)^2}}$

$= t_{0.95}$ for $n - 2$ degree of freedom

For df $= \infty$, $t_{0.95} = 1.64$ hence $n = 25.6 \approx 26$

For $n = 26$, df $= n - 2 = 26 - 2 = 24$, $t_{0.95} = 1.71$

$$t = \frac{0.32\sqrt{26-2}}{\sqrt{1-(0.32)^2}} = 1.65$$

For $n = 27$, df $= 27 - 2 = 25$, hence $t_{0.95} = 1.71$

$$t = \frac{0.32\sqrt{27-2}}{\sqrt{1-(0.32)^2}} = 1.69$$

For $n = 28$, df $= 28 - 2 = 26$, hence $t_{0.95} = 1.71$

$$t = \frac{0.32\sqrt{28-2}}{\sqrt{1-(0.32)^2}} = 1.72$$

Then the minimum sample size is $n = 28$.

Example: To study the correlation between stature of father and the stature of son, a sample of size 1600, is taken from the population of fathers and sons. The sample study gives the correlation between the two to be 0.80. Within what limits does it hold true for the population?2

Solution:

$$\text{The } S.\ E_r = \frac{1-r^2}{\sqrt{n}}$$

$r = 0.8,\ n = 1600$

$$S.\ E_r = \frac{1-(0.8)^2}{\sqrt{1600}} = \frac{1-0.64}{40} = 0.009$$

The correlation in the population probability lies between = $r \pm 3$ *S. E.* (when the sample is random and simple)

$R = S \pm S.\ E.$

$= 0.8 \pm 3 \times (0.009)$

$= (0.8 - 0.027,\ 0.8 + 0.027)$

$= (0.773,\ 0.827)$

SAMPLING THEORY OF REGRESSION

The regression equation of a normally distributed population is $y = a + bx$.

Let the regression equation of a sample drawn from it be

$y \ = a + dx.$

All you have done is, replaced the intercept (a) by c and the slope (b) by d.

To find *S. E.* of regression coefficient of y on x i.e.

$$S.\ E_{byx} \text{ use} \frac{\sigma x\sqrt{1-r^2}}{\sigma x\sqrt{n}}$$

To find *S. E.* of regressiojn coefficient of x on y i.e.

$$S.\ E_{bxy} \text{ use} \frac{\sigma x\sqrt{1-r^2}}{\sigma x\sqrt{n}}$$

Also *S. E.* of regression estimate of y on

$$x \text{ or } S.\ E_{xy} = \sigma x\sqrt{1-r^2}$$

S. E. of regression estimate of x on y or $S.\ E_{yx} = \sigma y\sqrt{1-r^2}$

To test $b = c$ use t = width $df = n - 2$.

This can be used to find confidence intervals for population regression coefficient from sample values.

Example: Find the regression coefficient of the prices of city A over the prices of city B given that:

	A	*B*
Average price per kg	120	130
Standard deviation	4	5

Coefficient of correlation 0.6

$n = 100$

Solution: Now regression coefficient of prices of city *A* (*x*) over the prices of city *B*.

$$b_{xy} = r.\frac{\sigma x}{\sigma y} = 0.6\left(\frac{4}{5}\right) = 0.48$$

Thus standard error of regression coefficient is

$$S.Eb_{xy} = \frac{\sigma y\sqrt{1-r^2}}{\sigma y\sqrt{n}} = \frac{4\sqrt{1-(0.6)^2}}{5\sqrt{100}} = 0.064$$

Thus the regression coefficient of prices of the city *A* over the prices of city *B* is 0.48 and its *S.E.* is 0.064.

Example: For a certain group of adults, the coefficient of correlation between height and weight is 0.7. Standard deviations of height and weights are 2 inches and 10 lb respectively and the means of heights and weights for the entire group are 70 inches and 130 lbs respectively. Find out the best estimate of weight of a member who is 65 inches tall. Assign limits to this estimate, within which all probability has actual weight would lie.

Solution: Weight (y) and height (x)

Regression of y on x is given by $y - \bar{y} = r.\frac{\sigma x}{\sigma y}(x - \bar{x})$

$\bar{y} = 130,\ \bar{x} = 70, \sigma y = 10,\ \sigma x = 2,\ r = 0.7$

$$y - 130 = 0.7\left(\frac{10}{2}\right)(x - 70)$$

$y - 130 = 3.5x - 245$ or $\quad y = 3.5x - 115$

When $x = 65$, $y = 3.5(65) - 115$

$y = 112.51b$

The standard estimate of y on x or $S.\ E_{yx}$ is given by

$$S.\ E_{yx} = \sigma y\sqrt{1-r^2} = 10\sqrt{1-(0.7)^2} = 7.411b$$

Thus the best estimate of weight of an member whose weight is 112.5 lb and height 65 inches cannot deviate from the actual weight by more than 3 *S. E.*

The estimate of all probabilities of his weight lies between

= 112.5 ± 3 (7.41)

= (112.5 – 22.23, 112.5 + 22.23)

= (90. 27 lb, 134.73 lb)

Area under standard normal curve (Z – score)

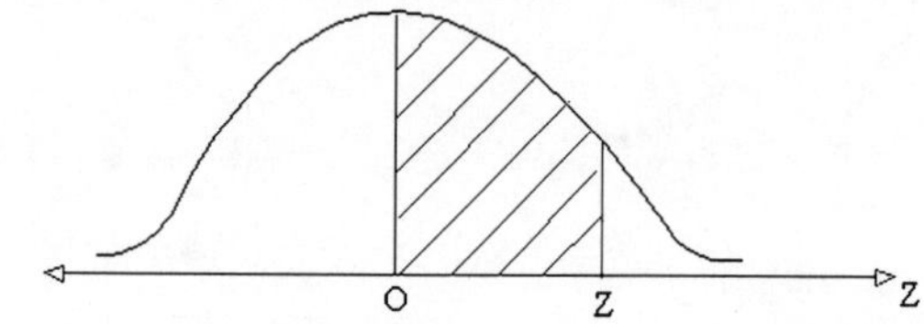

8

Graphic Method of Representation

We have discussed how to condense the mass of data by the method of classification and tabulation. It is not always easy for a layman to understand figures, nor is it is interesting for him.

Apart from that too many figures are often confusing. One of the most convincing and appealing ways in which statistical results may be represented is through graphs and diagrams. It is for this reason that diagrams are often used by businessmen, newspapers, magazines, journals, government agencies and also for advertising and educating people.

COMPARISON BETWEEN TABULAR AND DIAGRAMMATIC PRESENTATION

- Diagrams and Graphs are meant for a lay man.
- Tables are meant for statisticians for the purpose of further analysis.
- Diagrams give only an approximate idea.
- Tables contain precise figures. Exact values can be read from tables.
- Diagrams can be more easily compared, and can be interpreted by a layman.
- Comparison and interpretations of tables can only be done by statisticians and it is a difficult task.
- Diagrams and graphs cannot present much information.
- Tables can present more information.
- Diagrams are more attractive and have a visual appeal.
- Tables are dry for a layman (may be attractive to a statistician.)

William play fair - 1759 - 1823 said in his 'Commercial and political Atlas of 1801' that "Information take days through data presented in tables, but can be obtained in minutes through diagrams."

Cold figures are uninspiring to most people. Diagrams help us to see the pattern and shape of any complex idea, just as a map gives a bird's eye view of wide sketch of a country, so diagrams help us to visualize the whole meaning of a numerical complex at single glance. Diagrams register a meaningful impression almost before you think........." (Moroney).

DIFFERENCE BETWEEN DIAGRAMS AND GRAPHS

There is no clear-cut line of demarcation between a diagram and a graph yet–

- A graph needs a graph paper but a diagram can be drawn on a plain paper. In the technical way we can say that a graph is a mathematical relation between two variables. This however is not the case of a diagram.
- As diagrams are attractive to look at, they are used for publicity and propaganda. Graphs on the other hand are more useful to statisticians and research workers for the purpose of further analysis.
- For representing frequency distribution, diagrams are rarely used when compared with graphs. For example, for the time series graphs are more appropriate than diagrams.

GENERAL PRINCIPLES OF CONSTRUCTING DIAGRAMS

- The diagrams should be simple.
- Each diagram must be given a clear, concise and suitable title without damaging clarity.
- A proper proportion between height and width must be maintained in order to avoid an unpleasant look.
- Select a proper scale; it should be in even numbers or in multiples of five or ten. e.g. 25,50, 75 or 10, 20, 30, 40.... etc. But no fixed rule.
- In order to clear certain points, always put footnotes.
- An index, explaining different lines, shades and colors should be given.
- Diagrams should be absolutely neat and clean.
  - "The important point that must be borne in mind at all times that the pictorial representation chosen for any situation must depict the true relationship and point out the proper conclusion. Above all the chart must be honest."…. C. W. LOWE.

BAR DIAGRAMS

Simple 'Bar diagram'

It represents only one variable. For example sales, production, population figures etc. for various years may be shown by simple bar charts.

Since these are of the same width and vary only in heights (or lengths), it becomes very easy for readers to study the relationship.

Simple bar diagrams are very popular in practice. A bar chart can be either vertical or horizontal; vertical bars are more popular.

Illustration

The following table gives the birth rate per thousand of different countries over a certain period of time.

Country	Birth rate	Country	Birth rate
India	33	China	40
Germany	15	New Zealand	30
U. K.	20	Sweden	15

Represent the above data by a suitable diagram.

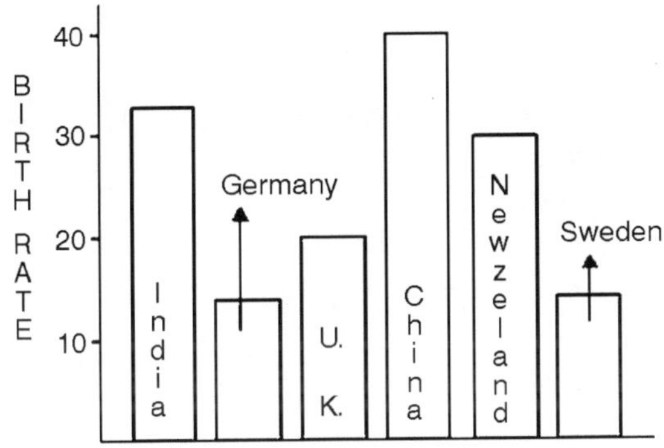

Fig. Birth Rate Per Thousan of Different Countries

Comparing the size of bars, you can easily see that China's birth rate is the highest while Germany and Sweden equal in the lowest positions. Such diagrams are also known as component bar diagrams.

Sub - divided Bar Diagram

While constructing such a diagram, the various components in each bar should be kept in the same order.

A common and helpful arrangement is that of presenting each bar in the order of magnitude with the largest component at the bottom and the smallest at the top.

The components are shown with different shades or colors with a proper index.

Illustration

During 1968 - 71, the number of students in University ' X ' are as follows. Represent the data by a similar diagram.

Year	Arts	Science	Law	Total
1968 - 69	20,000	10,000	5,000	35,000
1969 - 70	26,000	9,000	7,000	42,000
1970 - 71	31,000	9,500	7,500	48,000

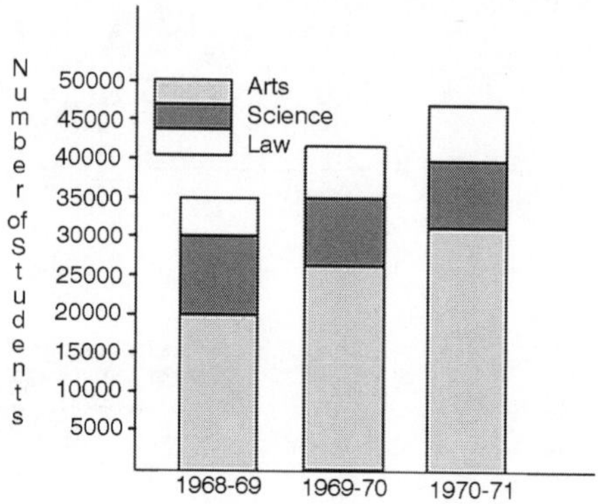

Multiple Bar Diagram

This method can be used for data which is made up of two or more components. In this method the components are shown as separate adjoining bars. The height of each bar represents the actual value of the component. The components are shown by different shades or colors. Where changes in actual values of component figures only are required, multiple bar charts are used.

Illustration

The table below gives data relating to the exports and imports of a certain country X (in thousands of dollars) during the four years ending in 1930 - 31.

Year	Export	Import
1927 - 28	319	250
1928 - 29	339	263
1929 - 30	345	258
1930 - 31	308	206

Represent the data by a suitable diagram

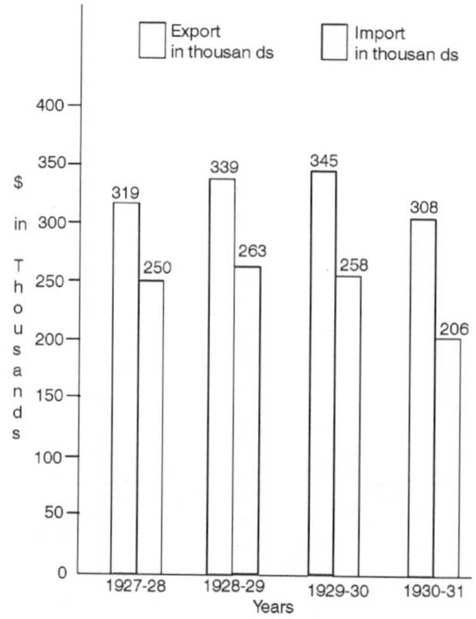

Deviation Bar Charts

Deviation bars are used to represent net quantities - excess or deficit i.e. net profit, net loss, net exports or imports, swings in voting etc. Such bars have both positive and negative values. Positive values lie above the base line and negative values lie below it.

Illustration

Years	*Sales*	*Net profits*
1985 - 86	10%	50%
1986 - 87	14%	–20
1987 - 88	12%	–10%

Present the above data by a suitable diagram showing the sales and net profits of private industrial companies.

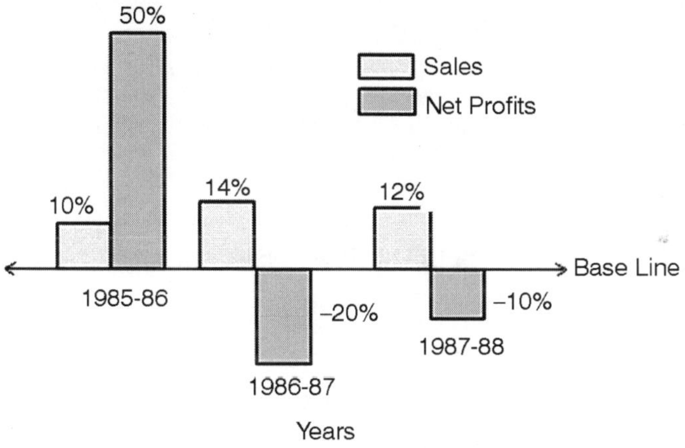

PIE CHART

- Geometrically it can be seen that the area of a sector of a circle taken radially, is proportional to the angle at its centre. It is therefore sufficient to draw angles at the centre, proportional to the original figures. This will make the areas of the sector proportional to the basic figures.

For example, let the total be 1000 and one of the component be 200, then the angle will be

$$\left(\frac{200}{1000}\right)\times 360^\circ = 72^\circ$$

In general, angle of sector at the centre corresponding to a component

$$= \left(\frac{\text{Component}}{\text{Total}}\right)\times 360^\circ$$

- When a statistical phenomenon is composed of different components which are numerous, bar charts are not suitable to represent them because, under this situation, they become very complex and their visual impressions are questioned. A pie diagram is suitable for such situations. It is a circular diagram which is a circle (pie) divided by the radii, into sectors (like slices of a cake or pie). The area of a sector is proportional to the size of each component.
- As an example consider the yearly expenditure of a Mr. Ted, a college undergraduate.

Tuition fees	\$ 6000
Books and lab.	\$ 2000
Clothes/cleaning	\$ 2000
Room and boarding	\$ 12000
Transportation	\$ 3000
Insurance	\$ 1000
Sundry expenses	\$ 4000
Total expenditure	= \$ 30000

Now as explained above, we calculate the angles corresponding to various items (components).

$$\text{Tuition fees} = \frac{6000}{30000} \times 360° = 72°$$

$$\text{Book and lab} = \frac{2000}{30000} \times 360° = 24°$$

$$\text{Clothes/ cleaning} = \frac{2000}{30000} \times 360° = 24°$$

$$\text{Room and boarding} = \frac{12000}{30000} \times 360° = 144°$$

$$\text{Transportation} = \frac{3000}{30000} \times 360° = 36°$$

$$\text{Insurance} = \frac{1000}{30000} \times 360° = 12°$$

$$\text{Sundry expenses} = \frac{4000}{30000} \times 360° = 48°$$

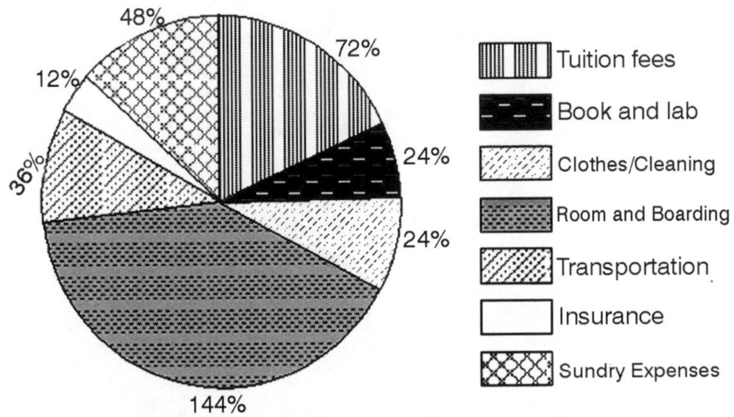

Uses:– A pie diagram is useful when we want to show relative positions (proportions) of the figures which make the total. It is also useful when the components are many in number.

Note:– The sectors of the circle (i.e. of a pie diagram) are ordered from largest to the smallest for easier interpretation of the data and they must be drawn in the counter-clockwise direction.

GRAPHS

A graph is a visual representation of data by a continuous curve on a squared (graph) paper. Like diagrams, graphs are also attractive, and eye-catching, giving a bird's eye-view of data and revealing their inner pattern.

Graphs of Frequency Distributions:–

The methods used to represent a grouped data are:-

- Histogram
- Frequency Polygon
- Frequency Curve
- Ogive or Cumulative Frequency Curve

Histogram

It is defined as a pictorial representation of a grouped frequency distribution by means of adjacent rectangles, whose areas are proportional to the frequencies.

To construct a Histogram, the class intervals are plotted along the x-axis and corresponding frequencies are plotted along the y - axis. The rectangles are constructed such that the height of each rectangle is proportional to the frequency of the that class and width is equal to the length of the class. If all the classes have equal width, then all the rectangles stand on the equal width. In case of classes having unequal widths, rectangles too stand on unequal widths (bases). For open-classes, Histogram is constructed after making certain assumptions. As the rectangles are adjacent leaving no gaps, the class-intervals become of the inclusive type, adjustment is necessary for end points only.

For example, in a book sale, you want to determine which books were most popular, the high priced books, the low priced books, books most neglected etc. Let us say you sold a total 31 books at this book-fair at the following prices.

$....2, $ 1, $ 2, $ 2, $ 3, $ 5, $ 6, $ 17, $ 17, $ 7, $ 15, $ 7, $ 7, $ 18, $ 8, $ 10, $ 10, $ 9, $ 13, $ 11, $ 12, $ 12, $ 12, $ 14, $ 16, $ 18, $ 20, $ 24, $ 21, $ 22, $ 25.

The books are ranging from $1 to $25. Divide this range into number of groups, class intervals. Typically, there should not be fewer than 5 and more than 20 class-intervals are best for a frequency Histogram.

Our first class-interval includes the lowest price of the data and, the last-interval of course includes, the highest price. Also make sure that overlapping is avoided, so that, no one price falls into two class-intervals. For example you have class intervals as 0 – 5, 5 – 10, 10 – 15 and so on, then the price $10 falls in both 5-10 and 10-15. Instead if we use $1–$5, $6 = $10, the class-intervals will be mutually exclusive.

Therefore now we have distribution of books at a book-fair

Class-interval	Frequency
$ 1- $ 5	6
$6 - $10	8
$11 - $15	10
$16 - $20	3
$21 - $25	4
Total	$n = \Sigma fi = 31$

Note that each class-interval is of equal width i.e. $5 inclusive. Now we draw the frequency Histogram as under.

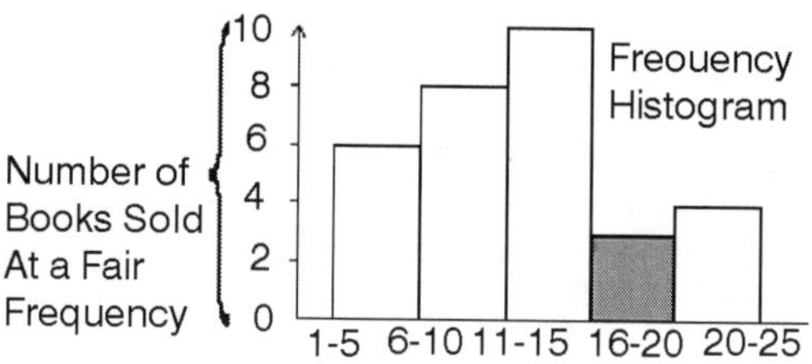

Relative Frequency Histogram

It uses the same data. The only difference is that it compares each class-interval with the total number of items i.e. instead of the frequency of each class-interval, their relative frequencies are used. Naturally the vertical axis (i.e. y-axis) uses the relative frequencies in places of frequencies.

In the above case we have

Class-interval	Frequency	Relative frequency
$ 1 - $ 5	6	6/31
$ 6 - $10	8	8/31
$11 - $15	10	10/31

\$16 - \$20	3	3/31
\$21 - \$25	4	4/31

The Histogram is same as in above case.

Construction of Histogram when Class-intervals are Unequal

In a Histogram, a rectangle is proportional to the frequency of the concern class-interval. Naturally, if the class-intervals are of unequal widths, we have to adjust the heights of the rectangle accordingly.

We know that the area of a rectangle = l. h. Now suppose the width (l) of a class is double that of a normal class interval, its height and thus the corresponding frequency must be halved. After this precaution has been taken, the construction of the Histogram of classes of unequal intervals is the same as before.

Note:– The smallest class-interval should be assumed to be " NORMAL "

Illustration:– Represent the following data by means of Histogram.

Classes:	11-14	16-19	21-24	26-29	31-39	41-59	61-79
Frequencies:	7	19	27	15	12	12	8

Solution: Note that class-intervals are unequal and also they are of inclusive type.

We have to make them equal and of the exclusive type.

Correct factor = (16 – 14)/ 2 = 1. Using it we have

Classes:	10-15	15-20	20-25	25-30	30-40	40-60	60-80
Frequencies:	7	19	27	15	12	12	8
Adjusted Heights: (Frequencies)	7	19	27	15	12/2 = 6	12/4 = 3	12/4 = 3

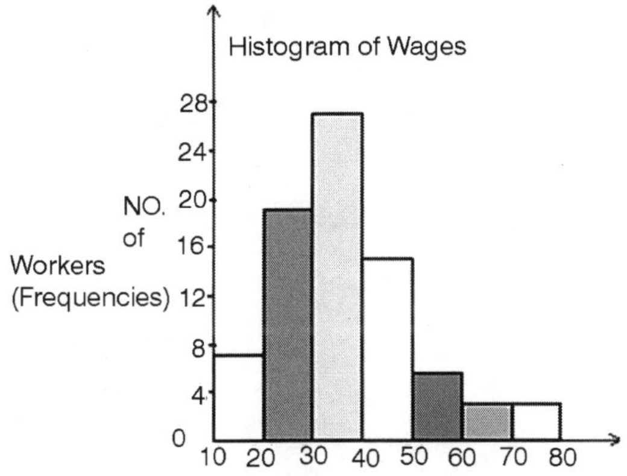

Frequency Polygon

Here the frequencies are plotted against the mid-points of the class-intervals and the points thus obtained are joined by line segments.

Example:

Height in cm.	150-154	154-158	158-162	162-166	166-170
No. of children	10	15	20	12	8

The polygon is closed at the base by extending it on both its sides (ends) to the midpoints of two hypothetical classes, at the extremes of the distribution, with zero frequencies.

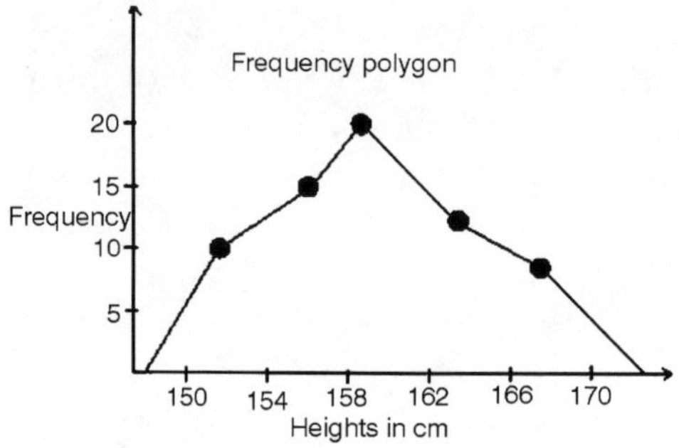

On comparing the Histogram and a frequency polygon, you will notice that, in frequency polygons the points replace the bars (rectangles). Also, when several distributions are to be compared on the same graph paper, frequency polygons are better than Histograms.

Frequency Distribution (Curve)

Frequency distribution curves are like frequency polygons. In frequency distribution, instead of using straight line segments, a smooth curve is used to connect the points. The frequency curve for the above data is shown as:

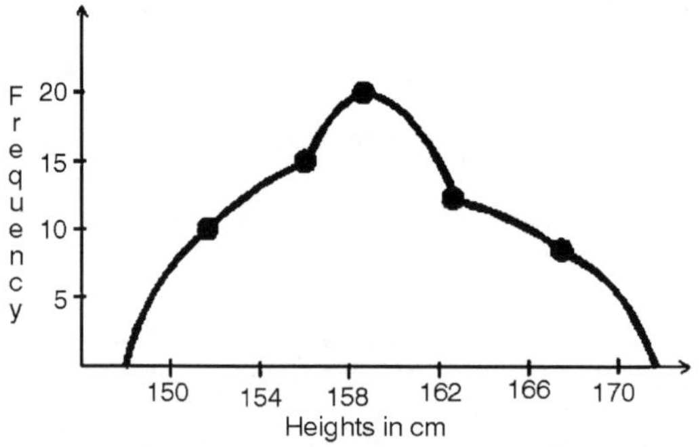

Shape of Distribution Curves:- We have seen what a distribution curve looks like. There are four types of distribution curves. (i) Symmetrical or bell-shaped (ii) Moderately symmetrical or skew (iii) J-shaped and (iv) U-shaped. We shall only study the first two.

Symmetrical distribution

As the name suggests, if the distribution is symmetrical, the curve rises gradually, reaches a maximum then falls equally gradually. The curve looks like a bell. This curve is symmetrical about the maximum frequency. For a perfectly symmetrical distribution, the mean, the mode and the median all coincide. This curve displays perfect symmetry, that is, its left half is the mirror image of the other right half. A bell-shaped or mound-shaped curve is also known as the normal curve, giving it special properties. This is an ideal situation and therefore, rarely found in practice.

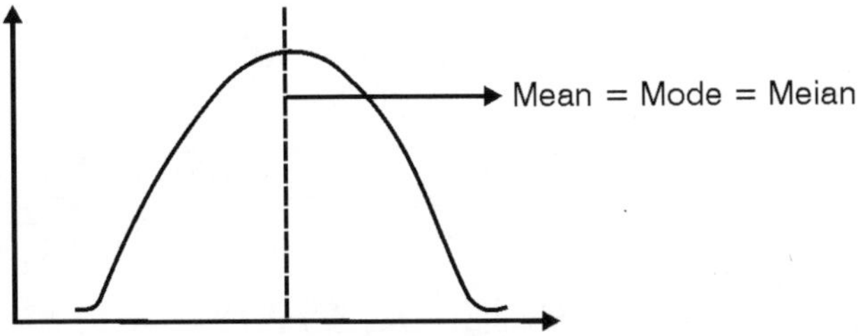

Moderately symmetrical or Skew

The curve is symmetrical but only moderately. If it rises rapidly, reaches a maximum and then falls slowly, it is a called a positively skewed curve. If it rises slowly, reaches a maximum and then falls rapidly, it is called a "negatively skewed curve". For these curves; the mean, the median and the mode do not coincide. In much of the economic and social phenomenon, we come across such curves.

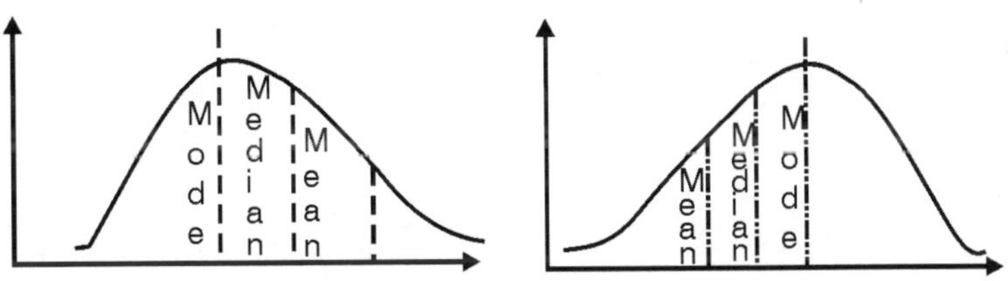

Ogives or Cumulative Frequency Curves

When frequencies are added, they are called cumulative frequencies. The curve obtained by plotting cumulating frequencies is called a cumulative frequency curve or an ogive (pronounced ojive).

To construct an Ogive:-

- Add up the progressive totals of frequencies, class by class, to get the cumulative frequencies.
- Plot classes on the horizontal (x-axis) and cumulative frequencies on the vertical (y-axis).
- Join the points by a smooth curve. Note that Ogives start at (i) zero on the vertical axis, and (ii) outside class limit of the last class. In most of the cases it looks like 'S'. Note that cumulative frequencies are plotted against the 'limits' of the classes to which they refer.
  - *Less than Ogive*:- To plot a less than ogive, the data is arranged

in ascending order of magnitude and the frequencies are cumulated starting from the top. It starts from zero on the y-axis and the lower limit of the lowest class interval on the x-axis.

– *Greater than Ogive*:- To plot this ogive, the data are arranged in the ascending order of magnitude and frequencies are cumulated from the bottom. This curve ends at zero on the the y-axis and the upper limit of the highest class interval on the x-axis.

Illustrations

On a graph paper, draw the two ogives for the data given below of the I.Q. of 160 students.

Class -intervals:	60-70	70-80	80-90	90-100	100-110
No. of students:	2	7	12	28	42

110 - 120	120 - 130	130 - 140	140 - 150	150 - 160
36	18	10	4	1

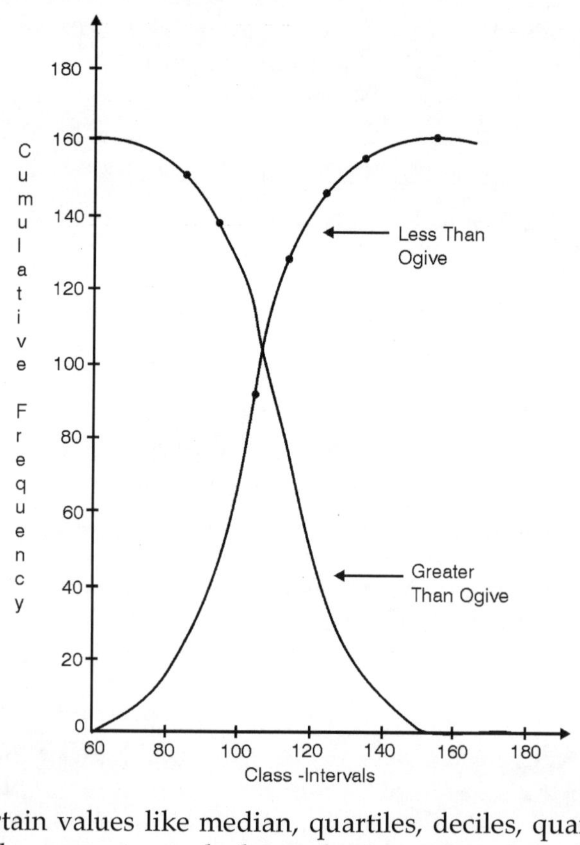

Uses:- Certain values like median, quartiles, deciles, quartile deviation, coefficient of skewness etc. can be located using ogives. it can be used to find the percentage of items having values less than or greater than certain value. Ogives are helpful in the comparison of the two distributions.

J-Shaped Curve

These curves are so called, as they have the shape of a 'J' or a 'U'. The distributions are extremely asymmetrical.

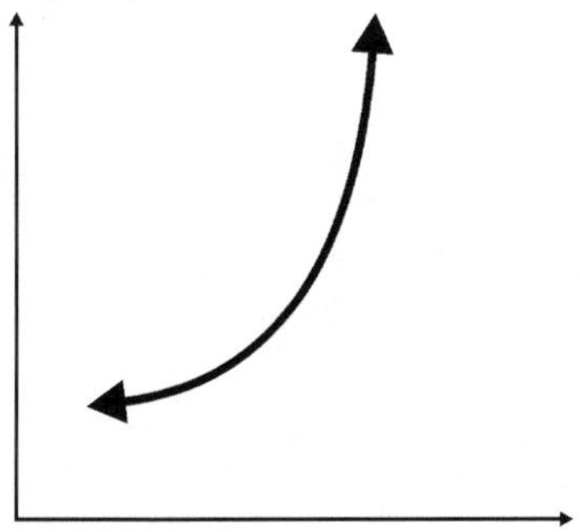

Biomodal Curve

Unlike a normal curve (symmetric distribution), a bimodal curve has two peaks or humps.

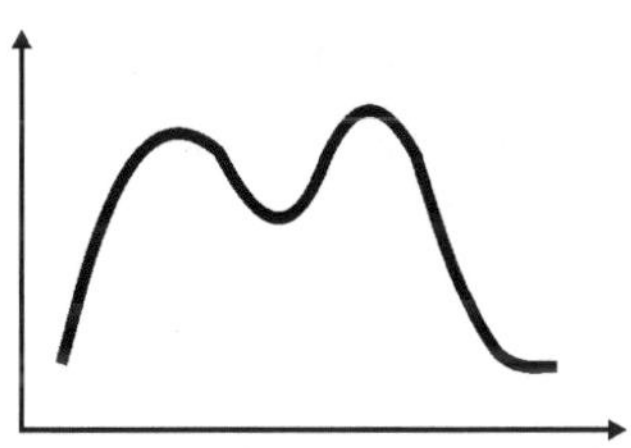

U-Shaped Curve

When a distribution is highly asymmetric we get this type of curve (U-type). U-Shaped curve exhibits the maximum frequencies at the ends of the range and the minimum towards the centre.

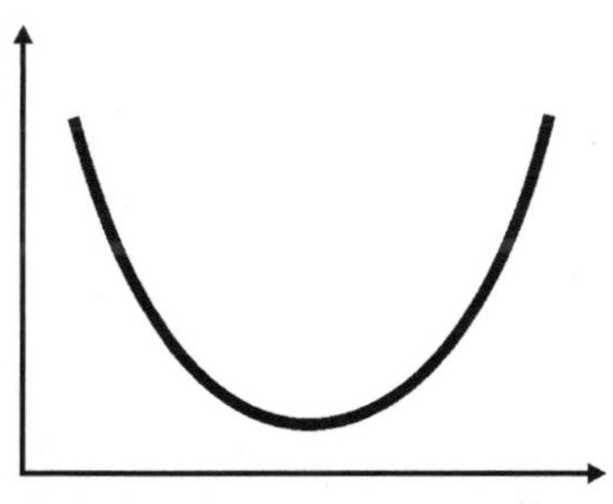

Box and Whiskers

It is one step further to stem-and-leaf. It displays a number of statistics like, median, lower quartile (Q1), upper quartile (Q3), Inter-quartile range

(IQR). It tells us about the symmetry of the distribution and also gives us the idea about the highest and the lowest values.

Example::

Verbal GMAT scores of 12 students 10, 22, 24, 27, 31, 33, 39, 40, 42, 43, 44, 45

Solution: The scores is arranged in the ascending order. 10, 22, 24, 27, 31, 33, 39, 40, 42, 43, 44, 45

- Since n = 12 (total items)

The two middle scores are $\frac{12+2}{2}$ = 6th and $\frac{12}{2}$ = 7th.

i.e. 33 and 39 respectively.

Therefore the average of the two is the median

i.e. Median $=\frac{1}{2}[33+39]=\frac{1}{2}[72]=36$

- The quartile (Q1) is the median of the bottom half. i.e. 25th percentile.

Thus Q_1 = N/4 = 3rd score = 24

- The upper quartile (Q3) is the median of the top half. i.e. 75th percentile.

Thus Now the box-plot is constructed as follows:-

- The line inside the box indicates the median.
- The left side of this box indicates the lower quartile (Q1).
- The right side of this box indicates the upper quartile (Q3).
- A straight line is then drawn from the lowest value of this distribution through the box to the highest value of this distribution. This horizontal straight line is called the "Whiskers".

Then the above GMAT score in box-plot will look like this:

0 10 20 30 40 50 60

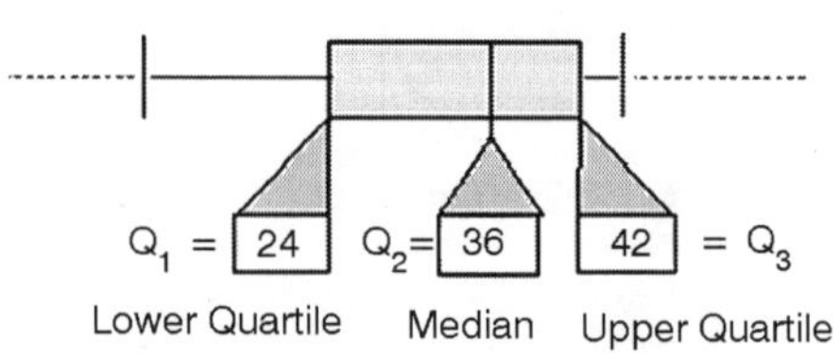

GRAPHICAL METHOD

A histogram is a graphical method of representing a probability distribution over an interval of the real number line. First, we discuss the formal representation of a histogram and follow this up with an informal discussion.

We assume that one has n data points from a particular probability distribution, $x_1 .....x_n$ over an interval [a, b]. To obtain histograms, we partition the interval [a, b] into m equally sized intervals called bins. Bin j is then: $B_j = [a + \frac{(b-a).(j-1)}{m},,, a + \frac{(b-a).j}{m}$ *for* j=1,....m

The endpoints a and b are usually taken to be the minimum and maximum of the data set. The number of data points in bin j is n_j. Of course it will turn out that

$$\sum_{1}^{j} n_j = n$$

Essentially, a histogram is the simplest non-parametric density estimator and is the that is used by most researchers.

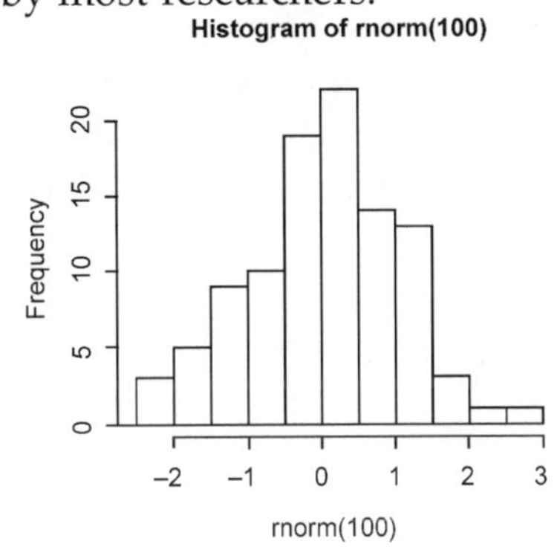

The figure depicts a histogram of 100 pseudo random numbers from a normal distribution with a mean of zero and standard deviation of one:

This histogram is constructed by dividing the interval covered by the data values into equal sub-intervals called bins. Each time a data point falls into a particular bin, then the bin is incremented by 1. The choice of endpoints and the choice of the number of sub-intervals can have marked effects on the shape of the histogram. Data can look bimodal when represented with a particular number of bins and bin width, but can appear uni-modal when represented with, for example, less bins and a wider bin width:

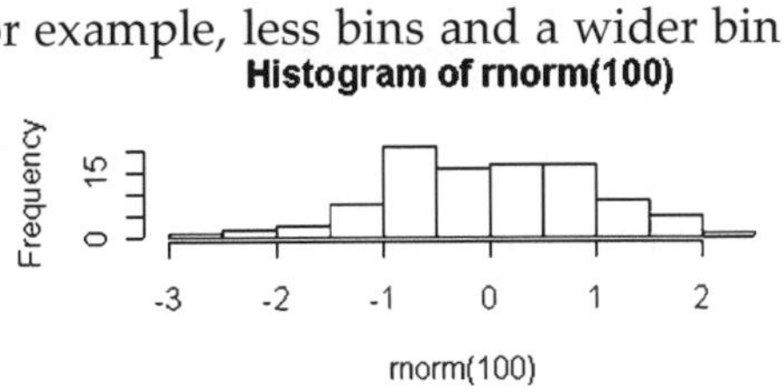

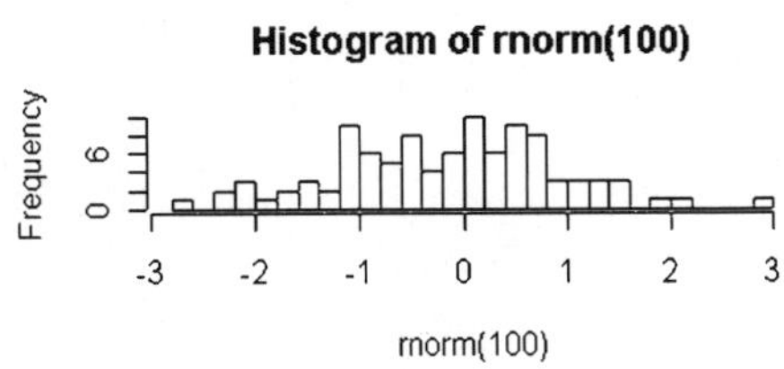

Thus, histograms have a few drawbacks: 1) they are not smooth, 2) the depend greatly on the end points of the bins, and 3) they depend on the width of the bins. These first two problems can be addressed by a histogram smoothing technique called "kernel density estimation". Before we look at kernel density estimation, we want to illustrate a method for simulating correlated bivariate and multivariate data sets. We will use a simulated data set with a known population correlation to illustrate kernel density estimation in two dimensions.

The effect is a rough approximation of the frequency distribution of the data. The groups of data are called *classes*, and in the context of a histogram they are known as *bins*, because one can think of them as containers that accumulate data and "fill up" at a rate equal to the frequency of that data class. Consider the exam scores of a group of students. By defining data classes each spanning an interval of 10 points and counting the number of scores in each data class, a frequency table can be constructed as in the following example:

Table. Frequency Table

Group	Count
0 - 9	1
10 - 19	2
20 - 29	3
30 - 39	4
40 - 49	5
50 - 59	4
60 - 69	3
70 - 79	2
80 - 89	2
90 - 99	1

To construct the histogram, groups are plotted on the x axis and their frequencies on the y axis. The following is a histogram of the data in the above frequency table.

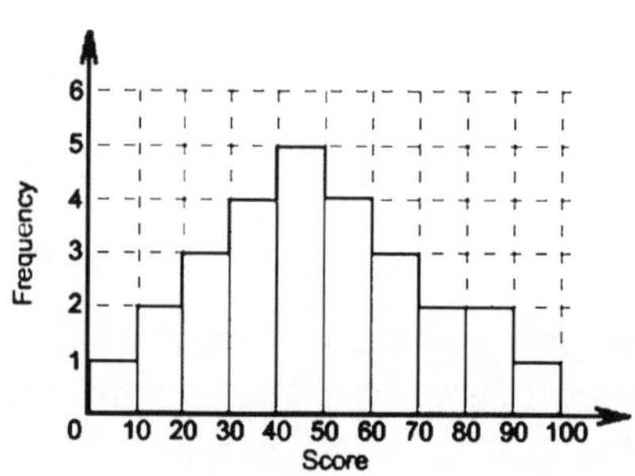

Fig. Histogram

Information Conveyed by Histograms

Histograms are useful data summaries that convey the following information:

- The general shape of the frequency distribution (normal, chi-square, etc.)
- Symmetry of the distribution and whether it is skewed
- Modality - unimodal, bimodal, or multimodal

The histogram of the frequency distribution can be converted to a probability distribution by dividing the tally in each group by the total number of data points to give the relative frequency.

The shape of the distribution conveys important information such as the probability distribution of the data. In cases in which the distribution is known, a histogram that does not fit the distribution may provide clues about a process and measurement problem.

For example, a histogram that shows a higher than normal frequency in bins near one end and then a sharp drop-off may indicate that the observer is "helping" the results by classifying extreme data in the less extreme group.

BIN WIDTH

The shape of the histogram sometimes is particularly sensitive to the number of bins. If the bins are too wide, important information might get omitted. For example, the data may be bimodal but this characteristic may not be evident if the bins are too wide.

On the other hand, if the bins are too narrow, what may appear to be meaningful information really may be due to random variations that show up because of the small number of data points in a bin.

To determine whether the bin width is set to an appropriate size, different bin widths should be used and the results compared to determine the sensitivity of the histogram shape with respect to bin size.

Bin widths typically are selected so that there are between 5 and 20 groups of data, but the appropriate number depends on the situation.

HISTOGRAMS AND BOXPLOTS

The histogram provides a graphical summary of the shape of the data's distribution. It often is used in combination with other statistical summaries such as the boxplot, which conveys the median, quartiles, and range of the data.

Purpose of A Histogram

A histogram is used to graphically summarize and display the distribution of a process data set.

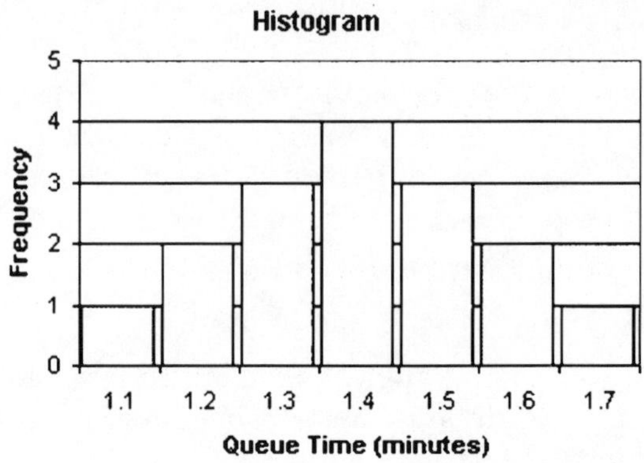

Fig. Sample Bar Chart Depiction

How To Construct A Histogram

A histogram can be constructed by segmenting the range of the data into equal sized bins (also called segments, groups or classes). For example, if your data ranges from 1.1 to 1.8, you could have equal bins of 0.1 consisting of 1 to 1.1, 1.2 to 1.3, 1.3 to 1.4, and so on.

The vertical axis of the histogram is labeled Frequency (the number of counts for each bin), and the horizontal axis of the histogram is labeled with the range of your response variable.

You then determine the number of data points that reside within each bin and construct the histogram. The bins size can be defined by the user, by some common rule, or by software methods.

What Questions The Histogram Answers

- What is the most common system response?
- What distribution (centre, variation and shape) does the data have?
- Does the data look symmetric or is it skewed to the left or right?
- Does the data contain outliers?

PROBABILITY

A Short History of Probability

"A gambler's dispute in 1654 led to the creation of a mathematical theory of probability by two famous French mathematicians, Blaise Pascal and Pierre de Fermat. Antoine Gombaud, Chevalier de Méré, a French nobleman with an interest in gaming and gambling questions, called Pascal's attention to an apparent contradiction concerning a popular dice game. The game consisted in throwing a pair of dice 24 times; the problem was to decide whether or not to bet even money on the occurrence of at least one "double six" during the

24 throws. A seemingly well-established gambling rule led de Méré to believe that betting on a double six in 24 throws would be profitable, but his own calculations indicated just the opposite.

This problem and others posed by de Méré led to an exchange of letters between Pascal and Fermat in which the fundamental principles of probability theory were formulated for the first time. Although a few special problems on games of chance had been solved by some Italian mathematicians in the 15th and 16th centuries, no general theory was developed before this famous correspondence. The Dutch scientist Christian Huygens, a teacher of Leibniz, learned of this correspondence and shortly thereafter published the first book on probability; entitled *De Ratiociniis in Ludo Aleae,* it was a treatise on problems associated with gambling. Because of the inherent appeal of games of chance, probability theory soon became popular, and the subject developed rapidly during the 18th century. The major contributors during this period were Jakob Bernoulli and Abraham de Moivre.

In 1812 Pierre de Laplace introduced a host of new ideas and mathematical techniques in his book, *Théorie Analytique des Probabilités*. Before Laplace, probability theory was solely concerned with developing a mathematical analysis of games of chance. Laplace applied probabilistic ideas to many scientific and practical problems. The theory of errors, actuarial mathematics, and statistical mechanics are examples of some of the important applications of probability theory developed in the l9th century.

Like so many other branches of mathematics, the development of probability theory has been stimulated by the variety of its applications. Conversely, each advance in the theory has enlarged the scope of its influence. Mathematical statistics is one important branch of applied probability; other applications occur in such widely different fields as genetics, psychology, economics, and engineering. Many workers have contributed to the theory since Laplace's time; among the most important are Chebyshev, Markov, von Mises, and Kolmogorov. One of the difficulties in developing a mathematical theory of probability has been to arrive at a definition of probability that is precise enough for use in mathematics, yet comprehensive enough to be applicable to a wide range of phenomena.

The search for a widely acceptable definition took nearly three centuries and was marked by much controversy. The matter was finally resolved in the 20th century by treating probability theory on an axiomatic basis. In 1933 a monograph by a Russian mathematician A. Kolmogorov outlined an axiomatic approach that forms the basis for the modern theory. Since then the ideas have been refined somewhat and probability theory is now part of a more general discipline known as measure theory."

Introductory Note

The term Probability, as the name suggests, refers to a calculation, a mathematical estimate concerning the possibility of a particular outcome in a situation where there are a number of different possible outcomes. If, for example, we know that in a certain situation (e.g., a roll of the dice) there is a determined number of possible outcomes (e.g., six possible faces of the die), we can calculate the probability of a particular outcome or of a particular sequence of outcomes if the event is repeated.

For example, with a normal die in a fair roll, there is a 1 in 6 chance of any particular face of the die showing on the top (since there are six surfaces on the cube); in a fair toss of a normal coin there is a 1 in 2 chance of a head appearing on top, a 1 in 2 chance of a tail appearing on top, and a 2 in 2 chance of a head or a tail appearing on top.

It is important to stress at the outset that probability is a *theoretical* calculation of the likelihood of a particular outcome. Thus, it is based, not upon observation of actual events (e.g., listing the results from several tosses of the coin) but on calculations which are based on certain assumptions (e.g., that the coin or die toss is fair, that there are no hidden factors, like cheating, influencing the outcome).

Because the probability of an outcome is a theoretical calculation, knowing the probability does not mean that we can always predict a particular outcome with certainty (please understand this very important point). Often the result of a particular event or series of events will not match the theoretical probabilities. For example, in a sequence of ten coin tosses, theory tells us that the most probable result will be 5 outcomes with heads on top and 5 outcomes with tails on top. But that calculation does not mean that, if we observe an actual 10-toss sequence, we will always get that most probable result.

Checking probabilities (that is, the theoretical calculations) against the observed outcomes of a real event is, as we shall see, an essential part of the study of probability and statistics (and a central exercise in this module). But always keep in mind this opening point: the probability of an event is a theoretical calculation; the observed frequency with which an event actually occurs is something different: the first is based upon mathematical analysis of an event (independent of observation); the second is based upon an actual experiment.

Probability theory has a number of extremely important uses. A simple but powerful application is its ability to assist us in establishing the mathematical likelihood of a particular outcome and thus to advise ourselves of the prudence of a certain action (e.g., betting). For instance, to take a very simple example, in a fair toss of a coin, theory indicates that the probability of the coin landing with heads on top is 50 per cent, with tails on top 50 per cent, and with either heads of tails on top 100 per cent. In a bet on the result of a coin toss, therefore, one would be unwise to wager, say, ten dollars that a head would appear against your opponent's bet of two dollars that a tail would appear. In the course of this module, we will become more familiar with a number of important applications of probability theory.

EXPRESSING PROBABILITY MATHEMATICALLY

We can express the probability of an event mathematically in a number of ways, but the most common is as a decimal between 1 and 0. Thus, a probability of 1 ($p = 1$) is certainty that the event will occur. A probability of 0 ($p = 0$) is certainty that event will not occur. Thus, all probabilities for an event are expressed as a decimal between 0 and 1.

The probability that a single fair coin toss will produce a head on top is expressed as follows: $p =.5$. This we might also express as meaning that the probability is 5 out of 10 or 50 per cent. The decimal notation is the most common and will be standard throughout the rest of this workbook.

In the same way, if $p =.75$, that means that the outcome will theoretically occur 75 times out of 100; if $p =.234$, that means that the outcome will theoretically occur 234 times out of 1000; if $p =.01345$, that means the outcome will theoretically occur in 1345 cases out of 100,000.

It will be clear that any value for p greater than.5 means that the result is theoretically more likely to occur than not; a value for p less than.5 means that the result is more likely not to occur than it is to occur. The smaller the value of p, the less likely that outcome.

Probability Theory and Observation

One of the major applications of probability is to check the theoretical possibility of a particular outcome (calculated mathematically) with the observed result of an event. If we find that the observed frequency of a particular occurrence departs widely from theoretical probabilities (i.e., the result is occurring more frequently than we would expect from our calculations), sometimes we have good reason to investigate the event more carefully.

For example, in a fair toss of a coin, we theoretically calculate p as.5 for a head to appear on any single toss. But what is the probability that someone will throw the coin four times in a row and have the outcome heads each time? We can calculate the probability by multiplying the probabilities together. Since there are four tosses and the probability of a head is.5 on each of these, the probability of a sequence of four heads is as follows:

$p =.5 \times.5 \times.5 \times.5 =.0625$

In other words, in a sequence of four consecutive coin tosses, probability theory indicates that in 625 cases out of 10,000 (or 1 outcome in 16) four heads will come up in a row. Thus, if you were making a bet in a number of different trials of four consecutive coin tosses that four heads would appear in a row, you could theoretically expect to win 1 out of every 16 trials and lose 15 out of 16 trials.

Now, this figure of 1 in 16 (p =.0625) does not claim that in every 16 trials of a four-coin-toss sequence, one result will *always* be four heads. The theory states that, on average, in a sequence of four-toss trials, the most likely outcome is that there will be four heads appearing in 1 out of every 16 trials. But in any particular series of four-toss trials, it is quite possible for more than sixteen four-toss trials to happen before the first four-head result appears or for a four-head result to occur before sixteen trials are completed or more than once in one sixteen four-toss sequence. As we shall see, the more times one repeats the four-toss sequence, the closer the observed result will come to the theoretically calculated result.

Thus, given that one four-head sequence every sixteen throws is the most likely (but not the inevitable) outcome of a series of four-toss sequences, if you were betting on the outcome of many four-toss sequences (that there would be four consecutive heads appearing), for the game to be truly fair, you should put up $1 against your opponent's $15 for each four-coin sequence (i.e., if four heads appear you win $15; if they do not your opponent wins $1). With a great many four-toss trials, you and your opponent should come out more or less equal.

Hence, if you are betting $1 that four heads will appear in a four-toss sequence of coins and if your opponent is unwilling to put up $15, you should not undertake the bet. If she is willing to put up more than $15, then you should take the bet.

An Introductory Note about Significance

When the probability of an event (theoretically calculated) is very low and yet the event occurs, sometimes we are entitled to be suspicious or alarmed at the result. Such moments are an invitation to investigate the event to see if there are hidden factors at work (e.g., loaded dice, cheating, trick coins, some hitherto unknown cause). When do such moments occur? At what point is the probability so unlikely (i.e., so low) that we should investigate further?

Well, let us first, as an example, consider the probability of someone's tossing a coin with ten consecutive heads appearing. Using the same way of calculating the probability as we did above (multiplying together the probabilities for a single event), we can calculate the theoretical probability of ten consecutive heads appearing as follows:

$p = .5 \times .5 \times .5 \times .5 \times .5 \times .5 \times .5 \times .5 \times .5 \times .5 = .000977$

This rounded off result indicates that the probability for ten consecutive heads in a series of ten fair coin tosses is 977 out of 1,000,000. Obviously the probability here is much smaller than for the four-head sequence (p =.0625), and we would be right to be much more surprised at such a result. But do we have the right to be suspicious? In other words, how improbable does an event have to get before we begin to think that there is something strange going on?

Scientists and social scientists have set conventional standards for how much an observed result has to differ from the theoretical expectation in order for the result to be considered significant (i.e., worthy of notice or of further investigation, because it is not likely to have occurred by chance). That level is p =.05 (or 5 results in 100). If there is more than a probability of.05 (i.e., if p is greater than.05) that an event could have occurred by chance, scientists do not usually pay much attention to it. If p is less than.05, however, then the result is considered significant and warrants analysis, because something other than chance may be affecting the outcome.

Thus, for example, someone's tossing a coin and getting four consecutive heads (where p =.0625) would not prompt any enquiry; the probability is low, but not so low that we need to start wondering about the fairness of the toss (remember the cut off point is p =.05). However, someone's tossing a coin and getting ten heads in a row (p =.000977 or, rounded off.001) is significant. The probability is so low (1 chance in 1000) that we have some grounds for thinking the result might not be produced by chance and that it is time to check the coin. The justification for this convention of a probability of.05 as the dividing line between significant and non-significant results is not mathematical but methodological and practical. Given the constraints, economic for example, upon investigation, it has been found to pay, in terms of success in explaining the world, to concentrate research in areas where such a degree of significance is obtainable. In some tests, as we shall see, where the procedure requires a much higher level of certainty, the cut-off line is sometimes reduced to.01 (or 1 chance in 100). In general, however, the figure of.05 probability is the accepted level below which results become significant and above which we can still ascribe the results to chance.

Note the very important point that a low probability (e.g., p =.001) does not indicate impossibility. It may well be that the ten-head coin-toss sequence, although very very improbable, is fair (i.e., produced by chance). The very low figure for p is a warning that something may be (and probably is) interfering with the result, but the figure does not *prove* such interference. These basic principles indicate one important aspect of probability, its use as a diagnostic tool, a means of recognizing that in a natural event something may be interfering with the results (e.g., cheating or some hidden factor). Significant discrepancies between theoretical calculations of probable outcomes and the observed results of actual outcomes are often the first clue that something needs investigating. And from this initial observation, the investigators often discover something they had not known about before (e.g., a new disease, like Legionnaire's Disease or AIDS, or a new natural phenomenon).

The Fundamental Basis of Probability Theory

The basis upon which the mathematical treatment of probability rests is as follows: we assume that the phenomenon we wish to investigate can be described in terms of a given number of different possible but equally probable outcomes. For instance, in a simple coin toss there are two equally probable outcomes, heads or tails. In one roll of a die, there are six equally probable outcomes, represented by the six sides of the die, each with a number of dots from 1 to 6. In drawing a card from a full and well shuffled normal deck with no jokers, we know that there are four equally probable outcomes for the suit of the drawn card (hearts, diamonds, spades, or clubs), there are two possible outcomes for the colour of the card (red or black), and there are thirteen possible outcomes for the value of the card. Naturally we are assuming that in all these trials the procedure is fair (i.e., no cheating).

Multiple outcomes (e.g., so many heads in consecutive coin tosses or so many sixes in consecutive rolls of a single dice) can be calculated from the probability of a single event (as we did above by multiplying the frequency of repeated events by the probability of the single outcome in one event). Events which cannot be described in terms of equally probable outcomes are beyond the scope of probability theory discussed here.

The probability of any specific outcome is given by the number which is equal to the number of possibilities which involve that outcome divided by the total number of possibilities. For example, in a simple coin toss, there is only one possibility that a head will appear, and the total number of possible outcomes is two. Thus, the probability that a head will appear is 1 divided by 2 or.5.

In a roll of a single die, there is one chance that a six will appear, and there are six possible outcomes. Therefore the probability of a six appearing on a single roll of a normal die is 1 divided by 6 (p =.1667). If we draw a card from a normal full deck, there is only one chance that a heart will be on the card, and there are four possibilities for different suits. Therefore the probability of drawing a heart from a full deck is 1 divided by 4 (p =.25).

What is the probability that on a single roll of a die, the result will be an even number? Well, there are three possible even outcomes (the numbers 2, 4, and 6) and there are 6 possible outcomes (1, 2, 3, 4, 5, 6). Thus, the probability that on a single roll of a die the result will be an even number of dots is 3 divided by 6: p =.5.

More complicated outcomes (e.g., four heads in a row in consecutive coin tosses, three sixes in a row in consecutive rolls of the die, four number 12 results in four consecutive spins of the roulette wheel, and so on) are more complicated, but we can work out the possible outcomes for such events and calculate the probabilities involved (as we did above for sequences of four and ten coin tosses).

Randomness

Random phenomenon...outcome cannot be predicted, but that has a regulardistribution over many repetitions. Probability...proportion of times an event occurs in many repeatedevents of a random phenomenon.

Independent events (trails)...outcome of an event (trial) does not influence theoutcome of any other event (trial).

Example:: of independent events: Rollinga single die twice. The result on the second roll is independent ofthe first.

Example:: of events not independent: Picking twocards from a deck, one at a time, without replacement. (If you pick acard, and don't put it back in the deck and reshuffle, then theprobability of a red card on the second pick is dependent upon whatthe first card happened to be.)

Probability Models

Overview: It is often important andnecessary to provide a mathematical description or model forrandomness. This section provides insights into how this can bedone.

Sample space: Theset of all possible outcomes of a random phenomenon.

Example:

Consider the sum obtained when two dice are rolled.

The following table displays the sums that can be obtained from thisevent.

		RED DIE					
		1	2	3	4	5	6
GREEN	1	2	3	4	5	6	7
DIE	2	3	4	5	6	7	8
	3	4	5	6	7	8	9
	4	5	6	7	8	9	10
	5	6	7	8	9	10	11
	6	7	8	9	10	11	12

The sample space contains 11 outcomes: S ={2,3,4,5,6,7,8,9,10,11,12}

Probability Rules

- If A is an event, then the probability P(A) is anumber between 0 and 1, inclusive.
- Prob(A does not happen) is 1 - P(A).
- Two events are disjoint if they have nooutcomes in common. If A and B are disjoint, then P(A or B) = P(A) +P(B). Some sources use the phrase mutuallyexclusive to describe events that aredisjoint.
  - In a roll of two dice, if A = "roll asum of 7" and B = "roll a sum of 2", then P(A or B) = 6/36 + 1/36 =7/36, since A and B are disjoint.
  - If C = "roll a sum of 7" and D = "roll an oddsum" then C and D are not disjoint since 7 is an odd sum. In thiscase, P(C or D) = P(C) + P(D) - P(C and D) = 6/36 + 18/36 - 6/36 =18/36 = 1/2.

Two events are independent if knowing that oneoccurs does not change the probability of the other. If events A andB are independent, then prob(A and B) = prob(A)xprob(B).

- If A is the event "getting a head onthe first coin toss" and B is the event "getting a head on a secondtoss of the coin." then A and B are independent, and prob(A and B) =(1/2)(1/2) = 1/4.
- If C is the event "getting a red card by pickinga card from a randomly shuffled deck," and D is the event "getting ared card by picking a second card from the deck" (when the first cardhas not been replaced), then C and D are not independent. Prob(C) =26/52 = 1/2. If the first card is red, then prob(C and D) =(26/52)(25//51), which is not equal to (26/52)(26/52). If the firstcard was replaced in the deck, and the deck reshuffled before eventD, then C and D would be independent.

More About Probability

Overview: There are basic laws thatgovern wise and efficient uses of probability. An understanding ofthese laws is important for those who wish to utilize statistics inpractical and meaningful ways..

For any two events A and B,

Prob(A or B) = Prob(A) + Prob(B) -Prob(A and B).

If A and B are disjoint, then Prob(A and B) =0.

Prob(B|A) = prob(A and B)/prob(A).

Consider a family with two children. There arefour possible boy/girl combinations, all equally likely.

Oldest	Youngest
G	G
G	B
B	G
B	B

Prob(at least one child is a girl) = 3/4.

Prob(two girls) = 1/4.

Prob(two girls|one child is a girl) = 1/3.Sample space is {(G,G), (G,B), (B,G)}.

Prob(two girls|oldest child is a girl) = 1/2.Sample space is {(G,G), (G,B)}.

Prob(exactly one boy|one child is a girl) =2/3.

Prob(exactly one boy|youngest child is a girl) =1/2.

OK, now suppose that a family unknown to you hastwo children. Here are two questions relating to this family.

(1) If one of the children is a boy,what is the probability that the other child is aboy?

(2) If the oldest child is a boy, whatis the probability that the other child is a boy?

Many intelligent people think that 50% is the answer to both (1) and(2). You should be able to show that this is not the case.

BINOMIAL DISTRIBUTION

The probability distribution of a random variable X which assumes integral values x=0..., n with the probabilities,

$$P\{X = x\}=b_x(n,p) = \binom{n}{x} P^x(1-p)^{n-x}$$

where p is a parameter of the binomial distribution, called the probability of a positive outcome, which can take values in the interval $0 \leq p \leq 1$. The binomial distribution is one of the fundamental probability distributions connected with a sequence of independent trials. Let $Y_{1,}$ $Y_{1...,}$ be a sequence of independent random variables, each one of which may assume only one of the values 1 and 0 with respective probabilities and (i.e. all are binomially distributed with). The values of may be treated as the results of independent trials, with if the result of the -th trial is "positive" and if it is "negative". If the total number of independent trials is fixed, such a scheme is known as Bernoulli trials, and the total number of positive results,

$$X = Y_1 + ... + Y_n, \quad n \geq 1,$$

is then binomially distributed with parameter P.

The mathematical expectation Ez^X (the generating function of the binomial distribution) for any value of is the polynomial $[pz+(1-p)]^n$, the representation of which by Newton's binomial series has the form,

$$b_0 + b_1 z + ... + b_n z^n$$

(Hence the very name "binomial distribution".) The moments of a binomial distribution are given by the formulas,

$$EX=np,$$

$$DX = E(X-np)^2 = np(1-p),$$

$$E(X-np)^3 = np(1-p)(1-2p)$$

The binomial distribution function is defined, for any real y,0<y<n, by the formula,

$$F(y) = P\{X \leq u\} = \sum_{x=0}^{[y]} \binom{n}{x} p^x (1-p)^{n-x},$$

where is the integer part of, and,

$$F(y) = \frac{1}{B([y]+1, n-[y])} \int_p^1 t^{[y]}(1-t)^{n-[y]-1} dt,$$

B(a, b) is Euler's beta-function, and the integral on the right-hand side is known as the incomplete beta-function. As, $n \to \infty$ the binomial distribution function is expressed in terms of the standard normal distribution function by the asymptotic formula (the de Moivre–Laplace theorem):

$$F(y) = \Phi\left[\frac{y - np + 0.5}{\sqrt{np(1-p)}}\right] + R_n(y, p),$$

where,

$$R_n(y, p) = O(n^{-1/2})$$

uniformly for all real. There also exist other, higher order, normal approximations of the binomial distribution.

If the number of independent trials n is large, while the probability P is small, the individual probabilities $b_x(n, p)$can be approximately expressed in terms of the Poisson distribution:

$$b_x(n, p) = \binom{n}{x} p^x (1-p)^{n-x} \approx \frac{(np)}{x!} e^{-np}$$

If $n \to \infty$ and $0 < c \leq y \leq C$ (where and are constants), the asymptotic formula,

$$F(y) = \sum_{x=0}^{[y]} \frac{\lambda^x}{x!} e^{-\lambda} + 0(n^{-2}),$$

where, is uniformly valid with respect to all in the interval.

$$\lambda = (2n - [y])p/(2 - P)$$

THE BINOMIAL DISTRIBUTION

Many events have only two possible results: success or failure. In tossing a coin, there are only two possible results—heads and tails—each with a probability of.5. Success in a coin toss is calling the correct result.

In answering multiple choice tests where there are four possible answers for each question, there are again only two possible results for each question, a correct answer or an incorrect one.

If we are trusting entirely to chance in answering such a test (i.e., guessing), we have a one in four chance of getting the answer for any question correct (i.e., on each question for success p =.25, for failure p =.75).

Sorting out the probabilities for a particular outcome requires us to figure out all the possible outcomes and to calculate the distribution for all those possible outcomes. And these calculations will vary depending on the number of possible outcomes.

Thus, there are many possible probabilities for different events (e.g., the distribution of outcomes—heads or tails—for a four coin-toss sequence will be different from the distribution of outcomes—heads or tails—for a ten coin-toss sequence; the distribution for the results of a repeated event with a.5 probability will be different from a similar sequence with a.1667 probability, and so on).

Constructing such a mathematical calculation for a particular series of outcomes is called calculating the binomial distribution. Constructing a binomial distribution for a particular sequence of events is not very difficult, but it is rather time consuming. Fortunately we have tables of binomial distributions so that we do not have to go through the calculations here.

However, in this section we are concerned with being above to read and use a simple binomial distribution table, so that we can judge the probabilities of simple events with only two possible outcomes (success or failure).

The simple table below provides an example of two binomial distributions. An explanation of the table follows immediately after it.

Table. Selected Binomial Distributions

p =.5					
n = 10			n = 20		
r	ind	com	r	ind	com
0	.001	1-	0	0+	1-
1	.010	.999	1	0+	1-
2	.044	.989	2	0+	1-
3	.117	.945	3	.001	1-
4	.205	.828	4	.005	.999
5	.246	.623	5	.015	.994
6	.205	.377	6	.037	.979
7	.117	.172	7	.074	.942
8	.044	.055	8	.120	.868
9	.010	.011	9	.160	.748
10	.001	.001	10	.176	.588
11	.160	.412			
12	.120	.252			
13	.074	.132			
14	.037	.058			
15	.015	.021			
16	.005	.006			
17	.001	.001			
18	0+	0+			
19	0+	0+			
20	0+	0+			

Note that the entry 1- means a probability larger than.9995 but less than 1 (about as certain as one can be); the entry 0+ means a probability less than.0005 but greater than 0 (extremely unlikely).

This table indicates two different binomial distributions. The one on the left side indicates the probabilities of success in a series of 10 coin tosses; the one on the right side indicates the probabilities of success in a series of 20 coin tosses; this distinction is indicated by the label $n = 10$ on the left and $n = 20$ on the right. For both tables the probability of success in any one toss is.5 (hence heading p =.5 below the title).

The first column on each side has the heading r. This indicates the number of successes in the sequence. So, for example, on the left side, the values go from 0 to 10, indicating the possible outcomes of 0 heads in 10 tosses of the coin to 10 consecutive heads in 10 tosses. On the right side, the *r* values go from 0 to 20, indicating the possible outcomes from 0 heads in 20 tosses to 20 heads in 20 tosses.

The *ind* (= individual) column in the middle of each side of the table gives the probability of one's achieving that exact r value in a full sequence of tosses. So on the left side, for example, the probability of getting exactly 5 heads in a sequence of 10 tosses is.246 (the *ind* value on the same line as the *r* value of 5).

In the right side of the table, the probability of getting exactly 5 heads in a sequence of 20 tosses.015.

The *cum* (= cumulative) column gives the probability of *r* or more successes in the total number of trials (or at least *r* successes). So, for example, on the left side of the table, the chances of getting 6 or more (or at least 6) heads in 10 consecutive tosses of a coin is.377; in the right side of the table, the probability of getting 5 or more (or at least 5) heads in 20 tosses of the coin is.994. Look on the right side of the table at the *r* value 4. As you would expect, the probability of getting exactly four heads in a 20-toss sequence (the *ind* value) is very low (.005), but the chances of getting at least 4 heads in a 20-toss sequence (the *cum* value) is very high (.999, close to certainty).

Table: Binomial Distribution for a Six-Sided Die

p =.1667
n = 24

r	**ind**	**cum**
0	.013	1-
1	.060	.987
2	.139	.927
3	.204	.788
4	.214	.584
5	.171	.371
6	.108	.200
7	.056	.091
8	.024	.035
9	.008	.012
10	.003	.003
11	.001	.001

The other *ind* and *cum* values from *r* =12 to *r* = 24 are 0

Some Observations on Binomial Distributions

The binomial distribution, is appropriate only when the events in the sequence are independent of each other (i.e., when the outcome of one event does not affect the outcome of another). For example, in any coin toss the probability of a head is always.5; it is not affected by the result of any outcome before it. In the roll of a single die, the probability of a 6 showing as the outcome is always the same (p =.1667), no matter what the results of previous rolls might have been. In other words in sequences of coin tosses or die rolls, the outcome of any single event is independent of the outcome of any other event.

This independence does not always apply in probability situations. For example, when one draws a single card from a full, well-shuffled deck, the probability of the outcome producing a red card is.5, because 26 of the 52 cards are red (26 divided by 52 equals.5). However, if we draw a red card and do not return it to the deck, then the probability of a second draw producing a second red card is no longer.5. Since one red card has been removed from the deck on the first draw, there are now only 51 cards in the deck, 26 black cards and 25 red ones. Therefore, the probability of drawing a red card on the second draw is now 25/51 (p =.4902); whereas, the chance of drawing a black card on the second draw with one red card removed is now 26/51 (p =.5098).

In this example, the probabilities in the second draw have been affected by the result of the first draw (one card less in the deck, one red card less in the deck). What this means is that the probability of a red card in the second draw is not independent of the first draw. Thus, the sort of binomial distribution which we have been considering in the coin toss or roll of the die (where the probability remains the same in each toss or roll) would not be appropriate.

In any card game where the deck is not full and shuffled before each event, the probabilities are constantly changing as cards are played and removed from the deck. This is the case, most famously, with blackjack, where after every hand the played cards are normally collected and placed on the bottom and a new hand dealt from the remaining cards. A careful player who keeps close track of the cards which have been played and not returned to the deck and who understands probabilities very well can calculate when the probabilities of a favourable outcome shift in her favour (i.e., when p for success becomes greater than.5). This is the basis for a number of well-known and successful legal systems for beating the casino dealer, since this is the only casino game in which the probabilities occasionally favour the player.

Here, for example, is a simple illustration. Suppose in playing blackjack at the casino (in a game between you and the dealer only), you keep careful track of all the cards which have been played and put on the bottom of the deck. Suppose, as a result of this careful observation, you know that there are only five cards left unplayed and, further, that these five are 3 eights and 2 sevens. In such a situation you pawn everything you have, sell your car, bet everything, and stand pat with the two cards dealt to you. Since in routine casino blackjack the dealer cannot stand pat with 16 or under (and you know that from the remaining cards he must have 16, 15, or 14), it is certain that the dealer will have to draw and that his hand will be over 21. In other words, the probability for your success here is 1 (certainty).

That is a very simple example. Sophisticated mathematicians have developed systems of keeping track of the shifting probabilities in blackjack, betting low when the probability is less than.5 and high when the probability for success shifts to above.5. Over time, given the fairness of the game, such players will win (and some have won enormous amounts).

Casinos routinely cope with such gamblers, when they recognize them, by shuffling the deck before every hand, thus restoring the favourable probabilities to the dealer in every hand. At this point, the sophisticated gambler with a system moves on down the strip to another casino.

BERNOULLI THEOREM

The (historically) original form of the (weak) law of large numbers. The theorem appeared in the fourth part of Jacob Bernoulli's book Ars conjectandi (The art of conjecturing). This part may be considered as the first serious study ever of probability theory. The theorem deals with sequences of independent trials, in each one of which the probability of occurrence of some event ("success") is *P*. Let *n* be the number of trials and let *m* be the random variable equal to the number of successful events. The Bernoulli theorem states that, whatever the value of the positive numbers ε and η, the probability $\supset$ of the inequality,

$$-\varepsilon \leq \frac{m}{n} - p \leq \varepsilon$$

will be higher than $1-\eta$ for all sufficiently large $\eta\left(n \geq n_0\right)$. The proof of this theorem, which was given by Bernoulli and which was exclusively based on a study of the decrease of probabilities in the binomial distribution as one moves away from the most probable value, was accompanied by an inequality which made it possible to point out a certain bound for the given $n_0$if and were given. Thus, it was found by Bernoulli that if p =2/5, the probability of the inequality,

$$-\frac{1}{50} \leq \frac{m}{n} - \frac{2}{5} \leq \frac{1}{50}$$

will be higher than 0.999 if $n \geq 25{,}550$. By introducing a slight improvement in the original reasoning of Bernoulli, it is possible to conclude that it is sufficient to select a value of n obeying the condition,

$$n > \frac{1+\varepsilon}{\varepsilon^2} \log \frac{1}{\eta} + \frac{1}{\varepsilon},$$

which gives in turn, for the probability $1-\mathrm{P}$ of the inequality,

$$\frac{m}{n} - p\Big| > \varepsilon,$$

an estimate of the form,

$$2\exp\{-\frac{1}{2}n\varepsilon^2\}$$

The condition obtained for the above example is $n \geq 17{,}665$ (more sophisticated estimates show that it is sufficient to take $n \geq 6502$; one may note, for the sake of comparison, that the de Moivre–Laplace theorem yields 6498 as the approximate value of n_0). Other estimates for $1 - \mathrm{P}$ may be obtained using the Bernstein inequality and its analogues.

An Investigation of Bernoulli's Theorem

The rest of this module describes an experiment to illustrate and test Bernoulli's Theorem, to see whether our observed results get closer and closer to the calculated probabilities as we increase the number of trials.

Equipment

For this experiment you need to collect together the following items:

- Ten coins, preferably all the same size and in good condition;
- A can or cup in which to shake the coins, which must be able to tumble freely in the container when you hold your hand over the opening and shake the coins;
- A tally sheet to keep track of the results (number of heads) of head throw (the tally sheet in given below)

LAW OF LARGE NUMBERS

A general principle according to which under certain very general conditions the simultaneous action of random factors leads to a result which is practically non-random.

That the frequency of occurrence of a random event tends to become equal to its probability as the number of trials increases (a phenomenon which was probably first noted for games of chance) may serve as the first example of this principle.

At the turn of the 17th century J. Bernoulli demonstrated a theorem stating that, in a sequence of independent trials, in each of which the probability of occurrence of a certain A event has the same value $p, 0 < p < 1$, the relationship,

$$\mathrm{P}\left\{\left\|\frac{\mu_n}{n} - \mathrm{p}\right| > \varepsilon\right\} \to 0$$

is valid for any $\varepsilon > 0$ if $n \to \infty$; here, μ_n is the number of occurrences of the event in the first n trials and *un*/*n* is the frequency of the occurrence. This

Bernoulli theorem was extended by S. Poisson to the case of a sequence of independent trials in which the probability of the occurrence of an event Avaries with the number of the trial. Let this probability in the k-th trial be $pk, k = 1, 2, ...,$ and let,

$$\overline{P}n = \frac{p_1 + ... + p_n}{n}$$

Then, according to the Poisson theorem,

$$\text{P}\left\{\left|\frac{\mu_n}{n} - \overline{p}\right| > \varepsilon\right\} \to 0$$

for any $\varepsilon > 0$ if $n \to \infty$. A rigorous proof of this theorem was first given in 1846 by P.L. Chebyshev, whose method was quite different from that of Poisson and was based on certain extremal considerations, whereas Poisson deduced from an approximate formula for the above probability, based on a law of Gauss which at that time had not yet been proved rigorously. Poisson was the first to use the term "law of large numbers", by which he denoted his own generalization of the Bernoulli theorem.

A further natural extension of the Bernoulli and Poisson theorems is a consequence of the fact that the random variables may be represented as the sum,

$$\mu_n = X_1 + ... + X_n$$

of independent random variables, where $X_K = 1$ if A occurs in the k-th trial and $X_K = 0$ otherwise. The mathematical expectation $\text{E}(\mu_n/n)$ (which is identical with the average of the mathematical expectations $EX_K, 1 \le k \le n$) is P in the case of Bernoulli and is in $\overline{P}n$ the case of Poisson. In other words, in both cases one deals with a deviation of the arithmetical average of the variables X_K from the arithmetical average of their mathematical expectations.

In his work "On average quantities", which appeared in 1867, Chebyshev established that the relationship,

$$p\left\{\left|\frac{X_1 + ... + X_n}{n} - \frac{EX_1 + ... + EX_n}{n}\right| > \varepsilon\right\} \to 0$$

is valid, for any if $\varepsilon > 0, n \to \infty$ for independent random variables $X_1, ..., X_n, ...,$ under fairly general assumptions. Chebyshev assumed that the mathematical expectations EX_K^2 are all bounded by the same constant, even though his proof makes it clear that the requirement of boundedness of the variances of,

$X_k, DX_k = EX_K^2 - (EX_K)^2$, or even the requirement

$$B_n^2 = DX_1 + ... + DX_n = o(n^2), \qquad n \to \infty$$

is sufficient. It was thus shown by Chebyshev that the Bernoulli theorem is susceptible of extensive generalizations. A.A. Markov noted the possibility of further extensions and proposed to apply the term "law of large numbers" to all extensions of the Bernoulli theorem (and, in particular, to). Chebyshev's method is based on a rigorous formulation of all the properties of the mathematical expectations and on the use of the so- called Chebyshev inequality in probability theory. For the probability it yields an estimate of the form,

$$n^{-2}\varepsilon^{-2}\sum_{K=1}^{n} DX_k$$

This estimate may be replaced by a more exact one — but under more restrictive conditions, Subsequent proofs of the law of large numbers are all, to varying extents, developments of Chebyshev's method. Using an appropriate "truncation" of the random variables X_k(replacement of these variables by auxiliary variables $X'_n k$, viz. $X'_{n,k} = X_k$ if $X_k - EX_k| \le L_n$ and $X'_{n,K} = 0$ if $X_k - E X_k| > L_n$, where L_n is a constant), Markov extended the law of large numbers to the case when the variance of the terms does not exist. He showed, for instance, that is valid if, for certain constants $\delta > 0$ and $L > 0$ for all *n*,

$$E|X_n - E X_n|^{1+\delta} < L$$

Khinchin's theorem (1929) is proved in a similar manner: If X_n have the same distribution and if EX_n exists, then the law of large numbers is valid.

It is possible to formulate more or less final versions of the law of large numbers for sums of independent random variables. To do this, it is expedient to adopt a more general point of view, involving the concept of a sequence of asymptotically-constant random variables. The random variables of a sequence $Y_1,\ldots,Y_n,\ldots,$ are said to be asymptotically constant if there exists a sequence of constants $C_1,\ldots,C_n,\ldots,$ such that for any $\varepsilon > 0$, if $n > \infty$,

$$\mathrm{P}\{|Y_n - C_n| > \varepsilon\} \to 0$$

(i.e. $Y_n - C_n$ converges to zero in probability). If is valid for C_n some, it is also valid for $C'_n = mYn$, where mY is the median of the random variable Y. Furthermore, instead of the $X_1,\ldots,X_n,\ldots,$ sequence of independent random variables, one may also take a so-called triangular array:

$$\begin{array}{c} X_{1,1},\ldots,X_{1,k_1}, \\ X_{2,1},\ldots,X_{2,k_2}, \\ \square\ldots\ldots, \\ X_{n,1},\ldots,X_{n,k_n}, \\ \square\ldots\ldots \end{array}$$

of random variables (the first subscript is the row number, while the second indicates the number of the variable within the row). The random variables of each individual row are assumed to be mutually independent. A sequence of partial sums is readily reduced to a triangular array if one assumes that $k_1 = 1, k_2 = 2,\ldots,$ $X_{n,k} = X_k / n$,

Let,

$$Y_n = X_{n,1+\ldots+}X_{n,k_n}.$$

The general problem of the applicability of the law of large numbers to sums of independent random variables may then be stated as follows: Under what conditions are the sums Y_n asymptotically constant?

This question was answered in 1928 by A.N. Kolmogorov. Assume, without loss of generality, that the medians of the variables $X_{n,k}$ are zero. Let $X_{n,k} = X_{n,k}$ if $|X_{n,}k| \leq 1$ and $X_{n,k} = 0$ if $X_{n,\ k}| > 1$. The simultaneous fulfillment of the two conditions,

$$\sum_{k=1}^{kn} \mathrm{P}\{|\mathrm{X}_{n,k}| > 1\} \to 0 \quad \textit{if } n \to \infty$$

and

$$\sum_{k=1}^{k_n} \mathrm{E}\tilde{X}^2_{n,k} \to 0 \quad \text{if } n \to \infty,$$

is necessary and sufficient for the sums Y_n to be asymptotically constant. The sum $\sum_k^{k_n} 1\mathrm{EX}_{n,k}$ may be taken as C_n. That these conditions are sufficient is readily demonstrated by Chebyshev's method. If the mathematical expectations $EX_{n,k}$ exist, it is easy to find supplementary conditions under which it is permissible to choose $C_n = \mathrm{E}Y_n$, which yields necessary and sufficient conditions for the law of large numbers in the classical formulation. For a sequence of independent identically-distributed variables $\{X_n\}$ these conditions are reduced — in accordance with Khinchin's theorem quoted above — to the existence of the mathematical expectation. At the same time, the condition,

$$n\mathrm{P}\{|X_1| > n\} \to 0 \text{ if } n \to \infty$$

is necessary and sufficient for the arithmetical averages Y_n to be asymptotically constant. Examples of cases in which condition is not met are easily found. Thus, the condition is not met if all X_n have a Cauchy distribution with density $1/\pi(1+x^2)$ (to which corresponds the characteristic function $\exp\{-|t|\}$).

Here, the arithmetical averages $Y_n = (X_1 + \ldots + X_n)/n$ have the characteristic function $\exp\{-n|t/n|\} = \exp\{-|t|\}$ and, as a result have the same distribution for any n as do the individual terms.

The most important cases to which the law of large numbers does not apply involve the times of return to the starting point in a random walk. Thus, in a symmetric Bernoulli random walk the time T_n passing prior to the n-th return to the starting point is the sum of the n independent random variables $X_1 .., X_n$ where X_1 is the time passed prior to the first return, is the time between the first and the second return, etc. The distribution of the variable $2T_{n/}\pi n^2$ converges as $\mathrm{n} \to \infty$ to a non-degenerate limit distribution with density,

$$P(x) = \frac{1}{\sqrt{2\pi}} e^{-1/2x} x^{-3/2} \, for \, x > 0$$

and zero for $x \leq 0$. Accordingly, in this case the distribution of the arithmetical average of X_i, i.e. $T_{n/}n$, is located, roughly speaking, on a segment of length of order n(whereas, in cases where the law of large numbers is applicable, it is located on segments of length) $_o(1)$.

The applicability of the law of large numbers to sums of dependent variables (both in its classical and in its more general formulations) is connected, first and foremost, with the asymptotic independence of the random variables X_i and X_j as the difference between their subscripts $|i - j|$ increases. The corresponding theorems were first proved by Markov in 1907 for variables connected in a Markov chain.

In fact, let be a homogeneous Markov chain with finite number of states, and let $X_1, \ldots, X_n, \ldots,$ all one-step transition probabilities be positive. Here, the asymptotic independence of X_j and X_i as $|i - j| \to \infty$ follows from the fact that the conditional distribution of X_j under a fixed value of X_i tends, as $n \to \infty$, to a limit which does not depend on the chosen value of X_i (Markov's ergodic theorem).

The law of large numbers is deduced from this theorem: It is first established that, as $n \to \infty$,

$$\mathrm{E}\left(\frac{X_1 + \ldots + X_n}{n} - \alpha\right)^2 \to 0,$$

where $a = \lim_{k \to \infty} EX_k$; hence it follows that as $n \to \infty$,

$$\mathrm{P}\left\{\frac{X_1 + \ldots + X_n}{n} - \alpha\right| > \varepsilon\left.\vphantom{\frac{X}{n}}\right\} \to 0,$$

The following, more general case, is governed by Bernstein's conditions: If $DX_j < L|R(X_i, X_j)| \leq \phi(|i - j|)$,, where L is a constant, R is the correlation coefficient and $\phi(n)$ is a function which tends to zero as $n \to \infty$, then the law of large numbers is applicable to the variables $\{X_n\}$.

For sequences $\{X_n\}$ which are stationary in the wide sense, the correlation condition may be weakened somewhat, by replacing it by,

$$\lim_{n \to \infty} \frac{1}{n} \sum_{j=1}^{n} R_j = 0,$$

where,

$$R_j = R(X_i, X_{i+j})$$

The above-mentioned results may be extended in various ways. First, only convergence in probability was considered so far. Other types of convergence may also be considered, including convergence with probability one, mean-square convergence, etc. (in fact, many of the above conditions ensure mean-square convergence, which implies convergence in probability). The case of convergence with probability one is important, and for this reason has been especially named the strong law of large numbers.

Furthermore, many of these theorems can be applied, with suitable modifications, to random vectors having values in Euclidean spaces of any dimension, in a Hilbert space or in certain Banach spaces. For instance, if $\{X_n\}$ is a sequence of independent identically-distributed random vectors with values in a separable Banach space, and if $\mathrm{E}\|X_n\|$ (where $\|x\|$ is the norm of x) is finite, one has,

$$\mathrm{P}\left\{\frac{X_1 + \ldots + X_n}{n} - \mathrm{EX}_1\| > \varepsilon\right\} \to 0$$

for any $\varepsilon > 0$ if $n \to \infty$.

The law of large numbers, when considered in its most general form, is closely related to ergodic theorems. Clearly, many theorems are also applicable to the case of the average $(1/T)\int_0^T X(t)dt$, where $X(t)$ is a random process depending on a continuous parameter.

Finally, instead of the sums of random variables one may consider other symmetric functions of them. This was in fact done by A.Ya. Khinchin (1951–1955) to prove certain conclusions in statistical mechanics. The result obtained by him may be illustrated by the following example. Let $X_{n},1 ,..., X_{n,n}$ be the coordinates of a point uniformly distributed on the surface of the sphere,

$$X_{n,1}^2 + \ldots + X_{n,n}^2 = n\mu, \qquad \mu > 0$$

The law of large numbers then applies to a wide class of symmetric functions $f(X_{n,1},..., X_{n,n})$ in the sense that as $n \to \infty$, their values are asymptotically constant (this is similar to the observation made in 1925 by P. Lévy to the effect that sufficiently regular functions of a very large number of variables are almost constant in a large part of their domain of definition).

BERNSTEIN INEQUALITY

Bernstein's inequality in probability theory is a more precise formulation of the classical Chebyshev inequality in probability theory, proposed by S.N. Bernshtein in 1911; it permits one to estimate the probability of large deviations by a monotone decreasing exponential function. In fact, if the equations,

$$\mathrm{EX}_j = 0, \quad \mathrm{EX}_j^2 = B_j, \quad j = 1, \ldots, n,$$

hold for the independent random variables $X_1 ,..., X_n$ with,

$$\mathrm{E}|X_j|^l \le \frac{b_j}{2} H^{l-2} l!$$

(where $l > 2$ and H is a constant independent of), then the following inequality of Bernstein (where $r > 0$) is valid for the sum $S_n = X_1 + \ldots + X_n$:

$$\mathrm{P}\{|S_n| > r\} \leq 2\exp\left\{-\frac{r^2}{2(B_n + Hr)}\right\},$$

where $B_n = \sum b_j$. For identically-distributed bounded random variables $X_j(EX_j = 0,\ EX_j^2 = \sigma^2$, and $|X_j| \leq L$,) inequality takes its simplest form:

$$\mathrm{P}\{|S_n| > t\sigma\sqrt{n}\} \leq 2\exp\left\{-\frac{t^2}{2(1+\alpha/3)}\right\}$$

where $\alpha = Lt/\sqrt{n\sigma}$. A.N. Kolmogorov gave a lower estimate of the probability in. The Bernstein–Kolmogorov estimates are used, in particular, in proving the law of the iterated logarithm. Some idea of the accuracy of may be obtained by comparing it with the approximate value of the left-hand side of which is obtained by the central limit theorem in the form,

$$\frac{2}{\sqrt{2\pi}}\int_t^\infty e^{-u^2/2}\,du = \frac{2}{\sqrt{2\pi t}}\left(1 - \frac{\theta}{t^2}\right)e^{-t^2/2},$$

where $0 < \theta < 1$. Subsequent to 1967, Bernstein's inequalities were extended to include multi-dimensional and infinite-dimensional cases.

Bernstein's inequality for the derivative of a trigonometric or algebraic polynomial gives an estimate of this derivative in terms of the polynomial itself. If $T_n(x)$ is a trigonometric polynomial of degree not n exceeding and if,

$$M = \max_{0 \leq x \leq 2\pi} |T_n(x)|,$$

then the following inequalities are valid for all x:

$$|T_n^{(r)}(x)| \leq Mn^r, \qquad r = 1, 2, \ldots.$$

These estimates cannot be improved, since the number $M=1$ for,

$$T_n(x) = \cos n(x - x_0)$$

is sharp:

$$\max_x |T_n^{(r)}(x)| = n^r.$$

Bernstein's inequality for trigonometric polynomials is a special case of the following theorem: If $f(x)$ is an entire function of order $\leq \sigma$ and if,

$$M = \sup_{-\infty < x < \infty} |f(x)|,$$

then one has

$$\sup_{-\infty < x < \infty} |f^{(r)}(x)| \leq M\sigma^r \qquad (r = 1, 2, \ldots).$$

Bernstein's inequality for an algebraic polynomial has the following form: If the polynomial,

$$P_n(x) = \sum_{k=0}^{n} \alpha_k x^k$$

satifies the condition,

$$|P_n(x)| \leq M, \quad \alpha \leq x \leq b$$

then its derivative $P_n^{'}(x)$ has the property,

$$|P_n^{'}(x)| \leq \frac{Mn}{\sqrt{(x-a)(b-x)}}, \quad \alpha < x < b,$$

which cannot be improved. As was noted by S.N. Bernshtein, this inequality is a consequence of the proof of the Markov inequality given by A.A. Markov.

Bernstein's inequalities are in fact employed in proving converse theorems in the theory of approximation of functions. There are a number of generalizations of Bernstein's inequality, in particular for entire functions in several variables.

SAMPLING METHODS

The need for accurate information in order to make informed decisions has been emphasized throughout this online publication. Statistics are an important type of information and statistical agencies play an important part in the production of such information.

In order to do this, the agencies rely on censuses, sample surveys and the use of administration records. These three sources, along with their advantages and disadvantages, have been explained.

Sampling allows statisticians to draw conclusions about a whole by examining a part. It enables us to estimate characteristics of a population by directly observing a portion of the entire population. Researchers are not interested in the sample itself, but in what can be learned from the survey—and how this information can be applied to the entire population.

It is essential that a sample survey be correctly defined and organized. If the wrong questions are posed to the wrong people, statisticians will not receive information that will be useful when applied to the entire population.

In the context of a national statistical agency like Statistics Canada, the following steps are needed to select a sample and ensure that this sample will fulfill its goals.

Establish the Survey's Objectives

The first step in planning a useful and efficient survey is to specify the objectives with as much detail as possible. Without objectives, the survey is unlikely to generate usable results. Clarifying the aims of the survey is critical to its ultimate success. The initial users and uses of the data should be identified at this stage. The pros and cons of a census versus a sample survey or the use of administrative records should be evaluated and a decision made as to the most appropriate method.

Define The Target Population

The target population is the total population for which the information is required. For example, if you were to conduct a survey about the most popular types of cars in Saskatchewan, then the target population would be every car in Saskatchewan. The units that make up the population must be described in terms of characteristics that clearly identify them. Specifically, the target population is defined by the following characteristics:

- Nature of data required: about persons, hospitals, schools, etc.
- Geographic location: the geographic boundaries of the population have to be determined, as well as the level of geographic detail required for the survey estimate (by province, by city, etc.).
- Reference period: the time period covered by the survey.
- Other characteristics, such as socio-demographic characteristics (interest in a particular age group, for example) or type of industry.

Decide on the Data to be Collected

The data requirements of the survey must be established. To ensure that the requirements are operationally sound, the necessary data terms and definitions also need to be determined.

Set The Level of Precision

As mentioned in the section on Sampling error, there is a level of uncertainty associated with estimates coming from a sample. For example, if you are trying to estimate the average distance between home and school for students in your class of 25 from a sample of 5 persons, your estimate will depend on who the 5 sampled students are.

If the 5 sampled students also live close to the school, the results will not be able to represent the class accurately. This sample-to-sample variation is what causes the sampling error. Statisticians can estimate the sampling error associated with a particular sampling plan, and try to minimize it.

When designing a survey, the acceptable level of uncertainty in the survey estimates has to be established. This level depends on what the end use of the results will be and on the size of the overall budget.

The bigger the budget, the more resources available, and thus, less chance for error. And if the end result is to serve a specific purpose, then the acceptable level of uncertainty would be smaller than an end result that is simply looking for general trends. The level of uncertainty will also be determined by the sample size. Increasing the sample size will decrease the sampling error. (If you sample 24 out of 25 students in your class, there will not be as much sample-to-sample variation as there would be if you only sampled 5 students from among the 25 possible samples.)

THE SAMPLE DESIGN

Once the objectives, guidelines and definitions have been worked out, the statistician can work on the survey plan. The survey plan is divided into three parts:

- Sample design: how the sample will be collected.
- Estimation techniques: how the results from the sample will be extended to the whole population.
- Measures of precision: how the sampling error will be measured.

The estimation techniques and measures of precision are discussed in a later section. For the moment, we will look at the sample design. The following steps lead to the complete determination of the sample design:

1. Determine what the survey population will be (e.g., students, men aged 20 to 35, newborn babies, etc.).
2. Choose the most appropriate survey time frame.
3. Define the survey units.
4. Establish the sample size (e.g., a sample of 100 from a population of 1,000).
5. Select a sampling method.

The Survey Population

The target population must be defined early in the survey-designing process. This is the population for which information is required. However, some members of the population have to be excluded because of operational constraints: the high cost of collecting data in some remote areas, the difficulty of identifying and contacting certain components of the target population, etc.

For example, because it would be too difficult to locate and survey each car owned by every resident in Saskatchewan, a survey population of just the major cities and towns might be conducted instead.

When some of the members of the target population are excluded, we call the included population the survey population or, what is sometimes called, an *observed population*. The target population is the population we want to observe while the survey population is the population we can observe.

The goal of this process is to have the survey population as close as possible to the target population. It is also very important that the users of the data be informed of the differences between the two populations, as the results of the survey will apply only to the survey population.

For example, a target population for a survey could be all Canadians aged 15 years and over (on a particular reference date), while the survey population could exclude residents of the Yukon, Nunavut and Northwest Territories, persons living on Aboriginal reserves, full-time members of the Canadian Armed Forces and residents of institutions. These Canadians might be excluded for various reasons: to survey people in the territories might prove to be difficult and expensive, military personnel may not be available for surveying if they are out on a mission, etc. Using this example, about 2% of the target population would be excluded from the survey population.

The Survey Frame

The survey frame, also called the sampling frame, is the tool used to gain access to the population. There are two types of frames: list frames and area frames. A list frame is just a list of names and addresses that provide direct access to 'individuals' (e.g., a list of hospitals, a list of restaurants, a list of students at a university). Area frames are a list of geographic areas that provide indirect access to individuals (e.g., the neighbourhoods in a city). This type of access is called indirect because first, a list of geographic areas must be selected and then, access to individuals within each selected area must be worked out.

For instance, suppose that you were surveying a rural town in Quebec to see what percentage of residents are farmers. If you were provided with an area frame, then you would be able to locate which roads to visit, but you would still have to find out the names and addresses of the residents on each road.

When there is no single frame that is appropriate, multiple frames can be used. Some sampling techniques using both types of frames will be discussed later.

A good frame should be complete and up-to-date; no member of the survey population should be excluded from the frame or duplicated on the frame (represented more than once); and no unit that is not part of the population (e.g., deceased persons) should be on the frame. The frame chosen will impact the selected survey population. For instance, if a list of telephone numbers is used to select a sample of households, then all households without telephones are excluded from the survey population.

The survey units

There are three types of units that have to be accurately identified in order to avoid problems during the selection, data collection and data analysis stages. They are as follows:

- The sampling unit is part of the frame and therefore subject to being selected.
- The respondent unit or reporting unit provides the information needed by the survey.
- The unit of reference or unit of analysis—the unit about which information is provided—is used to analyse the survey results.

For example, in a survey about newborns in Edmonton, the sampling unit might be a household, the reporting unit one of the parents or a legal guardian, and the unit of reference the baby. The sampling units may differ depending on the frame used. This is why the survey population, survey frame and survey units are defined in conjunction with one another.

The Sample Size

The level of precision needed for the survey estimates will impact the sample size. However, it is not as easy to determine the sample size as one may think. Generally, the actual sample size of a survey is a compromise between the level of precision to be achieved, the survey budget and any other operational constraints, such as budget and time.

In order to achieve a certain level of precision, the sample size will depend, among other things, on the following factors:

- The variability of the characteristics being observed: If every person in a population had the same salary, then a sample of one person would be all you would need to estimate the average salary of the population. If the salaries are very different, then you would need a bigger sample in order to produce a reliable estimate.
- The population size: To a certain extent, the bigger the population, the bigger the sample needed. But once you reach a certain level, an increase in population no longer affects the sample size. For instance, the necessary sample size to achieve a certain level of precision will be about the same for a population of one million as for a population twice that size.
- The sampling and estimation methods: Not all sampling and estimation methods have the same level of efficiency. You will need a bigger sample if your method is not the most efficient. But because of operational constraints and the unavailability of an adequate frame, you cannot always use the most efficient technique.

The Sampling Method

There are two types of sampling methods: probability sampling and non-probability sampling. The difference between them is that in probability sampling, every unit has a 'chance' of being selected, and that chance can be quantified. This is not true for non-probability sampling; every item in a population does not have an equal chance of being selected. The next section will describe features of both types of sampling and detail some of the methods related to each type.

PROBABILITY SAMPLING

Probability sampling involves the selection of a sample from a population, based on the principle of randomization or chance. Probability sampling is more complex, more time-consuming and usually more costly than non-probability sampling. However, because units from the population are randomly selected and each unit's probability of inclusion can be calculated, reliable estimates can be produced along with estimates of the sampling error, and inferences can be made about the population.

There are several different ways in which a probability sample can be selected. The method chosen depends on a number of factors, such as the available sampling frame, how spread out the population is, how costly it is to survey members of the population and how users will analyse the data. When choosing a probability sample design, your goal should be to minimize the sampling error of the estimates for the most important survey variables, while simultaneously minimizing the time and cost of conducting the survey.

Simple Random Sampling

In *simple random sampling*, each member of a population has an equal chance of being included in the sample. Also, each combination of members of the population has an equal chance of composing the sample. Those two properties are what defines simple random sampling. To select a simple random sample, you need to list all of the units in the survey population.

Example: To draw a simple random sample from a telephone book, each entry would need to be numbered sequentially. If there were 10,000 entries in the telephone book and if the sample size were 2,000, then 2,000 numbers between 1 and 10,000 would need to be randomly generated by a computer. Each number will have the same chance of being generated by the computer (in order to fill the simple random sampling requirement of an equal chance for every unit). The 2,000 telephone entries corresponding to the 2,000 computer-generated random numbers would make up the sample.

Simple random sampling can be done with or without replacement. A sample with replacement means that there is a possibility that the sampled telephone entry may be selected twice or more. Usually, the simple random sampling approach is conducted without replacement because it is more convenient and gives more precise results. For the purpose of these descriptions, when we discuss simple random sampling, we will refer to sampling without replacement.

Simple random sampling is the easiest method of sampling and it is the most commonly used. Advantages of this technique are that it does not require any additional information on the frame (such as geographic areas) other than the complete list of members of the survey population along with information for contact. Also, since simple random sampling is a simple method and the theory behind it is well established, standard formulas exist to determine the sample size, the estimates and so on, and these formulas are easy to use.

On the other hand, this technique makes no use of auxiliary information present on the frame (i.e., number of employees in each business) that could make the design of the sample more efficient. And although it is easy to apply simple random sampling to small populations, it can be expensive and unfeasible for large populations because all elements must be identified and labeled prior to sampling. It can also be expensive if personal interviewers are required since the sample may be geographically spread out across the population.

A lottery draw is a good example of simple random sampling. For example, when a sample of 6 numbers is randomly generated from a population of 49, each number has an equal chance of being selected and each combination of 6 numbers has the same chance of being the winning combination. Even though people tend to avoid combinations such as 1-2-3-4-5-6, it has the same chance of being the winning set of numbers as the combination of 8-15-21-28-32-40.

Example: Suppose your school has 500 students and you need to conduct a short survey on the quality of the food served in the cafeteria. You decide that a sample of 10 students should be sufficient for your purposes. In order to get your sample, you assign a number from 1 to 500 to each student in your school. To select the sample, you use a table of randomly generated numbers. All you have to do is pick a starting point in the table (a row and column number) and look at the random numbers that appear there. In this case, since the data run into three digits, the random numbers would need to contain three digits as well. Ignore all random numbers after 500 because they do not correspond to any of the students in the school. Remember that the sample is without replacement, so if a number recurs, skip over it and use the next random number. The first 10 different numbers between 001 and 500 make up your sample.

Example: Imagine that you own a movie theatre and you are offering a special horror movie film festival next month. To decide which horror movies to show, you survey moviegoers asking them which of the listed movies are their favourites. To create the list of movies needed for your survey, you decide to sample 100 of the 1,000 best horror movies of all time. The horror movie population is divided evenly into classic movies (those filmed in or before 1969) and modern movies (those filmed in or later than 1970). One way of getting a sample would be to write out all of the movie titles on slips of paper and place them in an empty box. Then, draw out 100 titles and you will have your sample. By using this approach, you will have ensured that each movie had an equal chance of selection.

You can also calculate the probability of a given movie being selected. Since we know the sample size (n) and the total population (N), calculating the probability of being included in the sample becomes a simple matter of division:

Probability of being selected (same for each horror movie)
$= (n \div N) \times 100\%$
$= (100 \div 1{,}000) \times 100\%$
$= 10\%$

This means that every movie title on the list has a 10% or a 1 in 10 chance of being selected.

You can see that that one disadvantage of simple random sampling (not the only disadvantage, but an important one) is that even if you know that the population is made up of 500 classic movies and 500 modern movies and you know each movie's release date from the sampling frame, no use is made of this information. This sample might contain 77 classic movies and 23 modern movies, which would not be representative of the whole horror movie population.

There are ways to overcome this problem (these will be briefly discussed in the Estimation section), but there are also ways to account for this information.

Systematic sampling

Sometimes called *interval sampling, systematic sampling* means that there is a gap, or interval, between each selected unit in the sample. In order to select a systematic sample, you need to follow these steps:

1. Number the units on your frame from 1 to N (where N is the total population size).
2. Determine the sampling interval (K) by dividing the number of units in the population by the desired sample size. For example, to select a sample of 100 from a population of 400, you would need a sampling interval of 400 ÷ 100 = 4. Therefore, K = 4. You will need to select one unit out of every four units to end up with a total of 100 units in your sample.
3. Select a number between one and K at random. This number is called *the random start* and would be the first number included in your sample. Using the sample above, you would select a number between 1 and 4 from a table of random numbers. If you choose 3, the third unit on your frame would be the first unit included in your sample; if you choose 2, your sample would start with the second unit on your frame.
4. Select every K^{th} (in this case, every fourth) unit after that first number. For example, the sample might consist of the following units to make up a sample of 100: 3 (the random start), 7, 11, 15, 19...395, 399 (up to N, which is 400 in this case).

Using the example above, you can see that with a systematic sample approach there are only four possible samples that can be selected, corresponding to the four possible random starts:

- 1, 5, 9, 13...393, 397
- 2, 6, 10, 14...394, 398

- 3, 7, 11, 15...395, 399
- 4, 8, 12, 16...396, 400

Each member of the population belongs to only one of the four samples and each sample has the same chance of being selected. From that, we can see that each unit has a one in four chance of being selected in the sample. This is the same probability as if a simple random sampling of 100 units was selected. The main difference is that with simple random sampling, any combination of 100 units would have a chance of making up the sample, while with systematic sampling, there are only four possible samples. From that, we can see how precise systematic sampling is compared with simple random sampling. The population's order on the frame will determine the possible samples for systematic sampling. If the population is randomly distributed on the frame, then systematic sampling should yield results that are similar to simple random sampling.

This method is often used in industry, where an item is selected for testing from a production line to ensure that machines and equipment are of a standard quality. For example, a tester in a manufacturing plant might perform a quality check on every 20th product in an assembly line. The tester might choose a random start between the numbers 1 and 20. This will determine the first product to be tested; every 20th product will be tested thereafter.

Interviewers can use this sampling technique when questioning people for a sample survey. The market researcher might select, for example, every 10th person who enters a particular store, after selecting the first person at random. The surveyor may interview the occupants of every fifth house on a street, after randomly selecting one of the first five houses.

Example: Imagine you have to conduct a survey on student housing for your university or college. Your school has an enrolment of 10,000 students and you want to take a systematic sample of 500 students. In order to do this, you must first determine what your sampling interval (K) would be:

Total population ÷ sample size = sampling interval

$N \div n = K$

$= 10{,}000 \div 500$

$= 20$

To begin this systematic sample, all students would have to be assigned sequential numbers. The starting point would be chosen by selecting a random number between 1 and 20. If this number were 9, then the 9th student on the list would be selected along with every 20th student thereafter. The sample of students would be those corresponding to student numbers 9, 29, 49, 69...9,929, 9,949, 9,969 and 9,989.

In the examples used thus far, the sampling interval K was always a whole number, but this is not always the case. For example, if you want a sample of 30 from a population of 740, your sampling interval (or K) will be 24.7. In these cases, there are a few options to make the number easier to work with.

You can round the number—either round it up to the nearest whole number or round it down. Rounding down will ensure that you select at least the number of units you originally wanted (and you can then delete some units to get the exact sample size you wanted). Techniques exist to adapt systematic sampling to the case where N (total population) is not a multiple of n (sample size), but still give a sample exactly the same as the n units. These techniques will not be discussed here.

The advantages of systematic sampling are that the sample selection cannot be easier and that the sample is distributed evenly over the listed population. The biggest drawback of the systematic sampling method is that if there is some cycle in the way the population is arranged on a list and if that cycle coincides in some way with the sampling interval, the possible samples may not be representative of the population. This can be seen in the following example:

Example: Suppose you run a large grocery store and have a list of the employees in each section. The grocery store is divided into the following 10 sections: deli counter, bakery, cashiers, stock, meat counter, produce, pharmacy, photo shop, flower shop and dry cleaning.

Each section has 10 employees, including a manager (making 100 employees in total). Your list is ordered by section, with the manager listed first and then, the other employees by descending order of seniority.

If you wanted to survey your employees about their thoughts on their work environment, you might choose a small sample to answer your questions. If you use a systematic sampling approach and your sampling interval is 10, then you could end up selecting only managers or the newest employees in each section. This type of sample would not give you a complete or appropriate picture of your employees' thoughts.

Sampling with Probability Proportional to Size

Probability sampling requires that each member of the survey population have a chance of being included in the sample, but it does not require that this chance be the same for everyone. If there is information available on the frame about the size of each unit (e.g., number of employees for each business) and if those units vary in size, this information can be used in the sampling selection in order to increase the efficiency. This is known as *sampling with probability proportional to size* (PPS). With this method, the bigger the size of the unit, the higher the chance it has of being included in the sample. For this method to bring increased efficiency, the measure of size needs to be accurate. This is a more complex sampling method that will not be discussed in further detail here.

Stratified Sampling

Using *stratified sampling,* the population is divided into homogeneous, mutually exclusive groups called strata, and then independent samples are selected from each stratum. Any of the sampling methods mentioned in this section (and others that exist) can be used to sample within each stratum.

The sampling method can vary from one stratum to another. When simple random sampling is used to select the sample within each stratum, the sample design is called *stratified simple random sampling*. A population can be stratified by any variable that is available for all units on the sampling frame prior to sampling (e.g., age, sex, province of residence, income, etc.).

Why do we need to create strata? There are many reasons, the main one being that it can make the sampling strategy more efficient. It was mentioned earlier that you need a larger sample to get a more accurate estimation of a characteristic that varies greatly from one unit to the other than for a characteristic that does not. For example, if every person in a population had the same salary, then a sample of one individual would be enough to get a precise estimate of the average salary.

This is the idea behind the efficiency gain obtained with stratification. If you create strata within which units share similar characteristics (e.g., income) and are considerably different from units in other strata (e.g., occupation, type of dwelling) then you would only need a small sample from each stratum to get a precise estimate of total income for that stratum. Then you could combine these estimates to get a precise estimate of total income for the whole population. If you were to use a simple random sampling approach in the whole population without stratification, the sample would need to be larger than the total of all stratum samples to get an estimate of total income with the same level of precision. Stratified sampling ensures an adequate sample size for sub-groups in the population of interest. When a population is stratified, each stratum becomes an independent population and you will need to decide the sample size for each stratum.

Example: Suppose you want to estimate how many high school students have part-time jobs at the national level and also in each province.

If you were to select a simple random sample of 25,000 people from a list of all high school students in Canada (assuming such a list was available for selection), you would end up on average with just a little over 100 people from Prince Edward Island, since they account for less than half of a per cent of the whole Canadian population. This sample would probably not be large enough for the kind of detailed analysis you had in mind.

Stratifying your list by province, again assuming that this information is available, and then selecting a sample size for each province would allow you to decide on the exact sample size needed for that specific province. Thus, in order to get good representation of Prince Edward Island, you would use a larger sample than the one allotted to it by the simple random sampling approach.

Example: An Ontario school board wanted to assess student opinion on dropping Grade 13 from the secondary school programme. They decided to survey students from Elmsview High School. To ensure a representative sample of students from all grade levels, the school board used a stratified sampling technique.

In this case, the strata were the five grade levels (grades 9 to 13). The school board then selected a sample within each stratum. The students selected in this sample were extracted using simple random or systematic sampling, making up a total sample of 100 students.

Stratification is most useful when the stratifying variables are

- Simple to work with,
- Easy to observe, and
- Closely related to the topic of the survey.

Cluster Sampling

Sometimes it is too expensive to spread a sample across the population as a whole. Travel costs can become expensive if interviewers have to survey people from one end of the country to the other. To reduce costs, statisticians may choose a *cluster sampling* technique.

Cluster sampling divides the population into groups or clusters. A number of clusters are selected randomly to represent the total population, and then all units within selected clusters are included in the sample. No units from non-selected clusters are included in the sample—they are represented by those from selected clusters. This differs from stratified sampling, where some units are selected from each group.

Examples of clusters are factories, schools and geographic areas such as electoral subdivisions. The selected clusters are used to represent the population.

Example: Suppose you are a representative from an athletic organization wishing to find out which sports Grade 11 students are participating in across Canada. It would be too costly and lengthy to survey every Canadian in Grade 11, or even a couple of students from every Grade 11 class in Canada. Instead, 100 schools are randomly selected from all over Canada.

These schools provide clusters of samples. Then every Grade 11 student in all 100 clusters is surveyed. In effect, the students in these clusters represent all Grade 11 students in Canada.

Example: Imagine that the municipal council of a small city wants to investigate the use of health care services by residents.

First, the council requests from Statistics Canada electoral subdivision maps that identify and label each city block. From these maps, the council creates a list of all city blocks. This list will serve as the sampling frame.

Every household in that city belongs to a city block, and each city block represents a cluster of households. The council randomly picks a number of city blocks. Using the simple random sample approach, then the council creates a list of all households in the selected city blocks; these households make up the survey sample. As mentioned, cost reduction is a reason for using cluster sampling. It creates 'pockets' of sampled units instead of spreading the sample over the whole territory. Another reason is that sometimes a list of all units in the population (a requirement when conducting simple random sample, systematic sample or sampling with probability proportional to size) is not available, while a list of all clusters is either available or easy to create.

In most cases, the main drawback is a loss of efficiency when compared with simple random sampling. It is usually better to survey a large number of small clusters instead of a small number of large clusters. This is because neighbouring units tend to be more alike, resulting in a sample that does not represent the whole spectrum of opinions or situations present in the overall population. In the two previous examples, students in the same school tend to participate in the same types of sports (depending on the facilities available at their school); similarly, elderly people have a tendency to live in specific neighbourhoods and to be heavy users of health services.

Another drawback to cluster sampling is that you do not have total control over the final sample size. Since not all schools have the same number of Grade 11 students and city blocks do not all have the same number of households, and you must interview every student or household in your sample, the final size may be larger or smaller than you expected.

Multi-stage Sampling

Multi-stage sampling is like the cluster method, except that it involves picking a sample from within each chosen cluster, rather than including all units in the cluster. This type of sampling requires at least two stages. In the first stage, large groups or clusters are identified and selected. These clusters contain more population units than are needed for the final sample.

In the second stage, population units are picked from within the selected clusters (using any of the possible probability sampling methods) for a final sample. If more than two stages are used, the process of choosing population units within clusters continues until there is a final sample.

Example: A cluster sample would choose 100 schools and then interview every Grade 11 student from those schools. Instead in multi-stage sampling, you could select more schools, get a list of all Grade 11 students from these selected schools and select a random sample (e.g., simple random sample) of students from each school. This would be a two-stage sampling design.

You could also get a list of all Grade 11 classes in the selected schools, pick a random sample of classes from each of those schools, get a list of all the students in the selected classes and finally select a random sample of students from each class. This would be a three-stage sampling design. Each time we add a stage, the process becomes more complex.

Now imagine that each school has on average 80 Grade 11 students. Cluster sampling would then give your organization a sample of about 8,000 students (100 schools x 80 Grade 11 students). If you wanted a bigger sample, you could select schools with more students; and for a smaller sample you could select schools with fewer students.

One way to control the sample size would be to stratify the schools into large, medium and small sizes (in terms of the number of Grade 11 students) and select a sample of schools from each stratum. This is called *stratified cluster sampling*.

With a three-stage design, you could select a sample of 400 schools, then select two Grade 11 classes per school (assuming that there are two or more Grade 11 classes per school). Finally, you could select 10 students per class. This way, you still end up with a sample of about 8,000 students (400 schools x 2 classes x 10 students), but the sample will be more spread out.

You can see from this example that with multi-stage sampling, you still have the benefit of a more concentrated sample for cost reduction. However, the sample is not as concentrated as other clusters and the sample size is still bigger than for a simple random sample size. Also, you do not need to have a list of all of the students in the population. All you need is a list of the classes from the 400 schools and a list of the students from the 800 classes. Admittedly, more information is needed in this type of sample than what is required in cluster sampling. However, multi-stage sampling still saves a great amount of time and effort by not having to create a list of all of the units in a population.

Multi-phase Sampling

A *multi-phase sample* collects basic information from a large sample of units and then, for a subsample of these units, collects more detailed information. The most common form of multi-phase sampling is two-phase sampling (or double sampling), but three or more phases are also possible.

Multi-phase sampling is quite different from multi-stage sampling, despite the similarities in name. Although multi-phase sampling also involves taking two or more samples, all samples are drawn from the same frame and at each phase the units are structurally the same. However, as with multi-stage sampling, the more phases used, the more complex the sample design and estimation will become.

Multi-phase sampling is useful when the frame lacks auxiliary information that could be used to stratify the population or to screen out part of the population.

Example: Suppose that an organization needs information about cattle farmers in Alberta, but the survey frame lists all types of farms—cattle, dairy, grain, hog, poultry and produce. To complicate matters, the survey frame does not provide any auxiliary information for the farms listed there.

A simple survey could be conducted whose only question is "Is part or all of your farm devoted to cattle farming?" With only one question, this survey should have a low cost per interview (especially if done by telephone) and, consequently, the organization should be able to draw a large sample. Once the first sample has been drawn, a second, smaller sample can be extracted from among the cattle farmers and more detailed questions asked of these farmers. Using this method, the organization avoids the expense of surveying units that are not in this specific scope (i.e., non-cattle farmers).

Multi-phase sampling can be used when there is insufficient budget to collect information from the whole sample, or when doing so would create excessive burden on the respondent, or even when there are very different costs of collection for different questions on a survey.

Example: A health survey asks participants some basic questions about their diet, smoking habits, exercise routines and alcohol consumption. In addition, the survey requires that respondents subject themselves to some direct physical tests, such as running on a treadmill or having their blood pressure and cholesterol levels measured.

Filling out questionnaires or interviewing participants are relatively inexpensive procedures, but the medical tests require the supervision and assistance of a trained health practitioner, as well as the use of an equipped laboratory, both of which can be quite costly. The best way to conduct this survey would be to use a two-phase sample approach. In the first phase, the interviews are performed on an appropriately sized sample. From this sample, a smaller sample is drawn. This second sample will take part in the medical tests.

NON-PROBABILITY SAMPLING

The difference between *probability* and *non-probability sampling* has to do with a basic assumption about the nature of the population under study. In probability sampling, every item has a chance of being selected. In non-probability sampling, there is an assumption that there is an even distribution of characteristics within the population. This is what makes the researcher believe that any sample would be representative and because of that, results will be accurate. For probability sampling, randomization is a feature of the selection process, rather than an assumption about the structure of the population.

In non-probability sampling, since elements are chosen arbitrarily, there is no way to estimate the probability of any one element being included in the sample. Also, no assurance is given that each item has a chance of being included, making it impossible either to estimate sampling variability or to identify possible bias.

Reliability cannot be measured in non-probability sampling; the only way to address data quality is to compare some of the survey results with available information about the population. Still, there is no assurance that the estimates will meet an acceptable level of error. Statisticians are reluctant to use these methods because there is no way to measure the precision of the resulting sample. Despite these drawbacks, non-probability sampling methods can be useful when descriptive comments about the sample itself are desired. Secondly, they are quick, inexpensive and convenient. There are also other circumstances, such as in applied social research, when it is unfeasible or impractical to conduct probability sampling. Statistics Canada uses probability sampling for almost all of its surveys, but uses non-probability sampling for questionnaire testing and some preliminary studies during the development stage of a survey.

Most non-sampling methods require some effort and organization to complete, but others, like convenience sampling, are done casually and do not need a formal plan of action.

Convenience or Haphazard Sampling

Convenience sampling is sometimes referred to as *haphazard* or *accidental sampling*. It is not normally representative of the target population because sample units are only selected if they can be accessed easily and conveniently.

There are times when the average person uses convenience sampling. A food critic, for example, may try several appetizers or entrees to judge the quality and variety of a menu. And television reporters often seek so-called 'people-on-the-street interviews' to find out how people view an issue. In both these examples, the sample is chosen randomly, without use of a specific survey method. The obvious advantage is that the method is easy to use, but that advantage is greatly offset by the presence of bias. Although useful applications of the technique are limited, it can deliver accurate results when the population is homogeneous.

For example, a scientist could use this method to determine whether a lake is polluted. Assuming that the lake water is well-mixed, any sample would yield similar information. A scientist could safely draw water anywhere on the lake without fretting about whether or not the sample is representative.

Examples of convenience sampling include:

- The female moviegoers sitting in the first row of a movie theatre
- The first 100 customers to enter a department store
- The first three callers in a radio contest.

Volunteer Sampling

As the term implies, this type of sampling occurs when people volunteer their services for the study. In psychological experiments or pharmaceutical trials (drug testing), for example, it would be difficult and unethical to enlist random participants from the general public.

In these instances, the sample is taken from a group of volunteers. Sometimes, the researcher offers payment to entice respondents. In exchange, the volunteers accept the possibility of a lengthy, demanding or sometimes unpleasant process.

Sampling voluntary participants as opposed to the general population may introduce strong biases. Often in opinion polling, only the people who care strongly enough about the subject one way or another tend to respond.

The silent majority does not typically respond, resulting in large selection bias.

Television and radio media often use call-in polls to informally query an audience on their views. The Much Music television channel uses this kind of survey in their CombatZone programme. The programme asks viewers to cast a vote for one of two music videos by telephone, e-mail or through their online website. Oftentimes, there is no limit imposed on the frequency or number of calls one respondent can make. So, unfortunately, a person might be able to vote repeatedly. It should also be noted that the people who contribute to these surveys might have different views than those who do not.

Judgement Sampling

This approach is used when a sample is taken based on certain judgements about the overall population. The underlying assumption is that the investigator will select units that are characteristic of the population. The critical issue here is objectivity: how much can judgment be relied upon to arrive at a typical sample? *Judgement sampling* is subject to the researcher's biases and is perhaps even more biased than haphazard sampling. Since any preconceptions the researcher may have are reflected in the sample, large biases can be introduced if these preconceptions are inaccurate.

Statisticians often use this method in exploratory studies like pre-testing of questionnaires and focus groups. They also prefer to use this method in laboratory settings where the choice of experimental subjects (i.e., animal, human, vegetable) reflects the investigator's pre-existing beliefs about the population.

One advantage of judgement sampling is the reduced cost and time involved in acquiring the sample.

Quota Sampling

This is one of the most common forms of non-probability sampling. Sampling is done until a specific number of units (quotas) for various sub-populations have been selected. Since there are no rules as to how these quotas are to be filled, *quota sampling* is really a means for satisfying sample size objectives for certain sub-populations.

The quotas may be based on population proportions. For example, if there are 100 men and 100 women in a population and a sample of 20 are to be drawn to participate in a cola taste challenge, you may want to divide the sample evenly between the sexes—10 men and 10 women. Quota sampling can be considered preferable to other forms of non-probability sampling (e.g., judgement sampling) because it forces the inclusion of members of different sub-populations. Quota sampling is somewhat similar to stratified sampling in that similar units are grouped together. However, it differs in how the units are selected. In probability sampling, the units are selected randomly while in quota sampling it is usually left up to the interviewer to decide who is sampled. This results in selection bias. Thus, quota sampling is often used by market researchers (particularly for telephone surveys) instead of stratified sampling, because it is relatively inexpensive and easy to administer and has the desirable property of satisfying population proportions. However, it disguises potentially significant bias.

As with all other non-probability sampling methods, in order to make inferences about the population, it is necessary to assume that persons selected are similar to those not selected. Such strong assumptions are rarely valid.

Example: The student council at Cedar Valley Public School wants to gauge student opinion on the quality of their extracurricular activities. They decide to survey 100 of 1,000 students using the grade levels (7 to 12) as the sub-population.

The table below gives the number of students in each grade level.

Table. Number of students enrolled at Cedar Valley Public School, by grade

Grade level of students	Number of students (%)	Percentage	Quota of studentsin sample of 100
7	150	15	15
8	220	22	22
9	160	16	16
10	150	15	15
11	200	20	20
12	120	12	12
Total	1,000	100	100

The student council wants to make sure that the percentage of students in each grade level is reflected in the sample. The formula is:

Percentage of students in Grade 10

= (number of students ÷ number of students) x 100%

= $(150 \div 1{,}000) \times 100$

= 15%

Since 15% of the school population is in Grade 10, 15% of the sample should contain Grade 10 students. Therefore, use the following formula to calculate the number of Grade 10 students that should be included in the sample:

Sample of Grade 10 students

= $(15\% \text{ of } 100) \times 100$

= 0.15×100

= 15 students

The main difference between stratified sampling and quota sampling is that stratified sampling would select the students using a probability sampling method such as simple random sampling or systematic sampling. In quota sampling, no such technique is used. The 15 students might be selected by choosing the first 15 Grade 10 students to enter school on a certain day, or by choosing 15 students from the first two rows of a particular classroom. Keep in mind that those students who arrive late or sit at the back of the class may hold different opinions from those who arrived earlier or sat in the front.

The main argument against quota sampling is that it does not meet the basic requirement of randomness. Some units may have no chance of selection or the chance of selection may be unknown. Therefore, the sample may be biased.

It is common, but not necessary, for quota samples to use random selection procedures at the beginning stages, much in the same way as probability sampling does. For instance, the first step in multi-stage sampling would be randomly selecting the geographic areas. The difference is in the selection of the units in the final stages of the process.

In multi-stage sampling, units are based on up-to-date lists for selected areas and a sample is selected according to a random process. In quota sampling, by contrast, each interviewer is instructed on how many of the respondents should be men and how many should be women, as well as how many people should represent the various age groups. The quotas are therefore calculated from available data for the population, so that the sexes, age groups or other demographic variables are represented in the correct proportions.

But within each quota, interviewers may fail to secure a representative sample of respondents.

For example, suppose that an organization wants to find out information about the occupations of men aged 20 to 25. An interviewer goes to a university campus and selects the first 50 men aged 20 to 25 that she comes across and who agree to participate in her organization's survey. However, this sample does not mean that these 50 men are representative of all men aged 20 to 25.

Quota sampling is generally less expensive than random sampling. It is also easy to administer, especially considering the tasks of listing the whole population, randomly selecting the sample and following-up on non-respondents can be omitted from the procedure.

Quota sampling is an effective sampling method when information is urgently required and can be carried out independent of existing sampling frames. In many cases where the population has no suitable frame, quota sampling may be the only appropriate sampling method.

ESTIMATION

The goal of conducting surveys is to obtain information about a particular population. When the sample has been selected and the information collected and processed, there still remains the task of linking the information gathered from the sample back to the overall population.

Estimation is the process of determining a likely value for a variable in the survey population, based on information collected from the sample. Researchers are usually interested in looking at estimates of many statistics—totals, averages and proportions being the most frequent—for different variables.

For example, a sample survey could be used to produce any of the following statistics: estimates for the proportion of smokers among all people aged 15 to 24 in the population; the average earnings of men and women with a university degree; or the total number of cars possessed by the whole survey population.

Underpinning the estimation process is the sampling weight of a unit, which indicates the number of units in the population (including the sampling weight) that are represented by this sampled unit. The sampling weight is the inverse of the unit's probability of selection.

Example: Suppose that the city of Winnipeg has decided to award bus travellers with free one-year bus passes as a way of promoting its services. A simple random sample of 10 people is selected from the 30 passengers on a city bus.

Since simple random sampling gives equal probability of selection to every member of the population (in this case, all passengers on the bus), each passenger had one chance out of three of being selected.

This translates into a sampling weight of three for every selected unit. This means that each person in the sample represents three persons in the population—himself or herself, plus two other persons.

To estimate this sampling weight, one could take the survey information for the 10 selected passengers and copy it three times to create an artificial population of 30. Totals, averages or proportions for the real population could then be estimated by the corresponding statistics computed using the artificial population. Instead of doing this, however, survey statisticians attach a sampling weight to each unit in the sample and take this weight into account when estimating.

If one person in a sample (with a sampling weight of 18) had blue eyes and brown hair, then it is as if a total of 18 people in the population had blue eyes and brown hair.

Example: You are conducting a survey to determine the total number of people living on your street and the average number of cars owned by each household.

You decide to select a systematic sample of 5 households from the 20 on your street and intend to use that sample to estimate the totals you are looking for. The following table summarizes the information that you gathered during your interviews with the sampled households:

Table. Sample of households on Redwood Street

Household number	Number of persons	Number of cars	Probability of selection	Sampling weight
1	1	0	1/4	4
2	4	2	1/4	4
3	2	1	1/4	4
4	2	1	1/4	4
5	3	2	1/4	4

The selection probability of 1 in 4 comes from the fact that systematic sampling gives an equal chance of being selected to each household on your street. The sampling weight of 4 is just the inverse of that probability. When estimating, you have to look at the characteristics of each sampled household. In this case, it is decided that 4 households from the population of 20 on your street have the same characteristics.

In order to estimate the total number of persons living on your street, you have to multiply the number of persons in a household by the number of households in that sampling weight, then add up all the final numbers.

For example, there are 4 one-person households (represented by Household number 1), 4 four-person households, 8 two-person households (four households represented by Household number 3 and four households represented by Household number 4) and 4 three-person households. The estimation of the total number of persons would then be:

Estimated number of persons living on your street

$= (4\times 1) + (4\times 4) + (8\times 2) + (4\times 3)$

$= 48$ people

To estimate the average number of cars per household, you proceed in the same manner. Get an estimate of the total number of cars owned by households on your street and then, divide the estimate by the actual number of households on the street. For example, there are 4 households without a car (represented by Household number 1), 8 households with two cars (represented by Household number 2 and Household number 5), 8 households with one car each (represented by Household number 3 and Household number 4).

Estimated number of cars

$= (4\times 0) + (8\times 2) + (8\times 1)$

$= 24$ cars

Estimated average

$= 24 \div 20$

$= 1.2$ cars per household

Self-weighting Designs

It is not always the case that all sampled units had the same sampling weight. Some designs give unequal probability of selection to units, resulting in units within the same sample having different sampling weights. Answers from one household or business could represent the answers for 200 units of the population, while the answers from another could represent only 50 units in the population.

When every unit in the sample has the same sampling weight, the sampling design is said to be self-weighted. This kind of design is time-saving and operationally convenient, particularly for large samples.

Because every unit has the same weight, those weights can be ignored when estimating averages and proportions. The average for the sample gives an appropriate estimate of the average for the whole population.

Simple random sampling and systematic sampling are examples of self-weighted designs. In that sense, calculations could have been made easier in example. For instance, to estimate the average number of cars per household in the population, we could have used the same average as the one used in the sample.

The 5 sampled households own a total of 6 cars, an average of 1.2 cars per household. This is the same result as that obtained using the sampling weight procedure.

Adjusting The Weights

Sometimes, the sampling weights are adjusted prior to estimation. There are basically two reasons for weight adjustment:

- Adjusting for non-response: Using sampling weights for estimation works fine when you have been able to interview all selected units. In Example:: 2, if two of the five sampled households refused to answer or were unavailable at the time of the survey, you would only have answers for three households, thus representing only 12 of the 20 households on the street. The two non-responding units represent four households each. This means that we have no information on the number of persons or cars for 8 households on your street. In order to adjust for that, survey statisticians usually increase the weights of responding units to account for the loss of representativeness caused by non-response. The goal would be to use only the 3 units for which we have information, but still represent the 20 households on the street.
- Adjusting for external information: Sometimes, we know the actual total for one or more variables measured in the sample. In Example:: of the Probability sampling section, a population of the 1,000 best horror movies was equally divided into 500 classic movies and 500 modern movies. Even though you knew this prior to sampling, you decided to select a simple random sample of 100 movies and ended up with 77 classic movies and 23 modern movies. Each of these

movies has a weight of 10 (because you selected 1 movie out of every 10 titles). Using the answers from the survey and the sampling weight, your sample would represent a population of 770 classic movies and 230 modern movies. This could lead to inaccurate estimates. One solution would be to decrease the weight of every sampled classic and increase the weight of every sampled modern movie so that your sample gives an estimate of 500 classics and 500 modern films in the population. This should reduce the distortion caused by a 'bad' sample.

Of course, stratifying by release date prior to sampling would have solved this problem. However, in a lot of cases, we have totals at the population level, but we don't know the attribute of each unit on the sampling frame. For example, from the Census of Population, we know how many men and women there are in a specific city, but all we have for sampling is a list of households. Thus, stratifying our population by sex would not be possible. Demographic projections by age and sex for each province are often used in social surveys to adjust sampling weights.

The weights adjusted for non-response and/or external counts are used for estimation, in the same way as the sampling weight was used in Example::.

Other Estimation Methods

Using the weights to inflate the sample results is not the only estimation method that exists, but it is the simplest one and the only one that we will cover. Nevertheless, it is important to know that there exist some other methods that could lead to more precise estimates (e.g., using auxiliary information). The estimation process has to take into account the sampling design that was used. Otherwise, the resulting estimates could be severely biased.

Estimating The Sampling Error

As mentioned before, any estimates derived from samples are subject to what is called the sampling error. This comes from the fact that only a part of the population was observed, instead of the whole. A different sample could have come up with different results. The amount of variation that exists among the estimates from the different possible samples is what makes the sampling error. (There are roughly 14 million different combinations of 6 numbers from 1 to 49, so imagine how many ways there are to select a sample of 25,000 Canadian households!) Of course, this sampling error is unknown, since we would need to know the answer for each unit of the population in order to calculate it. Nevertheless, it can be estimated by using the survey data.

The extent of the sampling error depends on many things, including the sampling method, the estimation method, the sample size and the variability of the estimated characteristic.

This is why each sample estimate has its own sampling error. This error should thus be approximated for each estimated total, average, proportion, etc. produced by the survey.

Examples of Estimation Using An Simple Random Sampling Design

Simple random sampling is the simplest of all sampling methods. Estimation using the simple random sampling method has been studied extensively. There are simple formulas to estimate the sampling error for many statistics when simple random sampling is used, especially since it is a self-weighting design. We present here the most common estimator for a population average (mean) and total, under simple random sampling.

Estimation of The Population Mean

In a simple random sample, the estimate of the population mean is identical to the mean of the sample:

$$\hat{x} = \frac{\sum x}{n}$$

where

x = an observed value $\hat{x}$

= estimate of the population mean

$\sum$ x= sum of all observed x values in the sample

n = number of observations in the sample.

Note: Lowercase x and n should be used if you are referring to a sample survey and upper case X and N should be used when referring to a population.

If the sample results have been summarized in a frequency table, then the estimate for the population mean is the same as the sample. Thus,

$$\hat{x} = \frac{\sum xf}{\sum f}$$

where

x = an observed value

f = the frequency of the value (the number of times that this value have been observed in the sample) $\hat{x}$

= estimate of the population mean $\sum xf$

= sum of all observed xf values (the product of the observed values times its frequency) in the sample $\sum f$

= sum of the frequencies in the sample.

Example: A farmer randomly selects 10 eggs from a gross of 12 dozen eggs (144 eggs) he finds in his hen house. He carefully weighs each egg.

The following weights were recorded in grams:
0.75, 0.70, 0.55, 0.50, 0.60, 0.65, 0.75, 0.65, 0.75, 0.50
What is the mean weight of the gross of eggs?

Using the above formula, we can determine the mean weight of all of the eggs:

$$\hat{x} = \frac{\sum x}{n}$$

$$= \frac{6.4}{10}$$

$$= 0.64 \text{ grammes}$$

Estimation of The Population Total

For a simple random sample, the estimation formula of a total for the population is,

$$\hat{x} = N\frac{\sum x}{n}$$

where

x = an observed value $\hat{x}$

= estimated population total $\sum x$

= sum of all observed x values in the sample

n = number of observations in the sample

N = total number of observations in the population.

It is just the estimate for the mean value multiplied by the number of units in the population.

In the previous example, the mean weight of an egg is 0.64 grams, so it is logical to think that the total weight of the 144 eggs would be 92.16 grams (144 × 0.64 = 92.16 grams).

9

Sampling Distributions

Suppose we have a population about which we want to know some characteristic, e.g. height, income, voting intentions. If it is a large population, it may be difficult to look at every individual. We therefore take a sample. For example, if we want to know the average height of the population, we might sample 100 people and take the average height of the sample.

But how good an estimate will this be? Is it likely to be biased upwards or downwards from the population average? How inaccurate is it likely to be? How big a sample do we need to be confident of getting a figure close to the true figure? These are the sorts of questions answered in this and subsequent sections. We discuss sampling with and without replacement, and from finite and infinite populations. We shall start by assuming that samples are randomly selected from the population, and that they are large, e.g. 30 observations or larger. Small samples will be dealt with later. Each type of sampling leads to a different sampling distribution. The sampling distribution of a parameter, such as sample mean or sample proportion is either a theoretical distribution, like the normal, or is obtained by taking many samples of the same size from a population and constructing a frequency distribution.

DEFINITION

The sampling distribution is a distribution of a sample statistic. While the concept of a distribution of a set of numbers is intuitive for most students, the concept of a distribution of a set of statistics is not. Therefore distributions will be reviewed before the sampling distribution is discussed.

THE SAMPLE DISTRIBUTION

The sample distribution is the distribution resulting from the collection of actual data. A major characteristic of a sample is that it contains a finite (countable) number of scores, the number of scores represented by the letter N. For example, suppose that the following data were collected:

32	35	42	33	36	38	37	33	38	36	35	34	37	40	38	36	35	31	37	36	33
36	39	40	33	30	35	37	39	32	39	37	35	36	39	33	31	40	37	34	34	37

In addition to the frequency distribution, the sample distribution can be described with numbers, called statistics. Examples of statistics are the mean, median, mode, standard deviation, range, and correlation coefficient, among others. Statistics, and procedures for computing statistics, have been discussed in detail in an earlier chapter.

If a different sample was taken, different scores would result. The relative frequency polygon would be different, as would the statistics computed from the second sample. However, there would also be some consistency in that while the statistics would not be exactly the same, they would be similar. To achieve order in this chaos, statisticians have developed probability models.

PROBABILITY MODELS - POPULATION DISTRIBUTIONS

Probability models exist in a theoretical world where complete information is available. As such, they can never be known except in the mind of the mathematical statistician. If an infinite number of infinitely precise scores were taken, the resulting distribution would be a probability model of the population.

This probability model is described with pictures (graphs) which are analogous to the relative frequency polygon of the sample distribution. The two graphs below illustrate two types of probability models, the uniform distribution and the normal curve.

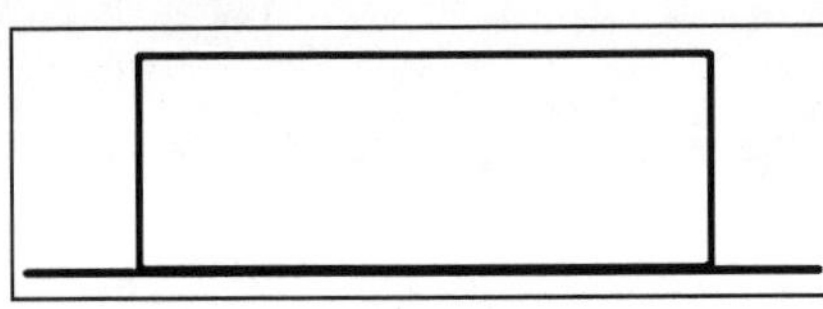

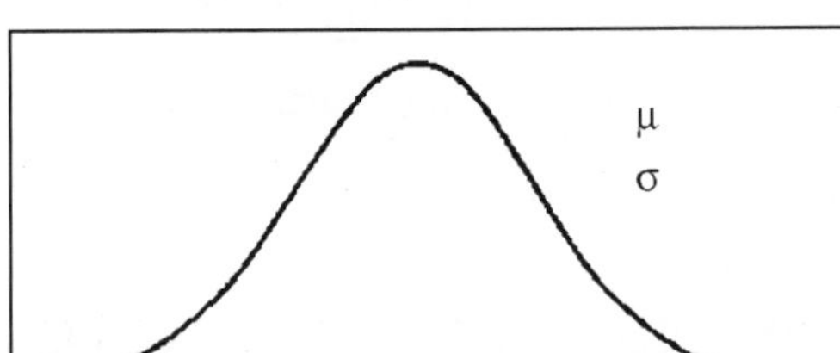

As discussed earlier in the chapter on the normal curve, probability distributions are described by mathematical equations that contain parameters. Parameters are variables that change the shape of the probability model. By setting these parameters equal to numbers, a member of that probability model family of models results.

A critical aspect of statistics is the estimation of parameters with sample statistics. Sample statistics are used as estimators of the corresponding parameters in the population model. For example, the mean and standard deviation of the sample are used as estimates of the corresponding population parameters μ and δ. Mathematical statistics texts devote considerable effort to defining what is a good or poor parameter estimation procedure.

THE SAMPLING DISTRIBUTION

Note the "-ING" on the end of SAMPLE. It looks and sounds similar to the SAMPLE DISTRIBUTION, but, in reality the concept is much closer to a population model.

The sampling distribution is a distribution of a sample statistic. It is a model of a distribution of scores, like the population distribution, except that the scores are not raw scores, but statistics. It is a thought experiment; "what would the world be like if a person repeatedly took samples of size N from the population distribution and computed a particular statistic each time?" The resulting distribution of statistics is called the sampling distribution of that statistic. For example, suppose that a sample of size sixteen (N=16) is taken from some population. The mean of the sixteen numbers is computed.

Next a new sample of sixteen is taken, and the mean is again computed. If this process were repeated an infinite number of times, the distribution of the now infinite number of sample means would be called the sampling distribution of the mean.

Every statistic has a sampling distribution. For example, suppose that instead of the mean, medians were computed for each sample. The infinite number of medians would be called the sampling distribution of the median.

Just as the population models can be described with parameters, so can the sampling distribution. The expected value (analogous to the mean) of a sampling distribution will be represented here by the symbol μ. The μ symbol is often written with a subscript to indicate which sampling distribution is being discussed.

For example, the expected value of the sampling distribution of the mean is represented by the symbol μ_{M_d}, that of the median by $\mu_{\overline{X}}$, etc. The value of μ_{M_d} can be thought of as the mean of the distribution of means. In a similar manner the value of $\mu_{\overline{X}_d}$ is the mean of a distribution of medians. They are not really means, because it is not possible to find a mean when $N=\infty$, but are the mathematical equivalent of a mean.

Using advanced mathematics, in a thought experiment, the theoretical statistician often discovers a relationship between the expected value of a statistic and the model parameters. For example, it can be proven that the expected value of both the mean and the median, $\overline{X}$ and M_d, is equal to μ_X.

When the expected value of a statistic equals a population parameter, the statistic is called an unbiased estimator of that parameter. In this case, both the mean and the median would be an unbiased estimator of the parameter μ_X.

A sampling distribution may also be described with a parameter corresponding to a variance, symbolized by σ^2. The square root of this parameter is given a special name, thestandard error. Each sampling distribution has a standard error. In order to keep them straight, each has a name tagged on the end of the word "standard error" and a subscript on the σ symbol. The standard deviation of the sampling distribution of the mean is called the *standard error of the mean* and is symbolized by $\sigma_{\overline{X}}$. Similarly, the standard deviation of the sampling distribution of the median is called the *standard error of the median* and is symbolized by σ_{M_d}.

In each case the standard error of a statistics describes the degree to which the computed statistics will differ from one another when calculated from sample of similar size and selected from similar population models. The larger the standard error, the greater the difference between the computed statistics.

Consistency is a valuable property to have in the estimation of a population parameter, as the statistic with the smallest standard error is preferred as the estimator of the corresponding population parameter, everything else being equal.

Statisticians have proven that in most cases the standard error of the mean is smaller than the standard error of the median. Because of this property, the mean is the preferred estimator of μ_X.

THE SAMPLING DISTRIBUTION OF THE MEAN

The sampling distribution of the mean is a distribution of sample means. This distribution may be described with the parameters $\mu_{\overline{X}}$ and $\sigma_{\overline{X}}$

These parameters are closely related to the parameters of the population distribution, with the relationship being described by the CENTRAL LIMIT THEOREM.

The CENTRAL LIMIT THEOREM essentially states that the mean of the sampling distribution of the mean ($\mu_{\overline{X}}$) equals the mean of the population (μ_X) and that the standard error of the mean ($\sigma_{\overline{X}}$) equals the standard deviation of the population (σ_X) divided by the square root of N as the sample size gets infinitely larger ($N \to \infty$).

In addition, the sampling distribution of the mean will approach a normal distribution. These relationships may be summarized as follows:

$$\mu_{\overline{X}} = \mu_X$$

$$\sigma\overline{X} = \frac{\sigma_X}{\sqrt{N}}$$

The astute student probably noticed, however, that the sample size would have to be very large (∞) in order for these relationships to hold true. In theory, this is fact; in practice, an infinite sample size is impossible. The Central Limit Theorem is very powerful.

In most situations encountered by behavioral scientists, this theorem works reasonably well with an N greater than 10 or 20. Thus, it is possible to closely approximate what the distribution of sample means looks like, even with relatively small sample sizes. The importance of the central limit theorem to statistical thinking cannot be overstated. Most of hypothesis testing and sampling theory is based on this theorem. In addition, it provides a justification for using the normal curve as a model for many naturally occurring phenomena.

If a trait, such as intelligence, can be thought of as a combination of relatively independent events, in this case both genetic and environmental, then it would be expected that trait would be normally distributed in a population.

MICROCOMPUTER SIMULATION OF SAMPLING DISTRIBUTIONS

The purpose of the microcomputer simulation exercise (named SIM-SAM) is to demonstrate how a sampling distribution is created. To run properly the programme requires the use Internet Explore 3.x.

The opening screen will appear as follows:

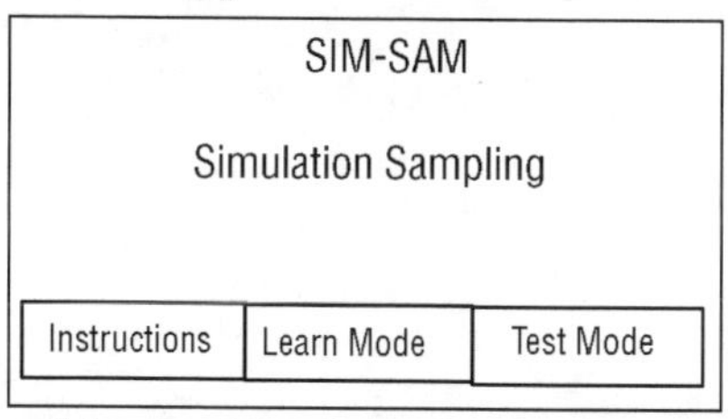

Although it is possible to skip directly to the test mode, it is suggested that the student spend some time familiarizing him or herself in the learning mode.

The learning mode screen will appear as follows:

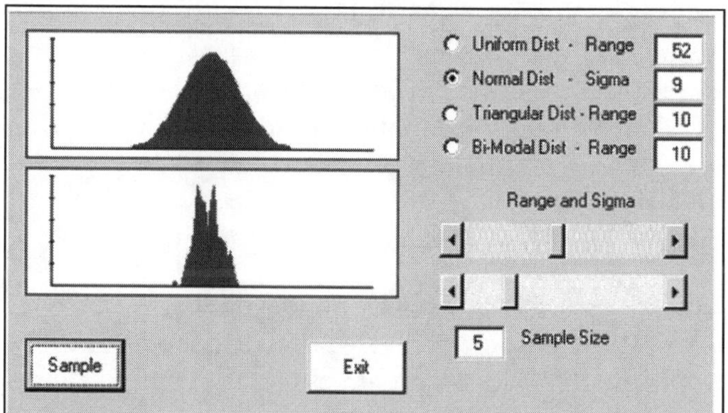

Selecting a distribution, a value for either the Range or Sigma, a sample size, and then clicking on the Sample button runs each simulation. The values for either the Range or Sigma and the Sample Size are changed using the scrollbar.

When the sample button is pressed, the computer generates 100 samples of the sample size selected, computes the mean for each sample, and then draws the sampling distribution of the mean below the population model.

The student should verify that the sampling distribution changes as a function of the type of population model, the variability of the population model, and the sample size.

In addition, the student should verify that the shape of the sampling distribution of the mean approaches a normal distribution as the sample size increases no matter what the population model looks like. When the student is comfortable and understands the above screen, he or she should Exit and proceed to the performance mode. The performance mode screen will appear as follows:

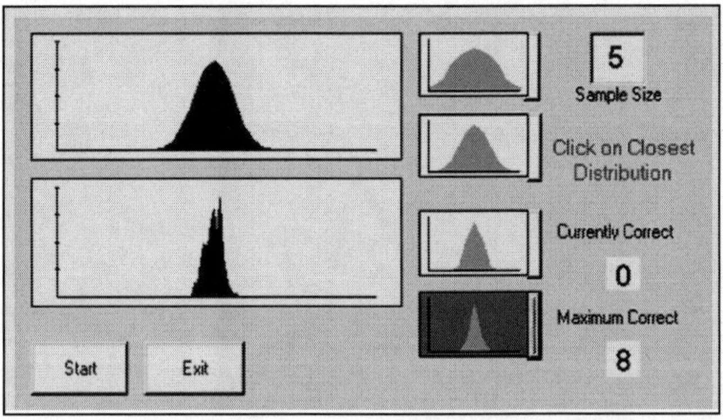

On each trial, the student is presented with a population model and a sample size. The student must guess which of the four potential sampling distributions will be closest to the sampling distribution of the mean that is generated by the computer. After selecting one of the four possibilities by clicking on the button next to the graph, the computer will generate 100 samples, compute the mean for each sample, draw the sampling distribution of the mean in the labeled box, and compare the observed sampling distribution of the mean with each of the four possibilities. Using a measure of "goodness of fit", the computer will select the distribution which is closest to the actual distribution. If that distribution is the one that the student selected, both the trial counter and the correct counter will be incremented by one, if not, only the trial counter will be incremented. The number of points given in this assignment will be the number appearing in the "Maximum Correct" box with a maximum of eight. When satisfied with the score, print this screen to turn in for the assignment and exit the programme.

SUMMARY

To Summarize:

- The sampling distribution is a theoretical distribution of a sample statistic.

- There is a different sampling distribution for each sample statistic.
- Each sampling distribution is characterized by parameters, two of which are μ and σ. The latter is called the standard error.
- The sampling distribution of the mean is a special case of the sampling distribution.
- The Central Limit Theorem relates the parameters of the sampling distribution of the mean to the population model and is very important in statistical thinking.

10

Linear Regression and Correlation

LEAST SQUARES LINE

The Least Squares Line is a method devoted to giving the line of best fit. As with other methods in statistics, the Least Squares Line has a population and a sample notation.

Population Line Notation: $y = \beta_0 + \beta_1 X$

Sample Line Notation: $\hat{y} = \hat{\beta}_0 + \hat{\beta}_1 x$

(This is the Least Squares Line)

The above notations may seem strange. However, try to remember back to algebra.

The equation of a line is the following: y = mx + b where m = slope and b = y-intercept. The Least Squares Line is using the same concept.

$(\hat{\beta}_0 = y - \text{intercept and } \hat{\beta}_1 = \text{Slope})$

$$\hat{\beta}_1 = \frac{SS_{xy}}{SS_{xx}} = \frac{\sum -xy \frac{(\sum x)(\sum y}{n}}{\sum X^2 - \frac{(\sum x)^2}{n}}$$

$$\hat{\beta}_0 = y - \text{int}\,\textit{ercept of Least Squares Line, and}$$

$$\hat{\beta}_0 = \bar{y} - \hat{\beta}_1 \hat{x}\ \textit{where the mean}\ \bar{y}\ \textit{is}\ \bar{y} = \frac{\sum y}{n}\ \textit{and the mean}\ \bar{x} = \frac{\sum x}{n}$$

The least-squares line uses a straight line:

$$y = a + bx$$

to approximate the given set of data, $(x_1y_1), (x_2y_2)\ldots, (x_ny_n)$, where $n \geq 2$ The best fitting curve f(x) has the least square error, i.e.,

$$\Pi = \sum_{i=1}^{n}[y_i - f(x_i)]^2 = \sum_{i=1}^{n}[y_i - (a + bx_i)]^2 = \min.$$

Please note that α and β are unknown coefficients while all x_i and y_i are given. To obtain the least square error, the unknown coefficients α and β must yield zero first derivatives.

$$\begin{cases} \frac{\partial \Pi}{\partial a} 2\sum_{i=1}^{n}\left[y_i - (a + bx_i)\right] = 0 \\ \frac{\partial \Pi}{\partial b} 2\sum_{i=1}^{n}\left[y_i - (a + bx_i)\right] = 0 \end{cases}$$

Expanding the above equations, we have:

$$\begin{cases} \sum_{i=1}^{n} y_i = \alpha \sum_{i=1}^{n} a + b \sum_{i=1}^{n} x_i \\ \sum_{i=1}^{n} x_i y_i = \alpha \sum_{i=1}^{n} x_i + b \sum_{i=1}^{n} {x_i}^2 \end{cases}$$

The unknown coefficients a and b can therefore be obtained:

$$\begin{cases} a = \dfrac{\left(\sum y\right)\left(\sum x^2\right) - \left(\sum x\right)\left(\sum xy\right)}{n\sum x^2 \left(\sum x\right)^2} \\ b = \dfrac{n\sum xy - \left(\sum x\right)\left(\sum y\right)}{n\sum x^2 \left(\sum x\right)^2} \end{cases}$$

where Σ... stands for,

$$\sum_{i-1}^{n} ...i$$

SLOPE OF A LINE

The three main choices for the null hypothesis and the alternative hypothesis are the following:

Null	Hypothesis Versus		Alternative	Hypothesis
H_o:	$b_1 = 0$	vs.	H_a: $b_1\ ^{1}0$	(Two-Tailed)
H_o:	$b_1\ ^{3}0$	vs.	H_a: $b_1 < 0$	(Left-Tailed)
H_o:	$b_1 < 0$	vs.	H_a: $b_1 > 0$	(Right-Tailed)

The critical number is dependent on which of the above tests (two-tailed, left-tailed and right-tailed) the problem involves. For a t-distribution, the following table is needed:

[t-distribution with degrees of freedom (df) = (n – 2)]

t-distribution

(a) $\hat{\beta}_1 = \dfrac{SS_{xy}}{SS_{xx}}$

(b) $SS_{yy} \sum y^2 - \dfrac{\left(\sum y\right)^2}{n}$

(c) $SSE = SS_{yy}\, \hat{\beta}_1\, SS_{xy}$

One main difference in the procedure occurs in the step that deals with the test statistic.

$$t = \frac{\hat{\beta}_1 - \hat{\beta}_1}{\sigma\hat{\beta}1} \; where \sigma t = \hat{\beta}1 = \sqrt{\frac{S^2}{SSxx}} \; and\; S^2 = \frac{SSE}{n-2}$$

ESTIMATING THE EXPECTED VALUE OF Y FOR A GIVEN VALUE OF X

(point estimator) ± *(margin of error)*

$$\hat{y} \pm t_{\alpha/2[n-2]} \sqrt{s^2 \left[\frac{1}{n} + \frac{(X_p - \overline{X})^2}{SS_{xx}}\right]}$$

$$and\; \hat{y} = \hat{\beta}_0 + \hat{\beta}_0\, x\, also\; s^2 = \frac{SSE}{n-2}$$

For a t-distribution, the following table is needed:

t-distribution

Predicting A Particular Value of y For A Given Value of x

$$\hat{y} \pm t_{\alpha/2[n-2]} \sqrt{s^2 \left[1 + \frac{1}{n} + \frac{(X_p - \overline{X})^2}{SS_{xx}}\right]}$$

$$and\; \hat{y} = \hat{\beta}_0 + \hat{\beta}_0\, x\, also\; s^2 = \frac{SSE}{n-2}$$

PEARSON'S CORRELATION COEFFICIENT

The notation for Pearson's Correlation Coefficient is r. This is also called Pearson's r. The three main choices for the null hypothesis and the alternative hypothesis are the following:

Null	Hypothesis	Versus	Alternative	Hypothesis
H_o:	r= 0	vs.	H_a: r ¹ 0	(Two-Tailed)

H_o:	$r^{3} 0$	vs.	H_a: $r < 0$ (Left-Tailed)
H_o:	$r < 0$	vs.	H_a: $r > 0$(Right-Tailed)

If the sample size greater than or equal to 30 than a normal disstribution exists with, $\sigma_r = 1/\sqrt{n}$

If the Sample size is less than 30 than a t-distrution exists with degrees of freedom (df) equal to (n – 2) and

$$\sigma_1 = \sqrt{\frac{1-r^2}{n-2}}$$

Peasson's r is,

$$r = \frac{SS_{xy}}{\sqrt{SS_{xx}SS_{yy}}}$$

$where -1 \leq r \leq 1$

What this means r = + 1 means a Perfect positive relationship between x and y

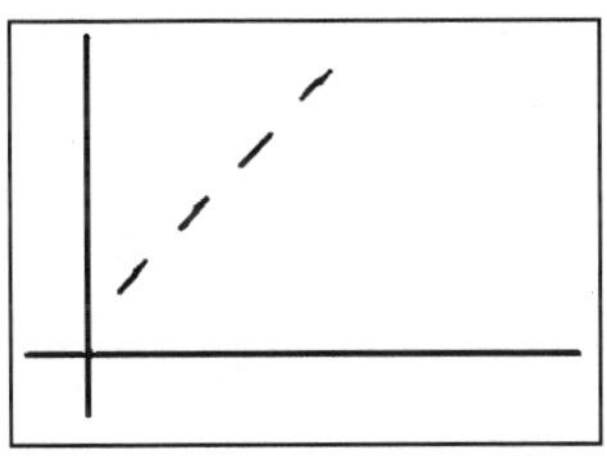

r = –1 means a perfect negative linear relationship between x and y

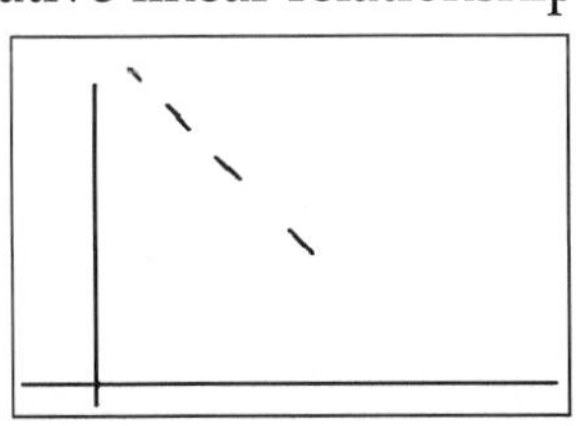

r close to 0 means no linear relation ship between x and y

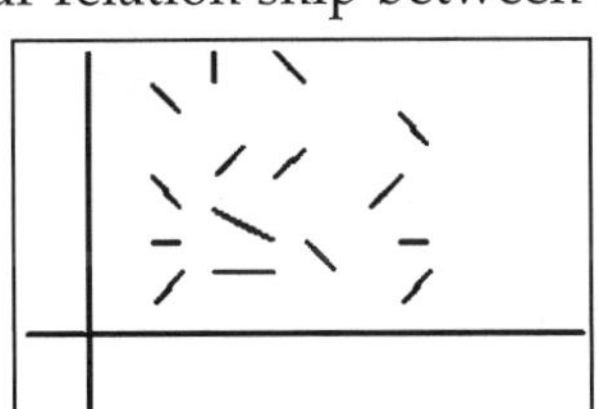

Test Statistic is r,

The z (or t) score for r is z (or t) =

$$\frac{r-0}{\sigma_r}$$

11

Time Series Analysis

A time series is a sequence of observations that are arranged according to the time of their outcome. The annual crop yield of sugar-beets and their price per ton for example is recorded in agriculture. The newspapers' business sections report daily stock prices, weekly interest rates, monthly rates of unemployment and annual turnovers. Meteorology records hourly wind speeds, daily maximum and minimum temperatures and annual rainfall.

Geophysics is continuously observing the shaking or trembling of the earth in order to predict possibly impending earthquakes. An electroencephalogram traces brain waves made by an electroencephalograph in order to detect a cerebral disease, an electrocardiogram traces heart waves.

The social sciences survey annual death and birth rates, the number of accidents in the home and various forms of criminal activities. Parameters in a manufacturing process are permanently monitored in order to carry out an on-line inspection in quality assurance.

There are, obviously, numerous reasons to record and to analyse the data of a time series. Among these is the wish to gain a better understanding of the data generating mechanism, the prediction of future values or the optimal control of a system. The characteristic property of a time series is the fact that the data are not generated independently, their dispersion varies in time, they are often governed by a trend and they have cyclic components. Statistical procedures that suppose independent and identically distributed data are, therefore, excluded from the analysis of time series. This requires proper methods that are summarized under time series analysis.

DEFINITIONS, APPLICATIONS AND TECHNIQUES

Definition of Time Series: *An ordered sequence of values of a variable at equally spaced time intervals.*

Applications: The usage of time series models is twofold:

- Obtain an understanding of the underlying forces and structure that produced the observed data
- Fit a model and proceed to forecasting, monitoring or even feedback and feedforward control.

Time Series Analysis is used for many applications such as:

- Economic Forecasting
- Sales Forecasting
- Budgetary Analysis
- Stock Market Analysis
- Yield Projections
- Process and Quality Control
- Inventory Studies
- Workload Projections
- Utility Studies
- Census Analysis and many, many more.

Techniques: The fitting of time series models can be an ambitious undertaking. There are many methods of model fitting including the following:

- Box-Jenkins ARIMA models
- Box-Jenkins Multivariate Models
- Holt-Winters Exponential Smoothing (single, double, triple)

The user's application and preference will decide the selection of the appropriate technique. It is beyond the realm and intention of the authors of this handbook to cover all these methods. The overview presented here will start by looking at some basic smoothing techniques:

- Averaging Methods
- Exponential Smoothing Techniques.

WHAT ARE MOVING AVERAGE OR SMOOTHING TECHNIQUES?

Smoothing data removes random variation and shows trends and cyclic components: Inherent in the collection of data taken over time is some form of random variation. There exist methods for reducing of canceling the effect due to random variation. An often-used technique in industry is "smoothing". This technique, when properly applied, reveals more clearly the underlying trend, seasonal and cyclic components.

There are two distinct groups of smoothing methods:

- Averaging Methods
- Exponential Smoothing Methods

Taking averages is the simplest way to smooth data

We will first investigate some averaging methods, such as the "simple" average of all past data. A manager of a warehouse wants to know how much a typical supplier delivers in 1000 dollar units. He/she takes a sample of 12 suppliers, at random, obtaining the following results:

Supplier	Amount	Supplier	Amount
1	9	7	11
2	8	8	7

3	9	9	13
4	12	10	9
5	9	11	11
6	12	12	10

The computed mean or average of the data = 10. The manager decides to use this as the estimate for *expenditure of a typical supplier.*

Is this a good or bad estimate?

Mean squared error is a way to judge how good a model is

We shall compute the *"mean squared error"*:

- The "error" = true amount spent minus the estimated amount.
- The "error squared" is the error above, squared.
- The "SSE" is the sum of the squared errors.
- The "MSE" is the mean of the squared errors.

MSE results for example

The results are:

The results are:Error and Squared ErrorsThe estimate = 10

The SSE = 36 and the MSE = 36/12 = 3.

Table of MSE results for example using different estimates

So how good was the estimator for the amount spent for each supplier? Let us compare the estimate (10) with the following estimates: 7, 9, and 12. That is, we estimate that each supplier will spend \$7, or \$9 or \$12.

Performing the same calculations we arrive at:

Estimator	**7**	**9**	**10**	**12**
SSE	144	48	36	84
MSE	12	4	3	7

The estimator with the smallest MSE is the best. It can be shown: The estimator with the smallest MSE is the best. It can be shown mathematically that the estimator that minimizes the MSE for a set of random data is the mean.

Table showing squared error for the mean for sample data

Next we will examine the mean to see how well it predicts net income over time.

The next table gives the income before taxes of a PC manufacturer between 1985 and 1994.

Year	**\$ (millions)**	**Mean**	**Error**	**Squared Error**
1985	46.163	48.776	–2.613	6.828
1986	46.998	48.776	–1.778	3.161
1987	47.816	48.776	–0.960	0.922
1988	48.311	48.776	–0.465	0.216
1989	48.758	48.776	–0.018	0.000

1990	49.164	48.776	0.388	0.151
1991	49.548	48.776	0.772	0.596
1992	48.915	48.776	1.139	1.297
1993	50.315	48.776	1.539	2.369
1994	50.768	48.776	1.992	3.968

The MSE = 1.9508.

The mean is not a good estimator when there are trends:

The question arises: *can we use the mean to forecast income if we suspect a trend?* A look at the graph below shows clearly that we should not do this.

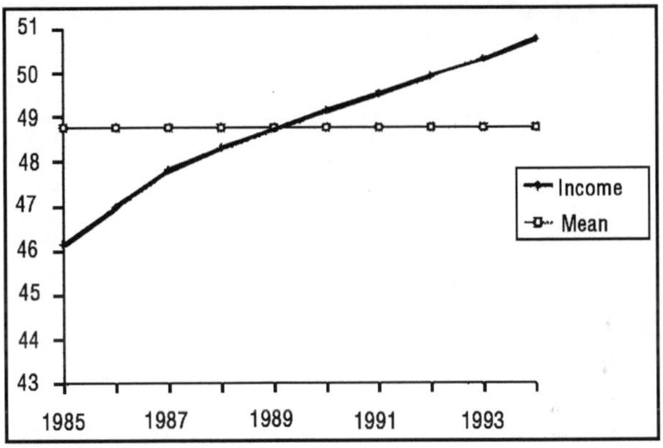

Average weighs all past observations equally

In summary, we state that:

- The "simple" average or mean of all past observations is only a useful estimate for forecasting when there are no trends. If there are trends, use different estimates that take the trend into account.
- The average "weighs" all past observations equally. For example, the average of the values 3, 4, 5 is 4. We know, of course, that an average is computed by adding all the values and dividing the sum by the number of values. Another way of computing the average is by adding each value divided by the number of values, or

  3/3 + 4/3 + 5/3 = 1 + 1.3333 + 1.6667 = 4.

  The multiplier 1/3 is called the *weight*. In general:

$$\bar{x} = \frac{1}{n}\sum_{i=1}^{n} x_i = \left(\frac{1}{n}\right)x_1 + \left(\frac{1}{n}\right)x_2 + \ldots + \left(\frac{1}{n}\right)x_n$$

  The, $\left(\frac{1}{n}\right)$ are the weights and of course they sum to 1.

Single Moving Average

Taking a moving average is a smoothing process: An alternative way to summarize the past data is to compute the mean of successive smaller sets of numbers of past data as follows:

Recall the set of numbers 9, 8, 9, 12, 9, 12, 11, 7, 13, 9, 11, 10 which were the dollar amount of 12 suppliers selected at random. Let us set M, the size of the "smaller set" equal to 3. Then the average of the first 3 numbers is: $(9 + 8 + 9)/3 = 8.667$.

This is called "smoothing" (i.e., some form of averaging). This smoothing process is continued by advancing one period and calculating the next average of three numbers, dropping the first number. *Moving average example*: The next table summarizes the process, which is referred to as *Moving Averaging*. The general expression for the moving average is

$$M_t = [X_t + X_{t-1} + ... + X_{t-N+1}]/N$$

Results of moving average:

Supplier	$	MA	Error	Error squared
1	9			
2	8			
3	9	8.667	0.333	0.111
4	12	9.667	2.333	5.444
5	9	10.000	-1.000	1.000
6	12	11.000	1.000	1.000
7	11	10.667	0.333	0.111
8	7	10.000	–3.000	9.000
9	13	10.333	2.667	7.111
10	9	9.667	–0.667	0.444
11	11	11.000	0	0
12	10	10.000	0	0

The MSE = 2.018 as compared to 3 in the previous case.

Centered Moving Average

When computing a running moving average, placing the average in the middle time period makes sense: In the previous example we computed the average of the first 3 time periods and placed it next to period 3. We could have placed the average in the middle of the time interval of three periods, that is, next to period 2. This works well with odd time periods, but not so good for even time periods. So where would we place the first moving average when $M = 4$?

Technically, the Moving Average would fall at $t = 2.5, 3.5...$

To avoid this problem we smooth the MA's using $M = 2$. Thus we smooth the smoothed values!

If we average an even number of terms, we need to smooth the smoothed values

Table. The Following Table Shows the Results Using $M = 4$.

Period	Value	Centered MA
1	9	
2	8	
3	9	9.5
4	12	10.0
5	9	10.75
6	12	
7	11	

DOUBLE MOVING AVERAGES FOR A LINEAR TREND PROCESS

Moving averages are still not able to handle significant trends when forecasting: Unfortunately, neither the mean of all data nor the moving average of the most recent M values, when used as forecasts for the next period, are able to cope with a significant trend.

There exists a variation on the MA procedure that often does a better job of handling trend. It is called *Double Moving Averages for a Linear Trend Process*. It calculates a second moving average from the original moving average, using the same value for M. As soon as both single and double moving averages are available, a computer routine uses these averages to compute a slope and intercept, and then forecasts one or more periods ahead.

WHAT IS EXPONENTIAL SMOOTHING?

Exponential smoothing schemes weight past observations using exponentially decreasing weights. This is a very popular scheme to produce a smoothed Time Series.

Whereas in Single Moving Averages the past observations are weighted equally, Exponential Smoothing assigns exponentially decreasing weights as the observation get older. In other words, recent observations are given relatively more weight in forecasting than the older observations.

In the case of moving averages, the weights assigned to the observations are the same and are equal to 1/N. In exponential smoothing, however, there are one or more smoothing parameters to be determined (or estimated) and these choices determine the weights assigned to the observations.

Single, double and triple Exponential Smoothing will be described in this section. In statistics, exponential smoothing is a technique that can be applied to time series data, either to produce smoothed data for presentation, or to make forecasts. The time series data themselves are a sequence of observations. The observed phenomenon may be an essentially random process, or it may be an orderly, but noisy, process.

Whereas in the simple moving average the past observations are weighted equally, exponential smoothing assigns exponentially decreasing weights as the observation get older.

Exponential smoothing is commonly applied to financial market and economic data, but it can be used with any discrete set of repeated measurements. The raw data sequence is often represented by {xt}, and the output of the exponential smoothing algorithm is commonly written as {st} which may be regarded as our best estimate of what the next value of x will be. When the sequence of observations begins at time t = 0, the simplest form of exponential smoothing is given by the formulas,

$$s_0 = x_0$$
$$s_t = \alpha x_t + (1-\alpha)s_{t-1}$$

where α is the smoothing factor, and $0 < \alpha < 1$.

The Simple Moving Average

Intuitively, the simplest way to smooth a time series is to calculate a simple, or unweighted, moving average. The smoothed statistic st is then just the mean of the last k observations:

$$s_t = \frac{1}{k}\sum_{n=0}^{k-1} x_{t-n} = \frac{x_t + x_{t-1} + x_{t-2} + \ldots + x_{t-k+1}}{k} = s_{t-1} + \frac{x_t - x_{t-k}}{k},$$

where the choice of an integer k > 1 is arbitrary. A small value of k will have less of a smoothing effect and be more responsive to recent changes in the data, while a larger k will have a greater smoothing effect, and produce a more pronounced lag in the smoothed sequence. One disadvantage of this technique is that it cannot be used on the first k ?1 terms of the time series.

The Weighted Moving Average

A slightly more intricate method for smoothing a raw time series {xt} is to calculate a weighted moving average by first choosing a set of weighting factors $\{w_1, w_2 ..., w_k\}$ such that,

$$\sum_{n=1}^{k} w_n = 1$$

and then using these weights to calculate the smoothed statistics {st}:

$$s_t \sum_{n=1}^{k} w_n x_{t+1-n} = w_1 x_t + w_2 x_{t-1} + \ldots + w_k x_{t-k+1}.$$

In practice the weighting factors are often chosen to give more weight to the most recent terms in the time series and less weight to older data. Notice that this technique has the same disadvantage as the simple moving average technique (i.e., it cannot be used until at least k observations have been made), and that it entails a more complicated calculation at each step of the smoothing procedure.

The Exponential Moving Average

The simplest form of exponential smoothing is given by the formulae

$$s_0 = x_0$$

$$s_t = \alpha x_t + (1-\alpha)s_{t-1} = s_{t-1} + \alpha(x_t - s_{t-1})$$

where a is the smoothing factor, and 0 < ? < 1. In other words, the smoothed statistic st is a simple weighted average of the latest observation xt and the previous smoothed statistic st?1. Simple exponential smoothing is easily applied, and it produces a smoothed statistic as soon as two observations are available.

Values of a close to one have less of a smoothing effect and give greater weight to recent changes in the data, while values of a closer to zero have a greater smoothing effect and are less responsive to recent changes.

There is no formally correct procedure for choosing a. Sometimes the statistician's judgment is used to choose an appropriate factor.

Alternatively, a statistical technique may be used to optimize the value of a. For example, the method of least squares might be used to determine the value of a for which the sum of the quantities (sn-1 – a x_n)2 is minimized.

This simple form of exponential smoothing is also known as an"exponentially weighted moving average". Technically it can also be classified as an ARIMA(0,1,1) model with no constant term.

Why is it"Exponential"?

By direct substitution of the defining equation for simple exponential smoothing back into itself we find that

$$\begin{aligned} s_t &= \alpha x_t + (1-\alpha)s_{t-1} \\ &= \alpha x_t + \alpha(1-\alpha)x_{t-1} + (1-\alpha)^2 s_{t-2} \\ &= \alpha\left[x_t + (1-\alpha)x_{t-1} + (1-\alpha)^2 x_{t-2} + (1-\alpha)^3 x_{t-3} - \cdots\right] \\ &\quad + (1-\alpha)t_{x0}. \end{aligned}$$

In other words, as time passes the smoothed statistic st becomes the weighted average of a greater and greater number of the past observations xt?n, and the weights assigned to previous observations are in general proportional to the terms of the geometric progression {1, (1 – α), (1 – α)^2, (1 – α)^3, ...}. A geometric progression is the discrete version of an exponential function, so this is where the name for this smoothing method originated.

Single Exponential Smoothing

SES is a method for smoothing a time series or for forecasting where the mean is either stationary or changes only slowly with time. The name is misleading, as this is a moving average method where the weight declines as the lag between the current time increases.

As this is smoothing method which relies on previous values, the smoothed value, lags the current value. The weight given to the current and previous values is given by the formula:

Weight= A(1 – A)k$_2$g

where Ais smoothing factor $(0 < A \leq 1)$

If the smoothing value is small, fluctuations will be heavily damped and the smoothed value will tend towards the mean, if it is large, fluctuations will be significant and the smoothed value will tend towards the current value.

The table below shows the weights applied to current and preceding values using a smoothing factor of 0.5.

Lag	Weight (4 d.p.)	Y	YS
0 (current)	0.5000	10	5.0000
1	0.2500	9	2.2500
2	0.1250	8	1.0000
3	0.0625	7	0.4375
4	0.0313	6	0.1878
5	0.0156	5	0.0780
6	0.0078	4	0.0312
7	0.0039	3	0.0117
8	0.0020	2	0.0040
9	0.0010	1	0.0010
10	0.0005	0	0.0000
		Smoothed Value	9.0012

Calculation

The process for calculating the smoothed value simplifies to:

$$YS_t AY_t + (1 - A)YS_{t-1}$$

Initial Values

Ideally the initial value of YS in formula 4.1.20 should be calculated using appropriated weights as shown in the above table, however, this means discarding a number of data points at the start of the series, this may not be a problem in long series, but with short ones and small smoothing coefficients, this may not be desirable. A pragmatic approach may be required: If the mean value is static or only changing slowly with time, an average of first few values can be used. If the mean is fluctuating, setting the first smoothed value to the first observed value may be a workable option.

Variation in Smoothing Coefficients

The graphs below show a time series which moves from one level to another, in the first case it is a smooth curve, in the second it is the same function with some added noise.

Time Series without "noise"

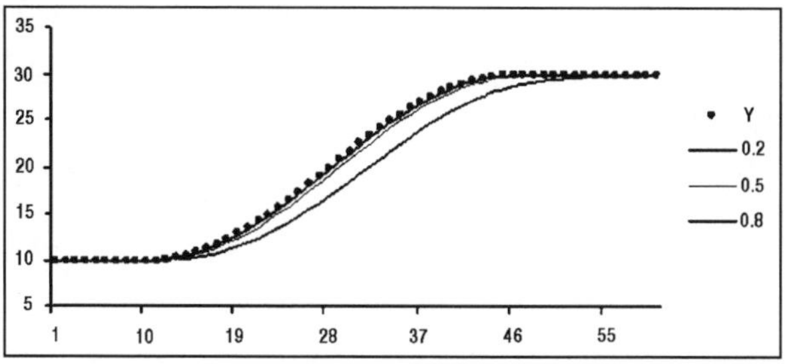

Time Series with added "noise"

The two curves illustrate the relationship between smoothing an lag. A smoothing coefficient of 0.2 produces a smooth curve which lags the source by as much as 6 periods,

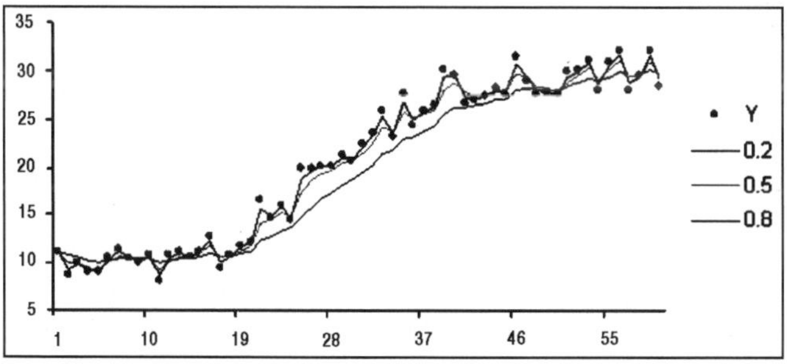

whilst 0.8 reduces the lag to approx. 1 period, but there are significant fluctuations in the smoothed value.

Forecast

The forecast value is the last smoothed value, this is only meaningful for a stationary time series.

Example

The example is based on the maximum monthly average temperature for London for the period 1860 to 1990. A smoothing coefficient of 0.05 has been used to damp down the fluctuations to the point where an slow, upward trend can be observed.

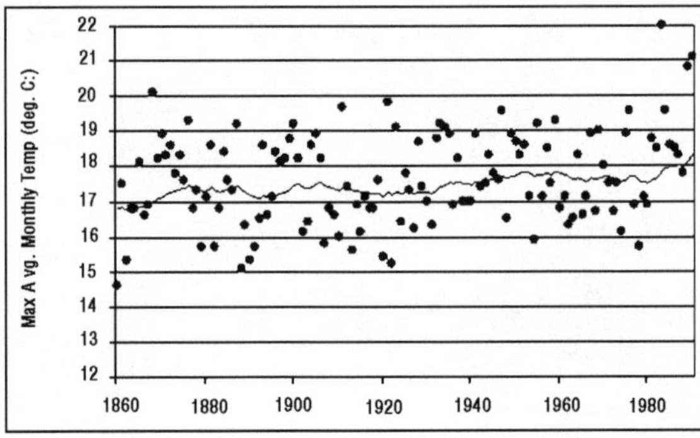

It should be pointed out changing the smoothing coefficient gives a significantly different visual impression.

Exponential smoothing weights past observations with exponentially decreasing weights to forecast future values

This smoothing scheme begins by setting S_2 to y_1, where S_i stands for smoothed observation or EWMA, and y stands for the original observation.

The subscripts refer to the time periods, 1, 2..., n. For the third period, $S_3 = \alpha y_2 + (1-\alpha) S_2$; and so on. There is no S_1; the smoothed series starts with the smoothed version of the second observation. For any time period t, the smoothed value S_t is found by computing:

$$S_t = \alpha y_{t-1} + (1-\alpha)S_{t-1} \; 0 < \alpha \leq 1 t \geq 3$$

This is the *basic equation of exponential smoothing* and the constant or parameter α is called the *smoothing constant.*

Note: There is an alternative approach to exponential smoothing that replaces y_{t-1} in the basic equation with y_t, the current observation. That formulation, due to Roberts (1959), is described in the section on EWMA control charts. The formulation here follows Hunter (1986).

Setting the First EWMA

The first forecast is very important: The initial EWMA plays an important role in computing all the subsequent EWMA's. Setting S_2 to y_1 is one method of initialization. Another way is to set it to the target of the process.

Still another possibility would be to average the first four or five observations.

It can also be shown that the smaller the value of α, the more important is the selection of the initial EWMA. The user would be wise to try a few methods, (assuming that the software has them available) before finalizing the settings.

Why is it Called "Exponential"?

Expand basic equation: Let us expand the basic equation by first substituting for S_{t-1} in the basic equation to obtain

$S_t = \alpha y_{t-1} + (1-\alpha)\ [\alpha y_{t-2} + (1-\alpha)\ S_{t-2}]$
$= \alpha y_{t-1} + \alpha(1-\alpha)\ y_{t-2} + (1-\alpha)^2\ S_{t-2}$

Summation formula for basic equation

By substituting for S_{t-2}, then for S_{t-3}, and so forth, until we reach S_2 (which is just y_1), it can be shown that the expanding equation can be written as:

$$S_t = \alpha \sum_{i=1}^{t=2} (1-\alpha)^{i-1} y_{t-i} + (1+\alpha)^{t-2} S_2, t \geq 2$$

Expanded equation for S_5: For example, the expanded equation for the smoothed value S_5 *is:*

$$S_5 = \alpha\left[(1-\alpha)^0 y_{5-1} + (1-\alpha)^1 y_{5-2} + (1-\alpha)^2 y5-3\right]$$
$$+(1-\alpha)^3 S_2$$

Illustrates exponential behaviour: This illustrates the exponential behaviour. The weights, $\alpha(1-\alpha)^t$ decrease geometrically, and their sum is unity as shown below, using a property of geometric series:

$$\alpha \sum_{i=0}^{t-1} (1-\alpha)^i = a\left[\frac{1-(1-\alpha)^2}{1-(1-\alpha)}\right] = 1(1-\alpha)^t$$

From the last formula we can see that the summation term shows that the contribution to the smoothed value S_t becomes less at each consecutive time period.

What is the "Best" Value for α?

How do you choose the weight parameter?

The speed at which the older responses are dampened (smoothed) is a function of the value of α. When αis close to 1, dampening is quick and when αis close to 0, dampening is slow.

Calculate for different values of α: The MSE was again calculated for α =.5 and turned out to be 16.29, so in this case we would prefer an αof.5.

Can we do better? We could apply the proven trial-and-error method. This is an iterative procedure beginning with a range of α between.1 and.9.

We determine the best initial choice for α and then search between α– Δ and α + Δ. We could repeat this perhaps one more time to find the best α to 3 decimal places.

Nonlinear optimizers can be used: But there are better search methods, such as the Marquardt procedure. This is a nonlinear optimizer that minimizes the sum of squares of residuals.

In general, most well designed statistical software programs should be able to find the value of α that minimizes the MSE.

Sample plot showing smoothed data for 2 values of α y x orogomal Y α - alpha =.10 alpha = 5

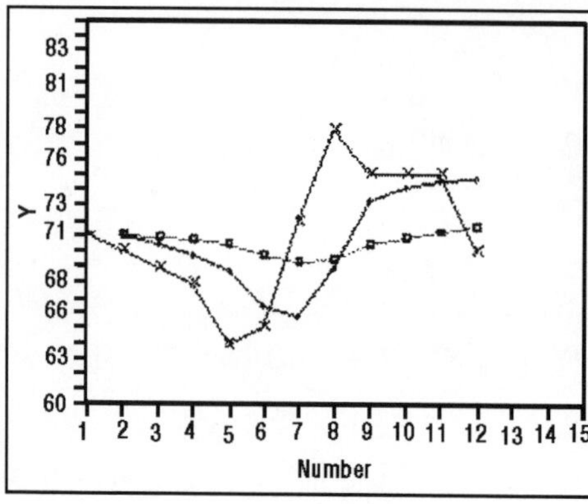

Fig. Exponential Smoothing: Original and Smoothed Values

Forecasting with Single Exponential Smoothing

Forecasting Formula

Forecasting the next point: The forecasting formula is the basic equation.

$$S_{t+1} = \alpha y_t + (1-\alpha)S_t\ 0 < \alpha \leq 1 t > 0$$

New forecast is previous forecast plus an error adjustment
This can be written as:

$$S_{t+1} = S_t + \alpha(S_t)$$

where ϵ_t is the forecast error (actual - forecast) for period t.

In other words, the new forecast is the old one plus an adjustment for the error that occurred in the last forecast.

Bootstrapping of Forecasts

Bootstrapping forecasts: What happens if you wish to forecast from some origin, usually the last data point, and no actual observations are available? In this situation we have to modify the formula to become:

$$S_{t+1} = \alpha y_{Oirigin} + (1-\alpha)S_t$$

where y_{origin} remains constant. This technique is known as *bootstrapping.*

Example of Bootstrapping

Example: The last data point in the previous example was 70 and its forecast (smoothed value S) was 71.7. Since we do have the data point and the forecast available, we can calculate the next forecast using the regular formula,

$$S_{t+1} = \alpha y_{Oirigin} + (1-\alpha)S_t$$

$$= .1(70) + .9(71.7) = 71.5 \quad (\alpha = .1)$$

But for the next forecast we have no data point (observation). So now we compute:

S_{t+2} =. 1(70) +.9(71.5)= 71.35

Single Exponential Smoothing with Trend

Single Smoothing (short for single exponential smoothing) is not very good when there is a trend. The single coefficient α is not enough.

Sample data set with trend: Let us demonstrate this with the following data set smoothed with an α of 0.3:

Data	Fit
6.4	
5.6	6.4
7.8	6.2
8.8	6.7
11.0	7.3
11.6	8.4
16.7	9.4
15.3	11.6
21.6	12.7
22.4	15.4

Plot demonstrating inadequacy of single exponential smoothing when there is trend

The resulting graph looks like:

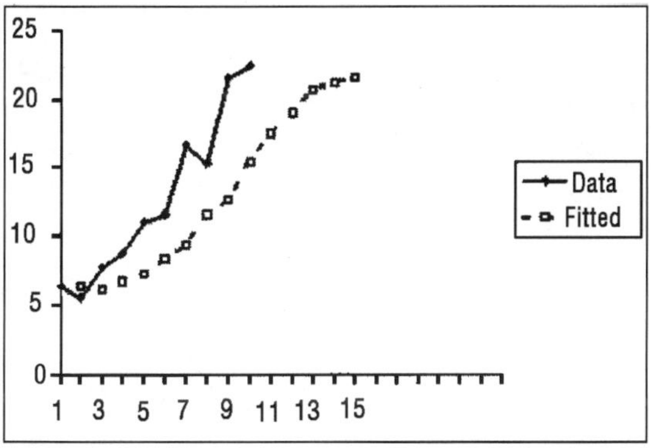

Floating Averages and
Double Exponential Smoothing

The best well-known and most commonly applied smoothing technique is the *Floating Average*. The idea is very simple: for any odd number of consecutive points, replace the centre-most value with the average of the other points:

$$x_i \rightarrow \frac{1}{2k+1} \sum_{i=-k}^{k} x_i + k$$

In this formula, all the x_i have the same weight, but it may be reasonable to require points towards the centre of the smoothing interval to be more important relative to the others. We can introduce weight factors into the sum to obtain a *weighted floating average*:

$$x_i \rightarrow \sum_{i=-k}^{k} w_k x_i + k \sum_{i=-k}^{k} w_k = 1$$

The weights are usually chosen symmetrically around the mid-point, for instance

$$\left(\frac{1}{4}, \frac{1}{2}, \frac{1}{4}\right) \text{ for } k=1 \text{ or } \left(\frac{1}{16}, \frac{1}{4}, \frac{3}{8}, \frac{1}{4}, \frac{1}{16}\right) \text{ for } k=2.$$

More complicated sets of weights exist for special applications, such as the 15-point "Spencer" moving average, which is used to calculate mortality statistics for the insurance industry and which contains *negative* weights as well as positive ones.

Straightforward as this approach is, it has nevertheless several problems:

- The first and last a points cannot be smoothed. While the beginning of a time series is usually not of great interest, it can be a real drawback not to have a smoothed value at the leading edge, where all the action is happening — in particular if a large k is required to achieve the desired smoothness.
- The calculation is slightly tedious, since for each smoothed point the entire interval has to be summed again, in particular if we use unequal weights. This implies that we must keep track of a sufficient amount of history, even if all we want to do is update the leading edge of the smoothed curve.
- It is not possible to extract something like a trend from the floating average, making extrapolation of the time series impossible.

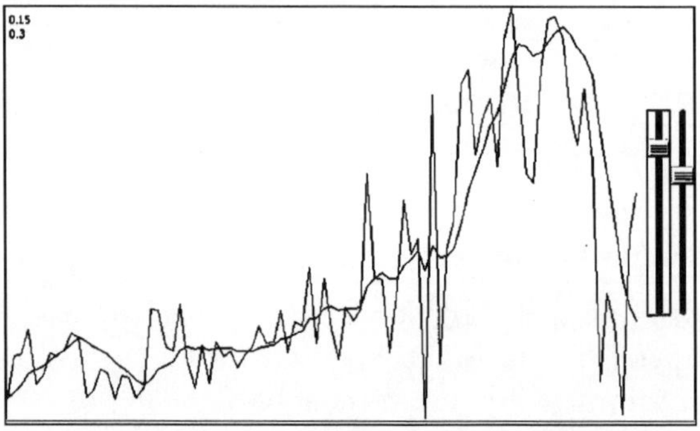

Fig. A Time Series with a Double-exponential Smoothed Curve

Interestingly, there exists a surprisingly unknown, simple little scheme called *Exponential Smoothing*, which addresses all of these points. There are three different forms of exponential smoothing, known as single, double (*Holt-*), and triple (*Holt-Winters-* exponential smoothing. The first one finds a smooth approximation to a noisy signal, the second also allows to extract a linear trend, and the third one takes into account periodic (i.e. regularly recurring) variations.

Forecasting with Double Exponential Smoothing

As a first step in improving on "naive" forecasting models, nonseasonal patterns and trends can be extrapolated using a *moving-average* or *smoothing* model.

The basic assumption behind averaging and smoothing models is that the time series is "locally stationary" with a slowly varying mean. Hence, we take a *moving* (i.e., local) average to estimate the current value of the mean, and use this as the forecast.

This can be considered as a compromise between the mean model and the random walk model. The moving average is often called a "smoothed" version of the original series, since short-term averaging has the effect of smoothing out the bumps in the original series.

By adjusting the degree of smoothing (i.e., the "width" of the moving average), we can hope to strike some kind of optimal balance between the performance of the mean and random walk models.

Simple (equally-weighted) Moving Average:

$$\acute{Y}(t) = (Y(t-1) + Y(t-2) + ... + Y(t-k))/k$$

Here, the one-period-ahead forecast $\acute{Y}(t)$, made at time t-1, equals the simple average of the last k observations. This average is "centered" at period t-(k+1)/2, which implies that the estimate of the local mean will tend to lag behind the true value of the local mean by about (k+1)/2 periods. Thus, we say the average age of the data in the simple moving average is (k+1)/2 relative to the period for which the forecast is computed: this is the amount of time by which forecasts will tend to *lag behind turning points* in the data.

For example, if you are averaging the last 5 values, the forecasts will be about 3 periods late in responding to turning points. Note that if k=1, the simple moving average (SMA) model is equivalent to the random walk model (without growth). If k is very large (comparable to the length of the estimation period), the SMA model is equivalent to the mean model. As with any parameter of a forecasting model, it is customary to adjust the value of k in order to obtain the best "fit" to the data, i.e., the smallest forecast errors on average.

Here is an example of a series which appears to exhibit random fluctuations around a slowly-varying mean. First, let's try to fit it with a random walk model, which is equivalent to a simple moving average of 1 term:

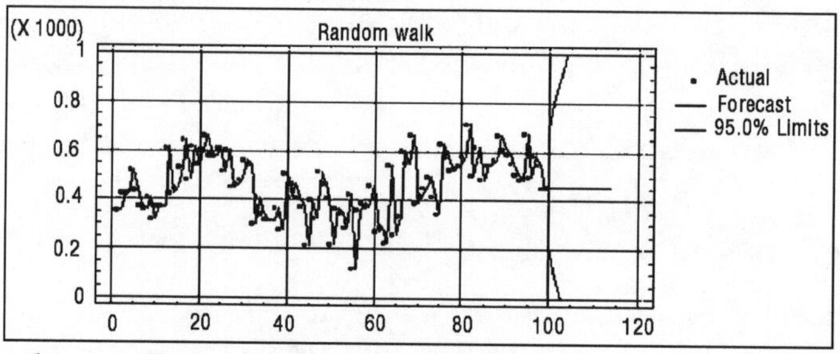

The random walk model responds very quickly to changes in the series, but in so doing it picks much of the "noise" in the data (the random fluctuations) as well as the "signal" (the local mean). If we instead try a simple moving average of 5 terms, we get a smoother-looking set of forecasts:

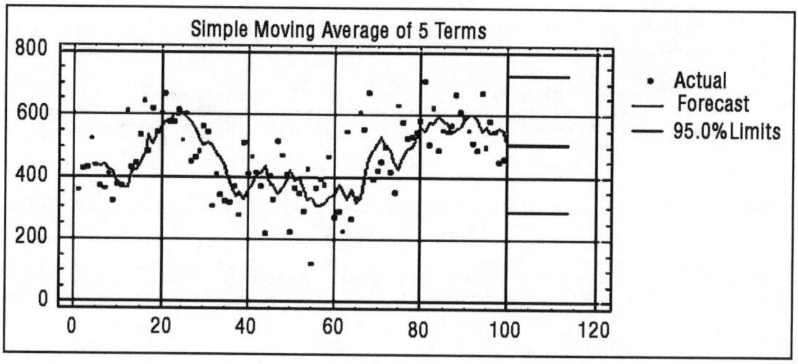

The 5-term simple moving average yields significantly smaller errors than the random walk model in this case. The average age of the data in this forecast is 3 (=(5+1)/2), so that it tends to lag behind turning points by about three periods. (For example, a downturn seems to have occurred at period 21, but the forecasts do not turn around until several periods later.)

Notice that the long-term forecasts from the SMA model are a *horizontal straight line*, just as in the random walk model. Thus, the SMA model assumes that there is *no trend* in the data. However, whereas the forecasts from the random walk model are simply equal to the last observed value, the forecasts from the SMA model are equal to a *weighted average of recent values*.

Interestingly, the confidence limits computed by Statgraphics for the long-term forecasts of the simple moving average do *not* get wider as the forecasting horizon increases. This is obviously not correct! Unfortunately, there is no underlying statistical theory that tells us how the confidence intervals ought to widen for this model.

If you were going to use this model in practice, you would be well advised to use an *empirical estimate* of the confidence limits for the longer-horizon forecasts.

For example, you could set up a spreadsheet in which the SMA model would be used to forecast 2 steps ahead, 3 steps ahead, etc., within the historical data sample.

You could then compute the sample standard deviations of the errors at each forecast horizon, and then construct confidence intervals for longer-term forecasts by adding and subtracting multiples of the appropriate standard deviation. If we try a 9-term simple moving average, we get even smoother forecasts and more of a lagging effect:

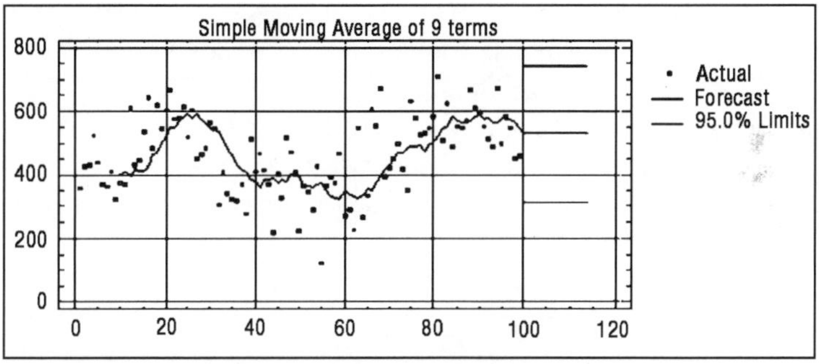

The average age is now 5 periods (=(9+1)/2). If we take a 19-term moving average, the average age increases to 10:

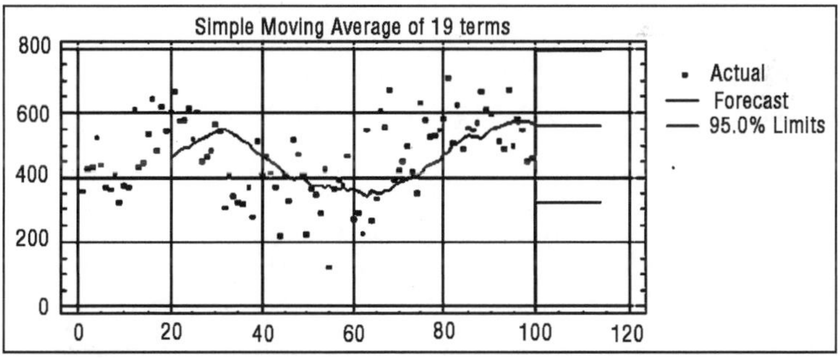

Notice that, indeed, the forecasts are now lagging behind turning points by about 10 periods.

Brown's Simple Exponential Smoothing (exponentially weighted moving average)

The simple moving average model described above has the undesirable property that it treats the last k observations equally and completely ignores all preceding observations. Intuitively, past data should be discounted in a more gradual fashion—for example, the most recent observation should get a little more weight than 2nd most recent, and the 2nd most recent should get a little more weight than the 3rd most recent, and so on.

The simple exponential smoothing (SES) model accomplishes this. Let αdenote a "smoothing constant" (a number between 0 and 1) and let S(t) denote the value of the smoothed series at period t. The following formula is used recursively to update the smoothed series as new observations are recorded:

$$S(t) = \alpha Y(t) + (1-\alpha)\, S(t-1)$$

Thus, the current smoothed value is an interpolation between the previous smoothed value and the current observation, where α controls the closeness of the interpolated value to the most recent observation. The *forecast* for the *next* period is simply the current smoothed value:

$$\acute{Y}(t+1) = S(t)$$

Note: we will henceforth use the symbol Ý to stand for a forecast of the time series Y, because Ý is the nearest thing to a "y-hat" that can be displayed on a web page. Equivalently, we can express the next forecast directly in terms of previous forecasts and previous observations, in any of the following ways:

$\acute{Y}(t+1) = \alpha Y(t) + (1-\alpha)\acute{Y}(t)$...forecast=interpolation between previous *forecast* and previous *observation*

$\acute{Y}(t+1) = \acute{Y}(t) + \alpha e(t)$...forecast=previous *forecast* plus fraction αof previous error, where $e(t) = Y(t) - Y(t)$

$\acute{Y}(t+1) = Y(t) - (1-\alpha)e(t)$...forecast=previous *observation* minus fraction 1–α of previous error

$\acute{Y}(t+1) = \alpha\ [Y(t) + (1-\alpha)Y(t-1) + ((1-\alpha)\hat{}2)Y(t-2) + ((1-\alpha)\hat{}3)Y(t-3)$ +......forecast=*exponentially weighted (i.e. discounted) moving average* with discount factor 1–α

The preceding four equations are all *mathematically equivalent*—any one of them can be obtained by rearrangement of any of the others.

The first equation above is probably the easiest to use if you are implementing the model on a spreadsheet: the forecasting formula fits in a single cell and contains cell references pointing to the previous forecast, the previous observation, and the cell where the value of is stored.

Note that if α=1, the SES model is equivalent to a random walk model (without growth). If α=0, the SES model is equivalent to the mean model, assuming that the first smoothed value is set equal to the mean.

The average age of the data in the simple-exponential-smoothing forecast is 1/α relative to the period for which the forecast is computed. (This is not supposed to be obvious, but it can easily be shown by evaluating an infinite series.)

Hence, the simple moving average forecast tends to lag behind turning points by about 1/α periods. For example, when α = 0.5 the lag is 2 periods; when α= 0.2 the lag is 5 periods; when α = 0.1 the lag is 10 periods, and so on.

For a given average age (i.e., amount of lag), the simple exponential smoothing (SES) forecast is somewhat superior to the simple moving average (SMA) forecast because *it places relatively more weight on the most recent observation*—i.e., it is slightly more "responsive" to changes occuring in the recent past. Another important advantage of the SES model over the SMA model is that the SES model uses a smoothing parameter which is continuously variable, so it can easily optimized by using a "solver" algorithm to minimize the mean squared error. The optimal value of α in the SES model for this series turns out to be 0.2961, as shown here:

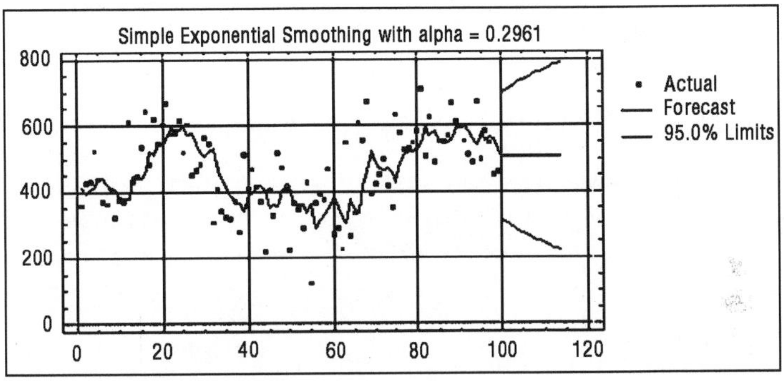

The average age of the data in this forecast is 1/0.2961 = 3.4 periods, which is similar to that of a 6-term simple moving average.

The long-term forecasts from the SES model are a *horizontal straight line*, as in the SMA model and the random walk model without growth. However, note that the confidence intervals computed by Statgraphics now diverge in a reasonable-looking fashion, and that they are substantially narrower than the confidence intervals for the random walk model. The SES model assumes that the series is somewhat "more predictable" than does the random walk model.

An SES model is actually a special case of an ARIMA model, so the statistical theory of ARIMA models provides a sound basis for calculating confidence intervals for the SES model. In particular, an SES model is an ARIMA model with one nonseasonal difference, an MA(1) term, and *no* constant term, otherwise known as an "ARIMA(0,1,1) model without constant".

The MA(1) coefficient in the ARIMA model corresponds to the quantity 1–α in the SES model. For example, if you fit an ARIMA(0,1,1) model without constant to the series analysed here, the estimated MA(1) coefficient turns out to be 0.7029, which is almost exactly one minus 0.2961.

It is possible to add the assumption of a non-zero constant linear trend to an SES model. To do this in Statgraphics, just specify an ARIMA model with one nonseasonal difference and an MA(1) term *with* a constant, i.e., an ARIMA(0,1,1) model *with* constant. The long-term forecasts will then have a trend which is equal to the average trend observed over the entire estimation period.

You cannot do this in conjunction with seasonal adjustment, because the seasonal adjustment options are disabled when the model type is set to ARIMA.

However, you can add a constant long-term exponential trend to a simple exponential smoothing model (with or without seasonal adjustment) by using the inflation adjustment option in the Forecasting procedure.

The appropriate "inflation" (percentage growth) rate per period can be estimated as the slope coefficient in a linear trend model fitted to the data in conjunction with a natural logarithm transformation, or it can be based on other, independent information concerning long-term growth prospects.

Brown's Linear (i.e., Double) Exponential Smoothing

If the *trend* as well as the mean is varying slowly over time, a higher-order smoothing model is needed totrack the varying trend.

The simplest time-varying trend model is Brown's linear exponential smoothing (LES) model, which uses *two* different smoothed series that are centered at different points in time. The forecasting formula is based on an extrapolation of a line through the two centers.

The algebraic form of the linear exponential smoothing model, like that of the simple exponential smoothing model, can be expressed in a number of different but equivalent forms. The "standard" form of this model is usually expressed as follows: Let S′ denote the *singly-smoothed* series obtained by applying simple exponential smoothing to series Y.

That is, the value of S′ at period t is given by:

$$S'(t) = \alpha Y(t) + (1-\alpha)S'(t-1)$$

(Recall that, under simple exponential smoothing, we would just let $\acute{Y}(t+1) = S'(t)$ at this point.) Then let S″ denote the *doubly-smoothed* series obtained by applying simple exponential smoothing (using the same α) to series S′:

$$S''(t) = \alpha\, S'(t) + (1-\alpha)S''(t-1)$$

Finally, the forecast $\acute{Y}(t+1)$ is given by:

$$\acute{Y}(t+1) = a(t) + b(t)$$

where:

$a(t) = 2S'(t) - S''(t)$...the estimated *level* at period t

$b(t) = (\alpha/(1-\alpha))(S'(t) - S''(t))$...the estimated *trend* at period t.

Forecasts with longer lead times made at period t are obtained by adding multiples of the trend term. For example, the k-period-ahead forecast (i.e., the forecast for Y(t+k) made at period t) would be equal to a(t)+kb(t).

For purposes of model-fitting (i.e., calculating forecasts, residuals, and residual statistics over the estimation period), the model can be started up by setting S′(1)=S″(1)=Y(1), i.e., set both smoothed series equal to the observed value at t=1.

A mathematically equivalent form of Brown's linear exponential smoothing model, which emphasizes its non-stationary character and is easier to implement on a spreadsheet, is the following:

$$\acute{Y}(t) = 2Y(t-1) - Y(t-2) - 2(1-\alpha)e(t-1) + ((1-\alpha)^2)e(t-2)$$

or equivalently:

Ý(t) – Y(t–1) = Y(t–1) – Y(t–2) – 2(1–α)e(t–1) + ((1–α)^2)e(t–2)

In other words, the *predicted difference* at period t (namely Ý(t) – Y(t–1)) is equal to the previous observed difference (namely Y(t–1) – Y(t–2)) minus a weighted difference of the two previous forecast errors. Caution: this form of the model is rather tricky to start up at the beginning of the estimation period.

The following convention is recommended: first set Ý(1) = Y(1), which yields e(1) = 0 (i.e., cheat a bit, and let the first forecast equal the actual first observation), then also set Ý(2) = Y(1), which yields e(2) = Y(2) – Y(1), then continue from this point using the equation above.

This would yield the same fitted values as the formula based on S′ and S″ if the latter were started up using S′(1) = S″(1) = Y(1).

Once again, you can use your spreadsheet the "solver" or any nonlinear least squares algorithm to optimize the value of α. The optimal value of α in the LES model fitted to this series by Statgraphics is 0.1607.

Note that the long-term forecasts of the LES model for this time series appear to track the local trend observed in the last 10 periods. Also, the confidence intervals for the LES model widen faster than those of the SES model.

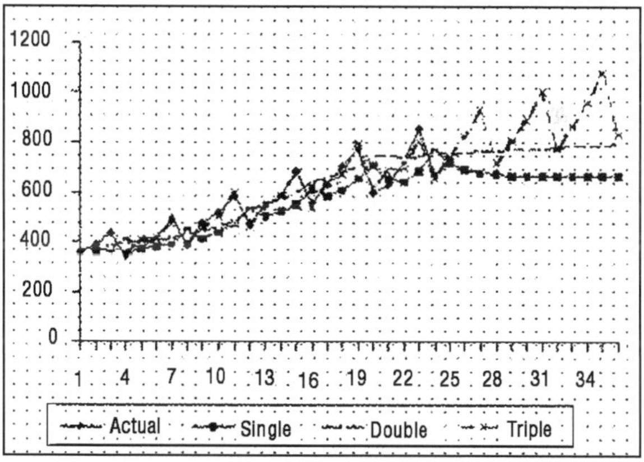

What's best for this particular time series? Here is a model comparison report for the models described above. It appears that the SES model performs better than the SMA models, and LES model is close behind. Whether you choose SES or LES in this case would depend on whether you really believe that the series has a local trend.

Brown's quadratic (i.e., triple) smoothing model...uses *three* smoothed series centered at different points in time and extrapolates a *parabola* through the three centers. This is rarely used in practice, though, since true quadratic trends are rare and the model is highly unstable.

Which Type of Trend-Extrapolation is Best: Horizontal, Linear, or Quadratic?

Empirical evidence suggests that, if the data have already been adjusted (if necessary) for inflation, then it may be imprudent to extrapolate short-term linear (or worse, quadratic) trends very far into the future. Trends evident today may slacken in the future due to varied causes such as product obsolescence, increased competition, and cyclical downturns or upturns in an industry.

For this reason, simple exponential smoothing often performs better out-of-sample than might otherwise be expected, despite its "naive" horizontal trend extrapolation.

Damped trend modifications of the linear exponential smoothing model are often used in practice to introduce a note of conservatism into its trend projections—alas, these are not available in Statgraphics.

In principle, it is possible to calculate confidence intervals around long-term forecasts produced by exponential smoothing models, by considering them as special cases of ARIMA models.

Beware: not all software does this correctly. In particular, a number of popular automatic forecasting programs use highly suspect methods for calculating confidence intervals for exponential smoothing forecasts.

The width of the confidence intervals depends on:

- The RMS error of the model,
- The value of a,
- The level of smoothing (single, double, or triple); and
- The number of periods ahead you are forecasting.

In general, the intervals spread out faster as α gets larger and/or or as the order of smoothing increases from single to double to triple.

Triple Exponential Smoothing

What happens if the data show trend and seasonality?

To handle seasonality, we have to add a third parameter: In this case double smoothing will not work.

We now introduce a third equation to take care of seasonality (sometimes called periodicity). The resulting set of equations is called the "Holt-Winters" (HW) method after the names of the inventors.

The basic equations for their method are given by:

$$S_1 = x\frac{y_1}{l_{t-L}} + (1-\alpha)(S_{t-1} + b_{t-1})\text{Overall Smoothing}$$

$$\mathrm{b_t} = \chi(S_t - S_{t-1}) + (1-\beta)l_{t-L}\textit{Trend Smoothing}$$

$$l_t = \beta\frac{y_t}{S_t} + (1-p)l_{t-L}\textit{Seasonal Smoothing}$$

$$F_{t+m} = (S_t + mb_t)l_{t-L+m}\textit{Forecast}$$

where,

- *y* is the observation

- *S* is the smoothed observation
- *b* is the trend factor
- *I* is the seasonal index
- *F* is the forecast at *m* periods ahead
- *t* is an index denoting a time period

and α, β, and γ are constants that must be estimated in such a way that the MSE of the error is minimized. This is best left to a good software package.

Complete season needed: To initialize the HW method we need at least one complete season's data to determine initial estimates of the seasonal indices I_{t-L}.

L periods in a season: A complete season's data consists of *L* periods. And we need to estimate the trend factor from one period to the next. To accomplish this, it is advisable to use two complete seasons; that is, 2*L* periods.

Initial Values for the Trend Factor

How to get initial estimates for trend and seasonality parameters

The general formula to estimate the initial trend is given by,

$$b = \frac{1}{L}\left(\frac{YL+1}{L} + \frac{YL+2}{L} + \ldots + \frac{YL+L-YL}{L}\right)$$

Initial Values for the Seasonal Indices

As we will see in the example, we work with data that consist of 6 years with 4 periods (that is, 4 quarters) per year.

Then:

Step 1: compute yearly averages

Step 1: Compute the averages of each of the 6 years,

$$A_P = \frac{\sum_{i=1}^{4} yi}{4} \quad P = 1, 2, \ldots, 6$$

Step 2: divide by yearly averages

Step 2: Divide the observations by the appropriate yearly mean

1	2	3	4	5	6
y_1/A_1	y_5/A_2	y_9/A_3	y_{13}/A_4	y_{17}/A_5	y_{21}/A_6
y_2/A_1	y_6/A_2	y_{10}/A_3	y_{14}/A_4	y_{18}/A_5	y_{22}/A_6
y_3/A_1	y_7/A_2	y_{11}/A_3	y_{15}/A_4	y_{19}/A_5	y_{23}/A_6
y_4/A_1	y_8/A_2	y_{12}/A_3	y_{16}/A_4	y_{20}/A_5	y_{24}/A_6

Step 3: Form seasonal indices

Step 3: Now the seasonal indices are formed by computing the average of each row. Thus the initial seasonal indices (symbolically) are:

$$i_1 = (y_1/A_1 + y_5/A_2 + y_9/A_3 + y_{13}/A_4 + y_{17}/A_5 + y_{21}/A_6)/6$$

$$i_2 = (y_2/A_1 + y_6/A_2 + y_{10}/A_3 + y_{14}/A_4 + y_{18}/A_5 + y_{22}/A_6)/6$$
$$i_3 = (y_3/A_1 + y_7/A_2 + y_{11}/A_3 + y_{15}/A_4 + y_{19}/A_5 + y_{22}/A_6)/6$$
$$i_4 = (y_4/A_1 + y_8/A_2 + y_{12}/A_3 + y_{16}/A_4 + y_{20}/A_5 + y_{24}/A_6)/6$$

We now know the algebra behind the computation of the initial estimates. The next page contains an example of triple exponential smoothing.

The Case of the Zero Coefficients

Zero coefficients for trend and seasonality parameters

Sometimes it happens that a computer programme for triple exponential smoothing outputs a final coefficient for trend (γ) or for seasonality (β) of zero. Or worse, both are outputted as zero!

Does this indicate that there is no trend and/or no seasonality? Of course not! It only means that the initial values for trend and/or seasonality were right on the money. No updating was necessary in order to arrive at the lowest possible MSE. We should inspect the updating formulas to verify this.

Example of the Computation of the Initial Trend

Computation of Initial Trend

The data set consists of quarterly sales data. The season is 1 year and since there are 4 quarters per year, $L = 4$. Using the formula we obtain:

$$b_1 = \frac{1}{4}\left[\frac{y_5 - y_1}{4}\right] + \left[\frac{y_5 - y_2}{4}\right] + \left[\frac{y_7 y_3}{4}\right] + \left[\frac{y_5 - y_4}{4}\right]$$
$$= \frac{1}{4}\left[\frac{382 - 362}{4}\right] + \left[\frac{409 - 385}{4}\right] + \left[\frac{498 - 432}{4}\right] + \left[\frac{387 - 341}{4}\right]$$
$$= \frac{5 + 6 + 16.5 + 11.5}{4} = 9.75$$

Example of the Computation of the Initial Seasonal Indices

Table. Initial Seasonal Indices

	1	2	3	4	5	6
1	362	382	473	544	628	627
2	385	409	513	582	707	725
3	432	498	582	681	773	854
4	341	387	474	557	592	661
$\overline{X}$	380	419	510.5	591	675	716.75

In this example we used the full 6 years of data. Other schemes may use only 3, or some other number of years. There are also a number of ways to compute initial estimates.

UNIVARIATE TIME SERIES MODELS

Structural Time Series Models for Univariate Time Series

The underlying principle in structural time series models is that the time series are modelled in terms of a trend, seasonal component, cycle, explanatory variables and noise. Each of these components is allowed to be stochastic. This means that a trend is not restricted to be a straight line and the cyclic and seasonal components are not necessarily neat cosine functions but can change over time. Obviously, if the time series are measured on an annual basis for a period of only 25 years, the seasonal component can be dropped.

Furthermore, using a cyclic component for such short time series is less suitable. The resulting model for a univariate time series becomes:

1 time series = trend + explanatory variables + noise (1)

The mathematical formulation of the'explanatory variables' component is similar to that in linear regression models, namely: Xt* b, where Xt is a vector containing the explanatory variables at time t and b is a vector containing unknown parameters. Brodgar gives estimated values and 95% confidence intervals for b and these can be used to asses whether explanatory variables are related to the time series. The'trend' component in (1) is based on a so-called random walk and takes the form:

Trend at time t = trend at time t–1 + noise at time t (2)

Structural Time Series Models for Multivariate Time Series

Now suppose that there are N time series. The univariate structural time series model can be applied on each individual time series. However, such an approach has two major disadvantages, namely:

- For each time series, a model validation has to be carried out. This means that a lot of information (residuals plots, fitted values, estimated parameters, etc.) has to interpreted.
- Interactions between the time series are ignored.

An approach which overcomes these two disadvantages is dynamic factor analysis. This technique applies a dimension reduction on the N time series. Instead of the N time series, it estimates M common trends, where M is (hopefully) much smaller than N. This is the same principle as in dimension reduction techniques like principal component analysis, factor analysis, correspondence analysis, etc. The main difference is that dynamic factor analysis is designed for time series.

The dynamic factor model, in words, is given by:

N Time series =	linear combination of M common trends +	explana-
tory variables +		
	level parameters +	
	noise	

The mathematical formulation of the dynamic factor model can be found in Zuur et al. (2003a), Harvey (1989), Lütkepohl (1991), among others (see also the Brodgar manual for further references).

To illustrate the underlying principle, the model formulation is presented for 5 time series (N=5) and 2 common trends (M=2):

y_{1t} =	$a_{11} * z_{1t} + a_{21} * z_{2t} + X_t * b_1 + level_1 + noise_{1t}$
y_{2t} =	$a_{12} * z_{1t} + a_{22} * z_{2t} + X_t * b_2 + level_2 + noise_{2t}$
y_{3t} =	$a_{13} * z_{1t} + a_{23} * z_{2t} + X_t * b_3 + level_3 + noise_{3t}$
y_{4t} =	$a_{14} * z_{1t}$ + a24 * z2t + $X_t * b_4 + level_4 + noise_{4t}$
y_{5t} =	$a_{15} * z_{1t} + a_{25} * z_{2t} + X_t * b_5 + level_5 + noise_{5t}$

where y1t is the value of the first time series at time t, z1t and z2t (in blue) are the two common trends at time t, the term Xt * b1 represents the effect of the explanatory variables on y1t, and level1 represents a constant level parameter for the first time series. The terms ai1 and ai2 (in red) are the factor loadings.

Hence, each time series is modelled as the sum of:

- A factor loading * the first common trend
- Another factor loading * the second common trend
- Effects of explanatory variables
- A level parameter
- Noise

The factor loadings determine how important a particular common trend is for the time series. For example, if a11 is large and a21 is close to zero, then this indicates that the first time series is mainly determined by the first common trend (except for possible effects of the explanatory variables). It is interesting to compare factor loadings with each other.

For example, if a12 is large and a22 is close to zero (as was the case for the first time series), then this indicates that the second time series is related to the first common trend as well, and hence the first two time series are driven by the same mechanism. On the other hand, if a12 is close to zero and a22 is large, then this indicates that the two time series are driven by two different underlying mechanisms. Another scenario is that a11 is large and positive, a21 is close to zero, a12 is large and negative and a22 close to zero. In this case, both time series are driven by the same process, but behave in an opposite way. Hence, by comparing factor loadings of different time series, interactions between time series can be inferred. Besides factor loadings, dynamic factor analysis estimates common trends. The common trends are required to be smooth functions (they are modelled as in equation (2)). The common trends represent the patterns in the data which cannot be explained with the measured explanatory variables.

Number of Common Trends

Just as in principal component analysis, one has to choose the number of common trends. A convenient choice is to use 2 common trends because factor loadings can then be plotted versus each other in one graph. Obviously, a more formal tool is needed to choose the number of common trends, for example the Akaike's Information Criterion (AIC). The AIC is a function a the measure of fit (value of maximum likelihood function) and the number of parameters.

MODELING THEORIES

Neural Network Models

Studies on the time series modeling of monthly reservoir inflows sequences using neural network method are presented.

Based on multilayer perceptron (MLP) and radial basis function (RBF)methods, two types of neural network models were proposed to forecast the net inflow series into Pedu-Muda reservoir system in Kedah, Malaysia.

The analyses determine the feasiblity and accuracy of neural network model in univariate forecasting of net inflows. Results of neural network forecast were compared with seasonal autoregresive integrated moving average (ARIMA) and adaptive fuzzy model (FM).

The illustrative model's application indicates that MLP, RBF and FM models provide a promising forecast of net inflow series into a reservoir.

The autoregressive integrated moving average, ARIMA models have been extensively used in hydrology and water resources for modeling of streamflow sequences. The natural hydrological processes that often contain the seasonal component could be handled by using multiplicative seasonal ARIMA model.

Applications of multiplicative seasonal ARIMA in flow forecasting are illustrated by. Recently, there are increasing number of works attempting to apply the neural network method for solving various problems in different branches of science and engineering.

The characteristics of the neural networks is that they provide a computational or mathematical technique which is powerful for modeling systems where explicit form of the relationship between the variables involved is unknown. It was discovered by various researchers that neural network method is successful in capturing non-linearity in the natural process after exposed to sufficient learning or training process.

There have been various applications of neural networks in the field of hydrology and water resources such as for modeling rainfall-runoff processes; river flow prediction; and water demand time series forecasting.

The neural network method is applied in the univariate forecasting using monthly net inflow series in the Pedu-Muda reservoir system in Kedah, Malaysia. Based on multilayer perceptron and radial basis function methods, two types of univariate forecasting model were proposed. The performance of the proposed neural network models is assessed using errors criteria.

Results of the univariate net inflow forecast are compared to the multiplicative seasonal ARIMA and adaptive fuzzy models. The relationship between the current and previous net inflow series is believed to be highly non-linear, time varying, and possesses a stochastic behaviour.

Hence the application of multilayer perceptron and radial basis function methods in the univariate net inflow forecasting is appropriate. In the univariate net inflow forecasting models, the input and output node consist of the net inflow series itself. The models are designed having several input nodes and one output node. In the proposed model the input nodes are the previous net inflow series and the output node is the current net inflow data.

The first technique of neural network modeling is the multilayer perceptron (MLP) model. Basically the MLP consists of an input layer, a hidden layer, and an output layer. The proposed MLP model consists of an input layer linked to the input net inflow variables, a hidden layer, and an output layer that connects to the output net inflow variable.

Input layer is the previous net inflow data and the output layer constitute the current net inflow data. The information of previous net inflow in the input layer transfer to the next consecutive layers in the system of feed forward networks. The binary sigmoid activation function will process the signal send by net inflow input that passes from each node. Associated with each incoming net inflow signal is a weight. Each input node unit in input layer broadcast the net inflow signal to hidden layer.

The input signal resulting from the input net inflow data. Each hidden node sums its weighted input signals, applies its activation function to compute its output signal from net inflow, and sends this signal to all units in the hidden layer, which is the weight between input layer and hidden layer, is the weight for the bias; and is the input net inflow signal.

The binary sigmoid activation function will process the signal that passes from each node. Then from second layer the signal is transmitted to third layer. The output unit sums its weighted input signals, and applies its activation function to compute its output signal, where is the weight between second layer and third layer; and is the weight for the bias.

The output node receives a target pattern corresponding to the input training pattern, computes its error (between target output and computed output) information term, calculates its weight correction term (used to update later), calculates its bias correction term (used to update later). The error information is conveyed from the output layer back to early layers. This is known as the back propagation of the output error to the input nodes to correct the weights. This method uses partial derivatives of error with respect to weights to update the weights of the connections that allows a multilayer network to change its weights in response to the output error.

The weights are updated continuously until minimum error is achieved. In this study the steepest descent method with momentum constant is applied for a faster convergence. The second technique of the neural network modelling is the radial basis function (RBF). It is recognized that the RBF neural networks is a curve fitting problem. Therefore the learning process is to find the best fit to the training data.

Seasonal Arima Model

The seasonal autoregressive integrated moving average, ARIMA model is designed as the univariate time series forecasting of reservoir net inflows. The development of seasonal ARIMA models requires three steps: identification, estimation and diagnostic checking.

The best model of seasonal ARIMA is chosen based on the minimum Akaike Information Criterion (AIC) and the white noise of residuals. The Box-Ljung test is used to assess the white noise of residuals.

Adaptive Fuzzy Model

The univariate forecasting of net inflow have been carried out by using the adaptive fuzzy model (FM). The methodology related to training and forecasting had been described details in their work.

Basically, the number of input nodes for FM is similar to the neural network. employed M = 12 number of rules, one possible rule for every month.

The spread of the membership functions of the input variables was chosen s = 60, and the learning rate for all models was a = 0.2.

Applecation and Discussions

Record of 27 years of monthly net inflow series of Pedu-Muda dams (Kedah, Malaysia) is selected to evaluate the performance of the neural network, adaptive fuzzy and seasonal ARIMA models. The two dams are connected by a free flow Saiong Tunnel and can be treated as a single reservoir system. For model development, 18 years of data are used, and for model testing, data for the remaining period of 9 years are considered.

The models are proposed to forecast the next net inflow yt+1, with known previous net inflow series. The optimal number of input node is important in the neural network and fuzzy model design and it is determined based on the following methods:

- Correlation method - analysis of partial autocorrelation function (PACF):
  yt, yt–1, yt–3, yt–7, yt–8, yt–10, yt–11
- Regression method - using stepwise regression:
  yt, yt–2, yt–7, yt–10
- Adopt the whole 12 months data:
  yt, yt–1, yt–2, yt–3, yt–4, yt–5, yt–6, yt–7, xt–8, xt–9, xt–10, xt–11

Basically, the number of input nodes considered for MLP, RBF and FM are, respectively 4, 7 and 12 nodes. For the neural network training process, the best hidden nodes is chosen based on the minimum root mean square errors (RMSE) computed for the training data. During modeling stage, the autocorrellation function of residuals is plotted to check for independence. The prediction of each model is evaluated using the root mean square error (RMSE), mean absolute error (MABE) and mean absolute relative error (MARE) stated in percentage. The seasonal ARIMA model requires logarithmic transformation and seasonal difference to remove the non-stationarity in the net inflow series. As the net inflow have non-positive values, the lower bound is determined in the natural log transformation, zt = ln (y + a). Where a is tested for several values until the skewness of zt is zero or almost zero; y is the original net inflow data; and zt is the transformed data.

In this work the seasonal ARIMA of order (2,0,0) × (0,1,1)12 is adopted with the parameters of model are f1 = 0.1788; f2 = 0.1318; Q = 0.8084; and the residual variance is 0.1857. Table presents the errors (RMSE, MABE and MARE) resulting from MLP, RBF, FM and ARIMA models. The seasonal ARIMA model gives a higher error than the MLP, RBF and FM models. It more obvious for the MARE. Results show that the neural network and adaptive fuzzy can provide more accurate net inflow forecast than classical method, multiplicative seasonal ARIMA. Analyses of errors reveal that although different input nodes (4, 7 and 12 input nodes) were used in the modeling, the neural and fuzzy display some flexibility to generalize their parameters and the results are in good agreement. In general, the neural network and adaptive fuzzy are adequate and reasonable methods for modeling of net inflow series.

Box-Jenkins Approach

Box-Jenkins Model

$$z_t = \varphi_1 z_{t-1} + \varphi_2 z_{t-2} + \dots + \varphi_p z_{t-p} + a_t - \theta_1 a_{t-1} - \theta_2 a_{t-2} - \dots - \theta_q a_{t-q}$$

where

$z_t, z_{t-1}, \dots$ is the observed time series

$\varphi_1, \varphi_2, \dots, \varphi_p, \theta_1, \theta_2, \dots, \theta_q$ are parameters

$a_t, a_{t-1}, \dots$, is a "white noise" sequence (a sequence of uncorrelated random variables having zero mean) or, in compact, "operator," notation:

$$\Phi(B)z_t = \Theta(B)a_t$$

where,

$Bz_t = z_{t-1}$ (I.E., B denotes the backward difference operator)

Iterative Procedure For Developing Box-Jenkins Models

- Statistics suggest model structure
- Parameters estimated
- Diagnostic checking
- If model inadequate, repeat procedure

Preliminary Statistical Analysis

Identify degree and structure of ρ(B) and è(B) polynomials
Two useful functions to assist model identification
Autocorrelation function (acf):

$$\rho_k = \text{corr}\ (z_t, z_{t-k}) = \text{cov}\ (z_t, z_{t-k})/\text{var}\ (z_t)$$

Partial Autocorrelation Function (PACF):
τ_k = k-th Coefficient Of Least-Squares Autoregressive (AR) model of order k
ACF "CUTS OFF" at order q of pure moving-average (MA) process (p=0)
PACF "CUTS OFF" at order of pure autoregressive (AR) process (q=0)

Estimation

Pure AR (NO θs) – linear statistical model:

$$z = Z'\underline{\varphi} + \underline{a}$$

$$\underline{\hat{\varphi}} = (ZZ')^{-1} Z\underline{z}$$

if θs present – nonlinear statistical model:

$$a_t = \Theta^{-1}(B)\ \Phi(B)\ z_t$$

I.E.,

$$a_t = a_t(\varphi, \theta, z) = a_t(\underline{\beta}, z)$$

Expanding in a taylor series around a "guess value," β_0:

$$\approx a_t \mid \beta = \beta 0 + \sum_{i=1}^{p+q} (\beta_i - \beta_{io}) \frac{\partial a_t}{\partial \beta_i} \mid \underline{\beta} = \underline{\beta} 0$$

which is a linear model with parameter $\underline{\delta} = \underline{\beta} - \underline{\beta_0}$. The parameter estimates are determined iteratively (e.g., the gauss-marquardt method or a numerical optimization method)

Optimal Forecaster

The optimal forecaster minimizes the mean squared error of prediction
$\hat{z}_t(1)$ = 1-ahead forecast made from time t

$$\hat{z}_t(1) = \hat{\varphi}_1 z_t + \cdots + \hat{\varphi}_p z_{t-p} - \hat{\theta}_1 \hat{a}_{t-1} - \cdots - \hat{\theta}_q \hat{a}_{t-q}$$

where,

$$\hat{a}_t = z_t - \hat{z}_{t-1}(1)$$

Seasonality

A reasonable model is:

$$\Phi_s(B^s) z_t = \Theta_s(B^s) e_t$$

where e_t is correlated with $e_{t-1}, e_{t-2}, \ldots$.

The Model Residuals May Be Represented By

$$\Phi(B)\ e_t = \Theta(B) a_t$$

where the at are white.

Hence, combining, the model is:

$$\Phi_s(B^s)\ \Phi(B)\ z_t = \Theta_s(B^s)\ \Theta(B)\ a_t$$

Exponential Smoothing

Exponential smoothing is a special case of

$$\Phi(B)\, z_t = \Theta(B) a_t$$

with

$$\Phi(B) = 1 - B \text{ AND } \Phi(B) = 1 - \alpha B,$$

I.E.,

$$z_t = z_{t-1} + a_t - \alpha a_{t-1}.$$

the least-squares forecaster is:

$$\hat{z}_t(1) = z_t - \alpha \hat{a}_t$$

or

- FORECASTING ACCURACY COMPARISONS

Criteria for Forecasting Performance

Forecast error variance, or mean squared error (mse) of prediction:
z_t = Observed value at time t $\hat{z}(\ell) = \ell$
- ahead forecast made from time t
mse $= v_\ell = E(z_{t+1} - \hat{z}_t(\ell))^2$
Theil coefficient:

$$U = \sqrt{\frac{\sum (Z_t - \hat{Z}_t)^2}{\sum (Z_t - Z_{t-1})^2}}$$

Box-jenkins vs. Brown's Method

Ref: box, jenkins and reinsel, *time series analysis, forecasting and control*
Brown's method:

- A forecast function is selected from a general class of linear combinations and products of polynomials, exponentials, sines and cosines
- The selected forecast functions are fitted to data by a "discounted least squares" procedure. Model parameters are chosen to minimize

$$\sum_{j=0}^{\infty} \beta^j (Z_{t-j} - \hat{Z}_t(j))^2$$

Data: Daily closing ibm stock prices, june 29, 1959 – november 2, 1962
Brown's model (triple exponential smoothing):

$$\hat{z}_t(\ell) = C_0(t) + C_1(t)\ell + (1/2) C_2(t) \ell^2$$

Where the c's are adaptive coefficients.
Box-jenkins model:

$$\nabla z_t = a_t - .1 a_{t-1}$$

Mean squared forecast errors:

Lead time (ℓ)	1	2	3	4	5	6	7	8	9	10	
Mse (brown)	102	158	218	256	363	452	554	669799		944	
Mse (b-j)		42	91	136	180	222	266	317371		427	483

Box-jenkins vs. Brown's Method (cont.)

IBM stock price series with comparison of lead-3 forecasts obtained from best ima(0,1,1) process and brown's quadratic forecast for a period beginning july 11, 1960. (from box, Jenkins, reinsel reference)

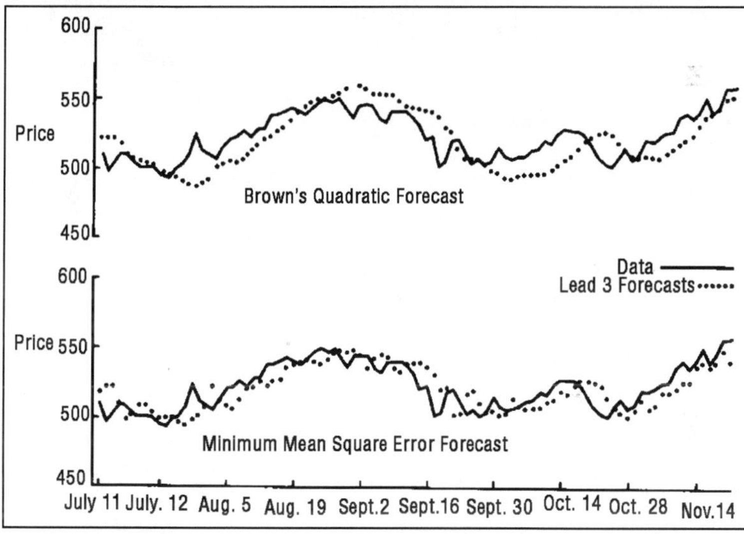

Fig. Model Building With The Box-Jenkins Methodology

Major Phases of the Box-jenkins Methodology

Estimation:

- Estimate model parameters
- Analyse model residuals, revise model if necessary

Forecasting (using the finished model):

- Optimal forecasts
- Tolerance limits

Simulation (using the finished model):

- Input to other models (e.g., an economic analysis of alternative modes of pharmaceutical manufacture)
- Used to test models or decision rules (e.g., to compare inventory restocking rules)

Stochastic model buildin:

- Identification
- Fitting
- Diagnostic Checking

Diagnostic Checks Suggest Modifications: Model Identification Autocorrelation Function (ACF) And Partial Autocorrelation Function (PACF) Need A Stationary Variate Homogeneous Nons-tationarity Is Common – Acf Does Not Die Out

Achieve Stationarity By Differencing Until The ACF Dies Out

Homogeneous nonstationarity:

$$\Phi(B)\, z_t = \Theta'(B)(1 - B)^d z_t$$
$$= \Phi'(B) \quad {}^d z_t$$
$$= \Phi'(B) w_t$$

$\Phi(B)$ has d zeros (roots) on the unit circle – z_t nonstationary

φ' has all zeros outside the unit circle – w_t stationary (recall $\nabla z_t = (1-B)z_t = z_t - z_{t-1}$)

Seasonal Homogeneous Nonstationarity

If seasonal nonstationarity is present, the acf has periodic peaks that do not die out

Approach: take seasonal differences:

$$w_t = (1 - B^s)z_t$$
$$= \nabla_s z_t$$

Stationary Time Series

ACF characterizes (uniquely defines) stationary series

PACF also aids identification

Pure autoregressive (ar) process:

$$\Phi(B)w_t = a_t$$

where

$$\Phi(B) = 1 - \varphi_1 B - \ldots - \varphi_p B_p.$$

PACF cuts off at order p (acf tails off)

Pure moving average (ma) process:

$$w_t = \Theta(B)a_t$$

where,

$$\Theta(B) = 1 - \theta_1 B - \ldots - è_q B_q$$

ACF cuts off at order q (pacf tails off)

Mixed Arma Process (Arima Process)

$$\Phi(B) \quad \nabla^d z_t = \Theta(B)a_t$$

Autoregressive-moving average (arma) process of order (p, d, q)

Usually called an autoregressive-integrated-moving-average (ARIMA) process

ACF tails off after order max (0, q–p)

PACF tails off after order max (0, p–q)

Identification Examples:

Behaviour of the autocorrelation functions for the d-th difference of an ARIMA process of order (p,d,q).

Order	Behavior of ρ_k	Behavior of ϕ_{kk}	Preliminary estimates from	Admissible Region
(1,d,0)	Decays exponentially	Only ϕ_{11} nonzero	$\Phi_1 = \rho_1$	$-1 < \phi_1 < 1$
(0,d,1)	Only ρ_1 nonzero	Exponential dominates decay	$\rho_1 = -\theta_1/(1 + \theta_1^2)$	$-1 < \theta_1 < 1$
(2,d,0)	Mixture of exponentials or damped sine wave	Only ϕ_{11} and ϕ_{22} nonzero	$\Phi_1 = \rho_1(1 - \rho_2)/(1 - \rho_1^2)$ $\Phi_2 = (\rho_2 - \rho_1^2)/(1 - \rho_1^2)$	$-1 < \phi_2 < 1$ $\phi_2 + \phi_1 < 1$ $\phi_2 - \phi_1 < 1$
(0,d,2)	Only ρ_1 and ρ_2 nonzero	Dominated by mixture of exponentials or damped sine wave	$\rho_1 = -\theta_1(1 - \theta_2)/(1 + \theta_1^2 + \theta_2^2)$ $\rho_2 = -\theta_1/(1 + \theta_1^2 + \theta_2^2)$	$-1 < \theta_2 < 1$ $\theta_2 + \theta_1 < 1$ $\theta_2 - \theta_1 < 1$
(1,d,1)	Decays exponentially from first lag	Dominated by exponential decay from first lag	$\rho_1 = (1 - \theta_1\phi_1)(\phi_1 - \theta_1)/(1+ \theta_1^2 - 2\Phi_1\theta_1)$ $\rho_2 = \rho_1\phi_1$	$-1 < \phi_1 < 1$ $-1 < \theta_1 < 1$

Caution:

- Estimated autocorrelations may be highly autocorrelated, and may have large variances
- Use the acf only to suggest models to fit (amount and type of differencing, number of φs and θs)
- Use least-squares procedure to obtain good estimates for the parameters
- Rely on diagnostic checks to accept or reject fitted models

Model Fitting:

- Specify p, q, and preliminary estimates (guess values) of parameters
- Use an available computer programme (statistical software package) to estimate the parameters
- For nonlinear models ($q > 0$ or seasonal components), estimation involves use of an iterative estimation procedure (e.g., gauss-marquardt, general nonlinear estimation routine)

Diagnostic Checking

Significance of various statistics is computed from the model "residuals" (error terms):

- Mean (t-test)
- PACF (t-test on each value)
- ACF (t-test on each value, ÷^{2} (chi-squared) test on entire function spectrum (grenander-rosenblatt test)

Example of Model Modification

Suppose the correct model is of order (0,2,2), but that the fitted model is:

$$\nabla z_t = (1+.68)e_t$$

Suppose that the model suggested for the residuals (e_t's) is:

$$\nabla e_t = (1+.68B)a_t$$

These results suggest that an improved model would be:

$$\nabla z_t = (1+.2B-.48B^2)a_t$$

This Suggests A Model Of Order (0,2,2) Should Be examined,

Model Simplification

A model of the form:

$(1 - \varphi B)(1 - B)z_t = (1 - \theta)a_t$

Might be reducible to:

$(1 - \varphi B)z_t = a_t$

If è is close to 1.

- Application to econometric and control problems

Basic Application

Pure stochastic model:

$\varphi(b)z_t = \theta(b)a_t$

Stochastic-dynamic Models

Econometric models

Physical models (e.g., radar tracking of a missile)

Control models:

$$\begin{aligned} z_t &= l_1^{-1}(b)\, l_2(b)\, b^b\, x_t + \varphi^{-1}(b)\theta(b)a_t \\ &= v(b)x_t + \varphi^{-1}(b)\theta(b)a_t \end{aligned}$$

Where x_t is a stochastic process (control variable, leading indicator); v(b) is the impulse response function of x_t

Identification of Stochastic-dynamic Models

The relationship is complicated if x_t is not "white" (uncorrelated, zero mean)

If we "prewhiten" x_t, the relationship is simple.

Prewhitening the Control (Input) Variable

Determine a stochastic-process model for x_t:

$$x_t = \varphi_x^{-1}(b)\ \theta_x(b)\ a_{xt}$$

the prewhitened series is:

$$a_{xt} = \theta_x^{-1}(b)\ \varphi_x(b)\ x_t$$

The original model becomes:

$$y_t = \varphi_x^{-1}(b)\ \theta_x(b)\ z_t = l_1^{-1}(b)\ l_2(b)\ b^b\ a_{xt} + \varphi_x^{-1}(b)\ \theta_x(b)\ \varphi^{-1}(b)\ \theta(b)\ a_t$$

Identification Using the Prewhitened Input Variable

The cross-correlation function of (a_{xt}, y_t) is:

$$\gamma_{ax,y}(k) = v_k \sigma_{ax}^2$$

So the transfer function v is directly proportional to the ccf

Hence we can deduce a tentative form of l_1, l_2 from:

$$v(b) = l_1^{-1}(b)\ l_2(b)\ b^b$$

Optimal Forecaster for Dynamic-stochastic Model

Econometric model with leading indicator x_t:

$$z_t = L_1^{-1}(B)\ L_2(B)\ B^b\ x_t + \Phi^{-1}(B)\ \Theta(B)\ a_t$$

OR

$$L_1(B)\ \Phi(B)\ z_t = \Phi(B)\ L_2(B)\ x_{t-b} + L_1(B)\ \Theta(B)\ a_t$$

OR

$$\Phi^*(B)\ z_t = \Lambda \times (B)\ z_{t-b} + \Theta \times (B)\ a_t$$

The optimal forecaster for this model is:

where

$$\hat{z}_t(\ell) = \varphi_1 z'_{t+\ell-1} + \cdots + \varphi_p z'_{t+\ell-p} + \lambda_0 x'_{t-b+\ell} - \cdots -$$

$$\lambda_r x'_{t-b+\ell-r} + a'_{t+\ell} - \theta_1 a'_{t+\ell-1} - \cdots - \theta_q a'_{t+\ell-q}$$

where t_0 is the point in time to which x_t is known, and the quantity is the optimal forecast from the stochastic model for x_t. Thus the optimal forecaster for an econometric model depends on the optimal forecaster of the stochastic model for the leading indicator.

Unless we know x_t for the entire future period over which we wish to forecast, we must use a stochastic model to forecast it in order to compute the optimal forecast for the econometric model.

Summary

The Box-Jenkins approach is a powerful method for determining mathematical models (representations) of a wide variety of stochastic-process phenomena. Although the method is relatively quick and produces "parsimonious" (not overly elaborate) models, the computations required to develop the model and to determine optimal forecasts from the model are complicated, and require the use of a statistical computer programme.

MULTIVARIATE TIME SERIES MODELS

The multivariate form of the Box-Jenkins univariate models is sometimes called the ARMAV model, for AutoRegressive Moving Average Vector or simply vector ARMA process.

The ARMAV model for a stationary multivariate time series, with a zero mean vector, represented by

$$x_l = (x_{1l}, x_{2l}, \ldots, x_{nl})^T \quad -\infty < t < \infty$$

is of the form

$$x_l = \phi_1 x_{l-1} + \phi_2 x_{l-2} + \ldots + \phi_p x_{t-p} + a_l$$
$$-\theta_1 a_{l-1} - \theta_2 a_{l-2} - \ldots - \theta_q a_{l-q}$$

where

- x_t and a_t are n x 1 column vectors
- $\phi_k = \{\phi_{k.ij}\}, k = 1, 2, \ldots, P$

  $\phi_k = \{\phi_{k.ij}\}, k = 1, 2, \ldots, q$

are n x n matrices for autoregressive and moving average parameters

- $E[a_t] = 0$
- $E[a_t, a_{t-k}] = D$, the dispersion or covariance matrix

As an example, for a bivariate series with $n = 2$, $p = 2$, and $q = 1$, the ARMAV(2,1) model is:

$$\begin{pmatrix} x_{1l} \\ y_{2l} \end{pmatrix} = \begin{pmatrix} \phi_{1.11} & \phi_{1.12} \\ \phi_{1.21} & \phi_{1.22} \end{pmatrix} \begin{pmatrix} x_{1l-1} \\ x_{2l-1} \end{pmatrix}$$
$$\begin{pmatrix} \phi_{2.11} & \phi_{2.12} \\ \phi_{2.21} & \phi_{2.22} \end{pmatrix} \begin{pmatrix} x_{1l-2} \\ 2_{l-2} \end{pmatrix}$$
$$+ \begin{pmatrix} a_{1l} \\ a_{2l} \end{pmatrix} - \begin{pmatrix} \phi_{1.11} & \phi_{1.12} \\ \phi_{1.21} & \phi_{1.22} \end{pmatrix} \begin{pmatrix} a_{1l-1} \\ a_{2l-1} \end{pmatrix}$$

Estimation of parameters and covariance matrix difficult: The estimation of the matrix parameters and covariance matrix is complicated and very difficult without computer software. The estimation of the Moving Average matrices is especially an ordeal.

If we opt to ignore the MA component(s) we are left with the ARV model given by: where,

- x_t is a vector of observations, $x_1, x_2 \ldots, x_n$ at time t
- a_t is a vector of white noise, $a_1, a_2 \ldots, a_n$ at time t
- xxxx is a an $n \times n$ matrix of autoregressive parameters
- $E[a_t] = 0$
- $E[a_t, a_{t-k}] = D$, the dispersion or covariance matrix

A model with p autoregressive matrix parameters is an ARV(p) model or a vector AR model.

The parameter matrices may be estimated by multivariate least squares, but there are other methods such as maximium likelihood estimation.

Interesting properties of parameter matrices: There are a few interesting properties associated with the phi or AR parameter matrices. Consider the following ARV(2) model:

As an example, for a bivariate series with n =2, p = 2, and q = 1, the ARMAV(2,1) model is:

$$\begin{pmatrix} x_l \\ y_l \end{pmatrix} = \begin{pmatrix} \phi_{1.11} & \phi_{1.12} \\ \phi_{1.21} & \phi_{1.22} \end{pmatrix} \begin{pmatrix} x_{l-1} \\ x_{l-1} \end{pmatrix} + \begin{pmatrix} \phi_{2.11} & \phi_{2.12} \\ \phi_{2.21} & \phi_{2.22} \end{pmatrix} \begin{pmatrix} x_{l-2} \\ 2_{l-2} \end{pmatrix} + \begin{pmatrix} a_{1l} \\ a_{2l} \end{pmatrix}$$

Without loss of generality assume that the X series is input and the Yseries are output and that the mean vector = (0,0). Therefore, tranform the observation by subtracting their respective averages.

Diagonal Terms of Phi Matrix

The diagonal terms of each Phi matrix are the scalar estimates for each series, in this case:

$\phi_{1.11}, \phi_{2.11}$ for the input series X,

$\phi_{2.11}, \phi_{\cdot 2.22}$ for the output series Y.

Transfer mechanism: The lower off-diagonal elements represent the influence of the input on the output.

This is called the "transfer" mechanism or transfer-function model as discussed by Box and Jenkins in Chapter 11. The ϕ terms here correspond to their δ terms.

The upper off-diagonal terms represent the influence of the output on the input.

Feedback: This is called "feedback". The presence of feedback can also be seen as a high value for a coefficient in the correlation matrix of the residuals. A "true" transfer model exists when there is no feedback.

This can be seen by expressing the matrix form into scalar form:

$$x_t = \phi_{1.11}x_{t-1} + \phi_{2.22}y_{t-2} + \phi_{1.112}y_{t-1} + \phi_{2.12}y_{t-2} + a_{1l}$$

$$y_t = \phi_{1.22}y_{t-1} + \phi_{2.22}y_{t-2} + \phi_{1.21}x_{t-1} + \phi_{2.21}x_{t-2}$$

Delay

Finally, delay or "dead' time can be measured by studying the lower off-diagonal elements again.

If, for example, $_{1.21}$ is non-significant, the delay is 1 time period.

Index